Mastering Microsoft Dynamics AX 2012 R3 Programming

A comprehensive guide to developing maintainable and extendable solutions with Microsoft Dynamics AX 2012 R3

Simon Buxton

Mat Fergusson

[PACKT] PUBLISHING enterprise
professional expertise distilled

BIRMINGHAM - MUMBAI

Mastering Microsoft Dynamics AX 2012 R3 Programming

First published: June 2015

Production reference: 2260615

Published by Packt Publishing Ltd.
Livery Place
35 Livery Street
Birmingham B3 2PB, UK.

ISBN 978-1-78217-601-5

www.packtpub.com

Credits

Authors
Simon Buxton
Mat Fergusson

Reviewers
Janet E. Blake
Martin Winkler
Ahsan Murshed
Kishor Jadhav

Commissioning Editor
Usha Iyer

Acquisition Editor
Vinay Argekar

Content Development Editor
Neeshma Ramakrishnan

Technical Editors
Ankita Thakur
Prajakta Mhatre
Anushree Arun Tendulkar

Copy Editors
Shambhavi Pai
Merilyn Pereira
Vikrant Phadke
Swati Priya

Project Coordinator
Danuta Jones

Proofreaders
Safis Editing
Paul Hindle

Indexer
Priya Sane

Graphics
Sheetal Aute

Production Coordinator
Shantanu N. Zagade

Cover Work
Shantanu N. Zagade

About the Authors

Simon Buxton has worked with Dynamics AX since its earliest incarnations, starting out as a consultant and developer in early 1999 when Dynamics AX was known as Damgaard Axapta 1.5.

Simon quickly became a team leader at Columbus IT Partners and carried out one of the first AX implementations in the UK before joining a new reseller, Sense Enterprise Solutions, as its technical director. Sense Enterprise Solutions enjoyed a global reach through the AxPact alliance and Simon was placed as AxPact's technical lead. Simon played a major role in expanding the company to become a successful Microsoft partner and was the technical lead on a number of highly challenging technical projects around the world, from the UK, to Bahrain, to the USA. These projects included developing solutions for third-party logistics, multichannel retail, and eventually developing an animal feed vertical, as well as integrating Dynamics AX into production control systems, government gateways, and e-commerce solutions, among others.

Sense Enterprise Solutions was sold to a major PLC and since then, Simon has teamed up with Binary Consultants as their technical architect, where he works with some of the most technically able AX and Microsoft .NET professionals in Europe. Binary Consultants are involved in the implementation, upgrade, and support of Microsoft Dynamics AX, the development of add-ons for AX 2012 and AX 7 (under the name Axponents), and vertical solutions in animal feed.

Simon was the author of *Microsoft Dynamics AX 2012 R2 Administration Cookbook*, published in 2013, by Packt Publishing, and was a reviewer on *Implementing Microsoft Dynamics AX 2012 with Sure Step 2012*, which was published by Packt Publishing in March 2013.

I would like to thank my colleagues at Binary Consultants, especially Josh Townson for his continued support throughout the writing process. I would also like to thank all those that helped review this book, Martin and Janet in particular, without whom this wouldn't be possible. Finally, I have to thank my partner, Evi, for her patience and support as I disappeared for hours each night working on another book. Of course, no bio would be complete without mentioning my children, Tyler and Isabella, and my parents for inspiring me to always want to be better.

Mat Fergusson started his journey into software development in 1998 by studying software engineering at Sheffield University. After graduating, Mat took to working in IT infrastructure, quickly progressing from desktop support to infrastructure implementation and management.

Armed with real-world experience of supporting users and seeing how applications and infrastructure are actually used, Mat began moving back into full-time application development, building classic ASP applications at the tail end of the .com boom.

Mat was among the very early adopters of Microsoft's next generation development platform, .NET. Over the next few years, Mat would develop numerous web applications and integration projects using VB.NET and later C#, and in 2005, he started developing mobile business applications built on the Windows CE platform years before the iPhone made mobile applications ubiquitous.

After completing the first release of an award-winning hosted health and safety mobile application, Mat decided to gain some broader experience and embarked on a one and a half year world tour, which saw him broadening both his IT and life skills by working for the Enterprise Applications division of HP in New Zealand and becoming a certified dive master in Thailand.

Returning to the UK, Mat teamed up with his old colleagues and between them, they founded Binary Consultants, where he continues to work today. In the last 6 years, Mat has continued to refine his .NET development skills in his role as .NET Lead at Binary, and has been responsible for several highly specialist web applications for the cosmetic industry in Russia and the rapidly growing online gaming industry in Malta.

In the last 2 years, Mat has started cross training in AX development, an experience that has helped him directly in writing this book with Simon. Mat's current specialty however, is the development of .NET applications for Binary's clients that extend the capabilities of AX by interfacing with the WCF services exposed by the AIF, introducing rich visualization and interactions that simply aren't possible with the AX client.

It is imperative that I acknowledge my wife for her understanding as I tried to cram in writing a book in the run up to our wedding. Caroline, I love you very much. We had a great 2 days and I'm looking forward to many more to come.

About the Reviewers

Janet E. Blake was introduced to Axapta 3.0 in 2006 by a friend who promised she "would never get bored" and kept that promise. She is now a development manager on the mcaConnect Product Development team. She holds two degrees from New York University and spends her free time blogging at `http://janeteblake.wordpress.com`, searching for AX books, and pondering over her next certification.

Janet has been a reviewer on *Microsoft Dynamics AX 2012 R2 Administration Cookbook* and *Microsoft Dynamics AX 2012 R2 Services*, both of which are published by Packt Publishing.

> I'd like to thank the authors and publishers for the opportunity to review this terrific book. Endless thanks to my management, colleagues, and clients for keeping it interesting and fun, and to the family for nodding thoughtfully when I discuss an AX question out loud!

Martin Winkler has over 12 years of experience with Microsoft Dynamics AX.

After receiving his master's degree in mathematical computer sciences at the Vienna University of Technology, he gained experience as an IT consultant at Capgemini and later as a BI consultant at an Austrian consulting company specializing in CFO-targeted services.

In 2003, Martin joined Solutions Factory, a newly-founded Austrian company that specialized in Microsoft Dynamics AX services. Starting as a developer and head of IT, he later became head of a development of up to 10 developers. From 2007 onwards, he also built a team of AX performance experts. In 2008, the company (then FWI) became the largest Microsoft Dynamics AX partner in Austria.

While still in development, he mostly worked as a technical lead consultant for Microsoft Dynamics AX for several corporate customers with international implementations in Europe, the Middle East, North Africa, and North America, and with up to 1,000 users. He also carried out numerous projects in the areas of Microsoft Dynamics AX performance and Microsoft BI for these customers.

Together with two long-term colleagues, he founded his own company, Semantax, in 2013, providing products and expert consulting services based on Microsoft Dynamics AX. In 2014, the experts of Semantax teamed up with two further long-term colleagues with vast know-how in industry processes and corporate ERP projects to relaunch Solutions Factory.

Solutions Factory (`www.sf-ax.com`) is dedicated to shaping customer processes and mapping them to Microsoft Dynamics AX in an efficient and optimal way, thereby aligning people, processes, and technologies. The team aims to contribute significantly to the increased competitive capability of European manufacturing companies.

Over the last decade, Martin has met the author of this book at several technical conferences on Microsoft Dynamics AX. He was impressed, not only with the author's in-depth technical knowledge, but also with his understanding of the business and process sides of the ERP branch. He enjoyed reviewing *Microsoft Dynamics AX 2012 R2 Administration Cookbook* by the same author and was honored to be asked to review this book as well. He hopes the readers will enjoy this book as much as he did.

Ahsan Murshed is an ex MVP (Microsoft Most Valuable Professional) from 2011-2013. He is currently working as a senior software engineer, with over 8 years of experience in the design, prototyping, development, and deployment of various scales of business solutions. His interest lies in working on large scale business applications such as MS SharePoint, MS Dynamics CRM, and so on.

I would like to dedicate this book to my family—parents, wife, and Ayesha—and also to my friends who give me tremendous support from time to time. Thanks friends for all your support.

Kishor Jadhav is currently working as a Microsoft Dynamics AX senior technical consultant with 42 Hertz INC. He has completed his master's degree in computer application from the University of Mumbai, and his bachelor's degree in information technology from Vidyalankar School of Information Technology, Mumbai.

Kishor has around 6 years of IT experience. He has worked with Godrej Infotech, Mumbai as a Dynamics AX technical consultant and has a deep understanding of the Microsoft Dynamics AX ERP system. He has worked with different versions of AX, such as AX 5.0 (AX 2009), and AX6.0 (AX 2012, AX 2012 R2, and AX 2012 R3). He has a good knowledge of Microsoft technologies, such as SQL, VB 6.0, C#, SSRS, and SSAS.

He can be contacted via Skype (`kishorworld`) or e-mail (`kishoworld1@gmail.com`), and he blogs at `http://kdynamics.blogspot.in`.

I would like to give a thanks to my friends and colleagues, who have guided me and encouraged me to pursue my passion. Also, special thanks goes to Danuta Jones and Packt Publishing for giving me the opportunity to review this book.

www.PacktPub.com

Support files, eBooks, discount offers, and more

For support files and downloads related to your book, please visit www.PacktPub.com.

Did you know that Packt offers eBook versions of every book published, with PDF and ePub files available? You can upgrade to the eBook version at www.PacktPub.com and as a print book customer, you are entitled to a discount on the eBook copy. Get in touch with us at service@packtpub.com for more details.

At www.PacktPub.com, you can also read a collection of free technical articles, sign up for a range of free newsletters and receive exclusive discounts and offers on Packt books and eBooks.

PACKTLIB

https://www2.packtpub.com/books/subscription/packtlib

Do you need instant solutions to your IT questions? PacktLib is Packt's online digital book library. Here, you can search, access, and read Packt's entire library of books.

Why subscribe?

- Fully searchable across every book published by Packt
- Copy and paste, print, and bookmark content
- On demand and accessible via a web browser

Free access for Packt account holders

If you have an account with Packt at www.PacktPub.com, you can use this to access PacktLib today and view 9 entirely free books. Simply use your login credentials for immediate access.

Instant updates on new Packt books

Get notified! Find out when new books are published by following @PacktEnterprise on Twitter or the *Packt Enterprise* Facebook page.

Table of Contents

Preface

Microsoft Dynamics AX is an ERP solution for complex single site and multi-site, multilanguage global enterprises. This flexible and agile solution provides both advanced built-in functionality and an industry leading integrated development environment, allowing an organization to provide even higher levels of fit. This book should be in the tool belt of any software engineer who works with Dynamics AX.

This book aims at providing software engineers and those involved in developing solutions within Dynamics AX with clear guidance of best practices, and theory and practical examples covering broad areas of the Dynamics AX integrated development environment and surrounding technologies. Even for experienced software engineers, this book will provide a good source of reference for efficient software development. The book's easy-to-follow practical guidance will help your solutions to be easier to maintain, extend, and upgrade.

In order to facilitate this, the book follows the development of a solution as a means to explain the design and development of data structures, classes, forms, BI, menu structures, and security. Concepts such as models, layers, software development patterns, and frameworks are explained and have been given a real-world context and perspective using the authors' experiences to point out the many traps that lay in wait, demonstrating not only how to write flexible solutions, but also why a design approach has been taken.

The structure of the book was designed so that it is useful in a practical sense from the initial chapters, without sacrificing the required theory that is needed to provide the necessary depth of knowledge when working with Dynamics AX. By *Chapter 3, Creating the User Interface*, we have a working solution for maintaining data, and by the end of *Chapter 7, Designing Your Security Model*, we cover most of what is required from many solutions. The earlier chapters provide a fast-paced tutorial for new developers to AX and a refresher for those already developing in AX using the latest best practices and software development patterns. The later chapters cover advanced development techniques and features that will help even the experienced Dynamics AX software engineers.

The sample solution was designed and developed as the book was written, and is available for download. It was co-developed by two authors living in different countries using Team Foundation Server with Visual Studio Online.

With this comprehensive tutorial, you will be armed with the knowledge and insight you need to develop well design solutions that will help your organization to get the most value from this comprehensive solution for both this and upcoming releases of Microsoft Dynamics AX.

What this book covers

Chapter 1, Preparing Our Solution, provides both the theory and practical steps that are followed when starting work on a new solution. This includes minimizing code footprint; creating a model, project, and label file; configuring source control; and designing the technical solution and test plans.

Chapter 2, Creating Data Structures, guides us through the creation of the data structures used for our hypothetical solution, bringing in new concepts such as table inheritance, extended data types, enumerated types, and referential integrity.

Chapter 3, Creating the User Interface, includes the creation of the user interface using standard design patterns for development of the forms and menu structure. We also demonstrate how to make form logic reusable by moving code to a class.

Chapter 4, Creating Business Logic and Hooking into Core AX, covers how to handle table events in a class for easier reusability by adding navigation and using number sequences. It also includes how to hook into core AX using eventing and delegates to minimize the footprint on standard code.

Chapter 5, Adding Business Intelligence, provides practical hands-on guidance for the creation of parts in order to provide real-time, pervasive business intelligence to our users through Info parts, Form parts, Cues, and Cue groups. Also covered is the interaction between form parts and the host form and how to control queries programmatically.

Chapter 6, Extending the Solution, lets you dive deeper into the solution we have developed by adding secondary list pages, drop dialogs, and reusable business logic with data contracts and exposing business logic to external applications through services.

Chapter 7, Designing Your Security Model, covers the design and development of the security of our solution, including roles, duties, privileges, and process cycles. We also cover code access permissions and how to secure data through the use of data policies (extensible data security).

Chapter 8, Customizing Standard AX, provides guidance on how (and where) to modify standard or third-party code without suffering the maintenance cost associated with upgrading the modified code. Also included is using standard frameworks, demonstrated by example of vendor electronic payments.

Chapter 9, Advanced Features and Frameworks, demystifies the more advanced topics such as the SysOperation framework, global address book, and the financial dimension framework through clear practical examples of how these should be used.

Chapter 10, Advanced Development Techniques, covers date effective tables, exception handling, computed columns on views, and controlling the tier our code runs on. We also step into the world of using metadata, making sense of advanced techniques many may shy away from.

Chapter 11, Unit and Performance Testing, covers practical guidance on unit and performance testing, including how to create automated test plans that help us avoid the regression that changes often incur. Performance testing and diagnosis is explained through the use of the code profiler, which covers analysis on both the code and database performance.

Appendix A, Efficient Design and Development with Microsoft Dynamics AX, covers the technical overview of Dynamics AX, models, layers, and the integrated development environment.

Appendix B, Using Version Control, provides guidance on how to use version control covering the interaction between version control and models and layers, how to build your solution, and how version control works with label files.

Appendix C, Code Editor Scripts, provides information and code samples on how to extend the standard code editor scripts, saving your time while developing code.

What you need for this book

The easiest way to follow the code samples in this book is to use one of the Microsoft Dynamics 2012 R3 solution demonstration VMs available from Partnersource or Customersource. You should use the latest available; this book was written to use CU8, with the differences to CU7 (or prior) explained.

Who this book is for

If you are a software developer, who has started developing in Dynamics AX 2012 or an experienced software engineer migrating from an earlier version of Dynamics AX, this book is an ideal tutorial to help you make the most of this advanced technology. This book is also useful if you are a technical solution architect or technical consultant as it provides a deeper insight into the technology behind the solution.

Conventions

In this book, you will find a number of text styles that distinguish between different kinds of information. Here are some examples of these styles and an explanation of their meaning.

Code words in text, database table names, folder names, filenames, file extensions, pathnames, dummy URLs, user input, and Twitter handles are shown as follows: "In our example, we will use `6015GettingStarted` as the project name."

A block of code is set as follows:

```
public Common resolveReference(FormReferenceControl
                                           _formReferenceControl)
{
    Common category;
    EcoResCategoryHierarchy     hierarchy;
    EcoResCategoryHierarchyRole role;

    select firstonly * from hierarchy
        join role
            where hierarchy.RecId == role.CategoryHierarchy
```

```
                && role.NamedCategoryHierarchyRole ==
                   EcoResCategoryNamedHierarchyRole::Procurement;

    category = EcoResCategory::resolveCategoryHierarchy(
                                _formReferenceControl, hierarchy);

    return category.RecId ? category : null;
}
```

When we wish to draw your attention to a particular part of a code block, the relevant lines or items are set in bold:

```
public Common resolveReference(FormReferenceControl
                                          _formReferenceControl)
{
    Common category;
    EcoResCategoryHierarchy     hierarchy;
    EcoResCategoryHierarchyRole role;

    select firstonly * from hierarchy
        join role
            where hierarchy.RecId == role.CategoryHierarchy
                && role.NamedCategoryHierarchyRole ==
                   EcoResCategoryNamedHierarchyRole::Procurement;

    category = EcoResCategory::resolveCategoryHierarchy(
                                _formReferenceControl, hierarchy);

    return category.RecId ? category : null;
}
```

New terms and **important words** are shown in bold. Words that you see on the screen, for example, in menus or dialog boxes, appear in the text like this: "Press **OK**."

> Warnings or important notes appear in a box like this.

> Tips and tricks appear like this.

Reader feedback

Feedback from our readers is always welcome. Let us know what you think about this book—what you liked or disliked. Reader feedback is important for us as it helps us develop titles that you will really get the most out of.

To send us general feedback, simply e-mail `feedback@packtpub.com`, and mention the book's title in the subject of your message.

If there is a topic that you have expertise in and you are interested in either writing or contributing to a book, see our author guide at `www.packtpub.com/authors`.

Customer support

Now that you are the proud owner of a Packt book, we have a number of things to help you to get the most from your purchase.

Downloading the example code

You can download the example code files from your account at `http://www.packtpub.com` for all the Packt Publishing books you have purchased. If you purchased this book elsewhere, you can visit `http://www.packtpub.com/support` and register to have the files e-mailed directly to you.

Downloading the color images of this book

We also provide you with a PDF file that has color images of the screenshots/diagrams used in this book. The color images will help you better understand the changes in the output. You can download this file from `https://www.packtpub.com/sites/default/files/downloads/6015EN_ColorImages.pdf`.

Errata

Although we have taken every care to ensure the accuracy of our content, mistakes do happen. If you find a mistake in one of our books—maybe a mistake in the text or the code—we would be grateful if you could report this to us. By doing so, you can save other readers from frustration and help us improve subsequent versions of this book. If you find any errata, please report them by visiting `http://www.packtpub.com/submit-errata`, selecting your book, clicking on the **Errata Submission Form** link, and entering the details of your errata. Once your errata are verified, your submission will be accepted and the errata will be uploaded to our website or added to any list of existing errata under the Errata section of that title.

To view the previously submitted errata, go to `https://www.packtpub.com/books/content/support` and enter the name of the book in the search field. The required information will appear under the **Errata** section.

Piracy

Piracy of copyrighted material on the Internet is an ongoing problem across all media. At Packt, we take the protection of our copyright and licenses very seriously. If you come across any illegal copies of our works in any form on the Internet, please provide us with the location address or website name immediately so that we can pursue a remedy.

Please contact us at `copyright@packtpub.com` with a link to the suspected pirated material.

We appreciate your help in protecting our authors and our ability to bring you valuable content.

Questions

If you have a problem with any aspect of this book, you can contact us at `questions@packtpub.com`, and we will do our best to address the problem.

1
Preparing Our Solution

Dynamics AX provides one of the best development environments of any ERP product. It is often easy to forget that the purpose of this environment is to create or extend functionality in order to satisfy a business requirement. The purpose of this chapter is to provide a short refresher on some of the core concepts and the preparation work required, before we start cutting code to put us on the right track to develop or extend functionality in Dynamics AX. This will enable your solutions to be maintainable and extendable, and minimize the impact on future updates and upgrades.

This chapter does not cover the installation and configuration of the required environments; it is assumed that this has already been done. We assume that our development environment has the AX client, management tools, and Visual Studio Professional 2013 installed. If you are using a version prior to **cumulative update 8** (**CU8**), you will need to use Visual Studio 2010 Professional.

If we have to use **Team Foundation Server** (**TFS**), each developer must have their own development environment. Typically, we will have a virtual server as a single box AX installation.

In this chapter, we will cover the following topics:

- The technical architecture of a solution
- Minimizing the footprint of customizations
- Selecting the appropriate layer for our solution
- Creating the models
- Creating a label file
- Configuring source control
- Creating a project

- Setting up a default project and model
- Designing the technical solution
- Designing test plans

The technical architecture of a solution

In the first part of this chapter, we will briefly cover some key topics to refresh our memory. We will then cover some areas that we will expand on as we progress through the chapters. If you want to read in more detail about the technical infrastructure, the MorphX IDE, and development practices and patterns, refer to *Appendix A, Efficient Design and Development with Microsoft Dynamics AX*.

A good design is just as relevant to small change requests as it is for larger development. It has many attributes; some key points to consider are as follows:

- **Configurable**: As much of the decision making as possible should be stored in configuration and parameter tables. It may take longer, but it will save time when the development goes through integration testing.
- **Extendable**: The solution (no matter how small) should be designed such that it can be extended without rewriting. Using patterns can help with this.
- **Design around standard patterns**: This helps avoid reinventing the wheel and ensures a higher quality design that is more consistent. The solution we write should look and feel like any other part of AX. This means less training and better adoption by our users.
- **Validate the design**: This should be done against the requirement before the work on the design commences. In some cases, it is appropriate to prototype the solution.
- **Use the advanced features of AX appropriately**: Just because a cool feature exists, it doesn't mean that it should be used in this case.
- **Configuration and parameter tables should be rule-based**: For example, a property used to determine which mode of delivery is urgent is limiting. It implies that there can only be one urgent delivery mode.
- **Minimize changes to standard code**: The more standard code we change, the more work is required to maintain the system in terms of updates and upgrades. We will discuss minimizing this footprint in the next section.

Most of the functionality that we write in AX (a new solution or customization of an existing functionality) is data-based. We use forms to create, maintain, and view this data, tables to store and validate this data, and classes to act upon it.

Data structures

The first part to design is the data structures. Even though these may evolve, a lot of attention is required here. A simple analogy would be to compare this to building a house; you can change the furniture, even add a room, but you cannot add a basement garage.

There is some guidance to be found here, that is, the structure will normally fit into an existing pattern that is already being used by AX. We normally expect to have the following types of tables in our solution:

- **Parameter**: This is a single record table that typically contains the table's defaults and other behavioral properties, such as the default printer settings.
- **Group**: An example of this can be the customer group or delivery mode tables. They can act as lookup values, or even control functionality. For example, we may create a table that contains a user's default label printer.

> When you find yourself creating multiple fields of the same type (for example, the `Urgent delivery method`, `Normal delivery method`, and `Low priority delivery method` fields), they should be recorded in a table with a reference (enumerated type) so that you can identify them in code.

- **Main**: These are the master data tables, such as items and customers.
- **Worksheet header** and **Worksheet line**: These are the standard document entry tables, such as the sales order table and lines, where the dataset has a header and lines.
- **Worksheet**: This is a table used to enter data that is later processed in some way. This is not very common in AX as most documents have both a header and lines.
- **Transaction header** and **Transaction lines**: These are the result of the worksheet after posting or committing, such as the sales invoice header and sales invoice lines.
- **Transaction**: This is the table where the result of posting is a single-level transaction record. The stock transaction table called `InventTrans` is an example, which is viewed as a list of stock transactions.

> The preceding types are actually set as a property on the table when it is created, enforcing the pattern further.

During the course of this book, we will be writing a solution based on a hypothetical case of a fleet management system as Contoso's internal development team. Based on the previous guidance, we can take the following simple requirement and quickly turn it into a data structure: we require the ability to view and maintain records of vehicles and their utilization.

From this, we can see that we will need to store a list of vehicles, probably of varying types, and then a record of their utilization will be attached to each vehicle. This leads us to the following structure:

Table type	Example table name	Description
Parameter	`ConFMSParameters`	The main parameters
Group	`ConFMSVehicleGroup`	A list of vehicle types
Main	`ConFMSVehicleTable`	A list of vehicles
Transaction	`ConFMSVehicleTrans`	The utilization records

In this case, little thought was required as the requirement fits nicely into the standard AX patterns.

The naming was also straightforward: the organization's prefix is `Con`, the module's prefix is `FMS`, and the rest of the name comes from the entity name and the table type. You will see this type of naming throughout AX. As far as possible, we should be able to understand from the name alone what it is, what it does, how it does it, and why it does what it does.

The user interface

The next part of the structure is the user interface, where we again have a set of templates that suit most circumstances:

- **List page**: This is the main entry point to both the main tables and worksheet tables. The list page offers the ability to search and act upon the data. You can also open a details form from list pages that allows the record to be edited or a new entry to be created. An example can be found by navigating to **Forms** | **CustTableListPage**.
- **Details form, master**: This is designed to allow the maintenance of master data, such as customers and items. These are not entry points, but are opened from a related record or the list page. We sometimes use this form type to create data, but we typically use a specific creation form for this. An example can be found by navigating to **Forms** | **CustTable**.

- **Details form, transaction**: This is intended for the maintenance of worksheet tables, such as the sales order form. An example of this can be found by navigating to **Forms** | **SalesTable**. The term "transaction" may be confusing here; it is not related to the `TableGroup` property of the table.
- **Simple list**: This is useful for group and transaction tables that are a simple list of records with only a small number of fields to present. An example of this can be found by navigating to **Forms** | **CustClassificationGroup**.
- **Simple list, details**: This is where the group table has many fields that are better arranged in groups of fields. There is still a list element, but there is a pane that allows for easier entry of data. An example of this can be found by navigating to **Forms** | **DeliveryMode**.
- **Table of contents**: This template is used for parameter forms. An example of this can be found by navigating to **Forms** | **CustParameters**.
- **Dialog**: These forms follow a style design to be used as a popup to gather some information and return it to the caller. A form used to create data is likely to use this template as we enter data and then ask AX to create the record once complete.
- **Drop dialog**: These appear as if they drop down from the calling button, and are typically used to perform an action using the current record. They are designed to display a small number of form controls, which the user will update as required before pressing **OK**. The following screenshot shows this:

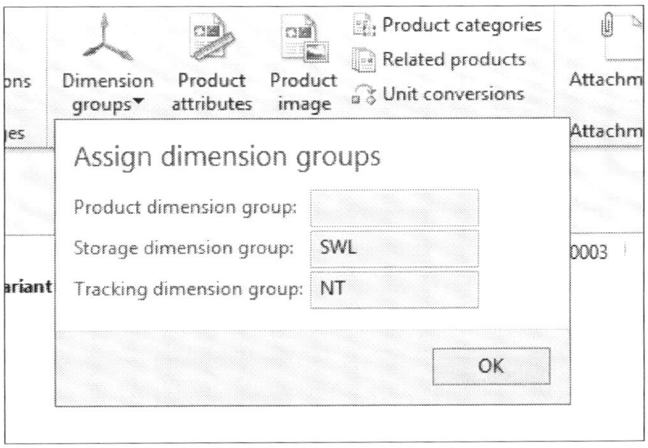

> The preceding templates are available for us to choose from when we create a form. Using these templates further assists us in creating a user interface consistent with AX.

Based on the preceding templates, we can create the following forms for our example requirement:

- **Table of contents**: `ConFMSParameters`
- **Simple list, details**: `ConFMSVehicleGroup`
- **List page**: `ConFMSVehicleTableListPage`
- **Details form, master**: `ConFMSVehicleTable`
- **Simple list**: `ConFMSVehicleTrans`

We normally name forms after the table they act on, except for list pages. The last example does not really have a true template; the simple list is the closest. The data structures and forms are taken directly from how other parts of AX behave. This should always be a design goal as it ensures that our users' incumbent knowledge of AX is used, reducing the time needed to learn the new feature and minimizing errors.

Application logic

Classes are used to store the main business logic. They are often used to handle user interface and table events as well. This allows the code to be reused and extended more easily.

The other key point is that we should also consider that we may want our solution to be available on mobile devices, and a careful thought about how we write the logic can make this much easier.

Classes in AX can be deployed as custom services that are consumed as WCF services in mobile or other Windows applications. This means that the logic should be simple to access, and have business logic in distinct classes, allowing the logic to be reused safely.

For example, we have a table with a status field that performs some validation and other events. We would write this in the data contract and service class pattern—a data contract to store the data to be acted upon and a service class to process the change. This can be used in a dialog form with the AX client or exposed as a service, allowing a mobile application to set the status.

Minimizing the footprint of changes

The footprint we make on existing objects is a key consideration when it comes to solution maintainability and the associated costs.

Microsoft has made key investments in the development environment in order to make it easier to write code in such a way that it sits alongside another party's solution. The advantage for Microsoft is that their customers can adopt multiple solutions or add-ons from ISVs with minimum effort.

Prior to AX 2012, this effort would have involved merging code from different partners and additional effort would have been required to ensure that a hotfix from one organization did not regress code in another add-on.

The next sections will highlight the practices and technologies that accomplish this.

Where to make the change

We are often asked to make changes to AX that require standard objects to be modified; often, the difficult decision is about where the change is to be made.

Firstly, we should consider how the code is structured by taking the example of a form that acts upon a table. Tables are structured into fields, field groups, indexes, relations, delete actions (for example, cascading the deletion to child tables), and methods. Forms are structured into form-level methods, data sources (a reference to a table), and controls. A request might be, "Can we make the vehicle field on the transport form mandatory?"

This is possible; the form control does have this property, as do the data source field and the equivalent field on the table—so, which of these to use? The answer is always as high in the stack as possible. The requirement is that the table always has this particular field filled in, so wherever this field is added, it should be mandatory.

The same pattern applies to code changes—always at the highest level and in this order: class, table, form data source field/method, form control.

> Making changes to form controls is very rarely required, and should be considered as a deviation from best practices.

Even hiding controls on forms should be handled in a method (which is usually called `enableControls`), as this makes the change more obvious and much easier to read, extend, and reuse.

The use of field groups

We may already use field groups, and it is best practice to do so. It may seem strange at first that we are creating what are essentially UI components in the data layer, but this pays off in terms of consistent UI and reduced footprint on standard AX. Forms dynamically display the fields that are in that field group; by adding a new field to the appropriate field group, the forms magically display this new field.

The reason this reduces footprint is because we are making one change that affects all forms that refer to the field group, and doesn't affect the form when applying updates.

Eventing

Eventing is a new key feature in AX 2012 that, along with models, is a key enabler for ISVs to write add-ons for AX.

Event subscription

This technology allows you to subscribe to an event in AX. So, instead of modifying the method, we simply subscribe to it as a pre- or post-event. We can then perform our logic elsewhere in an X++ or a .NET assembly, and even modify method parameters and return values.

This subscription is not a modification to the source method. Therefore, a method can have subscriptions in several different models in the same layer.

Delegates

Delegates are empty method stubs to which we subscribe. They are created by the original author and called from within their code. This is done so that you can subscribe to events that happen within a method without modifying a method.

For example, the following lines of code would be a delegate written by an ISV (`Axp` is the prefix used by this ISV):

```
delegate void weightCaptured(AxpWeighTicketContract _contract)
{
}
```

The ISV will then call this delegate at the appropriate time with the data contract. By subscribing to this delegate, you can handle the event and perform the necessary tasks with the supplier contract. This provides a hook into the supplied solution without modifying it. For more information about the guidelines on delegates, visit `http://msdn.microsoft.com/en-us/library/gg879953.aspx`.

Extending a class

Another method of modifying behavior with a minimal footprint is to extend the class. This should be done only if you cannot perform the task through an event subscription.

The pattern is implemented with the following steps:

1. Create a new class and use the `extends` keyword to extend the class you need to change.
2. Override the method you wish to change.
3. Modify the construct method on the base class so that it constructs your class based on the criteria you want.

Table-level form events

The table has several events that happen based on form events. In this example for the modified event, the mechanism is conceptualized as follows:

- A data bound field's `modified` event will call the data source field's `modified` method
- The bound data source field's `modified` event will call the table's `modifiedField` event with the field ID of the field being modified

The table's `modified` event is normally a large `switch` statement based on the field ID parameter with a case for each handled field. To modify this, we can simply add a case for our new field or change the behavior of an existing case.

In this situation, we should subscribe to the `modifiedField` method, but another option would be to create a new method with the same profile. This is preferable if we are the end-user organization, but is essential for VARs and ISVs. This is done by copying the method header. Let's take a look at the following example:

```
public void modifiedField(FieldId _fieldId)
```

We can then create a new method, as follows:

```
public void conModifiedField(FieldId _fieldId)
```

> **Downloading the example code**
>
> You can download the example code files from your account at `http://www.packtpub.com` for all the Packt Publishing books you have purchased. If you purchased this book elsewhere, you can visit `http://www.packtpub.com/support` and register to have the files e-mailed directly to you.

We can then create a `switch` statement to handle the fields we need to in this new method. In order to call this new method, we can then add a call to our new method in the original `modifiedField` method:

```
public void modifiedField(FieldId _fieldId)
{
    super(_fieldId);
    switch (_fieldId)
    {
        case fieldNum(<TableName>, <FieldName>):
            // code
            break;
    }
    // Con Var modification by SB 2014/06/09 handle custom fields
    this.conModifiedField(_fieldId);
}
```

Selecting the appropriate layer for our solution

This choice of layer is normally straightforward. As an ISV, we will use the ISV layer; as a VAR, the VAR layer; and so on.

We can sometimes choose, as the end user between the higher layers, CUS and USR. It does not normally matter which, as long as we stick to it. Incorporating more layers adds to the maintenance cost.

The main reason for using both CUS and USR is when we (as an end user organization) have multiple installations of AX that share a common base application. We would manage the CUS layer centrally, and each installation will be responsible for their installation-specific customizations in the USR layer.

The layer is selected in the AX Configuration Utility. To change the current layer, follow these steps:

1. Open **Microsoft Dynamics AX 2012 Configuration Utility**. This is accessed from the **Administrative Tools** Windows program group.
2. Select the desired configuration from the **Configuration** drop-down list and select the **Developer** tab.
3. Select the appropriate layer from the **Application object layer to open** drop-down list.

4. If the layer is not `usr`, you will need to enter the development license code in the field **Development license code**, and again in **Confirm license code**.
5. Press **OK**.

When we open the AX client the next time, the configured layer will be used.

Configuring source control

In this section, we will first configure the system to use MorphX VCS, and then reconfigure it to use **Team Foundation Services**.

Configuring AX to use MorphX VCS

If we are using MorphX VCS, which was designed for one to five developers, we will all be working on the same environment. This is called **shared development**.

MorphX VCS is set up within the MorphX IDE, as follows:

1. Navigate to the IDE (*Ctrl* + *D*).
2. From the main menu, go to **Version Control** | **Version Control Parameters** (or press *Ctrl* + *Shift* + *V*).
3. Configure the form as shown in the following screenshot:

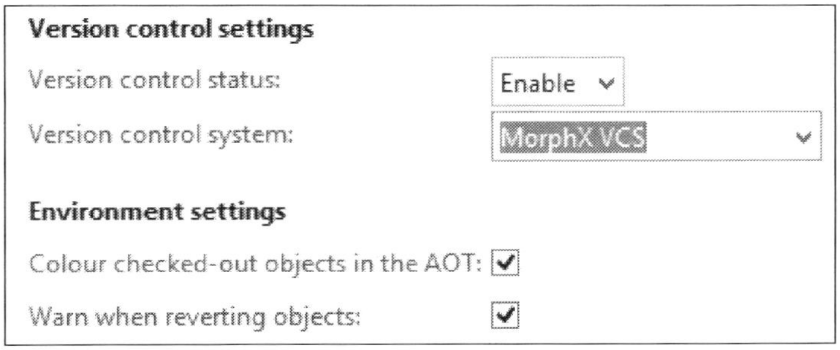

4. Press **OK**.

We can then configure the system settings for additional control over the VCS settings. This is covered towards the end of this section.

Configuring AX to use Team Foundation Services

In order to use TFS, we need access to a TFS server. This can be installed on premise, or we can use Visual Studio Online. For more information on Visual Studio Online, refer to http://www.visualstudio.com/en-us/products/what-is-visual-studio-online-vs.aspx.

If AX is cumulative update 8 or later, you will need Visual Studio 2013 professional or a higher edition. Ensure that you have started Visual Studio once and signed in with your Microsoft account.

Using Visual Studio Online with AX CU7 or prior

If you are using **cumulative update 7** (**CU7**) or prior versions, AX will not support Visual Studio 2013, which makes it incompatible with Visual Studio Online as this always uses the latest release. If we try to use Visual Studio Online, it will not be able to authenticate and we will be denied access to the online service.

In order to solve this, we need to install Microsoft Visual Studio Team Explorer 2013, which is a free download available at http://www.visualstudio.com/downloads/download-visual-studio-vs. Once this is installed, you need to start Visual Studio and log in with your Microsoft account. Team Explorer installs the Visual Studio 2013 shell in order to make it available for use with AX. This is where you manage the connection to Visual Studio Online.

Prior to Visual Studio 2010, we had to install Microsoft Visual Studio Team Foundation Server 2013 MSSCCI provider (MSSCCI). Further information on this is available at http://msdn.microsoft.com/en-us/library/dd997788.aspx#msscci. This needs to be installed in order for AX (prior to CU8) to connect to the latest TFS release.

> The Visual Studio Online service is a great way to gain access to TFS, and is currently free for up to five users.

Creating a new TFS project using Visual Studio Online

In this example, we will use Visual Studio Online. Registration is free but a Microsoft account is required to access the service. You will be given a portal URL that reads something such as `https://<yourorganisation>.visualstudio.com`.

Once the required steps have been done, we can create our new TFS project, as described in the following steps:

1. Open your Visual Studio Online portal.
2. Under **Recent projects and teams**, select **New**. This opens the following form:

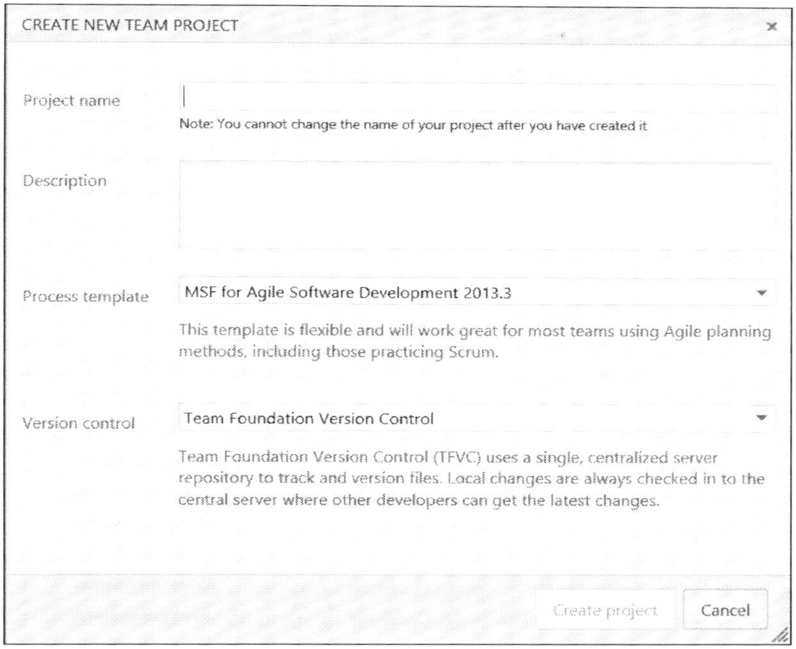

3. Configure the form as required. In our example, we will use `6015GettingStarted` as the project name.
4. Press **Create project**. After a short time, this message will be displayed:

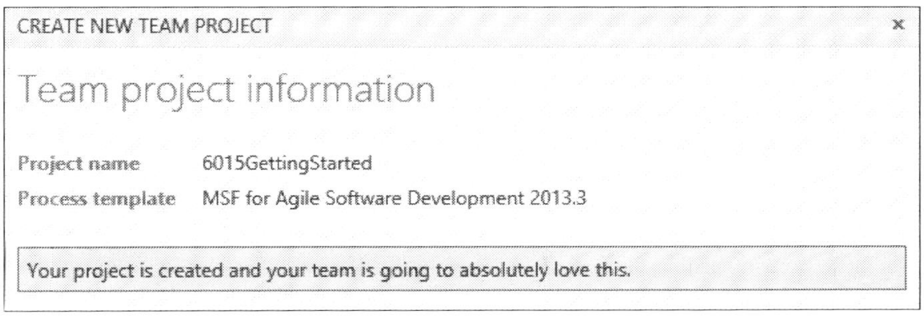

5. Click on **Navigate to project**.
6. This opens the new project. In this form, we should add the team members using their Microsoft account.
7. Once the team members are added, we can move on to configuring AX. The next step is done by each developer.
8. Create a folder in your local hard drive for the local files. For example, `C:\Projects\VCS\AX\6015GettingStarted`.

> The folder must be specific to AX and should be named the same as the TFS project name.

Configuring AX version control parameters to connect to TFS

The following steps complete the configuration:

1. Open the AX IDE and then the **Version Control Parameters** form.
2. Configure the **General** tab, as follows:

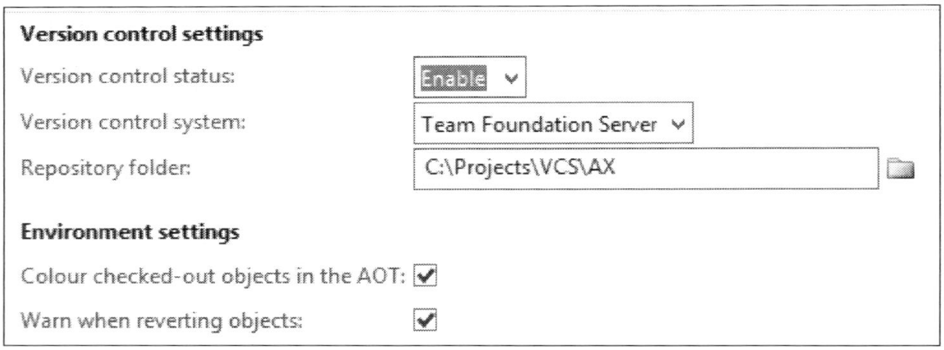

> The `Repository` folder is the structure below our project folder.

3. When **Version control system** is changed to **Team Foundation Server**, a **Team Foundation Server** tab appears on the left table of contents pane. Select this tab.

4. Configure **Team Foundation Server** options as follows:

Team Foundation Server URL	This is your local TFS address or your Visual Studio Online URL, for example, `https://<yourorganisation>.visualstudio.com/DefaultCollection`.
Team Foundation project name	This is the project name we created in TFS; in this case, `6015GettingStarted`.
Branch folder	We do not recommend branching at this stage. Enter `Trunk` in this case.
Application root folder	This is the folder name we created for the project, for example, `6015GettingStarted`.

5. Press **OK**.
6. AX will show the **Sign-In to Team Foundation Services** dialog, as shown here:

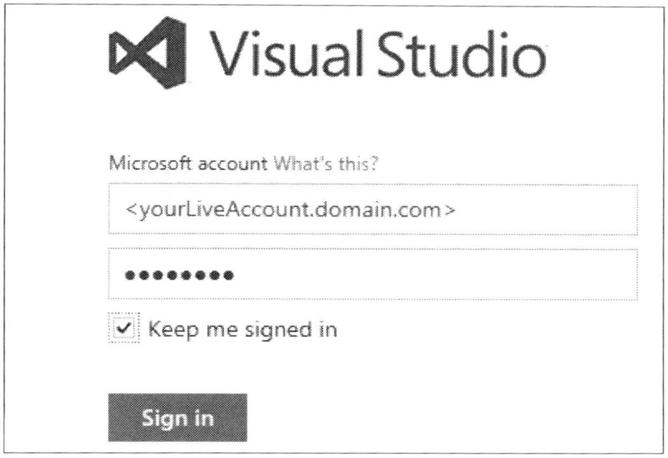

7. Complete the form with the same account details that you use to access the portal.
8. If successful, AX will show the following message:

```
Pending add on C:\Projects\VCS\AX\6015GettingStarted\Definition\
VCSDef.xml with status Getting
```

Troubleshooting

The most common error is as follows:

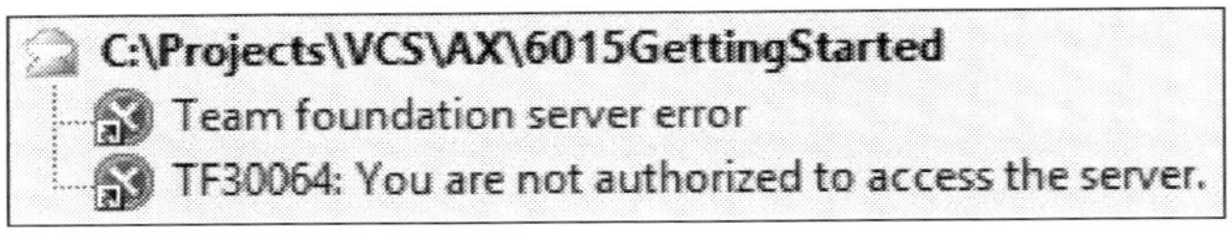

This has the following possible reasons:

- The URL was entered incorrectly; most likely, `DefaultCollection` was misspelt or missing
- MSSCCI was not installed—CU7 or prior releases of AX
- You do not actually have permission

If the URL is incorrect or you have no access to the Internet, the following message is displayed: Team Foundation services are not available from server `https://badnameeurl.visualstudio.com/defaultcollection`.

The best way to debug this is to open the URL (copied from the settings form) to a browser. If this works, try connecting to TFS through Visual Studio 2013, as shown in the following steps:

1. Open Visual Studio 2013 (or Team Explorer if using CU7 or prior releases).
2. Navigate to **TEAM | Connect to Team Foundation Server**.
3. In the **Connect to Team Project** dialog, click on **Servers...**.
4. In the **Add/Remove Team Foundation Server** dialog, click on **Add...**.
5. Configure the **Add Team Foundation Server** dialog, as shown in the following screenshot:

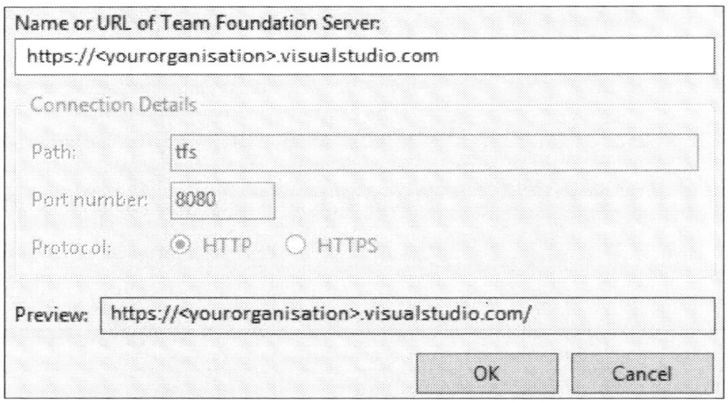

6. Press **OK**.
7. Visual Studio will now ask you to log in. Sign in using the credentials you used to access the Visual Studio portal.
8. Close the **Add/Remove Team Foundation Server** dialog.
9. The **Connect to Team Project** will now show the team project collections, but we can simply close this as we have completed the required authentication to Visual Studio Online.
10. Open the AX client again, and try the configuration again.

We can now add the elements we create or modify to source control. Refer to *Appendix B, Using Version Control*, for more information on using source control.

Creating the models

The models required depend on your organization's requirements, and these were discussed in the previous chapter. In this section, we will create the models based on our Fleet Management System, from a customer or end user perspective.

Models should also include your prefix. In this case, we will use the `Con` prefix for Contoso. We will create our models in the USR layer, as explained later in this section.

ISV models

ISVs will normally have a base model that contains shared code between all models, and a model per add-on or vertical solution. Some care is required in ensuring that there isn't a circular dependency chain between models; that is, both reference each other's models, requiring the installation to have special instructions.

Following the naming convention discussed in the previous chapter of prefixing elements—an ISV with the `Axp` prefix and an add-on named `Documental`—they can name the model `AxpDocumental`.

VAR models

If we are a VAR building a solution to customer-specific requirements, we will have three models: one for the actual modifications, another for changes to security, and the third for the labels. For example, if our prefix is `Bcl` and the customer is Contoso, we will have `BclContoso`, `BclContosoLabels`, and `BclContosoSecurity`.

Creating security in a separate model is not mandatory, but helps when implementing projects with the Sure Step methodology because it allows security to be worked on in separate streams.

Customer or end user models

If we are a global organization, with separate Dynamics AX installations, we may decide to develop a central application, which is then installed on each site. In this case, we will have three models placed in the CUS layer. For the Contoso example, we have `ConGlobalApplication`, `ConGlobalLabels`, and `ConGlobalSecurity`.

The most common scenario is to host Dynamics AX centrally, therefore having one application. The same three models are required, but this time in the USR layer: `ConApplication`, `ConLabels`, and `ConSecurity`.

It may make sense to place distinct sets of functionality in separate models, and this would certainly help in managing separate development streams. Over time, the models tend to develop cyclic dependencies, which require them to be merged in order to ensure that a complete set of code is deployed.

In our example, we will create a model for a specific functionality—our Fleet Management System—and it will make sense to hold it in a separate stream. However, it would be a particularly bad idea to hold each module's modifications in its own model.

Creating the models

Before we create the models, we must be in the correct layer; the USR layer in this case. The model creation is done by following these steps:

1. Open the Dynamics AX Client, and open the development environment (*Ctrl* + *D*).
2. From the main menu, go to **Tools** | **Model management** | **Create model**.
3. Complete the **Create model** form as shown here:

Field	Description
Model name	This is the name of the model. It can contain spaces, but it is normally the same as the display name.
Model Publisher	Your organization or department.
Layer	The layer the model should be created in. This should be the current layer.
Version	The version of the model. This becomes part of the strong name of the model during signing.
Model description	Long description of the model. It is a good idea to link this to a functional or technical design document.

4. Leave **Set as current model** checked and press **OK**.

An example of a completed **Create model** form is shown in the following screenshot:

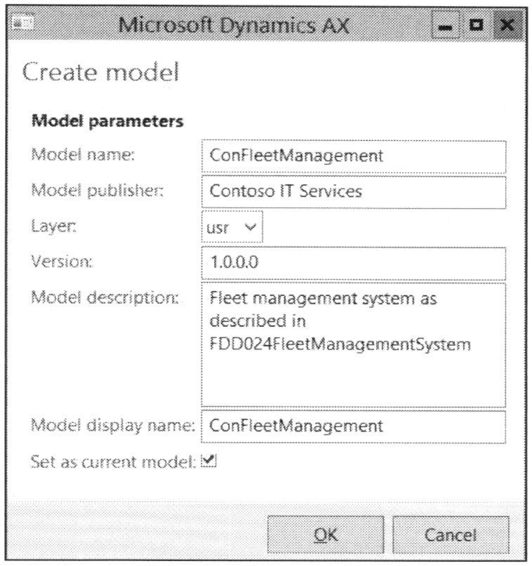

If we have version control enabled for TFS, we will also ask for the `Model` repository folder. It will suggest, in our example `C:\Projects\VCS\AX\6015GettingStarted\<Model folder>`. Replace `<Model folder>` with the model name, as shown in the following screenshot:

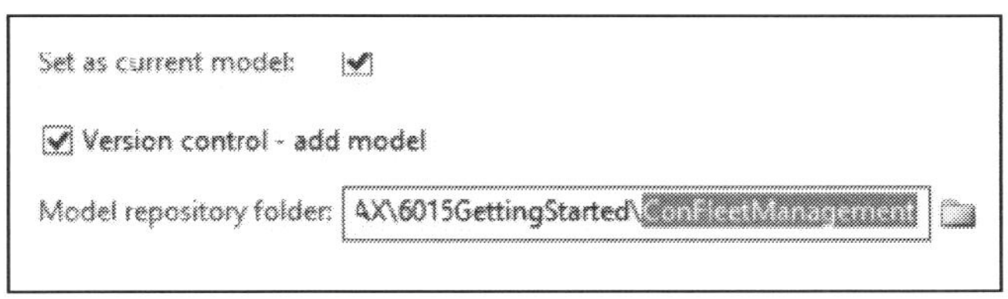

Using the preceding instructions as a guide, we will need to create the following models. Usefully, AX will remember the previous information, so we only need to populate **Model name** and **Model display name**:

- `ConFleetManagement`
- `ConLabels`
- `ConFleetManagementSecurity`

Creating a label file

Labels are not only a great feature of AX, giving an easy way to provide multilingual features, but are also required in order to comply with best practices. Labels should be placed in their own model, which we created earlier.

The label file is identified by three characters, and the list is global. The normal name is our prefix; for example, it could be `CON` for Contoso. `DYN`, `AX`, and `DAX` are particularly bad names as they may be used by Microsoft or an ISV at some point.

To create the label file, follow these steps:

1. Change to the `ConLabel` model by going to **Tools** | **Model management** | **Change current model**.
2. Ensure that the `ConLabel` model is shown in the lower status bar, as shown in the following screenshot:

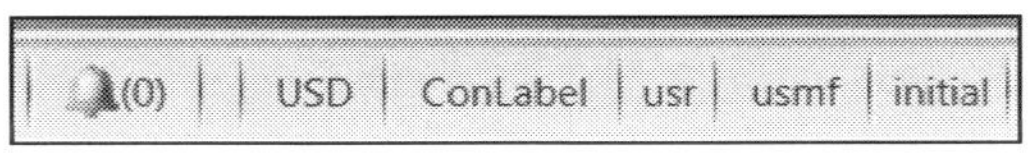

> If this does not display, navigate to **Tools** | **Options** | **Status bar** and check **Show current model**.

3. Go to **Tools** | **Label** | **Label file wizard** from the main menu.
4. On the **Add label file** page, accept the defaults (only **Create new label file ID** is checked) and press **Next**.
5. On the **New label file ID** page, enter the label file ID; in our example, it's `CON`. Pay attention to the warnings on this page!
6. Press **Next**. On the **Create the label files** page, press **Finish**.

The AX Client will appear unresponsive for a short time while it creates the label file. Once the **Label file wizard** closes, the label file will exist in the AOT.

Navigate in the AOT to **Label files**. You will see the new label file, **CON**, as shown in the following screenshot:

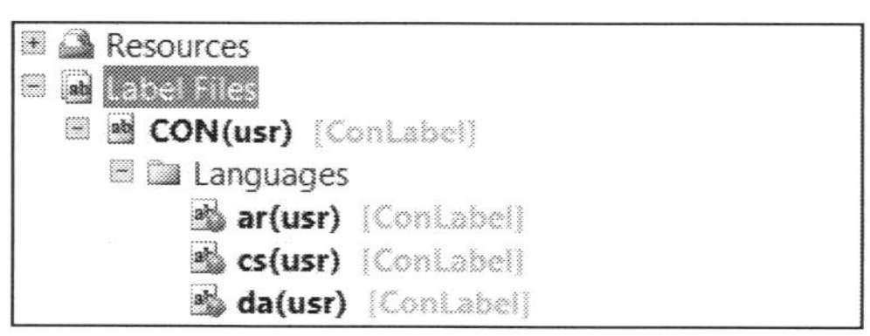

Creating a project

We should have a project for each area of work, for example, one project for each business requirement document. This helps spread the workload across the team, which is ideally split in such a way that the same objects are not modified by different developers.

If we are using source control, the object (form, class, table, and so on) will be locked until checked back in. This can become very inefficient if, for example, we have two different developers working on sales order requirements.

The naming is important; a common structure is as follows:

```
<Prefix><Requirement Id><Description>
```

For example, if we are working on a requirement to credit history fact panes to the sales order, as identified in the requirement document 2.4.1, we may name the project `BclFDD241_SalesOrderCreditHistoryFactPanes`.

To create a new project, follow these steps:

1. Change the model to `ConFleetManagement`.
2. Open the project window (*Ctrl* + *Shift* + *P*)
3. Right-click on the **Shared** node and go to **New** | **Project**.
4. Press *F2* to rename the project to `ConFleetManagementSystem`. We would normally include a reference number, which you may see referenced as a **Functional Definition Document** (**FDD**) or **Technical Definition Document** (**TDD**) reference.
5. Open the project by double-clicking or pressing *Enter*.
6. This opens a blank project, where we can create objects or drag from the AOT. However, we will create a structure similar to the AOT, as follows.
7. Right click on the root `ConFleetManagement` node and go to **New** | **Group**.

> We can see many options in this list, one for each AOT object type. Creating objects directly in the root node can make it difficult to manage. Having them grouped is much better as the project grows.

8. This will create a group object named `Object1`. Opening the **Properties** tab shows that this group can contain **All** AOT object types.

9. Since we are copying the AOT structure, we should change **ProjectGroupType** to `DataDictionary`, and **Name** to **Data Dictionary**, as shown in the following screenshot:

10. In the AOT, this node contains tables, so right-click on our new **Data Dictionary** node and select **New | Group**. This time set the **ProjectGroupType** property to `Tables`, and **Name** to `Tables`.
11. Continue to create at least the following, as per the AOT structure:

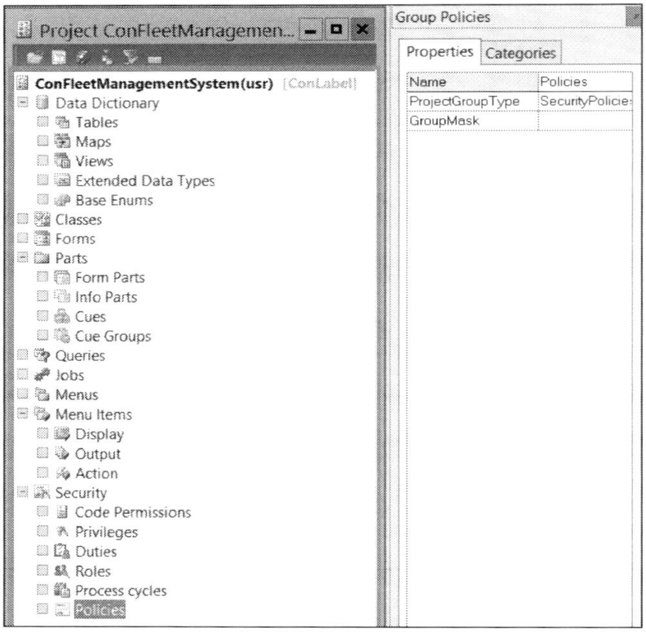

[The **ProjectGroupType** is the same as the AOT name, except for the **Security** subnodes. They are prefixed with `Security`.]

Since creating the project structure can be time-consuming, it is a great idea to create a project called `<prefix>ProjectTemplate`. We simply duplicate (right-click and choose **Duplicate** from the context menu) the project and rename it each time we need a new project.

[All new objects must be manually added to source control; this includes projects. This is done by right-clicking on the project and selecting **Add to Version Control**.]

Setting up the default project and model

AX will set the model to the default model whenever the client is opened. This will be `USR Model` if we are working in the USR layer. To avoid adding objects or changes to the wrong model, we can change this default. To do this, follow these steps:

1. In the development environment's main menu, go to **Tools** | **Options**. This will open your user options.
2. Select the **Development** tab and configure the form, as shown in the following screenshot:

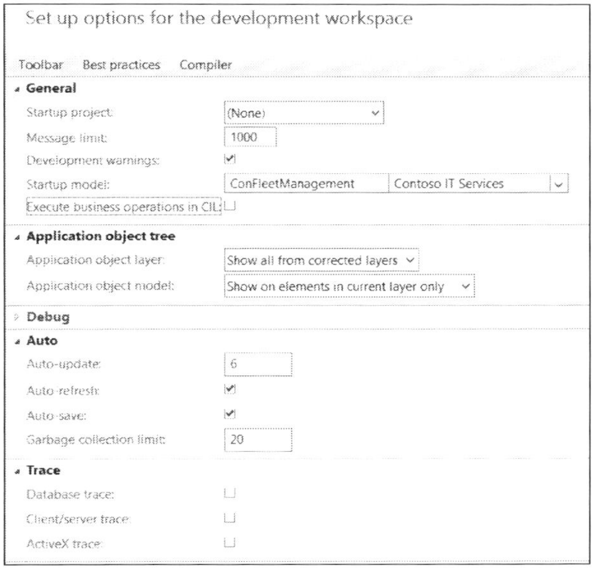

3. The key points on this form are as follows:

Startup project	The project AX will open by default. This can be useful when we work primarily in one project.
Startup model	The default model that AX will select when starting up. This is very important, and critical for users setting up security from the client (as the model is not obvious to them).
Execute business operations in CIL	Many events in AX, such as table events, will run automatically in IL (IL is the more common .NET term for this). This can cause confusion when we forget to generate the incremental CIL, especially when we don't configure the AX server to allow hot swapping of assemblies. During development, it is a good idea to uncheck this option and enable hot swapping of assemblies in the AX Server Configuration. Please see *Hot-swapping of .NET assemblies in the AOS [AX 2012]* at `https://msdn.microsoft.com/en-us/library/hh538487.aspx`.

Designing the technical solution

In most implementations, we have several roles involved in the solution design, build, and implementation. Our role is to design and develop a technical solution to a business requirement, and as discussed earlier, we will follow the design and build of a Fleet Management System.

The first steps in this are to analyze the business requirement and design a solution within Dynamics AX. This work will typically be led by a consultant, who will (in short) perform the following:

- Match the business requirements to the AX functionality. The requirement may require new functionality or an extension to existing functionality.
- Discuss the technical solution with a technical consultant/developer in order to design a solution that is feasible in AX in a suitable time frame.
- Work through the solution with the solution architect to ensure that it fits in the overall solution design.

Create functional design documents. These will be signed by the customer stakeholders and process owners.

The consultant may propose table structures as parts of the functional design, but these are only to reinforce the requirement. The technical designer may find a more appropriate solution to this. The process is intended to leverage the skills of all parties in the solution delivery, allowing all parties to use their skills by abstracting the solution. Here is its summary:

- The customer or process owner understands the process
- The consultant is an expert in AX and focuses on the solution, creating a FDD
- The solution architect validates the FDD against the solution design
- The technical architect (or lead/analyst developer) creates the technical design while validating that it fits with the overall technical solution

These roles often merge, but there should always be a separation of business requirement definition and technical design definition. This freedom over the technical design does not mean we have total freedom over the technical solution. At all levels, it has to both match the original requirement and fit in with the overall solution. Just because it is technically cool does not mean it is appropriate. Our purpose is to create a technical solution to a business requirement.

We will evolve the design throughout this book, and the reason for each decision will be explained. It is important to understand and follow these design goals:

- **Upgrades and system maintainability**: Minimize the footprint on standard AX.
- **Design for code reuse**: This could span from creating a general framework to a useful static function on a global class.
- **Design for a service-oriented architecture**: Always consider that your code might be used as a service or as part of a service. This paradigm also promotes code reuse.
- **Validate the design**: Always validate the technical design against the original requirement, which is a very common cause of time overruns and cost. A prototype can be useful for this.
- **Use design patterns**: Do not reinvent the wheel. Patterns save design time, reduce mistakes, and promote a solution that better conforms to best practice.

The technical design will include decisions on what technologies, frameworks, and patterns we will use. We may revert some decisions later on, but the majority we need to be sure we get right first time.

One such design element is the data structures. Once we start using them in code and the UI, it makes any changes to this more and more difficult. Some elements can't easily be reverted, such as whether to use table inheritance or not.

Table inheritance is a little like class inheritance. For example, we may have a core vehicle table, and specialized tables that inherit its properties (fields) and methods. As a more specific example, an articulated truck will have different attributes compared to a company car.

Data structure design considerations

The data structure architecture within Dynamics AX is breathtaking. When designing the technical structure, the tables and views should be considered along with classes as part of your static structure.

> We are not making the classes persist in the database. The table definition may be designed on **object-oriented** (**OO**) principles, but we are using this to define physical tables that are transacted on reliably.

The key concepts within this are described in the following sections.

Extended data types

In traditional database design, a field tended to be one of a limited set of primitive types, such as string, number, and so on. The **extended data type** (**EDT**) system in AX allows us to define types with extended properties.

With this, we can control the following categories of properties:

Appearance	For example, the label, help text, size (string), alignment, and other type-specific properties.
Behavior	Direction, for example, RTL and presence information.
Business intelligence	Information used by the system to generate the OLAP database.
Data	A reference table, internal ID information, or a reference form (the form used to open the record identified by the database relation).
Relationships	For the example of the `ItemId` EDT, this would specify that this EDT references `InventTable.ItemId`. In this way, the system knows when the EDT is associated with a field on a child table and which table and record it references. Additionally, the table will often have a reference to the form that is used to edit the data, allowing the user to quickly navigate to the details form.

The specific properties aren't important for now, but understanding the concept is. Using EDTs ensures database consistency (primarily type and size) and user interface consistency (label, help text, and so on). This is done with very little effort, as we only have to change the EDT properties. Even more powerfully, changing the size of an EDT will change the size of all fields that reference it.

Therefore, we will always use an EDT when creating a field, and almost always use EDTs as variable declarations and method parameters. We can override most of the other properties on the table field, but we rarely do this.

[A key benefit is that we can control these properties with little effort, ensuring consistency throughout the user interface.]

In some cases, we need to have a minor difference; for instance, we may wish to change a label when used in a specific context. Rather than changing the field label, it is better to create a new EDT that extends the primary EDT.

It is possible to change standard EDTs, but great care must be taken, as we need to know the full effects of the change. The choice between using standard EDTs (for example, for description fields) or creating new EDTs will be covered when we use them in the next chapter.

Base enums – enumerated types

Base enums are what is more commonly known as enumerated types. They provide a list of options that are stored as a number in the database; the user interface will always display the corresponding text. They are equivalent to integers, and can be cast between the integer and the symbol (text).

Enums are great for status fields, where we need to have code written against a specific value. Writing code against number or string literals is bad practice. Should the option not exist or be removed from the enum's definition, we will get a compilation error when the code is compiled.

An example enum is `SalesStatus`, which contains the following elements:

Symbol	Label (based on en-us)	Enum value
None	None	0
Backorder	Open order	1
Delivered	Delivered	2
Invoiced	Invoiced	3
Canceled	Canceled	4

You should always reference the symbol in the code. AX will understand that and translate it into the Enum value.

Tables

The table definitions stored within AX synchronize with the business database in SQL Server; often, this is automatic. No changes should be made to the SQL Server table definition, as this will be overwritten whenever the database is synchronized.

The table definition information controls both the user interface and how the physical table in SQL Server is created. This includes table properties, field definitions, and indexes. Relationships and referential integrity constraints are not created within SQL Server; these are managed within AX. They control what happens to a child table when a record is deleted or the primary key is renamed. The field definitions also control both the user interface and the physical field in SQL Server. These are usually set by the EDT it is associated with.

A key differentiator for tables is that we can create methods and override table event methods such as `validateField`, `validateWrite`, `modifiedField`, `insert`, `delete`, and so on. This allows us to place table-level validation and events on the table centrally and not on the interface.

In AX 2012, we can now have inheritance within tables and valid date/time states. Inheritance will allow us to have a base table, such as a vehicle table, and specialized tables that extend it, such as a bulk/loose product truck with silos and a vehicle designed to take pallets. The interface natively understands this relationship and can display records for all inherited tables in one grid control. This is covered in *Chapter 2, Creating Data Structures*.

The valid time state provides a way to version records. For example, as data about an employee changes, we can at any time ask the system what the data was at a specific point in time.

The key consideration here in the design is to determine the structure and events we need to handle, which in turn drives the required EDTs and base enums.

Views

Views are SQL view definitions, created by constructing a query of one or more tables. They can contain aggregates and also calculate view fields, which are essentially a piece of **Transact-SQL** that equates to a column in view.

These are useful when flattening data from normalized tables. The only real drawback is that they are read-only views, and when they are placed on the user interface in a grid control, the grid control becomes read-only. This means that if we add a column from a related table that is editable, it will become read-only in the grid control.

Maps

Maps provide a method of sharing code for similar tables. A good example of this is the pricing logic for sales and purchase order lines that is handled by the `SalesPurchLine` map.

Maps contain a list of reference fields, details of how these reference fields map to the actual table fields, and methods. This is best explained with an example, such as calculating the stocking unit quantity from the quantity ordered (for example, stored in cases and sold in each).

Rather than write this code on the sales order line and the purchase order line, we can do this once using a map. On the `SalesPurchLine` map, there are fields for `PurchSalesUnit`, `ItemId`, and `SalesPurchQty`. They are mapped as follows:

Map field	SalesLine field	PurchLine field
ItemId	ItemId	ItemId
PurchSalesUnit	SalesUnit	PurchUnit
SalesPurchQty	SalesQty	PurchQty

We can create a simplified method on the map that contains the following code snippet:

```
InventQty  calcQtyOrdered(Qty _qtySalesPurch = realMin())
{
    InventQty       qty;
    InventTable     inventTable;
    Qty             qtySalesPurch = _qtySalesPurch;

    if (qtySalesPurch == realMin())
        qtySalesPurch = this.SalesPurchQty;

    if (!qtySalesPurch)
        return 0;
```

```
        // this is actually calling a method that should exist
        // on the actual table, for example, SalesLine
        inventTable = this.inventTable();


        qty = UnitConvert::qty(qtySalesPurch,
                               this.PurchSalesUnit,
                               inventTable.inventUnitId(),
                               this.ItemId);

        return decround(qty,InventTable::inventDecimals(this.ItemId));
    }
```

On the sales and purchase order line table, we can call the preceding method. An example from the `PurchLine` table is as follows:

```
    AmountCur calcLineAmount(Qty  qty = this.PurchQty)
    {
        AmountCur ret;

        if (this.LineDeliveryType != LineDeliveryType::OrderLineWithMulti
    pleDeliveries)
        {
            ret = this.SalesPurchLine::calcLineAmount(qty);
        }

        return ret;
    }
```

The map will then automatically construct itself using the field mapping. Hence, we call methods on the map as if they are static methods with the `::` sign. So, when called from the sales order line, `this.PurchSalesUnit` becomes `SalesLine.SalesUnit` and `this.SalesPurchQty` becomes `SalesLine.SalesQty`.

This can be a useful feature for reusing code across tables that provide similar functionalities.

Classes

Class definitions with AX provide functionality similar to C++, C#, or Java classes, in that they support inheritance and encapsulation. Interfaces can also be used and implemented in a way similar to C#.

Classes are created for the following purposes:

- User interface interaction
- Table event handling
- Services
- General processing (for example data updates, batch routines, and so on)

Although it is common to use a class to handle table events, the table itself will handle the interaction with the database. Form interaction classes are not mandatory for list pages, such as **Accounts receivable** | **Common** | **Customers** | **All customers**, but should be used on data entry forms that require logic. This ensures consistency and allows easier maintenance of logic.

When designing the static (mainly table and class) structure, we should break the design down so that we can easily expose that task as a service. An example can be a class that takes a vehicle out of service. This may perform many tasks: checking whether it was planned on loads, replacing the vehicle on the basis of a rule set, changing the status of the vehicle, and so on.

We may have other requirements to simply change the status of vehicle or associate suitable vehicles with unallocated loads. We have already written the code to change the status and the code to find a suitable vehicle. If we had classes for finding a suitable vehicle, changing status, and so on, we could've reused them, be it on a form or from code or linked to a service that could be used by a mobile application.

The point here is that we should break discrete pieces of functionality down into separate classes, as it then become much easier to reuse later on.

Forms

Most forms will be built from templates, which help us provide a consistent user interface that will look and feel much like the rest of AX. The helps reduce training time, reduce user error, and improve end user acceptance.

The following templates are available:

- A list page
- A details form—master
- A details form—transaction
- A simple list
- A simple list, with a details section

- A table of contents
- A dialog
- A drop dialog

The list page is our main entry point to both master data (items, customers, and so on) and transactional forms, such as sales orders.

The list page provides the user with a searchable list of records, with a button ribbon allowing the user to interact with the record, for example, Post sales invoice. They also provide key business intelligence about the current record, which means we don't have to navigate to the details form to make a decision on the record in question.

There are two types of details forms: master and transaction. Master forms are like customer and item forms, while sales order details and purchase order details are transaction forms. Details forms are designed to be opened from a list page.

Simple lists are useful for setup groups, where the form contains only a grid of a few fields. These are useful for simple lists of setup data. The simple list with details version contains a grid on the left and a details section that can be arranged into tabs to present many fields. Both of these form types are designed to be opened from the content area or menu.

Tables of contents are designed to be used for parameter forms. Although they may act on more than one data source (table), the tables will typically have a single record.

Dialog and drop dialog are similar in that both are designed to ask for limited information and then trigger an action. Both are usually called from another form. The difference is in how they are presented. The drop dialog will appear to drop down and be a part of the calling form, whereas a dialogs appears as a pop-up window. The difference is cosmetic, but drop dialogs are often preferred as they can't fall behind the current window.

Designing test plans

There are two main types of testing: unit testing and integration (process) testing. We are more concerned with unit testing.

Unit testing primarily ensures that the code performs functions for the functional design. We may also have performance requirements, where we need to test the code under a simulated load. AX provides a method to do this through a test project, where we can extend the test framework to write specific test cases.

These work well when simulating the load against the live hardware environment. We can use a range of performance tools to ascertain where performance bottlenecks may lie and correct them. It is better to know before "go live" that we have a bottleneck.

Even with this framework in place, manual testing is often the best method, especially since we are typically writing code based on database and UI interaction.

Let's take an example of a vehicle status change requirement. In this case, we will list the conditions that allow the status change to occur, and what should happen.

Status changed to	condition	Result
Available	Status: created Vehicle: not acquired	Error "Vehicle not yet acquired" Status remains unchanged
Available	Status: created Vehicle: acquired	Success Status changed to Available
Not available	Status: created Vehicle: not acquired	Error "Vehicle not yet acquired" Status remains unchanged

We then test our code to ensure that these statuses are being followed. Because we have one class that handles the status change, the form button, service call, and code call should also work. "Should" does not mean "will" of course, so each should be tested individually.

One of the biggest fears and causes of end user complaints is regression. The users involved in testing are usually key users or process owners, who are already busy with additional work brought on by an implementation. It is often their job to train their users, and "sell" the system's benefits; user buy-in is critical for successful user adoption.

There are two causes of regression: code that breaks other code or a change to a process that is incompatible with another process. The latter is mitigated by getting a solution architect or lead consultant who is responsible for the solution as a whole.

Code regression can be caused by the simplest change, and these changes are often the main cause of regression, as testing is often skipped in these cases. This is mitigated by thinking of testing as a component of the technical design, and having good technical documentation. The risks are further reduced if developer notes points where regression might occur, as the code is being written. Since the code that might be affected is commented with the TDD or FDD reference, it should be easy to locate the test plan to check for regression.

Summary

In this chapter, we covered the steps that we take to start up a new project. The actual steps for each new development may vary, depending on the scale of the work required. The key points to take away are that we should target the correct layer, use a specific model, place our work in a project, produce test cases for our solution, design the technical design, and use source control.

This preparatory work may seem a lot to do before starting work on a new development, but it pays off in dividends later. In the next chapter, we will design and create the data structures required for our solution.

2

Creating Data Structures

In this chapter, we will design and build the initial data structures for our fleet management system. The goal is to illustrate, by example, the key parts of creating data structures in Dynamics AX 2012. We will be introducing ideas you may not yet be familiar with and refreshing the concepts you may be already using. The following are the topics we will cover in this chapter:

- Designing data structures for our solution
- Creating labels
- Creating the setup tables
- Creating extended data types
- Creating enumerated types
- Creating tables that support inheritance (vehicles of different types)
- Referential integrity—delete actions and validation

Designing the data structures for our solution

The solution we are going to create is a fleet management system for Contoso. We will be working with the Microsoft Dynamics AX 2012 R3 Demonstration Virtual Machine, available from PartnerSource and CustomerSource.

For the initial part of the solution, we require the following data to be stored:

- Vehicle data (Vehicles are of different types, and the attributes against each vehicle vary. They should be grouped into vehicle types for display and reporting purposes.)
- Vehicle service data
- Vehicle service schedule data
- Vehicle grouping data

Vehicle data is the main table, and we have a big design choice to make—to add fields for all attribute values for all vehicle types or to use inheritance.

Inheritance will allow us to define a base vehicle table, and then a table for each special case where we can add the additional fields. The problem with choosing this method is that, once it has been implemented, we are locked into this architecture without the need for a lot of rework—much like adding a basement garage to a house after it is built.

Another solution could be to add a child table to store the attribute values by vehicle where the possible attributes for that type of vehicle are stored in an attribute-type table. This is a nice solution as it allows the attributes to be changed through configuration and not in code. The downside is that it is difficult to handle the vehicle types in code as we are dealing with types not known at the time of design. Other problems are reporting and a potentially cumbersome interface, as it has to handle attribute values of different types.

Of course, we could also have one large table that holds all fields for all vehicle types, and use the UI logic to hide fields that aren't relevant. This is okay, but only really suits the scenario where we need some additional information for a special case; for example, a sales order return requiring additional information.

In our case, each vehicle type is not a special case. Vehicles such as cars and trucks share some base attributes, but are also distinct entity types with different information held against them.

We will not create a separate table per vehicle type; instead we will present a single view to the user. This means duplication of table handling logic, validation, relations, and so on as each table is distinct. In this case, we will use table inheritance.

Creating labels

In many steps of this chapter, we will create a label for various properties that are presented to the user. We should always create labels, and this is done by following these steps, which creates a label for the property **Label**.

1. In the **Label** property, enter the required label, such as `Vehicle group`, and press *Ctrl* + spacebar to open the **Label** editor, as shown in the following screenshot:

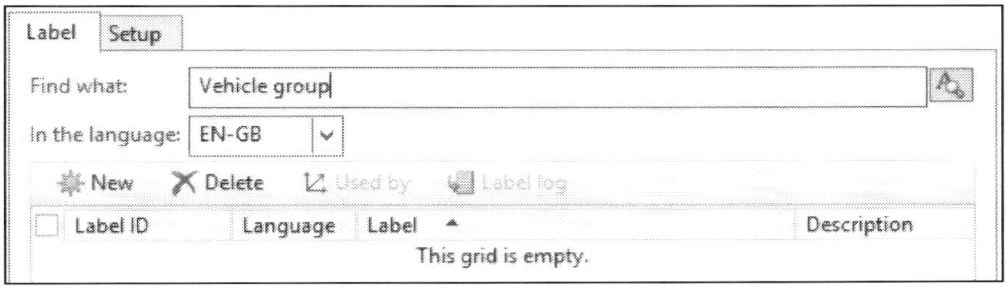

> If you're using source control, the label file must be checked out before a new label can be added. This is done by clicking on **Check out** on the **Label** editor. It isn't visible in the preceding screenshot as we have not yet added the label file to source control.

2. The **Find what** field is already populated with the label, and the language is chosen from our user options. We can simply click on **New** (or press *Ctrl* + *N*).

> The first time you create a label, select the **Setup** tab and verify that the current label file is `CON`.

3. In the new label record, enter the description of the label in the **Description** field. This helps us to understand the context if we reuse the label. It also makes it unique, as it can cause issues if the same label is created in the later upgrades or service packs.

> The **Description** field has a second purpose. It assists AX in determining whether the label is unique. As a minimum, enter your prefix here.

4. Press *Ctrl* + *S* to save the label record, and AX will populate the label ID with the next unique number, such as `@CON3`.

> When using TFS, the label will use a temporary label, such as `@$AA01`. This will be converted to the correct label when the label file is checked in.

5. Once done, paste the label ID back into your **Label** property by clicking on **Paste label** or pressing *Alt* + *P*).

> You will notice that the `@CON3` label ID is shown when the property is selected, but this is replaced by the label when you click on a different property.

Labels provide AX with multilingual capability. This is done by holding a dictionary of label IDs with a translation per language. By default, it will create a label in our current language, but if we are to deploy the solution for other countries, we may have to specify them for additional languages. To do this, we should change the setup of the **Label** editor to show multiple languages. This is done on the **Setup** tab of the **Label** editor, as shown in this screenshot:

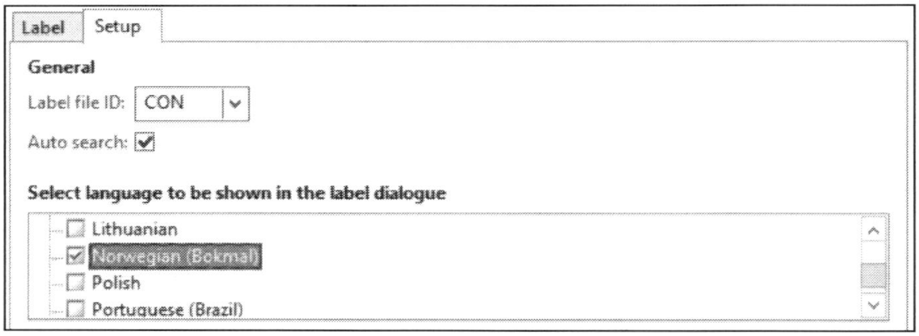

In this case, we will be given an option to specify both our native language and **Norwegian (Bokmal)**, as shown in the following screenshot:

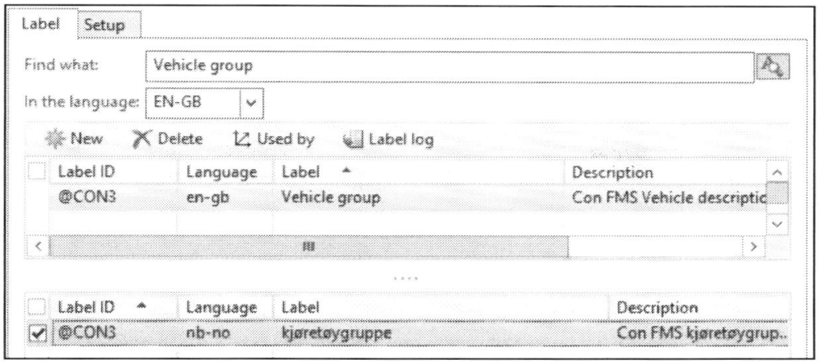

Only the label ID is stored in the metadata. The system looks up the label based on the label ID and user's language.

When creating labels, it is important to consider the context, as we may choose to reuse the existing labels if they are correct. Labels such as **Status** are unclear, and we can't know the true meaning just from the word **Status**. So, the label needs a description in order to have some context, for example, **Vehicle status**. In this way, another developer will know that this field can be used. Using labels that seem correct can cause issues if the original developer decides to change them, for example, from **Created** to **Manufactured**.

> We should never edit a label that we don't "own" because it can have repercussions later, especially after upgrades and hotfixes.

Creating the setup tables

Setup tables are normally created first as they are used on the main and transactional tables. Before a table is created, we must know which extended data types and enumerated types will be used or created.

The structure follows a common pattern, and you are welcome to create the tables based on the definitions described in the following section, using the detailed steps to check against. The tables and types created in the following section will be used in the upcoming chapters.

Creating the vehicle group table

The vehicle group table is a `Group` table, which is in common use in AX, and most main tables have a group field to assist in reporting, filtering, and other requirements. The definition is given here:

Table	**Label**	**Table group**	
`ConFMSVehicleGroup`	Vehicle groups	Group	
Field name	**Type**	**Size**	**EDT**
`VehicleGroupId`	String	10	`ConFMSVehicleGroupId`
`Description`	String	60	`Description`

> Although it would suffice in terms of naming conventions to use `Type` and `Group`, this would be bad practice as we shouldn't use SQL or AX keywords as field names. Examples of such keywords include `use`, `select`, `order`, `group`, and so on.

The table is prefixed with `ConFMS` so that we can easily see the objects that are specific to this solution. For smaller ad hoc changes, it may be sufficient to add the organization prefix. The fields are not prefixed as they are in "our" object.

Creating extended data types

The `VehicleGroupId` field is a standard field type, and will almost always be a string of length 10. It will have its own EDT, but will extend the standard group EDT of `SysGroup`. This is an EDT that most group EDTs extend, such as the customer, item, and vendor group EDTs.

`Description` is a standard EDT, and we will use this only when we create the table. There are several EDTs that we will see reused on many tables, such as `Name` and `Description`.

To create the `ConFMSVehicleGroupId` EDT, follow these steps from within the MorphX IDE:

1. Open the `ConFleetManagementSystem` project, which we created in the last chapter.
2. Expand the **Data Dictionary** node and right-click on **Extended Data Types**, navigating to **New** | **String**, as shown in the following screenshot:

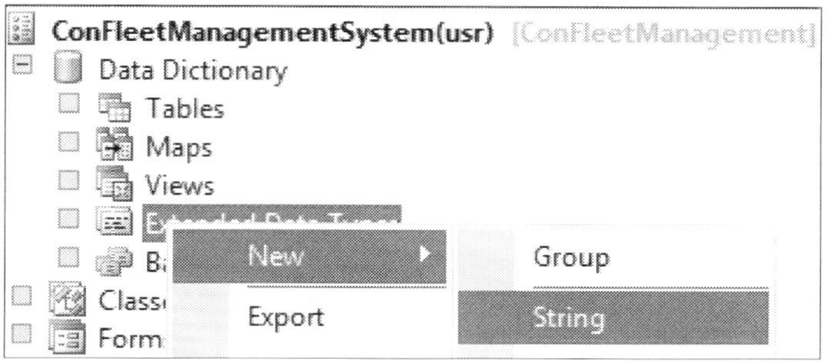

3. Rename the new EDT from `Type1` to `ConFMSVehicleGroupId`. You can use the option Rename from the context / right-click menu, but *F2* is quicker.
4. Open the properties for the new type: press *Alt* + *Enter* or choose **Properties** from the context/right-click menu.
5. In the **Label** property, enter `Vehicle group` and create a label.
6. Enter the **HelpText** in the same way. This is not mandatory but should be filled in because it helps the user. It appears as a popup when you move the mouse over the field linked to this EDT.
7. For now, we will skip to the **Extends** property and return to the other properties later. In the **Extends** property, enter `SysGroup`. Note that as soon as you enter `SysGr`, AX will enter the rest for you.

> The **Extends** property lets us specify which EDT we will inherit properties from. We can change all of these properties except **Size** and **Adjustment** (to ensure referential integrity of all child EDTs).

8. We should have three properties highlighted in bold, as we have changed from the default value, as shown in the following screenshot:

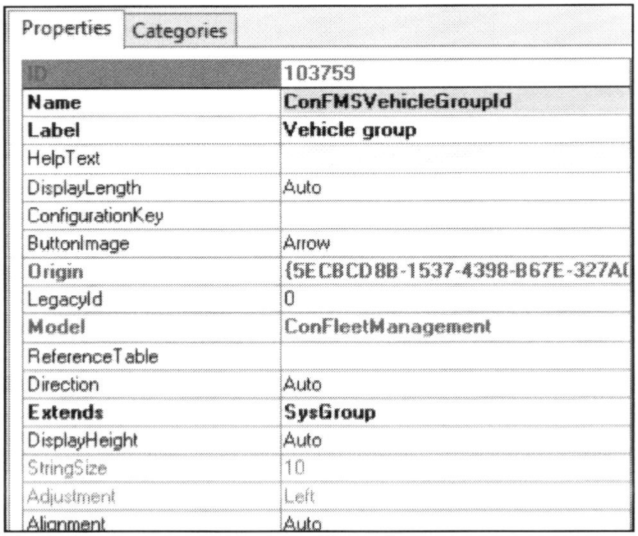

9. If there is a red vertical line next to our new EDT, it means it is not saved in the model store database. Press **save all** in the project window.

The EDT is not yet complete. We need to create the EDT's primary table, the vehicle group table.

> There is often an element of going back to finish an element's definition. In this case, we need the EDT to create the table, but we also need the table to complete the EDT.

Creating the table

The group tables are a common table type, and requires at least two fields, a group field and a description field.

There are some table properties that we will need to complete before we move on to creating the two methods. To create the table definition, follow these steps:

1. Using keyboard shortcuts where possible, create a new table called `ConFMSVehicleGroup` under the **Tables** node in your project.
2. Set the **Label** property `Vehicle groups`, and create a label as we did earlier.

3. Set **HelpText** to further describe the table for the user. This is part of best practice checks performed by the compiler.
4. Change the **TableGroup** property's value to **Group**.
5. Although not mandatory, it is a good idea to turn on the `ModifiedDateTime`, `ModifiedBy`, `CreatedDateTime`, and `CreatedBy` tracking fields.

> The **TableGroup** property tells AX what type of data the table will hold and also allows us to manage tables based on this. For example, we can choose to export data for all tables of the type Group.

Adding fields to the table

Next, we need to add our two fields, which can be done by right-clicking on the **Fields** node, but they are much quicker to create by dragging and dropping. To do this, follow these steps:

1. On the table `ConFMSVehicleGroup`, drag the `ConFMSVehicleGroupId` EDT onto top of the **Fields** node, and rename this to `VehicleGroupId`
2. This will be the primary key, so set the **Mandatory** property to `Yes`, set **AllowEdit** to `No`, and leave **AllowEditOnCreate** as `Yes`.
3. This creates a field of the same name. Rename this to `VehicleGroupId`.
4. Open the field's properties, set the **Mandatory** property to `Yes`, set **AllowEdit** to `No`, and leave **AllowEditOnCreate** as `Yes`.

> Since we will leave **AllowEditOnCreate** as `Yes`, we can enter the ID but not change it afterwards; this helps enforce referential integrity. It can still be changed using the **Rename** primary key function, but this should still be used with care after consultation with a developer or technical consultant.

5. Open a new AOT window (*Ctrl* + *D*) and position it side-by-side with your project window.
6. Expand the **Data Dictionary** node and the **Extended Data Types** node so as to navigate to the `Description` EDT.

> Remember that you can start typing to search, which causes AX to auto-search for the first matching node on the same level.

7. Drag `Description` onto your table's fields list.
8. Press the save all icon in the project window to ensure that your changes are saved.
9. Go back to the table's properties. Set the **TitleField1** property to `VehicleGroupId` and **TitleField2** to `Description`. AX can show these fields on forms that have this table as a data source.

Creating field groups

To aid the user interface design, we can place our fields in groups. This helps us provide a consistent interface for our users and also provides better and centralized control over the UI.

We only need one field group, as there is only a grid view of two fields. We will call this `Overview`. The following steps will create the field group:

1. Right-click on the **Field Groups** node and choose **New Group**.
2. Rename the group to `Overview`.
3. Open the properties and change **Label** to `Overview`.
4. Open the **Label** editor (press *Ctrl* and the *spacebar*) and wait a few seconds, as the first set of results is for specific contexts.
5. Select the first **Overview** label with no description and press **Paste** label.
6. Drag both the fields from the field list into the group. You can reorder them so that `VehicleGroupId` is first, using either the mouse or *Alt* and the up arrow key.

There are two other key field groups, `AutoLookup` and `AutoReport`. The `AutoLookup` field group governs the fields that appear when the system constructs a drop-down list against the table. The `AutoReport` field group governs the fields that appear should the user choose to create a quick report for the table. For this table, add all the fields to these two groups.

Creating indexes

The next part is to set up indexes. We set up indexes both for performance and to enforce unique constraints. There is another more fundamental reason. You may have noticed that the primary and clustered indexes were `SurrogateKey`. This is the default index, based on the record ID (`RecId`). Should we add a primary key relation, it will be based on that index and therefore on the `RecId` field. A record ID foreign key is of little use to us, as we intend the vehicle group ID to be placed on our vehicle table for grouping and reporting purposes.

So, we need to create a unique index based on the `VehicleGroupId` field, and tell the table to use this as its primary key. To create the primary index, follow these steps:

1. On the **Indexes** node of your table, right-click and choose **New Index**.
2. Rename the index from `Index1` to `VehGroupIdx`.
3. Drag the `VehicleGroupId` field onto `VehGroupIdx` to add this field to the index.
4. Go to the properties of the `VehGroupIdx` index and change the **AllowDuplicates** property to `No` and the **AlternateKey** property to `Yes`.

> Unless both of these are set, we won't be able to set the index as the table's primary key.

5. Press the save all icon in the project window. This causes the changes to be saved and the index to be created within SQL Server.
6. Go to the properties of the `ConFMSVehicleGroup` table.
7. Change `PrimaryIndex` and `ClusteredIndex` to `VehGroupIdx`.

Adding the find and exist methods

The final step before we hook up the user interface is to add a `find` and an `exists` method. These aren't used by the system, but it is a convention to create these methods on the tables we create. As the table's authors, we understand how to find records on this table and this saves time later as we avoid writing `select` statements to find the record.

These methods follow the same pattern for all tables we create, and are based on the primary key field, or fields. In our case, we have the `VehicleGroupId` key field, which is based on the `ConFMSVehicleGroupId` EDT (type).

The `find` method allows us to locate a record based (usually) on its primary key, and choose whether or not it should be selected for an update (locked). The method is a static method, which means we don't need to instantiate the table before calling it.

First, to create the find method, right-click on the **Methods** node and choose **New Method**. This will show a method template:

```
private void method1()
{
}
```

Methods marked as `private` are only visible for calls within this table. Our method is designed to be called from other objects and these methods are also declared as `static`, which is done as follows:

```
public static void method1()
{
}
```

The next part is the type of object the method returns. The method template assumes to be `void`. We want to return a record of the type `ConFMSVehicleGroup`, so replace `void` with the table name, but watch what happens as you type.

Replace `void` with the table name, but watch what happens as you type:

Use the arrow keys to choose the appropriate type from the pop-up list.
In this case, it is highlighted, so just press *Enter*.

Rename the method to `find`, and specify the parameters that the method accepts: the primary key field and whether or not the record should be selected for update.

These are specified as follows:

```
public static ConFMSVehicleGroup find(
                                    ConFMSVehicleGroupId _groupId,
                                    boolean _forUpdate = false)
{
}
```

> The underscore is the naming convention for parameters, and the `= false` assignment means that the parameter is optional and defaults to `false`.

We now have a vehicle group and know whether we should lock the record. We can now write the method's content.

The pattern for this method is similar each time we use it, and is done by:

- Declaring the table
- Using the `_forUpdate` parameter to mark the table as for update

- Writing a `select` statement to select the record
- Returning the record, even if not found

To save making a needless select call, we can also make the call only if the vehicle group is not empty. The final code will be like this:

```
public static ConFMSVehicleGroup find(ConFMSVehicleGroupId _groupId,
boolean _forUpdate = false)
{
    ConFMSVehicleGroup vehicleGroup;

    vehicleGroup.selectForUpdate(_forUpdate);
    if(_groupId != "")
    {
        select firstonly vehicleGroup
            where vehicleGroup.VehicleGroupId == _groupId;
    }
    return vehicleGroup;
}
```

> The `firstonly` keyword tells SQL to select only the first record it finds, which is the same as `TOP 1` in Transact-SQL. It doesn't make a great deal of difference here because we are searching the primary key. Nevertheless, if we intend to fetch only the first record, it gives a performance boost.

The `exists` method is similar but returns `true` or `false`, depending on whether the record was found. The way to determine whether a record was found is to check whether the record ID is zero or not.

To improve performance, we will select only the `RecId` column from the table. The method should look like this:

```
public static boolean exist(ConFMSVehicleGroupId _groupId)
{
    ConFMSVehicleGroup vehicleGroup;
    if(_groupId != "")
{
     select RecId
         from vehicleGroup
         where vehicleGroup.VehicleGroupId == _groupId;
}
    return (vehicleGroup.RecId != 0);
}
```

Close the code editor and press **Save All**.

> To create a new method while in the code editor, press *Ctrl* + *N*.

Aside from some user interface elements, our table is complete. You can browse the data in it using the table browser by choosing **Open** from the table's context menu on the table.

You will notice some system-generated fields here, which are as follows:

Field	Description
`RecId`	A system-generated and system-maintained unique record identifier.
`RecVersion`	This is used as part of the optimistic concurrency mechanism in order to determine whether the record we have is still current.
`DataAreaId`	For tables that store data per company, this contains the company ID and is automatically filtered to the current company.
`Partition`	This is the current partition, and is filtered at the kernel level.

Completing the primary key EDT

There is one key step remaining to complete the `ConFMSVehicleGroupId` EDT, that is, to tell the system how it relates to the vehicle group table.

Whenever we add an EDT that is also the primary key of a table, we need to give AX some information; this pays dividends later. To complete this setup, follow these steps:

1. Open the properties of the `ConFMSVehicleGroupId` EDT.
2. In the **ReferenceTable** property, enter `ConFMSVehicleGroup`.

> As soon as you type `ConFM`, AX will complete the rest for you.

3. Expand the `ConFMSVehicleGroup` node and right-click on **Table references**.
4. Go to **New** | **Table reference** from the context menu.
5. In the property sheet, AX has already populated the **Table** property with `ConFMSVehicleGroup`. Set the **RelatedField** property to `VehiceGroupId`.

AX will now understand that the `ConFMSVehicleGroup` EDT should be a foreign key to this table, and also will offer a drop-down list of vehicle groups.

More on indexes

A table index is a structure designed to make finding a specific record as fast as possible. The index is an ordered collection of keys and pointers to the actual records. Finding a record matching a given key involves going to the appropriate location in the index where that key is stored. Then you have to follow the pointer to the location of the actual record and the rest of the data. This, of course, requires two operations, an index seek and a lookup to get the actual data.

When we search for a record, SQL Server is able to determine the best index, or indexes, to use for that particular query. If we realize that we often require the same set of fields from a specific query, we can create an index that contains the keys we wish to search on and the fields we wish to fetch. This improves performance considerably, as SQL will use that index and can then simply return the values that already exist in the index.

We can improve this further by marking the fields we simply wish to return as **IncludedColumn** (a property of the fields in an AX index). So in our case, we may wish to select the description from the vehicle table where the vehicle group is `Artic`. Therefore, a solution can be to add the `Description` field to our `VehGroupIdx` index and mark it as **IncludedColumn**. However, there is a better solution in this case, which is to use clustered indexes.

A clustered index is similar to this, but the clustered index will contain the entire record, avoiding a lookup in the data for any field in the table. Clustered indexes are sorted by their keys; since the index contains the entire record, it can add a significant load to SQL Server if records are inserted, as opposed to being appended at the end of the table.

For setup tables where the number of records is small and changes infrequently, this isn't a problem and the read benefit far outweighs any drawback. For transactional tables, we must be careful. We should always have a clustered index, but the key must be sequential and the records must be added at the end of the table. In any case, we must have a clustered index.

An example of this is the sales order table, which has a clustered index based on `SalesId`. This is a great choice as we will often use this key to locate a sales order record, and the field is also controlled by a number sequence; records should always be appended at the end. However, should we change the number sequence so that records are inserted "mid-table", we will experience a delay in inserting records, adding an unnecessary load to SQL Server.

Creating the vehicle service schedule table

The next table will hold the various service schedules for the vehicles we have. This will be a simple, linear schedule of the distance or elapsed days. We could simply have this information held against the vehicle directly, but since this type of information will be the same for a make and model of vehicle, it is better to hold the schedule as a related record. In our solution, we will select the service schedule for each vehicle.

This is a common design decision, do we assign this directly to the entity, via a rule set, or by some other criteria? Perhaps the service schedule should be implied by other properties, for example, make and model year. This could be equally restrictive, so another option can be to limit the choices to a valid option when creating the vehicle.

The table we will create is as follows:

Table	**Label**	**Table group**	
`ConFMSVehicleSchedule`	Service schedule	Group	
Field name	**Type**	**Size**	**EDT**
`VehicleScheduleId`	String	10	`ConFMSVehicleSchedId`
`Description`	String	60	`Description`
`Distance`	Integer		`ConFMSDistance`
`Days`	Integer		`Days`

This time, we will just list the steps required:

1. Create the `ConFMSVehicleSchedId` EDT as a String type, extending `SysGroup` with **Label** as `Service schedule`.

   [Remember to create and paste the label as before.]

2. Create the `ConFMSDistance` EDT as an `Integer` type, and set **Label** to `Distance`.

> Since distance will never be negative, we can set the **AllowNegative** property to `No`; this helps reduce data entry errors. It also reinforces the power of EDTs. We can control these properties from one entity, wherever they are used.

3. Create the `ConFMSVehicleSchedule` table:
    1. Set **Label** to `Service schedules`.
    2. Add appropriate **HelpText**.
    3. Set **TableGroup** to `Group`.
    4. Set the required tracking fields.
    5. dd the following fields from EDTs, in the given order: `ConFMSVehicleSchedId`, `Description`, `ConFMSDistance`, and `Days`.

> As each field is created, it will be the first field in the listing. However, you will see that when the table refreshes (or if you restart your client), the fields will be ordered differently. They are ordered by their ID.

4. Remove the prefix from the field names as per the earlier table definition.

> Remember to make the primary key field `VehicleScheduleId` **Mandatory** and not **AllowEdit**.

5. Set the title field properties, `VehicleScheduleId` and `Description`.
6. Create the primary index, `VehicleScheduleIdx`. Add the `VehicleScheduleId` field.
7. Set **AllowDuplicates** to `No` and **AlternateKey** to `Yes`.
8. Set the table's primary and clustered indexes to the new index.
9. Create a field group for `Overview` (with a label as before) with the `VehicleScheduleId` and `Description` fields.
10. Create a field group called `Schedule` and create a label and add the `Distance` and `Days` fields.
11. Create the `find` and `exist` methods as per these code samples:

```
public static ConFMSVehicleSchedule find(
                                ConFMSVehicleSchedId _schedId,
                                boolean _forUpdate = false)
```

```
{
    ConFMSVehicleSchedule vehSched;

    vehSched.selectForUpdate(_forUpdate);
    if(_schedId != "")
    {
        select vehSched
            where vehSched.VehicleScheduleId == _schedId;
    }
    return vehSched;
}

public static boolean exist(ConFMSVehicleSchedId _schedId)
{
    ConFMSVehicleSchedule vehSched;
    if(_schedId != "")
    {
        select RecId
            from vehSched
            where vehSched.VehicleScheduleId == _schedId;
    }
    return (vehSched.RecId != 0);
}
```

12. Press the **Save All** button, and we're done!

After some time, creating tables like this becomes almost muscle memory, and we can do it without thinking. Moreover, if you learn the keyboard shortcuts, it becomes very quick.

We can create code snippets for the `find` and `exists` methods; code snippets are covered in *Appendix C, Code Editor Scripts*.

Creating enumerated types

Enumerated types, as discussed in the previous chapter, provide the user with a set of fixed options that we can code directly against. We understand at design time what they mean, as opposed to user-defined lists, which could represent anything.

Referenced as base enums in the AOT, they can be used directly on a table or referenced by an EDT, which, in turn, is added to the table. The reason for this is so that we can abstract and reuse a generic option list.

For example, the `NoYes` base enum has no label, but it offers the `No` and `Yes` options (`No` is first as it will be the default option). From this, we might create an EDT called `ConAreYouSure`, which has the `Are you sure` label. We can then use this label to create fields or dialog controls, and the interface can automatically use the `Are you sure` label and show the `No` and `Yes` options. This means we have one base enum that is reused in several places. This is ideal for general-purpose usage. We create new elements under the appropriate node in our project; the steps used to create a base enum are as follows:

1. In your project, right-click on the **Base enums** node and navigate to **New** | **Base enum**.
2. Rename it as required and open its property sheet.
3. Set the **Label** property and create a new label.
4. Use the **Style** property to control which type of user control AX will be created when added to a form by dragging and dropping; the default of `Combo box` is usually fine.
5. Change **UseEnumValue** to `Yes`; this tells AX to use the **EnumValue** property of each element, allowing us to manually specify the value that AX stores in the database.
6. We then add the elements by selecting **New element** from the context / right-click menu.
7. For each required element, rename it as required and set the **Label** property. Of course, don't forget to create a label.

> **Name** is the symbol we reference in the code, **Label** is what is displayed on the UI, and `EnumValue` is the value written to the database.

Creating the vehicle table

The vehicle table also follows a standard pattern; it is a main table, similar to the `Customer` or `Product` tables.

The structure of the table we will create is as follows:

Table	**Label**	**Table group**	
`ConFMSVehicleTable`	Vehicle table	Main	
Field name	**Type**	**Length**	**EDT**
`VehicleId`	String	20	`ConFMSVehicleId`
`Name`	String	60	Name
`VehicleGroupId`	String	10	`ConFMSVehicleGroupId`
`VehicleType`	Base enum		`ConFMSVehicleType`
`Status`	Base enum		`ConFMSVehicleStatus`
`ServiceSchedule`	String	10	`ConFMSServiceSchedId`

Creating the enumerated types for the vehicle table

Before we create the table, we need to create two base enums. The first base enum is `ConFMSVehicleType`, and should have the following elements:

Name	**Label**	**EnumValue**
Base	Base	0
Car	Car	1
Truck	Truck	2
Trailer	Trailer	3

The result should appear similar to what is shown in the following screenshot:

We now need the `Status` enum — `ConFMSVehicleStatus`. Create this from the following table:

Name	Label	EnumValue
Created	Created	0
Acquired	Acquired	1
Active	Active	2
Unavailable	Unavailable	3
Disposed	Disposed	4

Once complete, this should look similar to what is shown in the following screenshot:

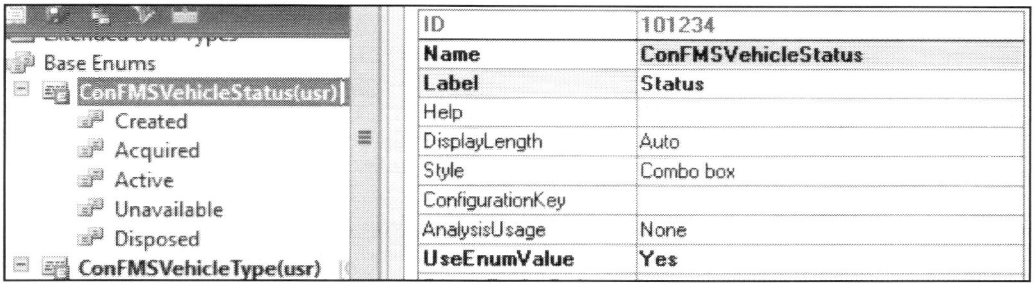

Finally, we create EDTs as follows:

1. Right-click on the **Extended Data Types** node. Navigate to **New** | **Enum.**
2. Rename the EDT to `ConFMSVehicleTypeId`.
3. Enter `ConFMSVehicleType` in the **EnumType** property.
4. Create a second EDT for the `ConFMSVehicleStatus` enum by following the same procedure.

There is no need to set the label as this has been set on the base enum. Often, when creating generic enumerated types, we won't add a label to the base enum; we will only add it to the EDT.

Creating the table that supports inheritance

First, we need to create the vehicle ID EDT, which we will do as before. This EDT will be controlled by a number sequence, so it should extend the `Num` EDT.

Create the `ConFMSVehicleId` EDT as shown here:

Name	`ConFMSVehicleId`
Label	`Vehicle Id`
Extends	`Num`

Entering the `Num` EDT will force **StringSize** to 20 and be left aligned; this is critical if we are to create IDs using a number sequence. Also, create an EDT based on the `Int64` type, called `ConFMSVehicleRelationType`, with the `Vehicle type` label. Reuse the same label that you created before.

We now have all the EDTs we need to create our table. Typically, the table structure of a `Main` table is the same as `Group` (Setup) table types. We just make the **TableGroup** property `Main`.

In this case, we are also going to enable this table to support inheritance:

1. Create the `ConFMSVehicleTable` table as before (it is a convention to suffix `Main` tables with `Table`)
2. Set the **Label** property to `Vehicle details`.
3. Set the **HelpText** property to something appropriate.
4. Set the **TableGroup** property to `Main`.
5. Set the tracking fields `CreatedBy`, `ModifiedBy`, `CreatedDateTime`, and `ModifiedDateTime`.
6. Set the **SupportInheritance** property to `Yes`.
7. We will then get the following compilation error:
8. Property InstanceRelationType must be set to an Int64 field for the root table.
9. We need to create a reference field that the system will use to tie the inherited tables together. Right-click on the table's **Fields** node and go to **New** | **Int64**.
10. Rename the field to **InstanceRelationType**. Set **ExtendedDataType** to **ConFMSVehicleRelationType**.
11. Save the table.
12. Set the table's **InstanceRelationType** property to **InstanceRelationType**.

13. Compile the project by selecting the root node in the project window and clicking on the compile icon (or pressing *F7*), as shown here:

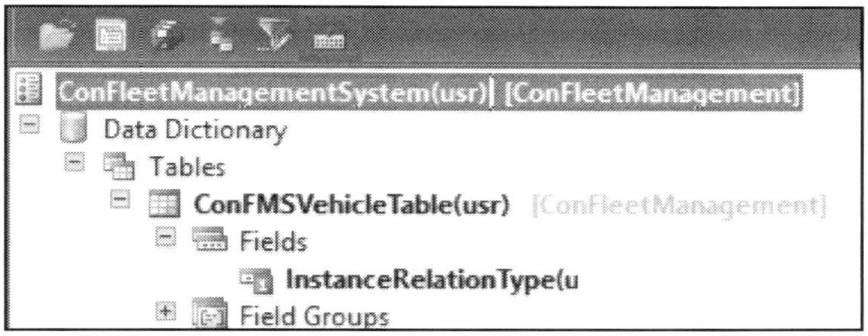

> See more on the **InstanceRelationType** property later in this section.

14. Now we can add the main fields to our table. Do this by dragging the following EDTs (in the given order) onto the table's Fields node:
    - `ConFMSVehicleId`
    - `Name`
    - `ConFMSVehicleGroupId`

> The system will ask you `Do you want to add the ForeignKey relation from the EDT to the current table?`. If you want to create a relation, click on **Yes**.
>
> If this message does not appear, remove the field and verify the EDT's relation.

    - `ConFMSVehicleTypeId`
    - `ConFMSVehicleStatusId`
    - `ConFMSServiceSchedId`

> As before, remove the `ConFMS` prefix; this is our table. To maintain consistency, rename the `ConFMSServiceSchedId` field to `VehicleScheduleId`.

15. Ensure that the following table properties are completed:
    - **TitleField1**: `VehicleId`
    - **TitleField2**: `Name`

Completing the table relations

Before we continue, we can now play with this table and you can learn a bit more about relations in AX.

To ensure that everything is synchronized, it is a good idea to force AX to synchronize its data dictionary with the physical database held in SQL Server. To do this, open the AOT (*Ctrl* + *D*), right-click on the **Data Dictionary** node, and select **Synchronize**. This may take 10-20 minutes, and may ask you to continue if there are any warnings. If it does, choose to continue.

> If this node is red, it means that AX has noticed that it is not in sync and needs to be synchronized.

Once this completes, go back to your project window and browse the `ConFMSVehicleTable` table (right-click on it and choose **Open**).

Press *Ctrl* + *N* to create a new record. Click through the fields, trying the drop-down options. The fields based on enums will show the appropriate elements and the system will automatically create dropdowns for the vehicle group and service tables—very powerful! This will get even better once we add the user interface.

The vehicle group and vehicle service fields are foreign keys to the respective tables, as defined in the relations on `ConFMSVehicleTable`. The following screenshot shows the definition of the `ConFMSVehicleGroup` relation:

The two relations are primary key relations, which has a special meaning with AX because it enables additional features over standard relations. One feature is that it can automatically create navigation methods. For this reason, we will always use primary key relations wherever possible.

The following screenshot shows the property sheet for the `ConFMSVehicleGroup` relation:

Properties | Categories

Name	ConFMSVehicleGroup
Table	**ConFMSVehicleGroup**
Validate	Yes
EntityRelationshipRole	
RelatedTableCardinality	NotSpecified
Cardinality	NotSpecified
RelationshipType	NotSpecified
UseDefaultRoleNames	**Yes**
RelatedTableRole	
Role	
CreateNavigationPropertyMethods	No
NavigationPropertyMethodNameOverride	
EDTRelation	No
Model	ConFleetManagement

Occasionally, we may have multiple relations to the same table (perhaps filtered to a subset of records in the foreign table), so we should change the name to specify this role. Most relations are one-to-many and we will configure the cardinality like this:

RelatedTableCardinality	**ZeroOne**
Cardinality	**ZeroMore**
RelationshipType	**Association**

> There is a quick way to achieve this configuration. Once you are in the **RelatedTableCardinality** property, press in the following order: *spacebar*, *Tab*, *spacebar*, *spacebar*, *spacebar*, *Tab*, and *spacebar*. We can complete the property sheet in this way in a couple of seconds.

The default role names are normally fine. A problem occurs if we add a second relation to the same table—we will get an error stating that role names are not unique. This is because the default role names are based on the table name, not the relation name.

You can easily overcome this by changing **UseDefaultRoleNames** to `No` and setting the **RelatedRoleName** and **RoleName** fields manually. These are normally set as follows: **RelationRoleName** as the foreign table name and **RoleName** as the foreign table name suffixed with the relation's role. Two examples of this are `VehicleGroup` and `VehicleGroup_VehicleTable`. These values are validated beyond being unique across this table.

All relations must have the correct cardinality set.

Completing the vehicle table

We still have a few tasks on the vehicle table to complete. These are as follows:

- Creating a primary index
- Completing the relation on the `ConFMSVehicleId` EDT
- Creating appropriate field groups
- Creating the find and exist methods

We have done this before and the process is the same as for other tables. Use the following checklist to complete the setup:

1. The `VehicleId` will be the primary key, so create an index called `VehicleIdIdx`. Then add `VehicleId` to it. Ensure that **AllowDuplicates** is **No** and **AlternateKey** is **Yes**.
2. Set the **PrimaryIndex** and **ClusteredIndex** properties to the new index.
3. On the `ConFMSVehicleId` EDT, enter `ConFMVehicleTable` in the **ReferenceTable** property.
4. Add the **TableReference** for the field `VehicleId`.
5. Create up to three field groups, including `Overview` and `Details`, as you see fit. Add the fields as appropriate. Do not add the `InstanceRelationType` field; this will be added to the form later.

The labels for `Overview` and `Details` should be standard labels, as these are standard field groups. Overview is the first with no description, and the `Details` label states the `Group` details in the description.

6. Create the `find` and `exist` methods, as follows:

```
public static ConFMSVehicleTable find(ConFMSVehicleId _vehicleId,
boolean _forUpdate = false)
{
    ConFMSVehicleTable vehicle;

    vehicle.selectForUpdate(_forUpdate);
    if(_vehicleId != "")
```

```
        {
            select vehicle
                where vehicle.VehicleId == _vehicleId;
        }
        return vehicle;
    }
    public static boolean exist(ConFMSVehicleId _vehicleId)
    {
        ConFMSVehicleTable vehicle;
        if(_vehicleId != "")
        {
            select RecId
                from vehicle
                where vehicle.VehicleId == _vehicleId;
        }
        return (vehicle.RecId != 0);
    }
```

Creating the inherited tables

Inherited tables are relatively quick to create. We just need to create the basic table definition as a main table and add the additional fields each type requires.

We will create tables for the following types:

- Car
- Truck
- Trailer

The car will require these fields and therefore the EDTs:

- `CarType`: The type of car, for example, Saloon, Sedan, Estate, and so on
- `TintedWindows`: To define whether or not the car has tinted windows

The truck will require these fields:

- `Artic`: To define whether or not it is an articulated truck

The trailer will require these fields:

- `TrailerId`: This is the trailer's ID number

We therefore need to create the EDTs first. It is sensible to create one for each of these fields and extend an EDT as appropriate.

Use this table to create the EDTs, setting the **Label** and **HelpText** properties as appropriate:

Name	**Type**	**Extends**	**Size**
`ConFMSCarType`	String		10
`ConFMSTintedWindows`	Enum	`NoYesId`	n/a
`ConFMSArtic`	Enum	`NoYesId`	n/a
`ConFMSTrailerId`	String	`Num`	n/a

Once the EDTs are created, we can create the tables, use the following table to create the tables:

Name	**Label**
`ConFMSVehicleTableCar`	Car details
`ConFMSVehicleTableTruck`	Truck details
`ConFMSVehicleTableTrailer`	Trailer details

In all cases, set the following properties:

TableGroup	`Main`
SupportsInheritance	`Yes`
Extends	`ConFMSVehicleTable`

There is no need to define `find` or `exist` methods on this table or create a primary index. Finally, note that the system automatically creates a relation to the base table based on `RecId`. This is part of the mechanics behind the inheritance functionality.

More on the InstanceRelationType property

The implementation of table inheritance is unique to AX and it is worth pointing out what we have done and why.

We are about to actually create an AX table for each type, all extending this base table. This will create a physical table in SQL Server to support them. SQL Server does not support table inheritance, so this technology is handled purely by AX.

As a user interface option, when we create a new record, the system will want to know which type it is (in our case, car, truck, and so on). It does this by offering the user a choice based on the tables that inherit from this table. AX will automatically create a dialog with one field labelled after the `InstanceRelationType` field (which is why it is labeled `Vehicle type`) and the options will be the labels of all tables, from the base table to all child tables.

Data will be physically stored in only one SQL table. AX knows what type each record is by looking at `InstanceRelationType`. This field is actually a table ID and it stores the AX table ID of the child table that the record belongs to. The child table does not exist as a table in its own right in SQL. This is shown in the following diagram of `ConFMSVehicleTable`:

InstanceRelationType	VehicleId	Car.CarType	Truck.Artic	Trailer.TrailerId
103649	V001	n/a	n/a	n/a
103650	V002	Saloon	n/a	n/a
103650	V003	Estate	n/a	n/a
103651	V004	n/a	No	n/a
103652	V005	n/a	n/a	T001

To see this for yourself, using the table browser, right-click on the table and select **Open**. You can use *Ctrl* + *N* to create records in any of the tables. You will see that the inherited tables show all fields from the parent and their own specific fields. Also, the records created in the inherited tables appear in both the base table and the specific table they were created in.

> From AX 2012 R2 onwards, the way table inheritance was achieved in SQL server changed.
>
> Before R2, a physical table was created for the parent table and its fields. Then another was created for each child table and those fields that it had and the parent did not. The `InstanceRelationType` field was used to determine which child table to look at in order to find the extra fields.
>
> Selecting data from SQL with this structure involved a complex set of SQL joins and, worse than that, updating one child record in AX would require updates to several tables in SQL.
>
> Now all the fields required by the parent table and all its child tables are kept in a single SQL table. This makes reading and updating much less complex, as there is just one table on the disk to read and write to.

Creating the vehicle service data table

This time, we will create a table that will hold service data. This is largely the same as the vehicle table, but doesn't require inheritance. The table will have the following structure:

Table	Label	Table group	
ConFMSVehServiceTable	Vehicle service table	Worksheet	
Field name	**Type**	**Size**	**EDT**
ServiceId	String	20	ConFMSServiceId
VehicleId	String	20	ConFMSVehicleId
ServiceDate	Date		ConFMSServiceDate
CurrentOdometer	Integer		ConFMSCurrentOdometer
ServicedBy	Int64		HcmWorkerRecId
NextServiceDueDate	Date		ConFMSNextServiceDate
NextServiceDueOdo	Integer		ConFMSNextServiceOdo

The reason **TableGroup** is `Worksheet` is that it is the data that we will enter directly that acts as dynamic data added against a main record. In a similar way, a sales order is dynamic data entered against a customer. This differs from tables of the `Transaction` type. These are created by a posting function, such as a sales invoice, from a worksheet record, and we will not allow the user to create, edit, or delete records directly from a table of type Transaction. However, we may add features to cancel or amend a transaction.

From this, we can determine that the following EDTs are required. Use these details to create the EDTs, setting **Label** and **HelpText** as appropriate:

Name	Type	Extends	Size
ConFMSServiceId	String	Num	n/a
ConFMSServiceDate	Date	TransDate	n/a
ConFMSCurrentOdometer	Integer		
ConFMSNextServiceDate	Date	TransDate	
ConFMSNextServiceOdo	Integer		

The obvious decision here was that service ID is the primary key, and will therefore be autogenerated. ID fields in AX are typically generated from the number sequence system. Even if they are not, primary key fields on anything but group tables should extend `Num`.

The decision to use `TransDate` comes from experience; it is already configured to use a nice date picker. The odometer fields are simple numbers, so there is no need to extend an EDT here. When creating the EDT, remember to specify and create labels for **Label** and **HelpText**.

The table creation is the same as before, so remember to:

- Set the **Label**, **HelpText**, **TableGroup** table properties and the tracking fields
- Create the primary index
- Configure the table's **PrimaryIndex** and **ClusteredIndex** properties
- Complete the relation properties for `ConFMSVehicleTable`
- Create the `find` and `exist` methods
- Complete `ReferenceTable` and `TableReference` on the `ConFMSServiceId` EDT

Referential integrity – delete actions and validation

It is critical that we enforce data integrity on the tables we create. AX assists us a lot with this by creating relations. AX will use the relations we created earlier to ensure that data entered through the user interface is valid. Simply put, we can only enter a vehicle group on the vehicle table that exists in the vehicle group table. It is more accurate in this example to say that the data entered in the vehicle group field is validated against the relation; the relation might have an additional constraint.

AX handles that data entry validation, but what happens when we want to delete a vehicle group? The system cannot know the answer to this because we have different scenarios here, as shown in the following table:

Foreign table	**Related table**	**Action**
`ConFMSVehicleGroup`	`ConFMSVehicleTable`	Restrict deletion
`ConFMSVehicleSchedule`	`ConFMSVehicleTable`	Restrict deletion
`ConFMSVehicleTable`	`ConFMSVehServiceTable`	Cascade

This is what delete actions are used for—to define this behavior. We configure this in the foreign table as per the following steps:

1. On the **DeleteActions** node for the `ConFMSVehicleGroup` table, right-click and select **New DeleteAction**.
2. Type `ConFMSVehicleTable` in the **Table** property (paying attention to autocompletion).

> **Relation** is set automatically to `ConFMSVehicleGroup`, which is great. For tables with multiple relations to this table, we can specify the correct relation using this property.

3. Set **DeleteAction** to **Restricted**.
4. Do the same for `ConFMSVehicleSchedule` > `ConFMSVehicleTable`.
5. Create the delete action for `ConFMSVehicleTable` > `ConFMSVehServiceTable`, but make **DeleteAction** property `Cascade`.

How this works

The delete action has the following options, `None`, `Restricted`, `Cascade`, `Cascade + Restricted`:

- `None`: This has no effect, and effectively disables the delete action. This is useful if you want to specifically state "do nothing" so that someone else doesn't try to correct what seems to be an omission.
- `Restricted`: This will prevent the record from being deleted if there are records in the related table that match the selected relation. This occurs within the `validateDelete` table event, which is called by the `delete` table event.
- `Cascade`: This will delete the record in the related table, based on the relation. A sales order line is of no use without a sales order. This is an extension of the `delete` table event.
- `Cascade + Restricted`: This is a little special. In a two-table scenario, it is the same as **Restricted**. It will stop the record from being deleted if a related record exists. But if the record is being deleted as part of a cascade from a table related to it, the records will be deleted.

> See *How to: Create Delete Actions* at `http://msdn.microsoft.com/en-us/library/bb315018.aspx`.

For example, in the following scenario we have invented a grandparent table above `ConFMSVehicleTable`, called `ConFMSHaulierTable`:

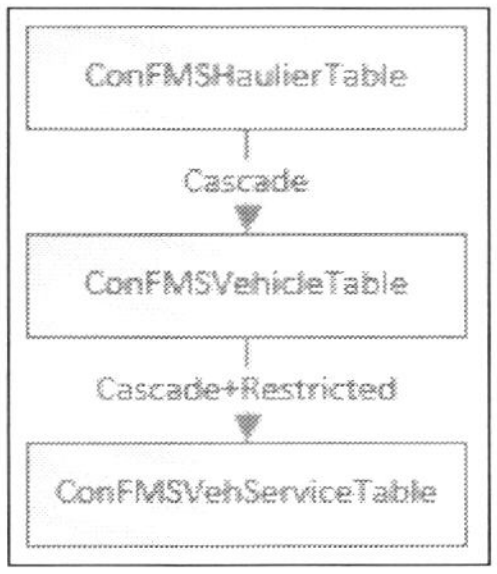

If we try to delete a record from `ConFMSVehicleTable` and there are related records in `ConFMSVehServiceTable`, the deletion will not be allowed.

If we delete a record from `ConFMSHaulierTable`, it will also delete related records in `ConFMSVehicleTable` and cascade the deletion so that the related `ConFMSVehServiceTable` records will be deleted as well.

Summary

In this chapter we covered a lot of ground with data structures, building on the concepts covered in the previous chapters. The functionality we worked through covers 90 percent of data dictionary functionality used within software development projects and the remainder we will cover in a later chapter in this book.

In the next chapter, we will add the user interface so that we can actually see these structures in action.

3

Creating the User Interface

In this chapter, we will create the user interface for our fleet management system. The interface design will follow standard AX patterns, explaining the design paradigm we should employ when writing interfaces for Dynamics AX.

We will cover the following:

- Creating the menu structure
- Understanding the patterns used in interface design
- Creating setup forms
- Creating the vehicle list page
- Investigating form events
- Taking more control over the form layout
- Creating the vehicle create form with the handler class

Creating a menu structure

All main entry points to the UI and reports are access though the menu structure. This is presented in three ways: the left-hand navigation pane, the content area, and the navigation bar (at the top of the client). The menu design is controlled from the **Menus** node in the AOT.

Each module will have a menu, which is created by adding a menu reference (or shortcut) to the main menu:

> This matches the list of modules shown in the client's left-hand navigation pane.

The module names are displayed as the menu's label and not the actual menu name. AX does this by using your client's language, so in the preceding case, **Sales ledger** is shown. This references the **AccountsReceivable** menu, which you can see by right-clicking on the menu reference and viewing the properties.

On expanding the **AccountsReceivable** menu, we see how the menu is structured; this is shown along with its key properties in the following screenshot:

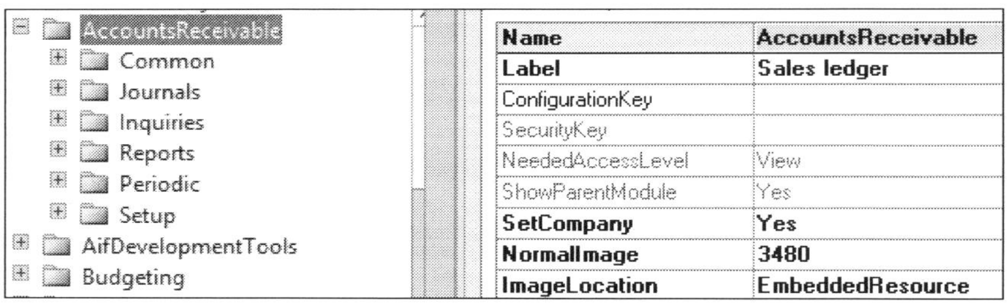

Each menu we create will have most of the following submenus that appear as sections in the content area in the client:

- **Common**: This hosts menu item pointers to list pages, the main entry point to our master or transactional data.
- **Journals**: This is for menu items that open journal entry forms, such as the vendor payment journal.
- **Inquiries**: These are menu items for general read-only inquiries into posted transactional or statistical data.

- **Reports**: These are menu items that allow us to print reports.
- **Periodic**: The menu items placed here are often routines that are accessed less frequently and are commonly placed in a periodic batch queue. For example, posting a set of sales invoices or performing a foreign currency revaluation.
- **Setup**: This includes forms used to configure the module.

Although we are free to design a menu structure as we see fit, we should adhere to this structure in order to meet the design goals of maintainability and ease-of-use.

We don't need to create all of the main submenus, but any items we add should fit under one of these submenus.

Each submenu can have further submenus. This can aid organization, but we should not nest submenus too far, as this will actually make the item harder to find. In terms of the number of items at each level, eight is a reasonable number. There is no rule here and user feedback is useful.

For our example system, we only need to provide interfaces to set up tables and the vehicle table. The vehicle table is master data and should be presented as a list page. We therefore require the **Common** and **Setup** submenus.

Before we create our main menu, we need to decide on its icon, which may likely be a logo we have designed. We will use AX's embedded resources (icons and images) for this example. This will be available when you navigate to **Tools** | **Embedded resources**, and the most suitable resources have a resource ID greater than 10,000. As this form will appear docked to the right of our development workspace, you will find it easier to use if you close the property sheet window first and if you have docked the property sheet window to the right side of the IDE.

To create the fleet management system menu, follow these steps:

1. Open our project `ConFleetManagementSystem`.
2. Right-click on the **Menus** node and select **New** | **Menu**.

> If the **New** option does not appear, it means the project is checked into source control. Right-click on the project name and select **Check Out**.

3. Rename the menu as `ConFleetManagementSystem` and open the property sheet.

4. Enter the label `Fleet management system` and create a label.
5. As this menu will be a module with company-specific information, set the **SetCompany** property to `Yes`.
6. Enter `10036` in the **NormalImage** property and set **ImageLocation** to `EmbeddedResource`.

> The **NormalImage** property will appear as the module's icon on the left-hand-side navigation pane.

7. Create the main submenus by right-clicking on the **ConFleetManagementSystem** menu and navigating to **New** | **Submenu**. Although we only need **Common** and **Setup** this time, a full table is listed as follows for reference:

Name	Label	NormalImage	ImageLocation
Common	`@SYS333846`	`3495`	**EmbeddedResource**
Journals	`@SYS333879`	`3475`	**EmbeddedResource**
Inquiries	`@SYS333856`	`3474`	**EmbeddedResource**
Reports	`@SYS333860`	`3477`	**EmbeddedResource**
Periodic	`@SYS333865`	`3476`	**EmbeddedResource**
Setup	`@SYS333869`	`3478`	**EmbeddedResource**

> You should enter **Name** before **Label**; otherwise you will get an error stating that the object already exists.

8. Once this is complete, press the **Save all** button on the project window.

For more information on menu properties, visit:

`http://msdn.microsoft.com/en-us/library/aa674461.aspx`

Finally, we need to add our menu as a module to the main menu, which is done as follows:

1. Place the AOT window next to our project window (if required, open the AOT window by pressing *Ctrl* + *D*).
2. Scroll down to **Menus** and expand **MainMenu**.

> The menus here are shortcuts, and you can't expand beyond the first level.

3. Right-click on **MainMenu** and navigate to **New** | **Menu** reference.
4. This opens a new window titled **Select: Menus**. Locate your **ConFleetManagementSystem** menu and drag it to **MainMenu**, as shown in the following screenshot (the title changes from **Select: Menus** to the path of the select node when you click on it):

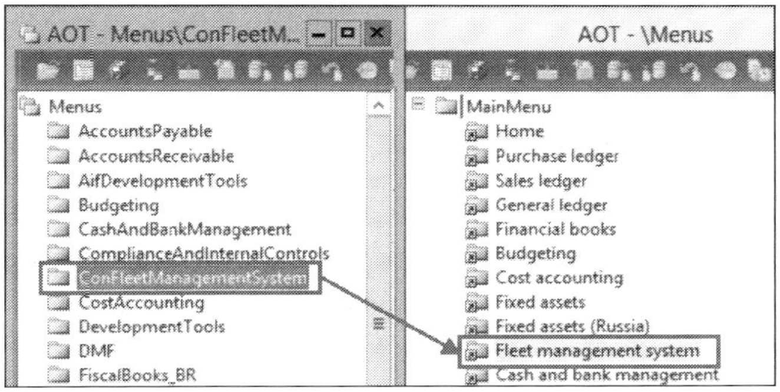

> Do not drag the **ConFleetManagementSystem** menu from your project!

5. Close the **Select: Menus** form. It is very easy for the IDE to get cluttered with forms and code windows, so it is best to close windows when they are no longer required.

6. Once complete, the new sub-menu should appear as a shortcut in **MainMenu**. Close the **Select: Menus** form and drag **MainMenu** to the **Menus** node of our project.
7. Restart the AX client or open a new workspace by pressing *Ctrl* + *W* to see the changes reflected in the client.

Customizing an existing menu

Sometimes, we may wish to add a list page or report to an existing menu; and, this list may grow over time. Try to avoid adding menu items directly to the menu. Instead, create a menu such as `ConInventReports` to hold all of our inventory reports and add this to the **Reports** node within the **InventoryManagement** menu as a menu reference. This way, we add a shortcut as we did in the preceding section, making it easier to maintain.

Understanding the patterns used in interface design

Most interfaces within Dynamics AX provide the user with the ability to search, amend, and perform actions based on data. For almost all interfaces we need to develop, there are standard patterns and templates provided to us to follow.

To help us, we are provided templates for most of these patterns. The templates available are as follows:

- **ListPage**: This provides a list of data (such as sales orders) and the ability to act on that data (post a sales order invoice). These are not used to edit or create data; this is what details forms are for.
- **DetailsFormMaster and DetailsFormTransaction**: Details forms have two types, master and transaction. Master detail forms are designed to amend and create master data, such as a customer. Transaction detail forms are used to amend data that normally has header and line views (for example, sales order details form). These forms are not normally used to create data; this is normally done in a custom form that allows the user to enter key information about the entity on a simple form.
- **SimpleListDetails and SimpleList**: These are usually used for setup forms, where the user opens the form directly from the menu. Simple list simply presents a grid of data that the user can edit directly. Simple list details shows a grid containing summary data with tabs containing the more detailed fields on the right-hand side.

Simple list is most suitable when the data is simply a list and the fields can fit without scrolling. Its details are more suitable where data benefits from being arranged in groups. The details version is also well suited to present data from a child data source.

- **TableOfContents**: These are used for parameter forms, where the table contains a record of parameters used for default or configuration options.
- **DropDialog**: This method shows a popup that allows the user to enter a small amount of information on a form, which appears to drop down from the button. This is useful to enter information about the current record, which requires a more assertive action, or to trigger a process. This is very similar in use to a dialog, but visually, it appears to be part of the calling form.
- **Dialog**: These are common for forms that start processes from the **Periodic** menu; although the **SysOperation framework** automatically creates dialogues for us, and therefore, reduces the number of times when this would be used.

The SysOperation framework is covered in *Chapter 9, Advanced Features and Frameworks*.

Form structure

Most of the forms we create will use a data source whose fields are added to the form as data-bound controls.

Forms are normally structured as one or more data sources, with a design that holds the controls to interact with them. The data source can be a table or view, and in some cases (such as dialogs), they will not have a data source.

The structure of a typical form is shown in the following screenshot:

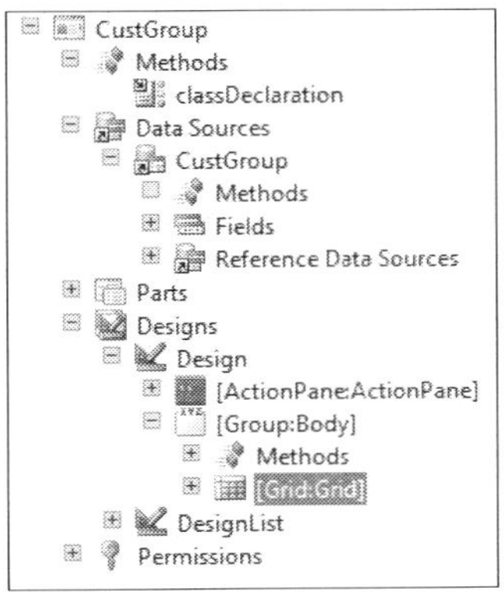

The form is based on the `FormRun` class. We can see this by opening (double-click) the **classDeclaration** for the **CustGroup** form:

```
public class FormRun extends ObjectRun
```

Therefore, you can think of the form as a definition file that `FormRun` instantiates with an order to build and execute the form.

> This is important and helps understand how forms are treated by the system.

Once the system has built the form design (using the `SysSetupFormRun` class), it will perform the initialization tasks and run the form. The key methods in this are `Init` and `Run`. These can be overridden on the form in order to perform additional initialization tasks.

One of the key tasks of the `FormRun` class's `Init` method is to construct the form's data sources. These aren't table references but `FormDataSource` objects constructed from the tables listed under the **Data Sources** node.

In the case of the `CustGroup` form, the system creates the following objects from the `CustGroup` data source for us:

- `CustGroup` as the `CustGroup` type
- `CustGroup_DS` as the `FormDataSource` type
- `CustGroup_Q` as the `Query` type
- `CustGroup_QR` as the `QueryRun` type

We aren't normally concerned with the `Query` and `QueryRun` objects, as we can access them through the `FormDataSource` object anyway. The `CustGroup_DS` data source is very useful, and will be explained in more detail in *Chapter 4, Creating Business Logic and Hooking into Core AX*, and *Chapter 6, Extending the Solution*.

The data sources are declared as global variables to the form, and provide a layer of functionality between the form and the table. This allows us to control the interaction between the bound form controls and the table.

For example, when a form control is modified, the control's modified method is called, which calls the data source field's `modified` method. This method in turn calls the table's `modifiedField` method with the ID of the field being changed.

The same goes for data source events. For instance, the `write` event on the form will call the data source's `write` event, which will call insert or update based on whether the record is new or not.

Based on this, we have a choice as to where we place our code. This decision is very important. The rule to follow here is to make changes at the lowest level possible: table, data source, and only at the form control if not possible at a lower level.

> It is critically important that code on a form must only be written to control the user interface and should not contain validation or business logic.

We can go further with this and write form interaction classes that allow user interface control logic to be shared across forms. For instance, controlling which buttons are available to a list page and the associated detail form.

Creating setup forms

The setup forms are usually simple list or simple list details forms. In our case, we will use both.

The vehicle group form

This form only has two columns and should be a simple list form. Since form templates can only be created on the main AOT window, it is useful to have both project and AOT windows open so that elements can be dragged on the project.

Feel free to create this form using the simple list form template, using the following steps as a guide:

1. Right-click on the **Forms** node and navigate to **New** | **New Form from template** | **SimpleList**.
2. This will open a new AOT window containing the object `CopyOSysBPStyle_SimpleList`. Rename this to match the table name `ConFMSVehicleGroup`. This is not technically required, but is the standard pattern.

> The **New Form from template** option simply copies a form that exists in the AOT. In this case, `SysBPStyle_SimpleList`.

3. Once renamed, drag this form onto the **Forms** node in our project.

> It is important to rename objects before adding them to a project, as they can occasionally be dropped from the project if renamed afterwards.

4. From the **Tables** node in our project, drag the `ConFMSVehicleGroup` table to the **Data Sources** node in the new form.
5. Expand the **Designs** node and open the properties of the **Design** node.

> The **DesignList** node is a flattened view of all controls on the form. We wouldn't normally use this view for development. It can be useful to locate a control by its name in order to change a property or even remove it. Be careful; controls in this list are the same as the controls in the **Designs** view.

6. The defaults are mostly fine, but we should change the following properties:
    - **TitleDatasource**: This is the data source to AX will use to display the title fields; these were set in the properties **TitleField1** and **TitleField2** on the table. Select the `ConFMSVehicleGroup` data source.
    - **Caption**: Set this to the label used on the table. In this case, the label for **Vehicle groups**.
    - **DataSource**: This property is inherited by controls that we add to the design, except for grid controls. Select the `ConFMSVehicleGroup` data source.
7. The `SimpleList` template has sections for an action pane (button ribbon), page title, filter controls, and a grid (contained in a grid container group). You can see these by expanding the **Design** node, as shown in the following screenshot:

8. The page title is hidden by default and is useful to show guidance to the user. To enable this, open the properties of the **PageTitleGroup** group and change the **Visible** property from `No` to `Yes`.
9. Right-click on the **PageTitleGroup** group and navigate to **New control** | **StaticText**.
10. Rename the control from `StaticText` to `StaticTextPageTitle`.

> Controls should always be given an appropriate name. This is particularly true when duplicating controls; controls starting with `CopyOf` is particularly bad.

11. The title is a brief instruction to the user. In this case, set the **Text** property to `Maintain vehicle groups` and create a label.
12. Depending on the type of control we can apply a style to, we should set the **Style** property to `MainInstruction`, which sets the text to a larger green style that stands out on the form.

> If detailed instructions are required, we would add a second control with **Style** set to `Auto`, which is the standard smaller black text. Don't add needless information; it will just clutter the interface.

13. Next, we should tell the grid control which data source to use. as this doesn't inherit the property from the parent container. Locate the grid control and set the **DataSource** property to the data source name.

> At this point, we could add fields to the grid by simply dragging them from the data source's field list, but as we created a field group for this purpose we don't have to.

14. Set **DataGroup** to `Overview` (the field group we created when creating the table).
15. Expand the **Grid** control to see that the fields are now added automatically.
16. To test the form, right-click on the form and select **Open**, which will display the following form:

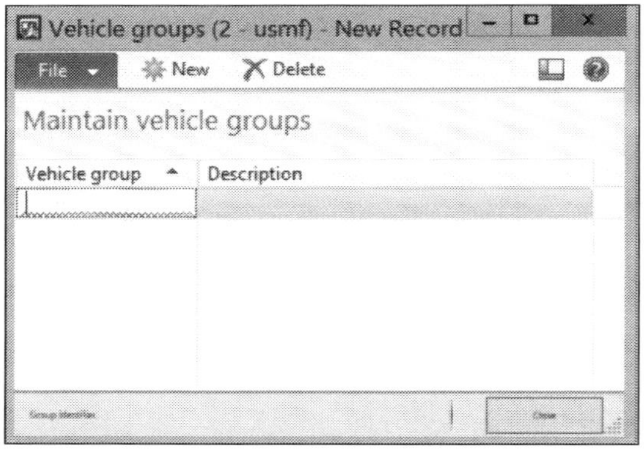

Because we made the **vehicle group** field mandatory, it is highlighted with a red underline. Should we enter a new vehicle group, we won't be able to change the vehicle group after the record is saved. This is good because it could cause vehicles to have vehicle groups that don't exist.

> You can use the **Rename** option from **Record info** in the right context menu. This will rename the vehicle group in all places it is used, using the table's relations thus maintaining referential integrity. This will work in all cases where relations are navigable, which is nearly all of them. There can be occasions when a foreign key is not renamed and would result in orphaned records. No warning or error will be displayed.

Creating the menu item

Although we have created a fully functional form, we can't open it from the main menu yet. We also need this to enable the **View details** option on related tables.

The first step is to create a menu item that acts as a shortcut to the form, with additional properties that can control the behavior of the form. We do this by dragging the form onto the **Display** node under **Menu** items on our project.

The menu items are of the following three types:

- **Display**: This includes forms or other user interface objects, such as info parts
- **Output**: This includes reports
- **Action**: This includes classes; which expects the class to have a method called `main` that accepts a single `Args` object.

Once created, we need to set the new menu item's **Label** property. Use the same label ID as we did for the table.

We can then add the menu item to the menu by dragging it onto the **Setup** node under our **ConFleetMaagementSystem** menu. The menu will be displayed as the menu item's label. If it is displayed as ***ConFMSVehicleGroup***, the label wasn't set, the label wasn't set in our language, or we didn't save the changes to the menu item.

To make the **View details** option work, we need to tell the table which form is used to edit the data; this is the **FormRef** property on the table. Simply paste in the menu item name. The property implies it wants a form name, but this actually requires a menu item.

The vehicle service data form

The vehicle service data table has more fields than can sit on a `SimpleList` form. So this time, we will create a form using the `SimpleListDetails` template.

This is done in the same way as we did earlier:

1. Right-click on the AOT window's **Forms** node and select **New** | **New Form from template** | **SimpleListDetails**.
2. Name the form `ConFMSVehicleSchedule`, and add this table to the form's data source
3. Set the properties of the **Design** node as follows:

Property	Value
TitleDatasource	`ConFMSVehicleSchedule`
Caption	Use the label from the table
DataSource	`ConFMSVehicleSchedule`

The design of this style of form consists of a grid on the left-hand side and one or more "fast tabs" on the right-hand side; as shown in the following screenshot:

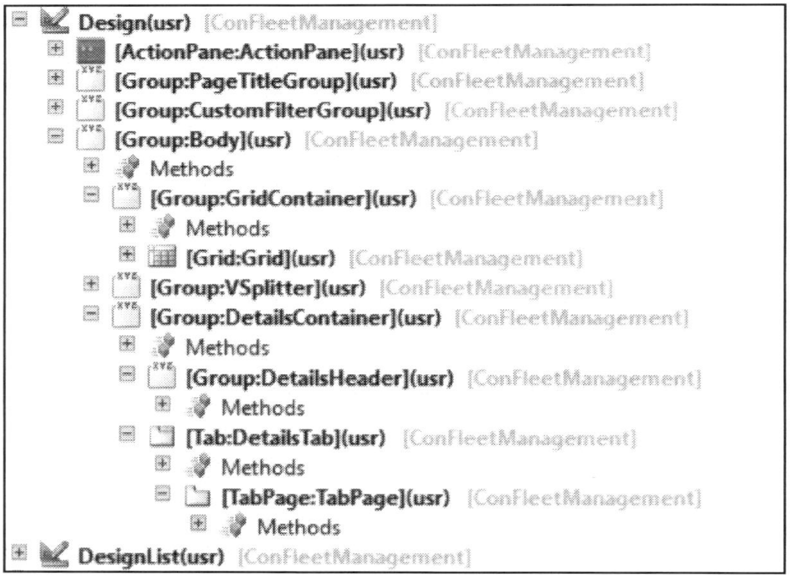

Complete the form as per the standard pattern for this form type, using the following steps as guidance:

1. The **Grid** control should contain fields that the user will use to identify the record, typically the ID and description fields. We will use the `Overview` field group, which is created (as earlier) by setting the grid's **DataSource** property to `ConFMSVehicleSchedule` and the **DataGroup** property to `Overview`.
2. The grid control is designed to be read only. We will add the `Overview` group to the `DetailsHeader` group, which is under the `DetailsContainer` group. To do this, right-click on the **Data Sources** node and choose **Open New Window**.
3. This opens a new AOT window from the selected node. Expand the new window's tree to reveal the fields and position it next to our form's window:

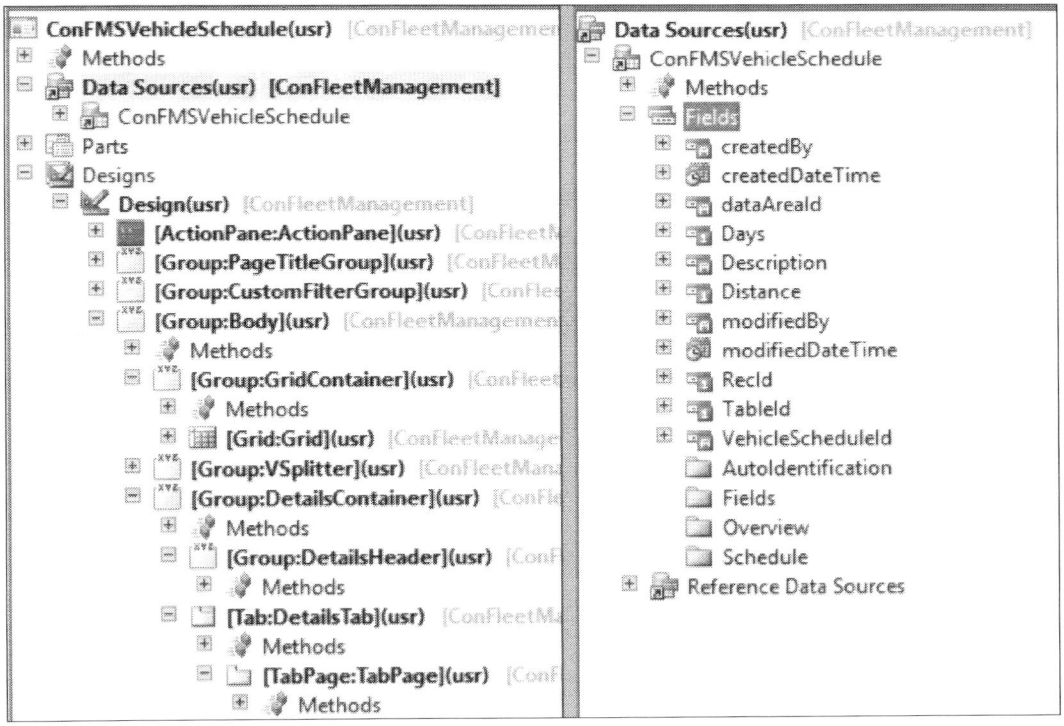

4. Right-click on the group control **DetailsHeader** and select **New Control | Group**. Rename the control to `GroupDetails`, set its **Caption** property to `Details`, and locate a label.

5. Drag the fields **VehicleScheduleId** and **Description** to our new group control.
6. Next, drag the **Schedule** group to the **TabPage** node. This creates a group control named after the field group. As all controls must be unique, we should rename them. Prefixing them with `Group` will suffice.
7. We should rename the **TabPage** control as per its purpose (for example, `TabPageSchedule`).
8. It also needs a caption. Enter `Schedule` and open the label editor. We already have a suitable label (@CON<#>) so select it and click on **Paste**.
9. If we open the form now, the fields **Days** and **Distance** appear vertically; they would be better suited in two columns. This is done on the group control's property sheet, by setting the property **Columns** to `2`.
10. Open the form again. They are displayed side-by-side.

Finally, as we did for the `ConFMSVehicleGroup` table, we need to create the menu item, add to the menu, and assign it to the **FormRef** property of the table.

Creating the vehicle list page

In order to complete the creation of a list page, we need to assign the actions to create and edit to reference a details form. Many developers create the list page first and then the details form. This would mean that we would need to go back to the list page to hook up the menu items to create and edit the data.

To simplify the process, let's create the details form first.

The list page pattern is typified by the released items list page (**Product information management** | **Common** | **Released products**). It is worth familiarizing yourself with this before continuing.

Creating the Details form

To create the `Details` form, right-click on the **Forms** node in the AOT and select **New Form** from **template** | **DetailsFormMaster**.

Rename the form to `ConFMSVehicleTable` and drag it onto the **Forms** node in our project.

To complete the `Details` form design, follow these steps:

1. Drag the `ConFMSVehicleTable` table to the form's **Data Sources** node.
2. Select the **Designs** | **Design** node, set the **Caption** field to `Vehicle details`, and find the label using the label editor.
3. Set the **DataSource** and **TitleDatasource** properties to the data source name.

> The action pane (button ribbon) on this form is not a simple strip of buttons. It behaves more like the action pane in a Microsoft Office application. This is controlled by the **Style** property on the action pane and was set from the template.

4. The only change required at this stage is to give the **Home** tab a caption. So expand **ActionPaneHeader** and change the **Caption** property of **HeaderHomeTable** to `Home` and select a label.
5. Expand the **Tab** control, which contains two pages, `TabPageDetails` and `TabPageGrid`. Depending on whether we are viewing the form in the list or details mode, it will display one of these tab pages.

> You change between these modes using the icons at the bottom of the form, as shown in the following screenshot:
>
> 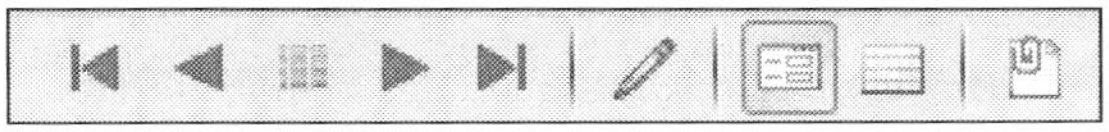

6. Expand the **TabPageGrid**, then expand **GridGroup**, and open the properties of the **HeaderGrid** control.
7. Set the **DataSource** field to `ConFMSVehicleTable` and the **DataGroup** field to `Overview`.

To create the details part of the form, we will add controls to the tab pages within the **Tab** | **TabPageDetails** | **HeaderDetailsTab** control, adding tab pages as required.

In our case, we only need the **HeaderGeneral** tab.

> Although we can create group controls and add the controls by dragging fields from the data source, it is better to use the field groups we created on the table. This saves time later and helps us create more consistent interfaces.

Under the `ConFMSVehicleTable` data source, there are four field groups, namely `AutoIdentification`, `Details`, `Fields`, and `Overview`. The `AutoIdentification` field group is created by the system from the primary key index, while `Fields` is maintained by the system to contain all fields.

Although using `Overview` and `Details` might seem to suffice, `Overview` is used to control the fields on the grids. We may wish to group fields differently on the details forms. So we need to adjust the field groups to cover the `VehicleId`, `Name`, `VehicleGroupId`, and `VehicleStatusId` fields. Use the following steps to adjust the group fields:

1. On the `ConFMSVehicleTable` table, create a new field group called `Identification` and use the first label without a comment.
2. Add the fields `VehicleId`, `Name`, `VehicleGroupId`, and `VehicleTypeId`.
3. Sort the fields into an appropriate order, using the mouse to drag or using the *Alt* + *Up*/*Down* arrow keys while the control is selected.
4. Save the table definition.
5. The form will not realize the table's definition has changed, so we must first ensure the form is saved (no red vertical line), then restore the form by right-clicking on the form, and choose **Restore**.
6. To make the dragging of field groups easier, open the **Data Sources** node in a new window and position it beside the project window.
7. Expand the design nodes by navigating to **Tab** | **TagPageDetails** | **HeaderDetailsTab** | **HeaderGeneral**.
8. From the Data Sources window, expand the **ConFMSVehicleTable** | **Fields** node and drag the field groups `Identification` and `Details`, so they appear as nodes under the **HeaderGeneral** tab page.
9. Save the form and open it to see our work in progress.

> To adjust the layout, the **Columns**, **Height**, and **Width** properties on any container control (such as group and tab page controls) are useful. Always use options from the drop-down lists when setting the height and width, as opposed to entering the width as a number. Also, try to avoid changing the **Left** and **Top** properties. Curiosity is good here, as is looking at forms written by Microsoft.

10. To see some reward for your earlier effort, right-click on the **Vehicle group** and **Service schedule** controls and select **View details**.
11. Once complete, create a menu item by dragging the form onto the **Menu items** | **Display** node of our project and then associate it with the **FormRef** property of the `ConFMSVehicleTable` table.

> Do not add it to the menu as `Details` forms are not main entry points; they access from a list page or other form.

The final step of finishing the `Details` form is to hook up a form whose purpose it is to create a new vehicle record. We will do this later in the chapter.

Creating the list page interaction class

This class will control the user interface interaction, including how the list page is constructed, and the state of various controls and columns.

In our case, we will simply create a basic interaction that we will extend later in the book.

Right-click on the **Classes** node in our project and choose **New** | **Class**.

Rename the class to `ConFMSVehicleTableListPageInteraction`, as per convention to name a list page interaction class.

Open **classDeclaration** (double-click on it) and change the definition to the following:

```
class ConFMSVehicleTableListPageInteraction extends
SysListPageInteractionBase
{
}
```

Save the class.

For further details and the inheritance hierarchy of `SysListPageInteractionBase`, go to `http://msdn.microsoft.com/en-us/library/syslistpageinteractionbase.aspx`.

Creating the base query for the list page

List pages are forms, but they are specifically designed to display lists of data and offer actions that act on the data. All data maintenance (except `delete`) is done by a details form.

These forms are based on a query defined in the AOT, which may seem like an additional step, but offers many advantages. One example is that you can quickly define secondary list pages that show a subset of the data without having to modify the list page itself.

To create the query, follow these steps:

1. Right-click on the **queries** node in our project and navigate to **New** | **Query**.
2. Rename the query to `ConFMSVehicleTableListPage`. It is convention to use the table name followed by `ListPage` for the primary list page query.
3. Expand the query to show the **Data Sources** node and drag the `ConFMSVehicleTable` table onto it. You may need to do this from the AOT, which is positioned to the side of the project window.
4. AX will name this `ConFMSVehicleTable_1`. Rename it to `ConFMSVehicleTable`. Again, this is purely convention; the suffix is not required.

> By default, no fields will be made available. This is useful when creating queries for views, as we won't want all fields to be available to a view. This simplifies the view creation by making only pertinent fields available. It can also help performance by restricting the fields that are available. In a view designed for high performance, we don't want memo or large string fields to be used.

5. Expand the `ConFMSVehicleTable` data source and open the properties of the **Fields** node.
6. Set the **Dynamic** property to `Yes`.

The query is now complete. We can proceed to create the list page.

Creating the list page

This is a reasonably simple process, now that we have most of the basics ready. Most of it may now seem more straightforward.

The following steps will create the list page and hook up the details form:

1. Right-click on the **Forms** node of the AOT and navigate to **New Form from template** | **ListPage**.

2. Rename the new form as `ConFMSVehicleTableListPage`, as per convention for the main list page, and drag it to the **Forms** node of our project.
3. Open the properties of the list page, and change the **InteractionClass** property to `ConFMSVehicleTableListPageInteraction`.

> This hooks up various events on the form, so we can handle them in code. This is useful as we can't add code directly to a list page.

4. You may notice that you can't add a data source manually. Again, by design, this forces us to use a query. To set the data sources in a list page, we use Data Sources' **Query** property; set this to `ConFMSVehicleTableListPage`.
5. Set the design properties as before (**TitleDatasource**, **Caption**, and **DataSource**).
6. Open the properties for the **ListPageGrid** control and set the **DataSource** property to `ConFMSVehicleTable` and **DataGroup** to `Overview`.

> The form will function at a basic level, but we need to hook up some action buttons to make it fully functional.

   When double-clicking on a row, the user expects to see the vehicle details form. The **DefaultAction** property on the grid references a button that is called when the user double-clicks on a row. The **DefaultActionLabel** property controls the text that appears on the menu that appears on right-clicking.

   This is fine in this particular case, although we may alter the **DefaultActionLabel** to something more specific, such as `View vehicle details`.

7. As the grid control references a button, in this case **ViewButton**. Locate this button on the action pane (**HomeTab** | **MaintainGroup** | **ViewButton**) and set the **MenuItemName** to `ConFMSVehicleTable`.

> There is also an edit button, but if we hook up the `ConFMSVehicleTable` menu item, it will open in the view mode, not the edit mode. We need a new menu item that opens the form in edit mode.

8. Right-click on the menu item `ConFMSVehicleTable` and choose **Duplicate**.
9. Rename the new menu item as `ConFMSVehicleTableForEdit`.
10. Change the **OpenMode** property Edit.
11. Change the **Label** property to `Edit vehicle details` and create a label.
12. On the `ConFMSVehicleTableListPage` form, navigate to **Designs** | **Design** | **ActionPane** | **HomeTab** | **MaintainGroup** | **EditButton**, and change the **MenuItemName** property to `ConFMSVehicleTableForEdit`.
13. We also need to hook up the new button, create another from `ConFMSVehicleTable`, and call it `ConFMSVehicleTableForNew`.
14. Change the **OpenMode** property to `New`.
15. Change the **Label** property to `New vehicle` and create a label.
16. Change the **NormalImage** property to `10874` (a nice new icon).
17. Change the **ImageLocation** property to `EmbeddedResource`.
18. Navigate to **Designs** | **Design** | **ActionPane** | **HomeTab** | **MaintainGroup** | **EditButton**, and change the **MenuItemName** property to `ConFMSVehicleTableForNew`.

You can test the form by opening it, which is a good idea as we progress, so we can see the effect of the changes we are making.

To add to the menu, we need to create a menu item of type display as per the vehicle details form, but set the label to `Vehicles`.

The menu item is added to the menu by dragging onto the **Common** submenu of `ConFleetManagementSystem`. Once it is added, you need to set the **isDisplayedInContentArea** field to `Yes` for it to display as a true list page.

We can open the form and it should all appear to work; but we aren't quite there yet. We need to create the `Create` form.

Investigating form events

We could use the debugger to trace through the events the system calls as part of handling the form. This can be difficult at first as the code jumps between methods on the form and the `FormRun` framework. We can also do this by simply overriding the key methods and displaying an info log message.

The command to display an info log message is `info("Message to be displayed")`.

We will override the methods called by the event by adding the `info` command after the call to `super()`, as highlighted in the following lines of code:

```
{
    super();
    info("<message>");
}
```

> As this method is overridden from the base class, AX automatically adds a line to call `super()`. This will call the base class' method, executing the code that would have normally run. We would not normally remove this line in the case of forms and framework classes as it can produce unexpected and undesirable results.

To create the demonstration, follow these steps:

1. This is a demonstration, so to make it easier to revert, we will work on a duplicate of the `ConFMSVehicleGroup` form. This is done by right-clicking on the form and selecting **Duplicate**.
2. Rename the form to `ConFMSTest`.
3. Right-click on **Methods**, which is under **ConFMSTest**, and navigate to **Override method | init**.
4. After the `super()` method call, add the following line:

   ```
   info("Form init called");
   ```

5. Right-click on **Methods**, which is under **ConFMSTest**, and navigate to **Override method | More...** and then select **run**.
6. After the `super()` call, add the following line:

   ```
   info("Form run called");
   ```

> This is placed deliberately after the `super()` call to highlight that the `run` method completes as soon as the form is displayed.

7. Right-click on **Methods**, which can be found by navigating to **ConFMSTest** | **Data Sources** | **ConFMSVehicleGroup**, and navigate to **Override method** | **write**.
8. After the `super()` call, add the following line:

   ```
   info("Data source write called");
   ```

9. Right-click on **Methods**, which can be found by navigating to **ConFMSTest** | **Data Sources** | **ConFMSVehicleGroup** | **Fields** | **Description**, and navigate to **Override method** | **modified**.
10. After the `super()` method call, add the following line:

    ```
    info("Data source field description modified");
    ```

11. Right-click on **Methods**, which can be found by navigating to **ConFMSTest** | **Designs** | **Design** | **GridContainer** | **Grid** | **Grid_Description** | **Methods**, and navigate to **Override method** | **modified**.
12. After the `super()` call, add the following line:

    ```
    info("Form control Grid_Description modified");
    ```

    1. Right-click on the **ConFMSTest** form and select **Open**. The system will display the following message in an **Infolog** window:

       ```
       Form init called
       Form run called
       ```

13. Close the info log and click on **New** to create a new vehicle group record.
14. Complete the **Vehicle group** and **Description** fields. Then, tab out of the **Description** field. This will show the following info log:

    ```
    Data source field description modified
    Form control Grid_Description modified
    ```

15. Close the info log and click on **New** again as if you are to create a new vehicle group. This causes the form to save the new vehicle group and display the following info log:

    ```
    Data source write called
    ```

These events also carry on to the table, as shown in the following simplified diagrams:

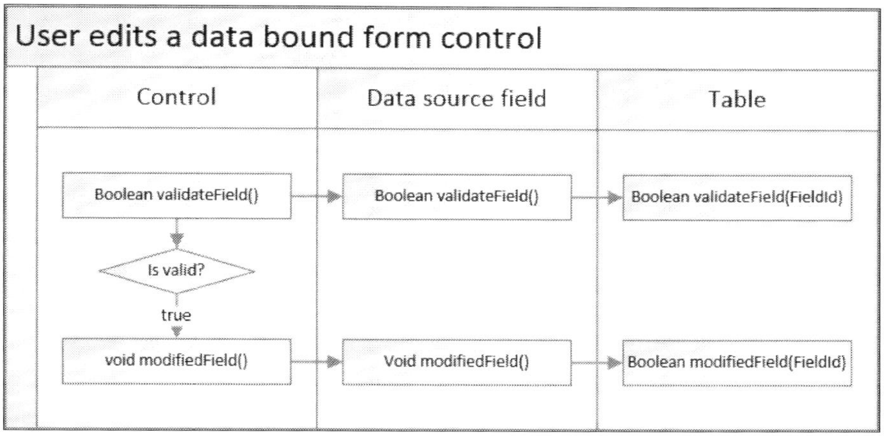

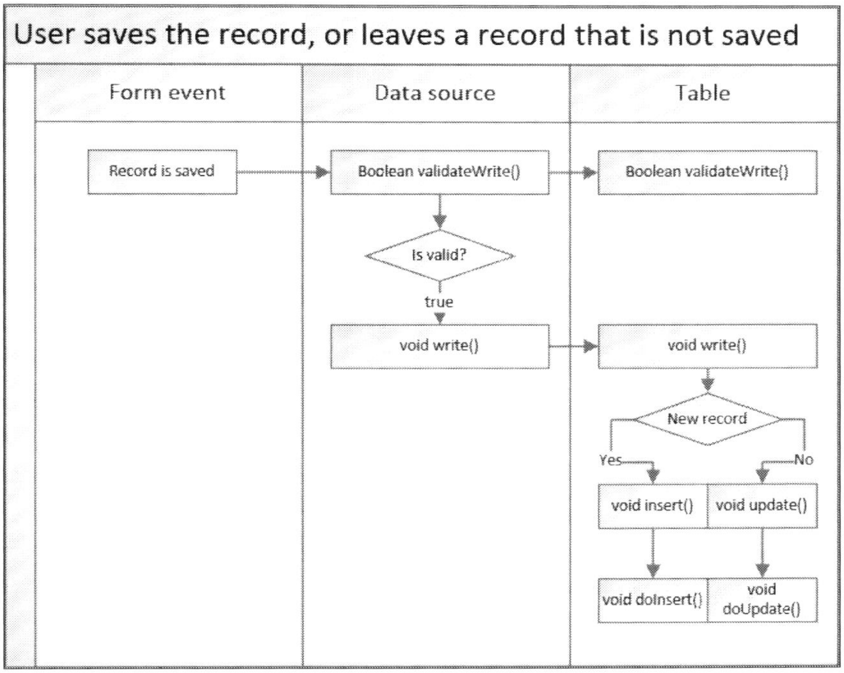

To delete the form, simply right-click on the form and choose **Delete**. If this is done from the project, we are asked if we wish to remove the object from the project or delete it. In our case, we wish to delete the object.

Taking more control over the form layout

Sometimes, we need to have more control of the form's design when data needs to be presented in a certain way. For example, when we want fields to be displayed in a vertical list and need two fields to be side by side (for example, a name for an ID field).

A good example is the form `SalesCreateOrder` where the design has the address information presented as follows:

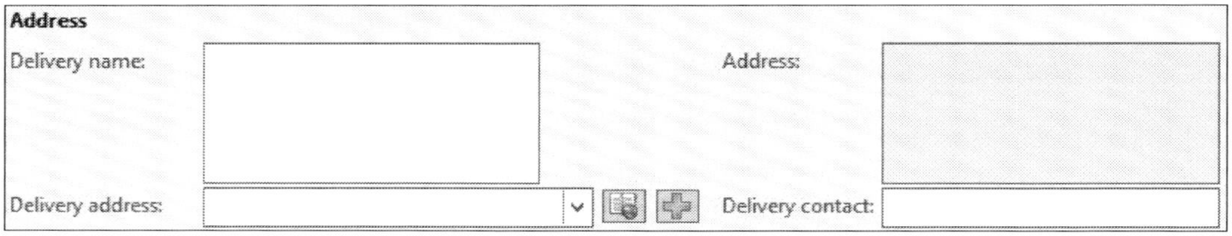

When we add controls to a group control, they appear according to the following properties on the group control:

Property	**Value**
Style	This controls the general settings such as margins, colors, and framing.
TopMargin, **BottomMargin**, **LeftMargin**, **RightMargin**	These are rarely set as the **Style** property is usually used. To set a value, click on the ellipses, and to revert back to **Auto**, click it again.
ArrangeMethod	This is usually `Vertical`, and is the default. The options `Horizontal`, `flush left and Horizontal`, and `flush right` can be used to prioritize the controls horizontally, but this is rare.
Columns	This sets the number of columns that controls are placed in.
ColumnSpace	The default is usually fine, but you can use this to change the spacing between columns.
AlignChildren	This controls whether the controls should be aligned after the longer label. In the preceding screenshot, the controls **Address** and **Delivery contact** are aligned in this way.

The properties we will usually use for layout control are **Style** and **Columns**. Continuing with the `SalesCreateOrder` form example, this was done by creating a set of nested group controls, as shown in the following screenshot:

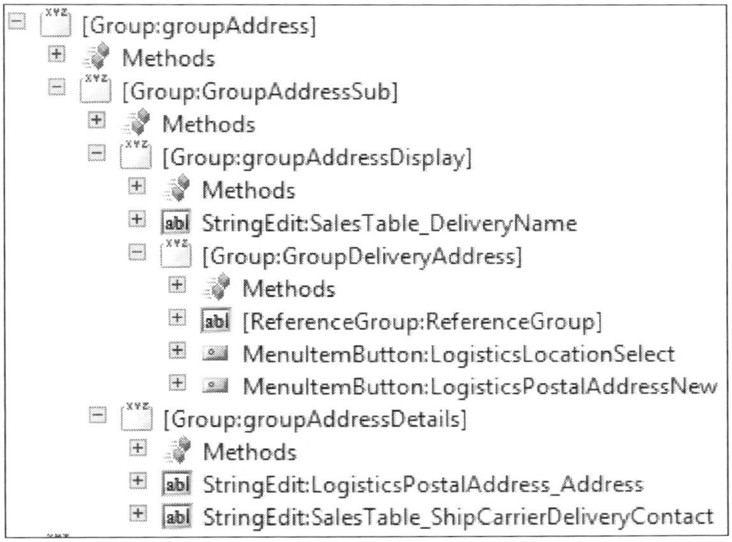

The structure was created by setting the properties as follows:

Control	Properties set
`groupAddress`	• **Style**: `Auto` • **ArrangeMethod**: `Vertical` • **Caption**: `Address`
`groupAddressSub`	• **ArrangeMethod**: `Vertical` • **Columns**: `2`
`GroupDeliveryAddress`	• **ArrangeMethod**: `Vertical` • **Columns**: `3` • **ColumnSpace**: `4`
`groupAddressDetail`	• **ArrangeMethod**: `Vertical`

The top level group is used to simply apply a caption, but why do we need `groupAddressSub`? In this case, we actually don't, but it can help when we want to make a group not to take part in the general form alignment. The property **AlignControl** can be used so that the controls in the group are not aligned with controls in other groups. This is a special case, so we would use this nesting technique so that the effect of the property only affects a limited set of controls.

We don't create forms using a graphical editor, and since MorphX is doing a great job of layout on the forms, we don't actually want that much manual control. We want the fields that are hidden by the user or through security rights to not leave holes in the form layout. We may also deploy AX to different counties, and the labels may have a different length.

So, even though we may need to design forms with a little trial and error, this is a small price to pay for the rewards we get. The best way to learn here is by trying it yourself, and looking for examples in the standard forms. It is very important that we follow the design patterns provided to us by Microsoft—we want our forms to look professional, and having forms that look and feel like the forms created by Microsoft, helps with user acceptance of our solutions.

Creating the vehicle create form with the handler class

The `Create` form is normally used when key data required to create the record is scattered through the details form. In our case, this isn't a mandatory step, given the data is easily accessible within the details form. However, it is included in order to complete the full pattern.

Our case has a little more to offer, as our vehicle table takes part in the inheritance. AX provides functionality at the kernel level to help us. Try creating a new vehicle from the list page created earlier. Once we click on **New vehicle**, the following dialog box is shown:

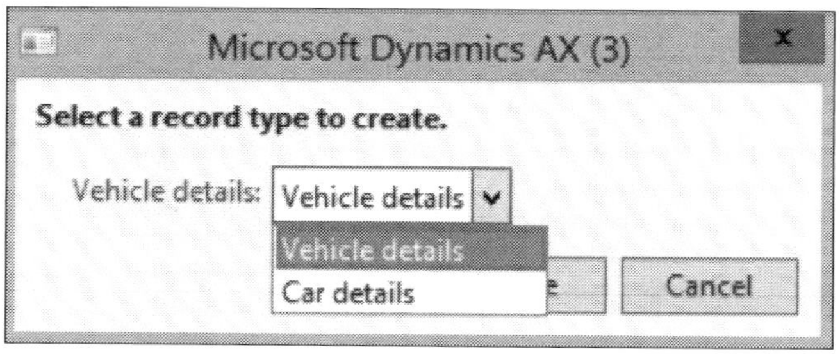

AX uses the metadata stored in the data dictionary to determine how many types of vehicles we have and also determine the label to display. It knows this from the inheritance we configured in *Chapter 2, Creating Data Structures*. The label is the table's label.

When we click create, an empty vehicle details form is shown, where we can complete the vehicle.

The dialog is not tied to the list page's **New vehicle** button but is actually triggered from the data source's create method on the `ConFMSVehicleTable` details form. The event occurs before the form is displayed, and therefore, it appears as though the dialog is created by the list page. This happens because the menu item referenced by the new button has **OpenMode** set to **New**.

To demonstrate this pattern, we will create a dialog whose purpose is to create a vehicle record. This means we can organize the form differently. This is very useful for more complicated forms, as we can place the key data in one place, making the form easier to use.

In order to do this, we need to tie our new `Create` form into the `Details` form's record create process. We do this by intercepting the standard process and returning the new record back to the form.

The process we will implement is shown in the following diagram:

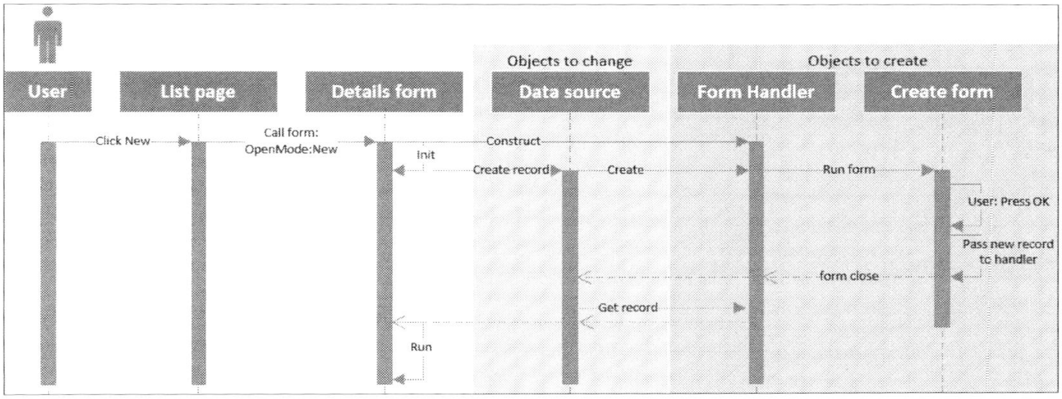

We need to create two objects, the handler class and the create form. As both depend on each other, we will create both objects at the same time.

First, we will create a blank create form, as we need this to finish the handler class; we will finish the form later. We will name this as the details form suffixed with `Create`. This places the form next to the details form in the AOT and describes the object sufficiently.

To do this, follow these steps:

1. Right-click on the **Forms** node in the AOT and navigate to select **Dialogue**, which is under **New Form from template**.
2. Rename the new form to `ConFMSVehicleTableCreate` and drag it to our project.
3. Ensure the form is saved.

First, we will create a basic form handler class. Unlike the list page interaction, there is no natural framework to hook into. This means, we will hook the class to the events manually, as required.

There are two ways of hooking up the interaction:

- Make the table a global variable to the handler class and set the current record using the data source's active method (which fires whenever a record becomes active).
- Use a `FormDataSource` object (again, a global variable to the class) as the connection to the form data source. Once set (during form initialization), the current record is always available from the data source.

The most common method used by Microsoft is the first option because it is easier to follow.

To create the initial part of the form handler class, follow these steps:

1. Right-click on the **Classes** node of the project and chose **New** | **Class**.
2. Rename the class to `ConFMSVehicleTableForm`.
3. Open **classDeclaration** and declare the vehicle table as as follows:

```
class ConFMSVehicleTableForm
{
    ConFMSVehicleTable vehicleTable;
}
```

4. Press *Ctrl* + *S* to save **classDeclaration**.
5. We now need a parameter method so that we can set this variable from other objects. Pressing *Ctrl* + *N* from **classDeclaration** will create a new blank method.

6. Delete the contents of the new method, type `parm`, and press *Tab* key.
7. This opens the **Create 'parm' method** form. type `ConFMSVehicleTable` in the **Type** field. In the **Name** field, enter `vehicleTable` (as we did in the class declaration), and click on **OK**.
   This will create a parameter method as follows:

```
public ConFMSVehicleTable parmVehicleTable(
            ConFMSVehicleTable _vehicleTable = vehicleTable)
{
    vehicleTable = _vehicleTable;

    return vehicleTable;
}
```

> Methods prefixed with `parm` are special methods in AX and produces automatic documentation. AX also understands what this method is, and in some frameworks, this naming is mandatory.

8. We will now use a method to return the name of the create form. This is a good practice, as we could extend the form later to display a different create form for a different type of vehicle. Within the code editor, press *Ctrl* + *N*.
9. Replace the method with the following code:

```
public str createForm()
{
    return formStr(ConFMSVehicleTableCreate);
}
```

10. Should the form not exist, the `formStr` command will cause the compiler to produce a compilation error. Now, press *Ctrl* + *N* again to write the method that will construct and run the form. The following method will do this:

```
public boolean create(RefRecId _instanceRelationType)
{
    Args                    args = new Args();
    FormRun                 createFormRun;
    ConFMSVehicleTable      currentRecord;
    // We need to call a method on the form that will
    // tell its data source to create a new record.
    // Since the method doesn't exist on the base
    // class FormRun we can't use it.
    // Assigning FormRun to an object of type Object
    // lets us call methods that the compiler
    // can't resolve.
```

```
Object                  createFormRunObj;

currentRecord = vehicleTable;
// args is a standard object (similar to a contract)
// that is used to construct a form.
args.name(this.createForm());
args.caller(this);
// The classFactory global class is used to construct
// the form from the args object.
createFormRun = classFactory.formRunClass(args);
// initialise and run the form
createFormRun.init();
createFormRun.run();
// We need to tell the create form's datasource to
// create a record, since we are using inheritance
// we need to tell which type we are creating.
createFormRunObj = createFormRun;
// we must check the method exists, and throw an
// appropriate error if not.
if(!formHasMethod(createFormRun, "createForType"))
{
    throw error(
        strFmt("Form %1 must have method %2",
               this.createForm(), "createForType"));
}
// strFmt is used to format strings, allowing numbered
// placeholders that are replaced at runtime.
// In this case it will replace %1 with the value
// returned from createForm() and %2 from
// 'createforType'.

createFormRunObj.createForType(_instanceRelationType);
if (!createFormRun.closed())
    createFormRun.wait();

//If the user presses OK, success!
if (createFormRun.closedOk())
{
    return true;
}
else
{
    // user cancelled, so set the vehicleTable record
```

```
        // back to the previous record the form will then
        // call parmVehicleTable to get this record back
        // as the current record
        vehicleTable = currentRecord;
        return false;
    }
}
```

> The preceding code has static text (`Form %1 must have method %2`) that hasn't be converted into a label. This will cause a best practice deviation message.

11. Create a label for the static text by selecting the text and then right-click on the selected text. Next, select **Lookup label/text** to create and paste the label back, replacing the text with a label ID.
12. Finally, we need a constructor. We will use the `construct` code snippet for this. Press *Ctrl* + *N* and remove the new method contents, type `construct`, and press *Tab*. This should create a method as follows:

```
public static ConFMSVehicleTableForm construct()
{
    return new ConFMSVehicleTableForm();
}
```

13. Close the code editor and save the class.

    The next task is to hook the handler class to the vehicle details form, where we need to initialize the class, maintain the current record via the active method, and override the data source's create method to call our new method.

14. In the `ConFMSVehicleTable` form, open **classDeclaration**.
15. Declare the `ConFMSVehicleTableForm` class as `formHandler`:

```
public class FormRun extends ObjectRun
{
    ConFMSVehicleTableForm formHandler;
}
```

16. Close the code editor and right-click on the form's **Methods** node and choose **Override method | init**. This opens the following code window:

```
public void init()
{
    super();
}
```

17. The super call handles the standard form initialization, so it must not be removed. After the super call, construct the form handler as follows:

    ```
    formHandler = ConFMSVehicleTableForm::construct();
    ```

18. Close the code editor and expand **Data Sources** and the `ConFMSVehicleTable` data source.
19. Right-click on the **Methods** node and choose **Override method | active**.
20. The `active` method is called whenever a record becomes active (which is also when we change records). Here, we need to update the vehicle record in our handler class. To do this, write the following code after the super call:

    ```
    public int active()
    {
        int ret;

        ret = super();
        formHandler.parmVehicleTable(ConFMSVehicleTable);
        return ret;
    }
    ```

> Remember that the form auto declares the `ConFMSVehicleTable` table as `ConFMSVehicleTable`. After the super call, we can be sure that this contains the data source's active record.

21. Close the code editor and override the method create. This is called when the user tries to create a new record, and we must intercept the process here so that we can interact with the form's data source.
22. The following code will be very similar each time we use a create form. The only big difference is that we are allowing `super()` be called in order to determine the `Vehicle type` option displayed to the user.

    ```
    public void create(boolean _append = false)
    {
        ConFMSVehicleTable newVehicleTable;
        RefRecId           instanceRelationType;

        // start: inherited table code
        // we need to let the create happen so the user can
        // choose the type
        super(_append);
        // store the type the user selected and remove the
        // record that was create above.
        instanceRelationType =
            ConFMSVehicleTable.InstanceRelationType;
    ```

```
        ConFMSVehicleTable_ds.delete();
        // end: inherited table code
        // call the create form
        if (formHandler.create(instanceRelationType))
        {
            // seems to be successful, but check
            // to see if the vehicle is created
            newVehicleTable = formHandler.parmVehicleTable();
            if (newVehicleTable)
            {
                super(_append);

                ConFMSVehicleTable.data(newVehicleTable);
                // research the current record set above from
                // the database, ensure we have the correct
                // data loaded.
                // The parameter controls whether the current
                // position is retained
                ConFMSVehicleTable_DS.research(true);
            }
        }
        else
        {
            // if new was called from a different form
            // (for example, the list page) close this form if a
            // record wasn't created.
            if (TradeFormHelper::isCalledFromForm(
                                            element.args()))
            {
                // close the form - since this method is called
                // before the form is drawn, it won't be shown
                // to the user.
                element.close();
            }
        }
    }
```

23. Close all code editors and save all changes to the class and form.

You may be surprised that we used a static method from the `TradeFormHelper` class. This is actually not specific to the trade module, and the `isCalledFromForm` method is very useful in this situation.

You can try and test this now. It will fail, but you will see from the error that the code is executing correctly. The error we are expecting is as follows:

Form `ConFMSVehicleTableCreate` must have method `createForType`.

We need to complete `ConFMSVehicleTableCreate`. The tasks here are as follows:

1. Add `ConFMSVehicleTable` as a data source.
2. Complete the form design.
3. Write the `createForType` method, which the form handler class needs to call.
4. Declare the form handler and initialize it from passed `args` object.

In `ConFMSVehicleTabeForm.create`, we constructed an `args` object and set the caller property to the `this` instance of the class. When `classFactory` created the `FormRun` instance for us, it copied the `args` object to the form.

We can then access the `args` object from within the form. There is a special object created that is constructed from the form definition; this is called **element** and it provides access to many parts of the form's instance, including the `args` object.

To complete these tasks, please follow these steps on the `ConFMSVehicleTableCreate` form:

1. Open the form level **classDeclaration** method and declare `ConFMSVehicleTableForm` as `formHandler`.
2. Override the form level method `init`.
3. Set `formHandler` to `element.args().caller()`:

   ```
   formHandler = element.args().caller();
   ```

4. Drag the `ConFMSVehicleTable` table from **Tables** onto the **Data Sources** node.

> As this is a create only form, we need to disable the research and reread methods (which happens when the user presses *F5* or *Ctrl* + *F5*),

5. Override the `reread` and `research` methods in **Data Sources | ConFMSVehicleTable** and comment on the `super()` call. Here's an example:

   ```
   public void reread()
   {
   //    super();
   }
   ```

6. Override the data source method `write`. We only need to save the record if the user presses **OK**. Then, we pass this new record back to the handler class. This is done using the following code:

   ```
   void write()
   {
       // if the user didn't press OK, or the record exists,
       // don't save the record.
       if (element.closedOk() && ConFMSVehicleTable.RecId ==
   0)
       {
           ConFMSVehicleTable.insert();
           formHandler.parmVehicleTable(ConFMSVehicleTable);
       }
   }
   ```

7. Create a new form level method. Right-click on **ConFMSVehicleTable | Methods** and choose **New method**.

8. Normally, we only need to call the data source create method, which we could have done by overriding the run method. Creating a table that takes part in the inheritance needs to be done by calling the data source's `createTypes` method, which needs to be told the type in the form of a map object.

9. Therefore, the `createForType` method needs to construct the map and call `ConFMSVehicleTable_DS.createTypes`:

   ```
   public void createForType(RefRecId _instanceRelationType)
   {
       Map tableType = new Map(Types::String, Types::String);
       tableType.insert(ConFMSVehicleTable_DS.name(), tableId2name(ta
   bleNum(ConFMSVehicleTable)));
       ConFMSVehicleTable_DS.createTypes(tableType);
   }
   ```

> A map is a typed collection with a unique key and a value. In our case, it holds a single item with the data source name and table name of the table to be created. The method is named `createTypes`, as `ConFMSVehicleTable` is a type of table. If you look under the **Derived Data Sources** node, which sits under the `ConFMSVehicleTable` data source node, you can see all tables (types) that inherit from the main table. To create a table of one of these types, you must use the appropriate table name.

10. We now need to complete the design. Complete this in the same way we created the `ConFMSVehicleTable` details form. However, this time add the field groups to the **DialogContent** group control. The field groups `Identification` and `Details` will suffice.
11. Once complete, save your changes.

You can test this now by opening the list page and pressing **New vehicle**. You will be asked for the type. Then, the create form is displayed. If you press **OK**, the details form is shown with the new record. If you press **Cancel**, you return to the list page.

Should we press **NewButton** on the details page, we get an error. We should delete this button and add `CommandButton` with the command `New` instead.

To do this, perform these steps on the `ConFMSVehicleTable` form:

1. Navigate through the design's action pane **ActionPaneHeader | HeaderHomeTab | NewGroup**.
2. Delete the menu item button **NewButton**.
3. Right-click on **NewGroup** and choose **New Control | CommandButton**.
4. Rename the new control from `CommandButton` to `cmdNewButton`.
5. Change the button's **Command** property to `New: 260` (you need to use the drop-down list to set this). Here, `260` refers the command number.
6. To see the progress, open the form.
7. This isn't in keeping with other controls, so we need to change more properties on the `cmdNewButton` control.
8. Set **NormalImage** to `10874`.
9. Set **ImageLocation** to `EmbeddedResource`.
10. Change **Big** to `Yes`.
11. Save the form changes and test the form.

The button appears with a new icon and is large like the rest. Clicking on **New** triggers the data source create method (which is why the create form is shown). This is because we set the command to **New** on the command button.

What this actually does is call the `task` method on the form with a parameter to trigger the current data source's `create` method.

Summary

In this chapter, we created the initial user-facing features of our fleet management system. We created forms, to manage our data, and a menu structure, to navigate between them.

We demonstrated how to intercept important form and data-source events. We also wrote a handler class to replace the standard create record process.

In the next chapter, we will dive deeper into AX development, extending our handler classes to work with number sequences and work with delegates to extend functionality in a cleaner way.

4

Creating Business Logic and Hooking into Core AX

We now have the basic table structure and user interface. In this chapter, we will extend the solution further to add business logic and initial integration with the transport management solution provided by Microsoft. We will also see some of the benefits of the investments we made in the earlier chapters.

In this chapter, we will cover the following topics:

- Moving table validation and logic into a class
- Adding navigation
- Creating a number sequence reference and hook into the form
- Hooking into standard AX logic using eventing
- Creating a delegate for our own use and by other parties

Moving table validation and logic into a class

We have discussed previously that there are various events we can hook into by overriding methods on a table. The typical events we override are shown in this table:

Method	**Occurs when**	**Description**
`validateField`	The `validate` method is called on one of the fields of the form's data sources.	Code can be written here to validate the user input. It will automatically verify that input is valid (for example, a foreign key relation). It can be called in code, but you should expect `infoLog` messages to be thrown, which are sometime undesirable.
`modifiedField`	The `modified` method is called on one of the fields of the form's data sources.	This performs actions based on the user input. It can be called in code, but don't assume that a developer will always call this method.
`validateWrite`	The form data source's `validateWrite()` is called on one of the form's data sources.	This performs special validation before the record is written. It will automatically check for required fields, but will not check whether a value is valid—this is done by `validateField`.
`update`	An existing record is saved through code or from the table's write method.	This method does not actually update the physical record, but simply calls `Common.doUpdate()`—`Common` being the base class for all tables. If the table takes part in inheritance, `update()` will call the base table's `update` method.
`insert`	A new record is saved, through code or from the table's write method.	Like `update`, this method calls `Common.doInsert()`. If the table takes part in inheritance, `insert()` will call the base table's `insert` method.

Method	Occurs when	Description
`validateDelete`	The `validateDelete` method is called on one of the form's data sources.	Code can be written here to perform special validation before the record is deleted. This method will automatically check whether there are any delete restrictions in place through `DeleteAction`.

Over the course of this chapter, we will override these methods as appropriate, but before we do this, we should decide where the code should be placed: directly on the table or in a class.

The decision to move table validation and other logic to a class is based on complexity. We will typically do this for tables of type worksheet (for example, sales orders and purchase orders), as the logic tends to become complicated. Main tables, such as `Customer`, `Item`, and our `Vehicle` table will not normally have their logic placed in a class, unless the table requires complicated business logic.

> We don't create a handler class for transaction tables, since the logic required goes into the class that posts the transaction, not the table itself.

Our example will be for the vehicle service data table, `ConFMSVehServiceTable`, as this is a worksheet table.

Apart from classes being a more suitable place to write more complicated code, they also allow us to construct a class based on the data in the record, for instance, the vehicle type field on the attached vehicle record.

A good example is the `validateField` method. Here, we would normally use a switch statement with a case per field. If we want different validation per vehicle type, we end up with a switch inside a switch.

This breaks two readability rules:

- The method should not be too long
- A nested switch should be avoided

A common pattern is to have just one switch statement, and then each case will be handled by a separate "check" method (such as `checkNextServiceDate()`). These methods can then be called from the `validateField` method and other places where a message to the user is required.

> Check methods are expected to display a message to the user on failure, and return false. A simple method is to use the `return checkFailed("<message>")` command. This always returns false and will display an error to the user as an **Infolog** window.

This simplifies our switch statement to a couple of lines per field, like this for example:

```
switch(_fieldIdToCheck)
{
    case fieldNum(ConFMSVehServiceTable, NextServiceDate)
        ret = this.checkNextServiceDate();
        break;
        // and so on
}
```

This is a good idea because we can reuse this method. There is another, more extendable solution to this: we can create a class that handles the service data logic and have a specialized class per vehicle type. Since the service data table is associated with a vehicle, we can easily determine the vehicle type by navigating back to the vehicle record. We will follow this approach in the following paragraphs.

Implementing the pattern

The pattern is implemented by creating a class named after the table, suffixed with `Type`. This will have a method per table event that we are handling.

To write code to this pattern, we will perform the following steps:

1. Create the table type class.
2. Create a method for each table event we will override (certainly the methods in the preceding table). These methods have the same parameter profile as the table method.
3. Create an instance method named type on the table that constructs the class based on the current record.
4. Override the table event methods to call `this.type().<eventMethod()>`.

In our case, the class will be called `ConFMSVehServiceTableType`.

The best way to describe this is by example. The following steps will create a template that we will extend over the course of the project:

1. In our project, right-click on the **Classes** node and go to **New** | **Class**.
2. Rename the class to `ConFMSVehServiceTableType`.
3. Open the **classDeclaration** and declare `serviceTable` as `ConFMSVehServiceTable`.
4. Create a `parm` method for this variable (press *Ctrl* + *N*, clear the method's content, type `parm`, press *Tab*, fill in the dialog, and press **OK**), the result of which should look like this:

```
public ConFMSVehServiceTableType parmServiceTable(ConFMSVehService
Table _serviceTable =
serviceTable)
{
    serviceTable = _serviceTable;
    return serviceTable;
}
```

5. Create a `construct` method, this time using the construct code snippet. This should result in the following:

```
public static ConFMSVehServiceTableType construct()
{
    return new ConFMSVehServiceTableType();
}
```

6. We should create a constructor that constructs the instance from a service table record, since this is how we will construct an instance of the class. This is done as follows:

```
public static ConFMSVehServiceTableType
newFromServiceTable(ConFMSVehServiceTable _serviceTable)
{
    ConFMSVehServiceTableType instance;

    instance = ConFMSVehServiceTableType::construct();
    instance.parmServiceTable(_serviceTable);
    return instance;
}
```

7. We can now write our code. We will create method stubs for the following table event methods:
    - `validateWrite`
    - `validateDelete`
    - `modifiedField`
    - `validateField`
    - `update`
    - `insert`
8. For each of the preceding methods, right-click on the **Methods** node of the `ConFMSVehServiceTable` table and select **Override method | <method name>**.
9. In the `ConFMSVehServiceTableType` class, create the new method as usual: right-click **New | Method** for the first method and press *Ctrl* + *N* while in the code editor for subsequent methods.
10. The method signature must match, so copy the method signature from the equivalent table method. The purpose at this point is to avoid interfering with what the system will normally do:

```
public boolean validateWrite()
{
    boolean ret = true;
    return ret;
}
public boolean validateField(FieldId _fieldIdToCheck)
{
    boolean ret = true;
    return ret;
}
public boolean validateDelete()
{
    boolean ret = true;
    return ret;
}
public void modifiedField(FieldId _fieldId)
{
}
public void update()
{
    serviceTable.doUpdate();
}
```

```
public void insert()
{
    serviceTable.doInsert();
}
```

> It is normal to allow validate and modified type methods to call `super()` and then call our table event handler, but in the case of `insert` and `update`, we will usually take full control and call the equivalent `do` method that performs the database operation.

11. We now need to wire the table's events to the class, but first, we need to create a `type` method that will construct an instance of the class. This must be an instance method on the table, as it will pass the current record to the class. This is done by creating a new method on the table and typing the following:

```
public ConFMSVehServiceTableType type()
{
    return ConFMSVehServiceTableType::newFromServiceTable(this);
}
```

12. We now need to modify the table methods so that they call our class. The code you need to write is highlighted:

```
public void modifiedField(FieldId _fieldId)
{
    super(_fieldId);
    this.type().modifiedField(_fieldId);
}
public boolean validateDelete()
{
    boolean ret;
    ret = super();
    // only perform our validation if the system's succeeds
    if(ret)
    {
        ret = this.type().validateDelete();
    }
    return ret;
}
public boolean validateField(FieldId _fieldIdToCheck)
{
    boolean ret;
    ret = super(_fieldIdToCheck);
    if(ret)
    {
```

```
            this.type().validateField(_fieldIdToCheck);
        }
        return ret;
    }
    public boolean validateWrite()
    {
        boolean ret;
        ret = super();
        if(ret)
        {
            ret = this.type().validateWrite();
        }
        return ret;
    }
```

13. The `insert` and `update` methods are slightly different, as we don't want to call `super();` it simply calls `doUpdate()` or `doInsert()`. We will do this in our class, and we can add code as required in our class. The methods will therefore be the following:

```
    public void update()
    {
        this.type().update();
    }
    public void insert()
    {
        this.type().insert();
    }
```

14. The main table events are now handled by the handler class, although we aren't adding any value to the process as yet. This comes later.

> There is another big benefit of using classes for this—we can create delegates that we can call within our class. Other developers can then subscribe to our delegates, adding new logic without directly modifying the code. This is covered towards the end of this chapter, in the *Creating a delegate for use by other parties* section.

Adding validation logic

Now that we have this framework in place, we can start adding validation and business logic. Some validation may be obvious, based on standard design patterns, and the rest will be provided in the functional requirements document.

The validation required in `ConFMSVehServiceTable` will be as follows:

- The primary key, `ServiceId`, must be filled in and can't be changed after creation
- `VehicleId` must be populated, and cannot be changed after creation
- `CurrentOdometer` must be filled in
- `ServiceDate` must be filled in
- `NextServiceDate` must be after `ServiceDate` and be set from the vehicle service schedule
- `NextServiceOdo` must be greater than `CurrentOdometer` and be set from the vehicle service schedule

In order to make fields mandatory, we will use the table fields' **Mandatory** property. This is checked by the standard `validateField` table method. Since we are calling `super()` before our method, this will still be processed. This property also highlights mandatory fields.

To make a field editable on creation, but read-only once it is saved, we set the field properties as follows: **AllowEdit** to `No` and **AllowEditOnCreate** to `Yes`.

We need to write code to handle the rest. To validate `NextServiceDate` and `NextServiceOdo`, we will modify the `ConFMSVehServiceTableType.validateField` method, as follows:

```
public boolean validateField(FieldId _fieldIdToCheck)
{
    boolean ret = true;
    switch (_fieldIdToCheck)
    {
        case fieldNum(ConFMSVehServiceTable, NextServiceDate):
            if(serviceTable.NextServiceDate <
               serviceTable.ServiceDate)
            {
                ret = checkFailed("The next service date must be
later than the service date");
            }
            break;
        case fieldNum(ConFMSVehServiceTable, NextServiceOdo):
```

```
            if(serviceTable.NextServiceOdo <
               serviceTable.CurrentOdometer)
            {
                ret = checkFailed("The next service odometer must
be greater than the current odometer reading");
            }
            break;
    }
    return ret;
}
```

> Remember to create labels for the string literals in the preceding code by selecting the text and pressing *Ctrl* + *Alt* and the spacebar.

Since `validateField` is called using the field ID and not the field's name, we need to look up the field ID from the data dictionary. This is done by calling the `fieldNum` method.

You can test this in the table browser by right-clicking on the table and selecting **Open**. You can then enter data that should succeed and fail to test the various cases.

Adding business logic

We now need to add some logic to set the `NextServiceDate` and `NextServiceOdo` fields. This will be done as we edit the `ServiceDate` and `CurrentOdometer` fields. It is done by adding logic to the class's `modifiedField` method, as shown in the following code:

```
public void modifiedField(FieldId _fieldId)
{
    switch (_fieldId)
    {
        case fieldNum(ConFMSVehServiceTable, ServiceDate):
            // TODO insert code to set NextServiceDate
            break;
        case fieldNum(ConFMSVehServiceTable, CurrentOdometer):
            // TODO insert code to set NextServiceOdo
            break;
    }
}
```

> Placing `TODO` as the first word in a comment causes the compiler to display the comment in the compiler output's to-do list.

The logic required in the preceding example is to check whether the vehicle has a service schedule. Then it has to look up the schedule to calculate the next service date and odometer settings. This would be too much code to place inside a case, so we will create a series of methods to do this.

We will create these methods on the class, since this is where they will be used.

Checking whether the record has a service schedule

Before we start, check whether that the relation `ConFMSVehicleTable` on `ConFMSVehServiceTable` has the **CreateNavigationPropertyMethods** property set to `Yes`. This will create a navigation property method that appears as the table name. You can change this using the **NavigationPropertyMethodNameOverride** property. This is useful because it is possible to have more than one relationship to the same table. This property allows you to give each relation method a unique name.

We will use this in the following code to get the service table's vehicle record in order to determine whether it has a schedule:

```
public boolean hasServiceSchedule()
{
    ConFMSVehicleSchedId serviceSchedId;

    serviceSchedId =
  serviceTable.ConFMSVehicleTable().VehicleSchedId;
    if(serviceSchedId != "")
    {
        if(ConFMSVehicleSchedule::exist(serviceSchedId))
            return true;
    }
    return false;
}
```

The choice to make this method `public` is because it may be useful outside the class.

The `ConFMSVehicleTable` method on `ConFMSVehServiceTable` was created for us by setting the relation's **CreateNavigationPropertyMethods** property to `Yes`. This method is not visible in the AOT; it is there just to be used. It uses the relation's definition, so if the relation changes, then so does the method. This saves time and simplifies navigation, especially when the tables become more complicated.

In the highlighted part of the preceding code, it may seem strange that we did not check whether a record was returned. AX will always return a record, and if none were found, the fields will be initialized with empty values; they will not be NULL. A normal way to check whether a record was returned is to check whether `RecId` is 0—its uninitialized value.

In this case, we are interested in the `VehicleSchedId` field. If a record is not found, then this will be an empty string. If a record that has no value for `VehicleSchedId` is found, then also it will be blank. In either case, it means the vehicle has no schedule.

Getting the service schedule record

The next method involves getting the service schedule record:

```
public ConFMSVehicleSchedule getServiceSchedule()
{
    ConFMSVehicleSchedId  serviceSchedId;
    ConFMSVehicleSchedule schedule;

    serviceSchedId =
  serviceTable.ConFMSVehicleTable().VehicleSchedId;
    if(serviceSchedId != "")
    {
        return ConFMSVehicleSchedule::find(serviceSchedId);
    }
    return schedule;
}
```

This method is similar, but what do we do if we don't have a schedule? Since the schedule is not mandatory, we shouldn't throw an error. We simply return the empty schedule record buffer, relying on the calling method to handle it properly.

We should therefore place a comment to this effect, which appears when we use the method.

Go to the top of the method and enter ///, like this:

```
///public ConFMSVehicleSchedule getServiceSchedule()
```

AX will replace this with the comment header template. Complete this as shown in the following code snippet:

```
/// <summary>
/// This method will lookup the <c>ConFMSVehicleSchedule</c>,
/// returning empty if not found
/// </summary>
/// <returns>
/// An instance of <c>ConFMSVehicleSchedule</c>, empty
/// if not found
/// </returns>
/// <remarks>
/// This method will not throw an exception if a record
/// is not found.
/// </remarks>
```

The special tag, `<c>ConFMSVehicleSchedule</c>`, can be read by AX, which understands that it is a type.

To see this in action, go to another method in the class and start typing `this.get`. Watch **IntelliSense** pick up the comment text, as shown in the following screenshot:

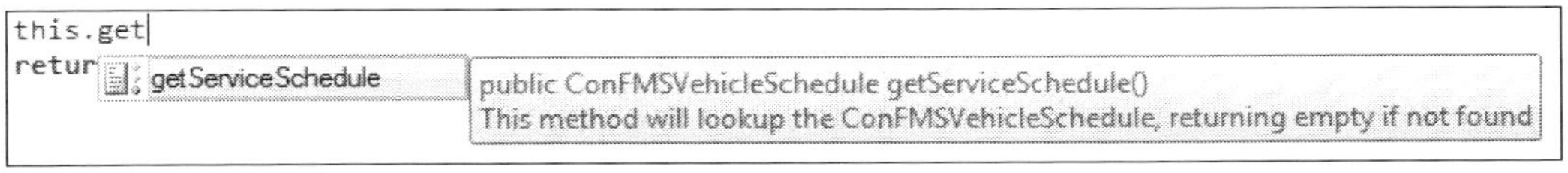

> IntelliSense is a feature of the MorphX IDE that assists us by offering a list of matching elements (types, variables, keywords, and others) as we type.

Creating the NextServiceDate and NextServiceOdo methods

We should now create the methods to set `NextServiceDate` and `NextServiceOdo`.

The service schedule definition stores the number of days and distance between services. We can add days to a date variable by simply adding the number of days to it, as shown in the `setNextServiceDate` method:

```
public void setNextServiceDate()
{
    if(this.hasServiceSchedule())
```

```
        {
            serviceTable.NextServiceDate =
                    serviceTable.ServiceDate +
                    this.getServiceSchedule().Days;
        }
    }
```

This sets `NextServiceDate` to `ServiceDate` plus the days returned from the vehicle's service schedule record. Again, if no record is found, the days will be zero and the next service date will be set to `ServiceDate`. We will therefore need to add validation to `ConFMSVehicleSchedule` to check whether days is greater than zero.

The next point of note is that this code will not trigger `modifiedField` or `validateField` for the change to `NextServiceDate`; remember that these are only called from the data bound form controls via the form data source. We can call `validateField` and `modifiedField` programmatically, but we run the risk of a recursive loop.

If we want to validate `NextServiceDate`, we should write a dedicated check method instead, like this:

```
public boolean checkNextServiceDate(TransDate _nextServiceDate =
serviceTable.NextServiceDate).
{
// validate logic on _nextServiceDate
}
```

This method can be used to test a future state by passing a proposed `NextServiceDate` value, or check the current record's value using the default parameter.

The next method, `setNextServiceOdo`, is similar:

```
public void setNextServiceOdo()
{
    if(this.hasServiceSchedule())
        serviceTable.NextServiceOdo = serviceTable.CurrentOdometer
                                 + this.getServiceSchedule().Distance;
}
```

Finally, we need to hook up these methods with the `modifiedField` method in our class so that they are triggered when the user alters the `ServiceDate` or `CurrentOdometer` fields.

In our class, open the `modifiedField` method and adjust it, as follows:

```
public void modifiedField(FieldId _fieldId)
{
    switch (_fieldId)
    {
        case fieldNum(ConFMSVehServiceTable, ServiceDate):
            this.setNextServiceDate();
            break;

        case fieldNum(ConFMSVehServiceTable, CurrentOdometer):
            this.setNextServiceOdo();
            break;

    }
}
```

This may seem complicated to create, but the way we have created specific methods simplifies readability and allows future changes to be made more easily than writing logic in a single method.

The preceding code is summarized by the following sequence diagram, which follows the events for a form control bound to the `NextServiceDate` field:

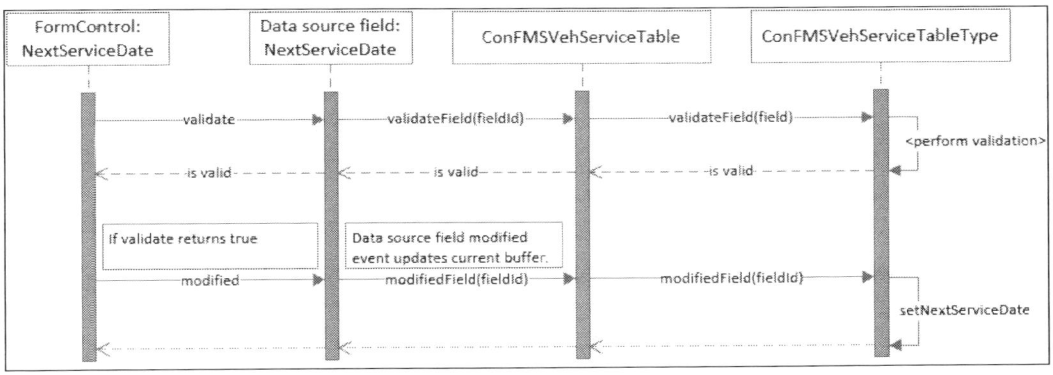

Testing

The test case for this is relatively straightforward, but necessary. In order to do this, some test data must be created. We should create the following test cases.

Open the form: `ConFMSVehicleSchedule` and create a record as shown in the following table:

VehicleScheduleId	**Distance**	**Days**
D180-10K	10,000	180

Then, open the form, `ConFMSVehicleTable`, and create the two records as defined in the following table:

VehicleId	**VehicleSchedId**
V0001	""
V0002	D180-10K

Next, we define the required test data for our test, as shown in the following table, we could create this in Excel in order to compare the test against what we expect:

Test			**Expected results**	
`VehicleId`	`ServiceDate`	`CurrentOdometer`	`NextServiceDate`	`NextServiceOdo`
V0001	1st January 2015	123000	1st January 2015	123000
V0002	1st January 2015	123000	30th June 2015	133000

To perform the test we need to create the test records in `ConFMSVehServiceTable` as defined in the preceding table. To create these test records, use the table browser by right-clicking on the `ConFMSVehServiceTable` table and selecting **Open**.

Create a new row by pressing *Ctrl* + *N* and select the vehicle created earlier. The table browser is an auto-generated form that triggers normal form events. You should see that the changes made to the current service schedule record are automatically updated in the table browser.

Adding navigation

At the end of the last chapter, we had the task of creating the user interface for the service records. We now need to add functionality so that we can create a service record from a vehicle and navigate to the service records from the vehicle list page or details.

The UI convention is that the details and list page should have the same action pane layout, with the only exception being that we don't need buttons to view or edit service records in the details form. This does present us with a level of duplication, but it is manageable.

Adding the ability to create a service record for a vehicle

The first task is to create a button on the vehicle list page that creates a new service. This will be one by dragging the menu item `ConFMSVehServiceTableForNew` on to a new button group in the action pane. The steps in detail are as follows:

1. Arrange the project window and AOT so they are side by side.
2. In the project, expand **Forms** | **ConFMSVehicleTableListPage** | **Designs** | **Design** | **Action Pane** | **HomeTab**.
3. Create a new `ButtonGroup` control named `ServiceGroup` on the **HomeTab** action pane tab (right-click and select **New Control** | **ButtonGroup**).
4. Change **Caption** to `Service details`.
5. Move the new control to just below **MaintainGroup** (select the control and use *Alt* and the down arrow key).

> The label should already exist if you've followed the naming conventions when creating the service details form.

6. In the AOT window, go to **Menu items** | **Display** and locate **ConFMSVehServiceTableForNew**. Drag this menu item onto the new button group control, `ServiceGroup`.
7. The button should be a large icon, so change the property **Big** to `Yes`.

Open the vehicle list page and test the new button. It should open the service create form, and once you create the service record, it will open the service details form.

Initializing the service record from the vehicle record

The form works, but we should not require the user to select a vehicle when it is opened from the vehicle list page. This is a common situation, and there is a pattern to follow for this.

The `args` object passed to the `ConFMSVehServiceTable` form will contain the record that the form was called from. From this, we can set the vehicle ID.

To implement this pattern, we will perform the following steps:

1. Create an `initFrom` method so that we can initialize the service record from a vehicle record.
2. Modify the form handler to store the calling vehicle's record.
3. Adjust the form so that it detects whether it was called from a vehicle record.
4. Adjust the create form so that when a record is created, it initializes from the vehicle record.

Creating the initFrom method

The first task is to create a generic `initFrom` method, which should be added anyway when the table is a child, such as tables of type `Worksheet` and `Transaction`. The purpose of this method is to set various defaults from the primary table and also set the key. Although this seems a lot of effort for simply setting one field, it is usual that the main table (for example, the vehicle table) stores defaults to use on worksheet tables (for example, the service record). It is also common for this list of defaults to grow, and having one method to handle this is good practice. Since it is the convention to have these methods, a developer will expect these to be created for them, removing the need to think about what data is transferred to the worksheet table.

To do this, right-click on the **Methods** node of the table `ConFMSVehServiceTable`, select **New Method**, and write a method, as follows:

```
public void initFromConFMSVehicleTable(
                                ConFMSVehicleTable _table = null)
{
    // is the parameter default; that is, no vehicle
    if(prmisDefault(_table))
    {
        // no initialization is required as
        // we are only setting the id
        // so simply return
        return;
        // should we require more fields to be
        // initialize from the vehicle record the
        // following code is required
        //if(this.VehicleId == "")
        //    return;
```

```
            //_table = ConFMSVehicleTable::find(this.VehicleId);
        }

        this.VehicleId = _table.VehicleId;
    }
```

In our case, it is just the key that we wish to store, but if we have more fields to initialize from the vehicle record, we will only have to modify this method and not the many places where a service record may be created for a vehicle. Should we add more fields later, which need copying from the vehicle table, we simply need to alter this method.

To trap the event when the user manually changes the vehicle, we should hook into the `modifiedField` method created earlier.

> To quickly navigate to the table handler class, open the `modifiedField` method on the table, click inside the text `modifiedField` after `this.type()`, and press *F12*.

The case statement should simply be like this:

```
case fieldNum(ConFMSVehServiceTable, VehicleId):
    if(serviceTable.VehicleId != "")
    {
        serviceTable.initFromConFMSVehicleTable();
    }
    break;
```

The `initFrom` method will actually not do anything yet, as we are using the default parameter.

Modifying the form handler to store a vehicle record

Because the list page is calling the details form using the `ConFMSVehServiceTableForNew` menu item (which has the `OpenMode` parameter set to New) the details form will call the create form. Unfortunately, the create form does not know that the details form was called with a vehicle record. Since we already have a class that we are using to pass data between the details and create forms, we will extend this so that it also stores a vehicle record.

This is achieved by simply adding `ConFMSVehicleTable` as a global variable to the class, and then adding an associated `parm` method. This is done by the following steps:

1. Open the **classDeclaration** field of `ConFMSVehServiceTableForm` and add the following line:

   ```
   ConFMSVehicleTable    vehicleTable;
   ```

2. Create a `parm` method (remember to use the `parm` code snippet for speed) that will look like this:

```
public ConFMSVehicleTable
parmVehicleTable(ConFMSVehicleTable _vehicleTable =
vehicleTable)
{
    vehicleTable = _vehicleTable;
    return vehicleTable;
}
```

Modifying the service details form to detect whether it was called with a vehicle

We now need to set this variable when we initialize the service details form, but only when it is called from a vehicle. This is done using the following steps:

1. On the `ConFMSVehServiceTable` form, open the `init` method.
2. We need to determine whether the calling dataset was the vehicle table, and then use the calling record buffer to set the vehicle table in our form handler class. This is done by the following code:

```
public void init()
{
    super();
    formHandler = ConFMSVehServiceTableForm::construct();
    switch(element.args().dataset())
    {
        case tableNum(ConFMSVehicleTable):
            formHandler.parmVehicleTable(element.args().record());
            break;
    }
}
```

> The `element` object is the instantiated form, and `args` is constructed automatically setting the dataset to the calling table ID and the record to the calling data source's current record.

Modifying the form handler to initialize from the vehicle

To complete the pattern, we need to add a method to the form handler and hook into the `initValue` method of the data source. The `initValue` method simply calls the table's `initValue` method, setting the defaults as required. In our case, we have to do this on the data source. The vehicle record is stored in the form handler class, which is a global variable to the form.

First, we need to add a new method on the form handler class to initialize the service table's fields as we require. This will be named `initValues` as a convention to be deliberately different from the `initValue` table event.

To do this, create a new method on `ConFMSVehServiceTableForm`, as follows:

```
public void initValues()
{
    if(vehicleTable.RecId != 0)
    {
        serviceTable.initFromConFMSVehicleTable(vehicleTable);
    }
}
```

The `vehicleTable` record will be set by the details form's `init` method if the form was called with a vehicle record.

We now need to tell the create form, `ConFMSVehServiceTableCreate`; to call this method. This is done in the `initValue` event, as shown in the following steps:

1. Navigate to **Forms** | **ConFMSVehServiceTableCreate** | **Data sources** | **ConFMSVehServiceTable** | **Methods**.
2. Right-click on **Methods** and select **Override method** | **initValue**.
3. Adjust the method so that it looks like this:

```
public void initValue()
{
    super();
```

```
        formHandler.parmServiceTable(ConFMSVehServiceTable);
        formHandler.initValues();
    }
```

4. Ensure that everything is saved and compiled without error.

In the preceding code, we have to set the current service table record because `initValue` is called before `active`. Before continuing, we need to test creating service records from the following forms:

- The vehicle list page
- The vehicle services list page
- The vehicle service details

You should also create several vehicles and one or more service records for each vehicle.

Viewing vehicle service records for a vehicle

It is natural navigation to move from the vehicle record to show the relevant service records. Since this is a one-to-many relationship, it should take the user to the vehicle service list page. We will also add the option to view the vehicle associated with a service, but since this is many-to-one, it should open the vehicle details form.

To do this, we simply drag the menu item onto the form, as shown in the following steps:

1. Position the project window and AOT side by side.
2. Drag the `ConFMSVehServiceTableListPage` menu item onto **ConFMSVehicleTableListPage** | **Designs** | **Design** | **ActionPane** | **HomeTab** | **ServiceGroup**.
3. On the new button control, set the **Big** and **NeedsRecord** properties to `Yes`.

> Setting **NeedsRecord** to `Yes` will disable the button if there is no vehicle selected.

4. Open the `ConFMSVehicleTableListPage` list page, select a vehicle, and click on **Vehicle services**.

Magically, it displays the appropriate service records for the vehicle. This is one of the many rewards we gain from our earlier efforts.

Let's try the same trick by adding the ability to open the vehicle details from a service record. This is done by the following steps:

1. On `ConFMSVehServiceTableListPage`, create a button group for reference data by navigating to **ActionPaneHeader** | **HeaderHomeTab,** called `RelatedInfoGroup`.
2. Set the **Caption** property to `Related information` and select a label (for example, `@SYS111665`)
3. Drag the `ConFMSVehicleTable` menu item onto the new group.
4. Set the **Big** and **NeedsRecord** properties to `Yes`.
5. Test the form.

Again, it magically opens the correct vehicle record, but how does it know? It may seem obvious because the form only contains one record, but what if the form contains many data sources? Which one does it choose?

It does this based on the **Datasource** property. We left this blank in the menu items, allowing it to be inherited from the parent container, all the way to the design. Should we wish to change this behavior, we can simply fill in this property.

We should now copy the new button groups from the list pages to the correct place on the equivalent details form. Each time we change the action pane, we must make the change in the other form.

Number sequences

The vehicle table is a main table, for which we normally provide the ability to control the primary ID, `VehicleId`, via a number sequence. A number sequence allows the user to control how numbers are generated in terms of format and what happens if a record is deleted. This section describes how to hook into it.

All forms that are `Main`, `Worksheet`, or `WorksheetHeader` should use the following pattern.

Defining a number sequence

The first step is to define a number sequence that can be applied to our `vehicleId` field. A number sequence is associated with a particular EDT, `ConFMSVehicld` in our case. So, it is that EDT for which we define the number sequence, not the field.

We create a number sequence reference to the EDT in code using the number sequence framework. To create a number sequence reference, the framework requires us to write a new class that extends the `NumberSeqApplicationModule` class. In it, we will define a number sequence and associate it with our EDT, as follows:

1. Create a new class. Name it `ConFMSNumberSeqModuleFleetManagement`.
2. View the code for the class and change the class declaration so that it extends `NumberSeqApplicationModule`:

    ```
    class ConFMSNumberSeqModuleFleetManagement
        extends NumberSeqApplicationModule
    {
    }
    ```

3. In the AOT, right-click on the class and override the `numberSeqModule` method.
4. The `numberSeqModule` method must return a value from the `NumberSeqModule` base enum. We will return `NumberSeqModule::TMS`:

    ```
    public NumberSeqModule numberSeqModule()
    {
        // This tells the framework which module our
        // sequence belongs to. We always place custom
        // sequences in a standard module, as changing
        // standard enums should be avoided.
        return NumberSeqModule::TMS;
    }
    ```

5. Next, override the `loadModule` method.
6. This method is where we will set up a `NumberSeqDatatype` class object that defines the reference:

    ```
    protected void loadModule()
    {
        NumberSeqDatatype datatype =
            NumberSeqDatatype::construct();
    ```

```
        // Datatype number sequence properties for Vehicle Id
        //Associate the number sequence definition to our EDT
        datatype.parmDatatypeId(
            extendedTypeNum(ConFMSVehicleId)
            );
        //Provide help text for the number sequence
        // Remember to create a label for this
        datatype.parmReferenceHelp(
            literalStr("Unique key for Fleet Vehicle")
            );
        //Set default values for the number sequence
        //don't force unused numbers to be reused, unless we
        //specifically need this feature
        datatype.parmWizardIsContinuous(false);
        datatype.parmWizardIsManual(NoYes::No);
        datatype.parmWizardIsChangeDownAllowed(NoYes::No);
        datatype.parmWizardIsChangeUpAllowed(NoYes::No);
        datatype.parmWizardHighest(999999);
        datatype.parmSortField(1);
        //There will be just one number sequence shared
        // by every DataArea
        datatype.addParameterType(
            NumberSeqParameterType::DataArea, false, false
            );
        //finally create the reference
        this.create(datatype);
    }
```

> In this example, by returning `NumberSeqModule::TMS`, we have assigned our number sequence to the transport management module. This is because we want this reference to appear in the parameters form within transport management.

7. Finally, to run the module and generate our number sequence definition, we create and run the following job:

```
static void ConFMSGenerateNumberSequences(Args _args)
{
    NumberSeqApplicationModule::loadAll();
}
```

You can now generate the number sequence. Guidance for this is available at `http://msdn.microsoft.com/en-us/data/hh242127`.

Configuring the table to automatically apply the number sequence

We now need to instruct our forms to use the number sequence to populate the **VehicleId** field.

> It is standard practice to apply the number sequence from the form, although it is also possible to do it from the table. The framework supports the ability to assign a number on creation, which is returned to the number sequence's free list of numbers if the user cancels the creation. This is controlled by the continuous option.

First, we need a way to get a reference to the number sequence from code. We will use an existing method as a template:

1. Find the `TMSParameters` table in the AOT and drag it into the **Tables** node of your project.
2. Press *Ctrl* + *N* to create a new method on the `TMSParameters` table.
3. Now replace the method with this:

```
server static
    NumberSequenceReference conFMSNumRefConFMSVehicleId()
{
    return NumberSeqReference::findReference(
        extendedTypeNum(ConFMSVehicleId));
}
```

> It may save time if you copy an existing number sequence method of this pattern, for example, `numRefTMSTransportationOrderNum`. Be careful, however, as copying and pasting is a main cause of errors that are hard to debug, and sometimes, detect.

The forms will use a `NumberSeqFormHandler` object to get number sequence values from the framework and, if necessary, return them to the pool if they aren't used. To do this, follow these steps:

1. Find the `ConFMSVehicleTableCreate` form in the AOT and view the class declaration code.

2. After the `ConFMSVehicleTableForm` object we added earlier, we will add a new `NumberSeqFormHandler` object:

```
public class FormRun extends ObjectRun
{
    ConFMSVehicleTableForm formHandler;
    NumberSeqFormHandler numberSeqFormHandlerVehicleId;
}
```

3. Create a new form level method called `numSeqFormHandlerVehicleId()`. This method will instantiate `numberSeqFormHandlerVehicleId`, if necessary, and then return it:

```
public NumberSeqFormHandler numSeqFormHandler()
{
    if (!numberSeqFormHandlerVehicleId )
    {
      numberSeqFormHandlerVehicleId =
        NumberSeqFormHandler::newForm(
          TMSParameters::conFMSNumRefConFMSVehicleId()
            .NumberSequenceId,
          element,
          conFMSVehicleTable_ds,
          fieldNum(ConFMSVehicleTable, VehicleId)
        );
    }
    return numberSeqFormHandlerVehicleId ;
}
```

> The `NumberSeqFormHandler` instance is created by passing the number sequence identifier as well as the specific form and data source to apply the number sequence to.

Now that we have a `NumberSeqFormHandler` instance, we can use it. It has methods to call when creating a new record, validating and writing the record, and closing the form:

1. Expand the **Data Sources** node and then the **ConFMSVehicleTable** node in the `ConFMSVehicleTableCreate` form.
2. Right-click on the **Methods** node and override the `create` method, as follows:

```
public void create(boolean _append = false)
{
    //Before create - validate the number sequence
```

```
        element.numSeqFormHandlerVehicleId()
            .formMethodDataSourceCreatePre();

        super(_append);
        //After create - get next number
        element.numSeqFormHandlerVehicleId()
            .formMethodDataSourceCreate();
    }
```

3. Next, override the `validateWrite()` method and use the number sequence form handler to validate that the vehicle ID conforms to the sequence definition:

```
public boolean validateWrite()
{
    boolean ret = super();
    if(ret)
    {
        // validate that the vehicle id conforms to
        // the sequence definition
        ret = element.numSeqFormHandlerVehicleId()
                .formMethodDataSourceValidateWrite();
    }
    return ret;
}
```

4. Now we are going to amend the `write` method on the data source. It was already overridden earlier, so now we simply add a new line after the call to `super()` but before we hand over the record to the form handler:

```
void write()
{
    // if the user didn't press OK, or the record exists,
    // don't save the record.
    if (element.closedOk() &&
        ConFMSVehicleTable.RecId == 0)
    {
        ConFMSVehicleTable.insert();

        //After write - call number sequence action
        element.numSeqFormHandlerVehicleId()
            .formMethodDataSourceWrite();

        formHandler.parmVehicleTable(ConFMSVehicleTable);
    }
}
```

5. Finally, override the `close` method in the actual form:

```
public void close()
{
    super();
    //after close - number sequence, form close action.
    element.numSeqFormHandlerVehicleId().formMethodClose();
}
```

Now open the `ConFMSVehicleTable` form and click on the **New** button. The create form will automatically fill in a vehicle ID from the number sequence. Save the record and create another; the next vehicle ID number will be used.

We have applied the number sequence pattern to the create process. To finish it, we must also apply it to the read, update, and delete processes. All of these are handled from the `ConFMSVehicleTable` form, so we must add code there as well.

To handle the update process on the `ConFMSVehicleTable` form, we will intercept the `validateWrite`, `write`, and `close` methods as we did on the create form. The form will require a `numSeqFormHandlerVehicleId` method of its own. The full code for this is as follows.

Here are the form-level methods:

```
public class FormRun extends ObjectRun
{
    ConFMSVehicleTableForm formHandler;

    NumberSeqFormHandler numberSeqFormHandlerVehicleId;
}

public NumberSeqFormHandler numSeqFormHandler()
{
    if (!numberSeqFormHandlerVehicleId )
    {
      numberSeqFormHandlerVehicleId =
        NumberSeqFormHandler::newForm
        (
        TMSParameters::
            conFMSNumRefConFMSVehicleId().NumberSequenceId,
        element,
        conFMSVehicleTable_ds,
        fieldNum(ConFMSVehicleTable, VehicleId)
        );
    }
    return numberSeqFormHandlerVehicleId;
}
```

The following is the code required to add to the `ConFMSVehicleTable` form data source:

```
public boolean validateWrite()
{
    boolean ret;
    ret = super();
    if(ret)
    {
        ret = element.numSeqFormHandlerVehicleId()
            .formMethodDataSourceValidateWrite();
    }
    return ret;
}

public void write()
{
    super();
    element.numSeqFormHandlerVehicleId()
        .formMethodDataSourceWrite();
}

public void close()
{
    super();
    element.numSeqFormHandlerVehicleId()
        .formMethodClose();
}
```

The `NumberSeqFormHandler` class has two more form event actions. These are `formMethodDataSourceDelete()` and `formMethodDataSourceLinkActive()`.

The `formMethodDataSourceDelete` method is to be called before the data source delete method calls to `super()`. It will let the number sequence know that the current vehicle ID is no longer in use. This is important if the number sequence is set up as a continuous number sequence:

```
public void delete()
{
    //release the number sequence value.
    element.numSeqFormHandlerVehicleId()
        .formMethodDataSourceDelete();
    //now delete the record
    super();
}
```

The `formMethodDataSourceLinkActive` method is to be called from within the `linkActive` data source method. It is called when the user changes the record on a linked data source (which could be a dynamic link to another form):

```
public void linkActive()
{
    super();
    element.numberSeqFormHandlerVehicleId()
        .formMethodDataSourceLinkActive();
}
```

The `linkActive` method is included to cover the case where a linked data source moves the record cursor. If this occurs and the current record cannot be saved, it will abort the number sequence generation.

More information on `linkActive()` is available at:

- `http://msdn.microsoft.com/en-us/library/formdatasource.linkactive.aspx`
- `http://msdn.microsoft.com/en-us/library/bb394995.aspx`

Hooking into standard AX logic using event handling

Event handling is a new and welcome feature in AX from version 2012 onwards. One of its biggest gains is that it helps reduce the footprint on standard software (or that provided by an ISV or a partner). The footprint is one of the biggest concerns when minimizing the impact of future updates and upgrades.

The scenario we are describing is where we subscribe to an event (such as a table's delete method) so that it will call a method that handles the event. Although we add this subscription to a standard object in the AOT, the standard object is not modified. AX stores only the subscription definition. It is represented against the standard code, but this is only to help us intuitively create and manage event subscriptions.

The functionality we are going to provide is as follows:

> *When scheduling an appointment in transport management, the system has to associate the tractor and trailer with our fleet management system, if it exists. No lookup or validation is required because we schedule third-party vehicles, since many deliveries and collections are made by third-party hauliers or subcontractors. This should match the trailer ID or vehicle registration number.*

Associating the appointment with a vehicle

The appointment table already has free text fields for tractors (vehicle) and trailers, so the solution to this is to trap when these fields are modified and relate them to our tables if a match is found.

We will do this by adding fields to the appointment table from our EDTs for the vehicle and trailer (and letting it create the relation), and setting them by hooking into the `modifiedField` method in order to trap when the tractor and trailer fields are modified.

> To quickly work out the AOT form (and therefore the table), open the form in the client, right-click on the form, and choose **Personalize**. On the **Information** tab, you can click on **Edit** next to the **Form name** field.

This is where events come in. We will add an event to the `modifiedField` method to call an event handler than we will create.

Adding custom fields to the appointment table

The first task is to add our fields, which is something we have done several times by now. However, this is the first time on a standard table. We do this by following these steps:

1. Place an AOT window next to your project window.
2. Locate the `TMSAppointment` table.
3. Expand the **Relations** node.
4. Right-click on **Relations** and choose **New relation**.
5. We open the property sheet for our new relation, set the **Table** property to `ConFMSVehicleTableTruck`, and copy this to the **Name** property (this saves typing).
6. Set the cardinality properties as usual for a foreign key.
7. Right-click on the new relation and select **New** | **ForeignKey** | **PrimaryKeyBased**.

> More magic happens, as it has created a field to hold the foreign key.

8. Do the same for the `ConFMSVehicleTableTrailer` table.
9. We drag the table onto the **Tables** node of our project. All objects we modify must be in a project.

You may notice that the type of field that AX created was `Int64`. This is because the primary key on the tables is a surrogate key, which is based on `RecId`.

AX makes performance gains using this type of relation. To make the apparently random number useful to the user, there are ways to hide the number behind more a useful representation of the related record. This is what happened when we added the `HCMWorkerRecId` field to the service record.

In this case, we actually don't want to present this data. It is only for us to store a relation if the user enters a vehicle and trailer that we have inside AX.

Creating a class to handle the modifiedField event

Now we can write the event handler, which we need to write in a class. The code has to perform a few tasks, so we will do this in a class specific to the event. We will first write the logic to determine whether the vehicle or trailer exists.

The first thing to note is that `ConFMSVehicleTableTruck` does not contain a registration number! Since registration is common to trucks and cars, we should add this to the base table, `ConFMSVehicleTable`. Create a `ConFMSVehRegNo` string EDT of suitable size. Add it to the table as a new field named `VehRegNo`. By dragging this field into the `Identification` and `Overview` field groups, the UI will be adjusted for us.

> You may decide that the trailer ID field is redundant, given that the vehicle type gives this identifier context. We won't use the trailer ID later in the book.

The class will be specific to linking the appointment to the vehicle. Its entry point will be an event handler that will set the foreign keys created earlier. To create the class, follow these steps:

1. Create a class as usual, name it `ConFMSAppointmentVehicleHandler`, and create a standard `construct` method.
2. Add class variables for the following types: `TMSAppointment` (for example, `appointment`) and `RefFieldId` (for example, `fieldId`). Create the `parm` methods as you have done previously.

3. Create a method that will get the record ID of the tractor or trailer, as follows:

```
public RefRecId getVehicleReferenceForType(str
_tmsVehicleId, RefTableId _vehicleTypeTableId)
{
    ConFMSVehicleTable  vehicle;
    ConFMSVehRegNo      searchStr = _tmsVehicleId;

    select firstOnly RecId
        from vehicle
        where
            vehicle.InstanceRelationType ==
                                       _vehicleTypeTableId
         && vehicle.VehRegNo            == searchStr;

    return vehicle.RecId;
}
```

This was a simple method, but we have introduced some new concepts. The `_tmpVehicleId` parameter is of the `str` type. This base type is an unbound string with no specific size. This makes the method more versatile, but also means we can't use it as part of a `where` clause of a `select` statement. To use it in a `where` clause, we should assign it to a variable based on the EDT of the field in question, `ConFMSVehRegNo` in this case.

In the `select` statement, we are selecting only the `RecId` field and the first record found (`firstOnly`). This increases performance by transferring less data between database and server tiers.

We are using the `InstanceRelationType` field in our where clause, as the registration may not always be globally unique across all vehicle types.

> This is a simple solution, and in real life, we will use a more sophisticated search mechanism, since the user isn't selecting a record from a drop-down list.

Finally, whenever we write a select statement in AX, we must verify that there is an index covering the fields in the `where` clause. Therefore, we need an index for `VehRegNo`.

We can now create the class following the patterns used previously:

1. Create a `validate` method:

```
public boolean validate()
{
    if(fieldId == 0)
    {
        return checkFailed(
            strFmt(
              "Vehicle handler %1 was called incorrectly",
              classStr(ConFMSAppointmentVehicleHandler)));
    }
    return true;
}
```

> The `classStr` method simply returns the name of the class as a string. But more importantly, it will cause a compilation error if the class not exist, for example, after refactoring.

2. Create methods to handle the `TractorNumber` and `TrailerNumber` fields:

```
private void handleTractorNumber()
{
    RefRecId vehicleTableRef =
                this.getVehicleReferenceForType(
                        appointment.TractorNumber,
                        tableNum(ConFMSVehicleTableTruck));
    // the reference will be 0 if not found.
    appointment.ConFMSVehicleTableTruck = vehicleTableRef;
}
private void handleTrailerNumber()
{
    RefRecId vehicleTableRef =
         this.getVehicleReferenceForType(
                  appointment.TrailerNumber,
                  tableNum(ConFMSVehicleTableTrailer));
    // the reference will be 0 if not found,
    // which is by design.
    appointment.ConFMSVehicleTableTrailer =
                                   vehicleTableRef;
}
```

3. Create the `run` method, which reflects that of the `modifiedField` pattern, as follows:

```
public void run()
{
    if(!this.validate())
        return;

    switch(fieldId)
    {
        case fieldNum(TMSAppointment, TractorNumber):
            this.handleTractorNumber();
            break;
        case fieldNum(TMSAppointment, TrailerNumber):
            this.handleTrailerNumber();
            break;
    }
}
```

Creating the event handler method

The final part of the class is to create the event handler method, which will serve as its primary entry point, even though the way we wrote the method means we can reuse it elsewhere. This method has a special declaration, to which all event handlers must conform, and it is similar to those found in C#. This declaration is as follows:

```
public static void eventHandlerNameEventHandler(XppPrePostArgs
_args)
```

Unlike C#, we aren't passed the calling object as a parameter. All of the interaction with the caller is done through the `XppPrePostArgs` object.

The event can subscribe to a publisher (in our case, the `modifiedField` method on the `TMSAppointment` table) as a pre or post-event subscription. This means that it can be called before the method is executed or after it completes.

This object has many useful methods. The key methods we will use are listed here:

Method	Description
`getThis`	Returns an instance of the calling object, or publisher. This could be a class instance or a record in a table.
`getArg`	Allows us to get the value of a named property.
`getArgNum`	Allows us to get a value of a property by the number from the left.

Method	Description
`getReturnValue`	Gets the return value of the method (this is effective only when it is a post-event subscription).
`setArg`	Modifies a named parameter of the publisher (this is effective only when this is a pre-event subscription).
`setArgNum`	This method is similar to `setArg`, but referenced by parameter number from the left.
`setReturnValue`	Modifies the return value of the caller. This is effective for post-event subscription.

In order to handle this event, we need to know the current `TMSAppointment` record and the field being modified. The current record is taken from `getThis`. The field being modified is a parameter of `modifiedField`, so we will use `getArg`. The event handler method is created as follows:

1. Right-click on the `ConFMSAppointmentVehicleHandler` class and select **New | Pre- or post-event hander**.
2. Rename the method to `tmsAppointmentModifFiedFieldEventHandler`. The `EventHandler` suffix is by convention.
3. Declare a `TMSAppointment` table variable as appointment and assign `_args.getThis()`, as shown here:

   ```
   TMSAppointment appointment = _args.getThis();
   ```

> You may notice that `getThis()` returns `AnyType`. This can be cast as any X++ type.

4. Next, we need to know which field we are handling, since we know that `modifiedField` has one parameter of `_fieldId` (we can simply look). We the use the `_args.getArg(str _argName)` method:

   ```
   RefFieldId     fieldId     = _args.getArg('_fieldId');
   ```

5. We now have the `TMSAppointment` record in appointment and the field being changed in `fieldId`.
6. Now we can declare, construct, and run our handler. The complete method is as follows:

   ```
   public static void tmsAppointmentModifiedFieldEventHandler(XppPreP
   ostArgs _args)
   {
   ```

```
        TMSAppointment appointment = _args.getThis();
        RefFieldId     fieldId     = _args.getArg('_fieldId');
        ConFMSAppointmentVehicleHandler handler;

        handler = ConFMSAppointmentVehicleHandler::construct();
        handler.parmAppointment(appointment);
        handler.parmFieldId(fieldId);
        handler.run();
    }
```

Adding a subscription to TMSAppointmentTable.modifiedField

This is a simple task. The only decision we have to make is whether it should run before or after the method has executed. This decision varies for each situation, but it should become clear if we imagine the code as running inline. The task of adding the subscription is as follows:

1. On the `TMSAppointment` table, expand the **Methods** node.
2. Right-click on the `modifiedField` method and choose **New Event Handler Subscription**.
3. Open the properties of the new subscription, **EventHandler1**.
4. Change **Name** to `ConFMSVehicleEventHandler`.
5. Change **CalledWhen** to **Post**.
6. Enter `ConFMSAppointmentVehicleHandler` in **Class** (copy and paste helps here)
7. **Method** will default to the first event handler method on the class, `tmsAppointmentModifFiedFieldEventHandler` in this case. Select the property and press *Enter*. This sets `AOTLink` to the full path to the method.

What happens when the code executes

The best way to test this code is through the debugger. If you want to try this, skip to *Chapter 11, Unit and Performance Testing*.

When an event occurs, AX builds an `XppPrePostArgs` object and passes it to the subscriber, that is, our event handler. The event handler method gets the current appointment record using `getThis()`, which is done by reference. It then constructs the class and passes the record to it, again by reference. The fact that the record is passed by reference by the `XppPrePostArgs` object means we don't write the change to the database.

Before we finish with this example, let's view the **Record Info** for the appointment record (right-click on the form and choose **Record Info** and **Show all fields**). Not only do our two new fields appear, but AX also displays the reference primary key automatically, as shown in the following screenshot:

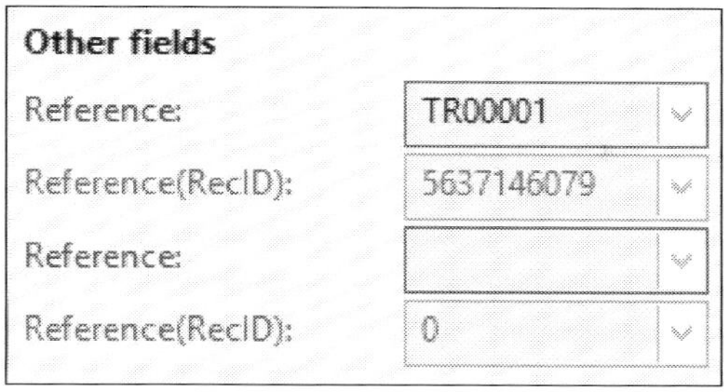

We will use this association later in *Chapter 6, Extending the Solution*.

Creating a delegate for use by other parties

In the previous section, we were using pre- and post-event subscriptions, which is fine when hooking into standard code. Another method, which is better, is the concept of delegate subscriptions. A delegate is represented in AX as a method with no code. Its sole purpose is to enable other parties to subscribe to it.

We can make a call to our delegate from any point in our code. When the delegate is called, any subscriptions are called as a result. A delegate subscription is preferable to pre- and post-event subscriptions for several reasons:

- It is easier for a third-party to know what to subscribe to. A delegate method is a clearly defined event.
- Subscribers to the delegate have the same method signature of the delegate. They are passed the same parameters that were passed to the delegate.
- The event is called from a specific point in our code.
- The event is called based on a condition.
- The clearly defined delegate has a fixed purpose. If we change our code later, any code that relies on it will not be broken as long as the delegate still serves the same purpose.

The same cannot be said for subscribing to a pre- or post-method handler of an arbitrary method. In our example, we will create a delegate that is called when an appointment's truck is changed, which was previously assigned to another vehicle. This is done by the following steps:

1. Create the delegate by right-clicking on the `ConFMSAppointmentVehicleHandler` class and going to **New** | **Delegate**.
2. Rename the delegate to `vehicleChanged`. The naming is important to explain what the event is. See `http://msdn.microsoft.com/en-us/library/gg879953.aspx`.
3. Add two reference record ID parameters for the original and new vehicle references, as follows:

```
delegate void vehicleChanged(RefRecId _originalVehicleRef,
                             RefRecId _newVehicleRef)
{
}
```

4. In the `handleTractorNumber` method, add the following lines before the vehicle reference is assigned:

```
private void handleTractorNumber()
{
    RefRecId vehicleTableRef =
            this.getVehicleReferenceForType(
                        appointment.TractorNumber,
                        tableNum(ConFMSVehicleTableTruck));
    // the reference will be 0 if not found.
    if(appointment.orig().ConFMSVehicleTableTruck != 0 &&
       appointment.orig().ConFMSVehicleTableTruck !=
                                              vehicleTableRef)
    {
        this.vehicleChanged(
            appointment.orig().ConFMSVehicleTableTruck,
            vehicleTableRef);
    }
    appointment.ConFMSVehicleTableTruck = vehicleTableRef;
}
```

The `orig` method allows us access to the appointment record when it was last read from the database. If the user changes the vehicle back to the original, the delegate won't be called. Finally, we create a test event handler. To do this, follow these steps:

1. Create a new class called `ConFMSEventTest`. Then create an event handler method like this: right-click on the class, select **New | Pre- or post-event handler**, and rename it to `vehicleChangedEventHandler`.
2. We must make the signature of our handler match the delegate, as shown in the following code:

```
public static void vehicleChangedEventHandler(
                                        RefRecId _origRef,
                                        RefRecId _newRef)
```

3. Declare two `ConFMSVehicleTable` instances for `origVehicle` and `newVehicle`, and select the respective records:

```
ConFMSVehicleTable  origVehicle;
ConFMSVehicleTable  newVehicle;

select origVehicle where origVehicle.RecId == origRef;
select newVehicle where origVehicle.RecId == newRef;
```

4. Then show an `infoLog` message to the user, using the following code:

```
info(strFmt("Vehicle was changed from %1 (%2) to %3 (%4)",
            origVehicle.VehicleId, origVehicle.VehRegNo,
            newVehicle.VehicleId, newVehicle.VehRegNo));
```

5. Add an event subscription to the delegate created earlier.

You may notice that the method does not appear in the drop-down list, so you have to manually enter or paste it in **Method** name field. AX will set the **AOTlink** property, as shown in the following screenshot:

Class	ConFMSEventTest
Method	vehicleChangedEventHandler
AOTlink	\Classes\ConFMSEventTest\vehicleChangedEventHandler
Model	ConFleetManagement

We should now test this by creating an appointment. Create an appointment where the vehicle will be associated, save the appointment (to `reread orig()`), and then change then vehicle to another.

Summary

We covered a lot in this chapter, and also saw the benefits of our earlier efforts. These benefits will become more and more apparent as we complete the solution. We placed the key business logic in classes, leveraged the number sequence framework, and touched on extending AX through event handling.

In the next chapter, we will get to use this information to add business intelligence and user interface helpers, showing how we can present key data to our users without them requiring to navigate away from where they are.

5
Adding Business Intelligence

One of the key features of AX 2012 is the ability to easily present key information to the user, placing more information more easily at hand and enabling quick decision making.

In this chapter, we will cover the following topics:

- What are parts?
- Creating info parts to show key business data
- Creating a form part
- Creating cues and cue groups
- Using form parts in a form

What are parts?

In terms of adding business intelligence to the UI, we will not use OLAP cubes (which provide statistical data that is not real-time), but instead add real-time key information to list pages and detail forms in the form of parts. OLAP is beyond the scope of this book.

There are three types of parts:

- **Info parts**: These are the most common, and you can see these on the right-hand side of most list pages and details forms. They show a small, key piece of information based on a query.
- **Form parts**: These are used in many places. They can show pop-up information as you hover over a field, or more complicated information on the right-hand-side pane.

- **Cues**: These are placed onto a form as a cue group. Cues are used on the role center and as parts on a list page or details form. On the list page, they are presented as a set of links that will take the user to a filtered set of data and show a count of the associated records, with an optional total.

In this chapter, we will add each of these parts to list pages, but you should also add them to the associated details form, as the information is often more valuable while the user is maintaining the data, for example, planning a load, taking a vehicle out of service, and so on.

Creating info parts to show key business data

Although AX is shipped with a standard set of info parts placed on key forms throughout the system, we often find that our users require different information to be made available. An example of an info part is displayed on the right-hand pane of the **All loads** list page found by navigating to **Transportation management** | **Common** | **Loads** | **All loads**.

The data that is displayed on the info part is determined by a query. We use the query to define the data that will be displayed, and also to define how this relates to the form where the info part is placed. To demonstrate this, we will add a part to the **All loads** list page that will show vehicle information.

First, we will construct a query that defines a path from the load table to our vehicle table. This will have to go through the appointment table's relations to link to the vehicle created in the previous chapter.

The query structure doesn't need to include the load table itself, as the appointment table already has a relation defined. Queries used in any part must be written for performance and should only contain fields actually used in the part. We therefore don't create a generic reusable query, but a query specifically for a part.

Our part will need the following fields:

- Vehicle ID
- Vehicle registration number
- Vehicle status
- Vehicle group
- The next service date

Creating a query for the part

Before we start, we need to create a new relation on the `TMSAppointment` table that connects the `ConFMSVehicleTableTruck` foreign key to `ConFMSVehicleTable.RecId`. This is because the current relation is to the inherited truck table, and we really need a relation to the base vehicle table. This becomes more apparent when we add parts to the vehicle list page, as this will show a combined list of all vehicle types. The only commonality is that they all extend `ConFMSVehicleTable`.

There are two ways we can do this, add a new foreign key relation on `TMSAppointment` and update the code to set the foreign key, or use the same field as the relation to `ConFMSVehicleTable`. We can justify using the same key as we can say that the main vehicle is a truck. To do this, follow these steps:

1. Create a relation on `TMSAppointment` to `ConFMSVehicleTable` and update the required properties as before. You must set the `RelatedTableRole` property. The relation should be done by right-clicking on the new relation and selecting **New | Foreign Key | Single field AlternateKey based**. We want `RecId` as the relation.
2. Now edit the relation to change it from `ConFMSVehicleTable` to `ConFMSVehicleTableTruck`.
3. As expected, it will have created a new field called `ConFMSVehicleTable`. We don't need this field now, as our relation is using `ConFMSVehicleTableTruck` as the foreign key. Delete this new field.

To create the query for the vehicle information info part, follow these steps:

1. In your project, right-click on the **Queries** node and go to **New | Query**.
2. Rename the query to `ConFMSVehicleAppointmentPart`. The `Part` suffix is a convention, and it is important to highlight to other developers that it is a part query.
3. The first data source will be the one used to link the form's data source, so add `TMSAppointment` to the **Data Sources** node.

> AX automatically adds the suffix `_1`. This is to ensure that the name is unique. We should remove this suffix. If we have two data sources for the same table, we should use a suffix that identifies the table better than a number.

4. On the **Fields** node, we change the **Dynamic** property to `No`, as we don't want any fields from this data source.

> Since our part doesn't require fields from this data source, we should not add any. This includes `ApptRefNum` and `AppRetType`, even though these fields are used in the relation to `WHSLoadTable` and `WHSShipmentTable`. Fields used in the relation don't need to be included in the fields list.

5. Add `ConFMSVehicleTable` to the **Data Sources** node under `TMSAppointment`.
6. On the **Fields** node, change the **Dynamic** property to `Yes`, noting that all of the table's fields have been automatically added under the **Fields** node. Now, change it to `No` and they are still there. This is a nice trick to add all the fields to the field list when we want most but not all fields.
7. Remove all fields except `VehicleId`, `VehicleStatusId`, `VehRegNo`, and `VehicleGroupId`. Verify that **Dynamic** is set to `No` once finished.
8. On the properties of `ConFMSVehicleTable`, set **Relations** to `Yes`.
9. Check whether the relation (the **Relations** node) has been added. In this case, it should have assumed the `ConFMSVehicleTable` relation, which happens to be correct.

> If it didn't choose this relation, you will need to set the **Relations** property back to `No` and add the relation manually, using the `ConFMSVehicleTable` relation.

10. Add `ConFMSVehServiceTable` to the **Data Sources** node under `ConFMSVehicleTable`.
11. Do the trick with the **Dynamic** property on the **Fields** node and ensure that you only have the `NextServiceDate` field. **Dynamic** must be set to `No` once finished.
12. On the properties of `ConFMSVehServiceTable`, set **JoinMode** to `OuterJoin` and **Relations** to `Yes`. We are using the outer join, as we will still want to show the vehicles without service data.
13. We also only want one service record, so we set **FirstOnly** and **FirstFast** to `Yes`.
14. To get the last service record, right-click on **Order By** and select **New Field**, setting the properties as follows: **DataSource** to `ConFMSVehServiceTable`, **Field** to `NextServiceDate`, and **Direction** to `Descending`.

The query structure should look like what is shown in the following screenshot:

You may notice that we didn't include the fields used in the joins to our tables. AX will handle this for us.

Creating the info part

Next, we can create the info part, which is done by the following steps:

1. In your project, right-click on **Form Parts** | **Info Parts** and select **New** | **Info Part**.
2. Rename the part to `ConFMSVehicleAppointmentPart`.
3. On the property sheet, set the **Query** property to `ConFMSVehicleAppointmentPart`.
4. Under the **Layout** node, add a new group (right-click and choose **New Group**).
5. Set **Name** to `VehicleGroup`.
6. We only have one group, so a caption will not help the user and just take up space. Leave **Caption** blank, and leave **ShowCaption** as `No`.
7. If we required a list of records in a grid, we would've set **Repeating** to `Yes`. In our case, we want just the information in a form view, so we leave it as **No**.

> If we had designed a field group for this purpose, we could use it to define this group. This can be useful when we have the same fields used in more than one part and it allows changes to be made once and reflected in all parts that use the field group.

8. Right-click on **VehicleGroup** and choose **New Field**. Set **DataSource** to `ConFMSVehicleTable` and **DataField** to `VehicleId`. Copy the `VehicleId` field name to the **Name** property.
9. Repeat this process for the remaining fields.
10. On the `VehicleId` field, set **Style** as `TitleField`.

Creating the part's menu item

We now have to create a display menu item so that it can be added to a form. This is done as follows:

1. In your project, right-click on **Display**, which is under **Menu Items**, and go to **New** | **Menu Item**.
2. Rename the menu item to `ConFMSVehicleAppointmentPart`.
3. Set **Label** to `Vehicle information` and create a new label (don't use the existing GLS label), remembering to set **Comments** to `Con Vehicle information`.
4. Finally, set **ObjectType** to `InfoPart` and **Object** to `ConFMSVehicleAppointmentPart`.

Adding the info part to the All loads list page

To add the **All loads** list page, our first task is to locate it in the AOT. The easiest way is to navigate the **Menus** node in the AOT as if you are navigating through the interface. The properties of the **All loads** node reveal that the menu item is `WHSLoadPlanningListPage`. The **Object** property of this menu item has the same name, so this is the form.

> List pages are normally named after the table and suffixed with `ListPage`, but it is acceptable to deviate from this naming convention based on the situation.

To add the `WHSLoadPlanningListPage` info part, follow these steps:

1. Drag the `WHSLoadPlanningListPage` form onto the **Forms** node of your project.
2. Drag the `ConFMSVehicleAppointmentPart` menu item onto the Parts node of `WHSLoadPlanningListPage`.
3. Move the part so that it is at the top of the list of parts using *Alt* and the arrow key; this simply arranges the part on the form to be at the top.
4. Go to the properties of the new part and note that `DataSource` is `WHSLoadTable`, which is correct, as this is how we intend to relate to `TMSAppointment`.
5. If you click on **DataSourceRelation**, it should set itself to `TMSAppointment.WHSLoadTable`. This is the relation defined between `WHSLoadTable` and `TMSAppointment`, which is also correct.

Completing the info part

First, we should test the info part. As part of our testing in *Chapter 4, Creating Business Logic and Hooking into Core AX*, we created a vehicle and linked it to an appointment. To test this part, we need to associate it to a load. This is done on the **Reference** fast tab in the **Appointment Scheduling** form.

To test the info part, right-click on the `WHSLoadPlanningListPage` form and select **Open**. Move through the records until you reach the load that was referenced against the appointment. It should display information as shown in the following screenshot:

The vehicle ID appears as a heading, and the other fields appear as a form, which is as expected. After clicking on **More**, we are shown the **Appointment Schedule** form, but the **Vehicle details** form would be more appropriate.

We can change this by the following steps:

1. On our info part, we expand the part, right-click on **Layout**, and show the property sheet.
2. Set **ShowMoreDataSource** to `ConFMSVehicleTable`.
3. Save the changes and open the list page again. Notice that the **More** button now opens the **Vehicle details** form.

If you open the other list pages by going to **Transportation management** | **Common** | **Loads**, you will see that they all contain our info part. These are secondary list pages, which are the same form configured to show subsets of the loads.

You can also add more actions to the part, but be careful not to clutter the design as this would detract from the purpose of showing key data.

To add another link to the **Appointment Schedule** form as an action, follow these steps:

1. Right-click on the part's **Actions** node and choose **New Action**.
2. In **MenuItemName**, enter `TMSAppointment` and copy the **Name** property also.
3. Save the changes and open the list page.

A new link is added below the **More** link, labeled **Appointment Scheduling**, as shown in the following screenshot:

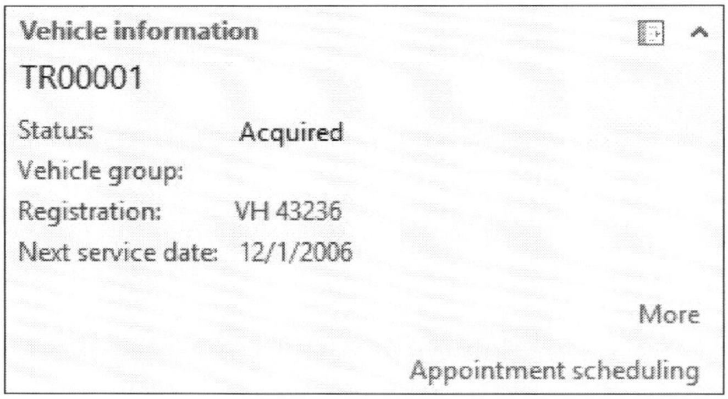

Finally, we should add the info part to the **All shipments** list page. The form is `WHSShipPlanningListPage` and you simply have to drag the part's menu item as before onto the **Parts** node. Remember to click on the **DataSourceRelation** property to ensure that this is correct.

Creating a form part

Form parts are another way to show pertinent information, reducing the need to navigate away from the user's current tasks. One example is that they can allow us to show a form designed to pop up automatically as the user hovers the mouse over a foreign key field.

In this example, we will create a form part for vehicle information that will show up as the user hovers over the vehicle ID field. It will show key vehicle information and a list of services the vehicle has had.

A form part is actually a normal form, but written in a certain way and using a `FormPart` style. The form is associated with a table so that it can be shown when the user hovers over a link to that table.

While we can design the form part any way we wish, we should consider only showing what the user needs. This is for both cleanliness of design and performance reasons.

Creating the form for the form part

To create the form for the form part, follow these steps:

1. There is no template for this, so we will create the form by right-clicking on the **Forms** node and going to **New | Form**.
2. Rename the form to `ConFMSVehicleTablePart`.
3. Drag the `ConFMSVehicleTable` table onto the form's **Data Sources** node.
4. Next, drag the `ConFMSVehServiceTable` table onto the same **Data Sources** node, ensuring that it is the second data source in the list. The order is important, as the vehicle table needs to be the first data source.
5. On both the data sources, set the **AllowEdit**, **AllowCreate**, **AllowDelete**, **InsertAtEnd**, and **InsertIfEmpty** data source properties to `No`.
6. On the `ConFMSVehServiceTable` data source, set the **JoinSource** property to `ConFMSVehicleTable`, as this is a child table of the vehicle table.
7. On the **Designs** node, set the style for `FormPart`.
8. To make dragging fields easy, open the **Data Sources** node in a new window (right-click and choose **Open New window**).

9. Create a group control called `TopGroup` (right-click on **Designs** and go to **New** | **Group**). Set the new group's **FrameType** property to `None` and **Columns** to `2`. This group is only used to help lay out the form, as we will add two field groups, which will look better side by side with the grid of services below.

10. From `ConFMSVehicleTable`, drag the `Identification` and `Details` field groups onto `TopGroup`. These two groups will be drawn side-by-side. The parent group has two columns.

11. Then add a new grid control by right-clicking on the **Designs** node and going to **New** | **Grid**. Move the new grid control below the `TopGroup` field group using *Alt* and the down arrow key. The layout should now look like what is shown in the following screenshot:

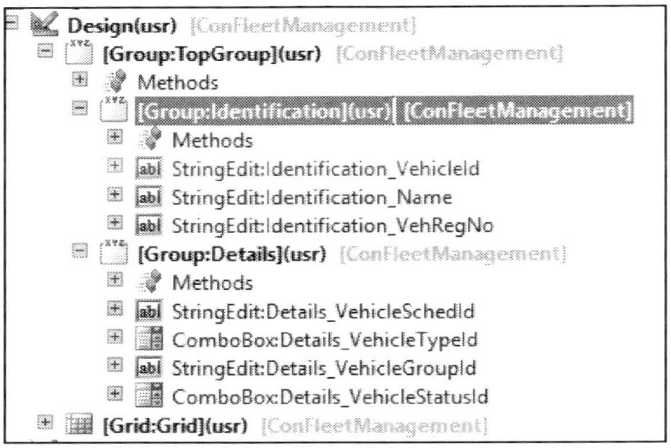

12. Set the grid's **DataSource** property to `ConFMSVehServiceTable` and the **Style** property to `SimpeReadOnly`.

13. From the `ConFMSVehServiceTable` data source, drag the `ServiceId`, `ServiceDate`, `NextServiceDate`, `NextServiceOdo`, and `HcmWorkerRecId` fields onto the new grid control.

14. To have a little fun with reference field groups, on the new grid control called `HcmWorkerRecId`, change the **ReplacementFieldGroup** property to `CaseMoreInformation`. AX will replace the record ID with the fields in the field group, as shown in the following screenshot:

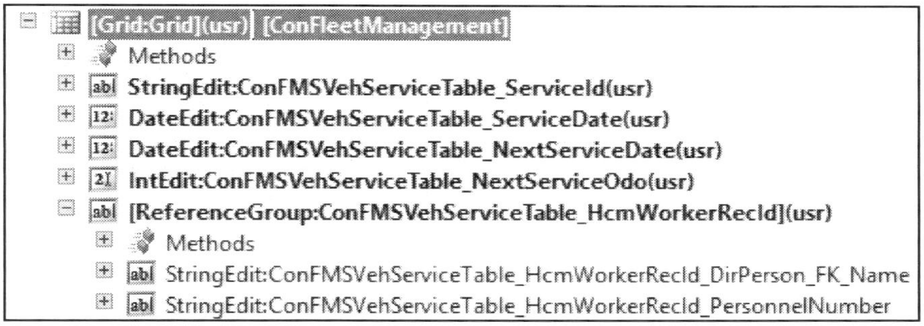

Creating the form part reference

This next task is to create a form part, which acts as a reference to the form we have just created. This is done as follows:

1. In your project, create a form part under the projects **Parts** | **Form Parts**, and select **New** | **Form Part**.
2. Rename the part to `ConFMSVehicleTablePart`.
3. Set the **Caption** property to `Vehicle details`, the same label as the vehicle table.
4. Enter `ConFMSVehicleTablePart` in the **Form** property.

Creating the menu item and associating it with the vehicle table

We now need to tell the table that it should use the new form part when showing preview information. In order to do this, we need to create a menu item.

We'll create a display menu item as we did for the info part, setting **ObjectType** to `FormPart` and `Object` to **ConFMSVehicleTablePart**. Finally, on the `ConFMSVehicleTable` table, set the **PreviewPartRef** property to the name of the new menu item (`ConFMSVehicleTablePart`).

To test, we simply need a form that has a vehicle ID, such as `ConFMSVehServiceTable`. Open this and hover the mouse pointer over the **Vehicle Id** control. The form should look like what is shown in the following screenshot:

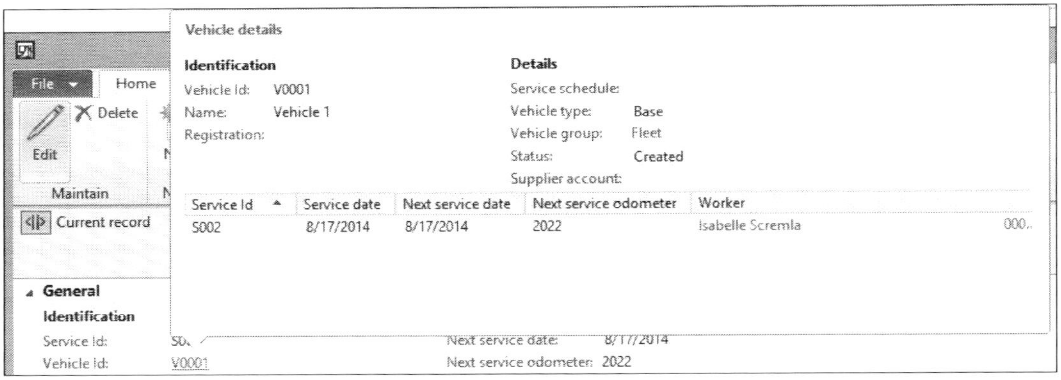

This form was designed this way to demonstrate that we can put a lot of information into a form part, which isn't always a good idea. The important point here is that we are showing *key data*. We should show only what the user needs, not everything they could ever want.

Creating cues and cue groups

Cues are a simple representation of the results of a query. They show the number of records returned by that query and, optionally, some aggregate data from those records.

A cue group is a part that displays one or more cues. Cue groups can be found in two places, on a role center, helping direct a user to what is important, (for example, quickly navigating to the list of orders on hold for a key customer), and also on a form, providing navigation to data related to the current record.

A good example of a cue group is on the **All customers list** page, which shows four cues, as shown here:

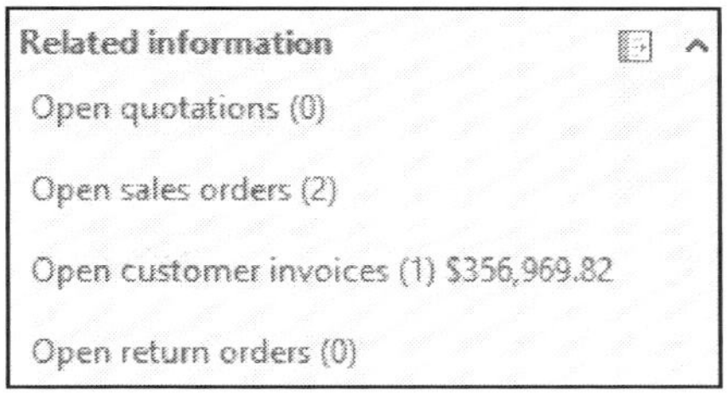

Cues require a menu item that targets the destination form and a query. The query can be the form's standard query, or one with additional filters and even additional data sources. The restriction is that the query must be compatible. This means that the root data source must be the same and it must have the same child data sources within its definition. We are free to add ranges to any data source in the query if we want to show a subset of data.

To ensure compatibility, we should use composite queries wherever possible, as these restrict us to only adding ranges. These are covered in *Chapter 6, Extending the Solution*.

Although cues show aggregate data (quantity and optionally value), they are intended to take you to a form, which is typically a list page. The system determines the query from the menu item associated with the cue using the menu item's **Query** property. To show data filtered to our needs, we need to create a query and a menu item first.

We will create a cue to show the service history of the vehicle and also the associated appointments. We will also create a preview part that shows summary information about the vehicle's service history, which may be all the user needs to see and will avoid having to navigate away from the vehicle form.

Creating the service history cue

In the case of a vehicle service list page, the target form's data source has a direct relation with the vehicle table. In this case, we need a menu item that references the target list page and a query.

The existing vehicle services menu item references the right form, but not a query, so we need a new menu item. This can be created by duplicating this menu item and associating it with the list page's query. We don't need to filter this beyond the current vehicle record, so using the list page's query is fine. Should there be a need, we could supplant the query on our menu item at that point.

> The query will actually replace the target form's query (even if the form is not based on a query), which means we aren't strictly limited to calling list pages.

We then create a cue referencing the menu item and add it to a cue group. It is the cue group that we add to a form, again via a menu item. The following steps are the way to do this:

1. Right-click on the `ConFMSVehServiceTableListPage` display menu item and select **Duplicate**.
2. Rename this to `ConFMSVehServiceTableListPageCue`.
3. Set the **Query** property to `ConFMSVehServiceTableListPage`.

> Although this is a very simple menu item, we should always test it so that it opens the target form and displays the expected data, all vehicle service records in this case.

4. Right-click on the node, go to **Parts** | **Cues**, and then go to **New** | **Cue**.
5. Rename this cue to `ConFMSVehServiceTableListPageCue`.
6. Set the caption to `Vehicle services` and locate the label.

> It is common to give a slightly longer description here, if it helps the user understand the information being shown.

7. Set the menu item to `ConFMSVehServiceTableListPageCue`.

> AX will check at this point whether the menu item has a query, and will reject it if it does not.

8. Right-click on the **Cue Groups** node, which is under **Parts**, and go to **New** | **Cue Group**.
9. This is meant to display related information to a vehicle, so rename it to `ConVehicleRelatedInfoCueGroup`.
10. Set the label to `Related information` and create a new label.
11. Save all changes.
12. Drag the cue `ConFMSVehServiceTableListPageCue` onto the new cue group.

13. Create a new menu item called `ConVehicleRelatedInfoCueGroup`, and set **ObjectType** to `CueGroup` and **Object** to `ConVehicleRelatedInfoCueGroup`.
14. Save all changes.
15. Drag the new menu item onto the **Parts** node in the `ConFMSVehicleTabeListPage` form.
16. On the form's new `ConVehicleRelatedInfoGroup` part, set the **DataSource** property to `ConFMSVehicleTable` and the **IsLinked** property to `Yes`.
17. In order to test this, we need to restart the client.
18. Once the client opens, open `ConFMSVehicleTableListPage` and note that there is a link to the **Vehicle services**, with a quantity showing the number of service records. Clicking on this link will open the service list page showing records related with the vehicle. This is shown in the following screenshot:

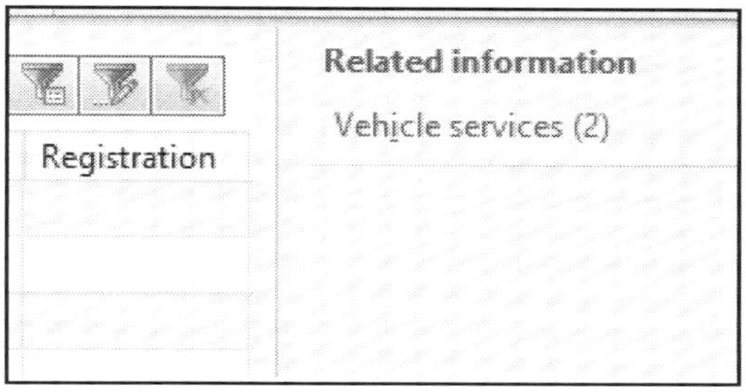

When you click on the **Vehicle services** cue, the data is automatically filtered based on the selected vehicle. This is done using a feature called a **Dynalink**. This is a mechanism that creates a dynamic link between the caller and the form that is opened.

To see this link, click on the new **Vehicle services** cue for a vehicle that has one or more services. Then right-click on this form and select **Personalize**.

The following screenshot shows the **Query** tab of this form. The **Dynalink** node does not filter on a specific value, but sets up a relation with the calling form's data source.

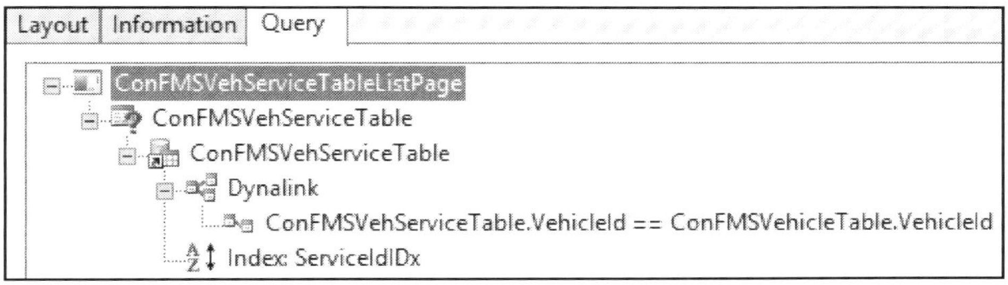

Creating a Preview part for the cue

We can take this further and display a form part that will display a list of services, removing the need to actually navigate to the vehicle service table if the user simply wants to see the list.

The form part is simple, create a form for the form part as before. Name the form `ConFMSVehServiceTableCuePart`, as we will use this only on a cue.

The form should have the table `ConFMSVehServiceTable` as a data source. Then, add a grid based on the **Overview** field group. Set the grid's **Width** and **Height** properties to `Column width` and `Column height` respectively.

Remember these key points about form parts:

- The data sources must have **AllowEdit**, **AllowCreate**, **AllowDelete**, **InsertAtEnd**, and **InsertIfEmpty** set to `No`.
- **Design** must have **Style** set to **FormPart**.

Once you have created the form part and the associated menu item, use this in the **PreviewPartReference** property of the cue.

To test this, simply hover the mouse over the **Vehicle services** link, as shown here:

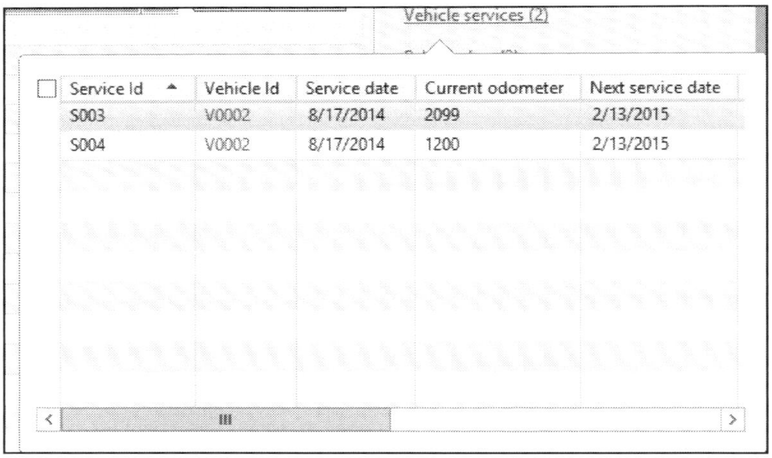

Creating an appointment cue

We can create a cue to any list page or form whose root data source has a relation with the list page's data source.

An important exception to this rule is where the target form clears dynamic links. Sometimes, we don't want the system to automatically filter the form based on the caller and in this case we can call a `clearDynalinks` function on the data source object.

An example of this behavior is to be found in the `TMSAppointment` form, which clears this link in **init** and can be found by navigating to **Data Sources** | **TMSAppointment** | **Methods**, as shown in the following code extract:

```
public void init()
{
    QueryBuildDataSource qbds;

    super();

    qbds = tmsAppointment_q.dataSourceTable(
                                    tableNum(TMSAppointment));
    qbds.clearDynalinks();
//...
```

In order to create a cue to the appointment form, we have to modify this form to not to clear the dynamic links when it is called from our form. This is best done using `element.args().dataset()`, as shown here:

```
public void init()
{
    QueryBuildDataSource qbds;

    // Con 2014/09/07 - 6015-06 - modification by SB:
    // Do not clear dynaLinks if called from a
    // ConFMSVehicleTable record
    boolean              conFMSDoNotClearDL;
    switch(element.args().dataset())
    {
        case tableNum(ConFMSVehicleTable):
            conFMSDoNotClearDL = true;
            break;
    }
    // Con - 6015-06 end
    super();

    qbds = tmsAppointment_q.dataSourceTable(tableNum(TMSAppointment));
    // Con 2014/09/07 - 6015-06 - modification by SB:
    // Do not clear dynaLinks if called from a
    // ConFMSVehicleTable record
```

```
// original code was to always qbds.clearDynalinks();
if(!conFMSDoNotClearDL)
    qbds.clearDynalinks();
// Con - 6015-06 end
```

The code to determine whether it should clear dynamic links should be in a method on the `TMSAppointment` table to make it reusable. Also, to remove the number of custom lines of code in a standard method, it is placed inline here for clarity. In any case, this example has been included to show you how this particular issue could be solved. However, most of the time, cues will be related to information in a list page or details form and we will probably never come across this problem.

> By making this change, we have added a task to any upgrade or hotfix that updates this form.

Now that the appointments form allows dynamic links, we can proceed to create our cue. The creation of this cue is the same as that of the service history cue, which is done with the following steps:

1. Create a `ConFMSAppointmentVehicleCue` query with a single data source named `TMSAppointment`.
2. Create a `ConFMSAppointmentVehicleCue` display menu item, setting **Object** to `TMSAppointment` and the query to `ConFMSAppointmentVehicleCue`.
3. Create a cue called `ConFMSAppointmentVehicleCue`, setting an appropriate label, and set **MenuItemName** to `ConFMSAppointmentVehicleCue`.
4. Drag the new cue onto the `ConFMSVehicleRelatedInfoCueGroup` cue group.
5. Save all changes and restart the client.

Feel free to write a preview part and attach this to the cue, as we did for the vehicle services cue.

Using form parts on a form

We can use form parts on a form, including list pages. We can also write code within the form part, but if we do this, we won't be able to see it if the list page is deployed on the Enterprise Portal. The Enterprise Portal cannot execute xpp/p-code directly.

The form part we will create will show a summary of load utilization, based on the number of items, load lines, and loads associated with the load, via the appointment.

To allow the user to use this form part to show future or past utilization, we need a date range. This is why we need a form part; otherwise, we could've accomplished this through an info part.

Creating a view to aggregate the data for the form part

Since the form part will show aggregate data (number of items, load lines, and loads), we should create a view make it simpler to create to simply its usage and so that we can filter on the columns in a view. This means we should create a query for the view. This is not mandatory, but provides a better interface than directly adding tables to the view's data source.

Creating a query for the view

The query will be designed to provide the view with the following information:

Column	Source/aggregation
A date to filter on	`WHSLoadTable.LoadSchedShipUTCDateTime`
Number of items	Sum of `WHSLoadLine.InventQty`
Number of order lines	Count of `WHSLoadLine.InventTransId`
Number of loads	Count of `WHSLoadTable.RecId`

Two decisions were made here, why use `RecId` on `WHSLoadTable` to count loads, but `InventTransId` to count load lines?

We could have used `LoadId` or `RecId` on `WHSLoadTable`; within a legal entity, they are equivalent. However, using `InventTransId` may seem an interesting choice because it is not unique within the `WHSLoadLine` table. The reason is that it is unique for order lines (transfer order lines, sales order lines, and purchase order lines). It is the primary relation between order lines and stock transactions. In this way, we actually get the number of order lines associated with the vehicle and not where it is split across multiple loads. In the next chapter, we will cover in more detail how the stock transaction relates to order lines.

To navigate from the vehicle to the load line, the query will be structured as follows:

```
ConFMSVehicleTable
    Inner join TMSAppointment
        Inner join WHSLoadTable
            Inner join WHSLoadLine
```

Since the relations are defined on the tables, we don't normally need to know how the tables are related, but we must always check whether a relation exists. In some cases, there are multiple relations; for example, the `TMSAppointment` table has three relations with `ConFMSVehicleTable`. In this case, we want to ensure that it is using the base table's relation. We construct the query using these steps:

1. Create a new query, `ConFMSVehicleUtilisation`.
2. Add the `ConFMSVehicleTable` table to the query's **Data Sources** node.
3. Set the **Fields** node's **Dynamic** property to `No`.
4. Manually add the **VehicleId** and **Name** fields by right-clicking on the **Fields** node and going to **New** | **Field**. Use the property sheet to select the correct field.
5. Drag the `TMSAppointment` table onto the **Data Sources** node under `ConFMSVehicleTable`.
6. In the `TMSAppointment` data source, set the **Relations** property to `Yes`.
7. Verify that the **Relations** node has selected the `ConFMSVehicleTable` relation. If it hasn't, change the **Relations** property back to `No` and add the relation manually.
8. On the **Fields** node, set the **Dynamic** property to **No**.

> Do not add any fields, as the view doesn't require fields from this data source.

9. Drag the `WHSLoadTable` table onto the **Data Sources** node under `TMSAppointment`.
10. Set the **Relations** property to `Yes`. On the **Fields** node, set the **Dynamic** property to `No`.
11. Add the `RecId` and `LoadSchedShipUTCDateTime` fields.
12. Finally, add the `WHSLoadLines` table, manually adding the `InventTransId` and `InventQty` fields.
13. Recheck the **Relations** nodes for all data sources.

The relation from `TMSAppointment` to `WHSLoadTable` is different, in that it contains two keys. This is because the `ApptRefNum` field can relate to more than one table. The `ApptRefType` field defines the related table through an enum, which is represented as a number.

The reason we chose to add only the required fields was not to improve performance but to make the creation of the view easier. The query defines the structure of the view (ranges, groups, sorting, relations, and so on) but not the actual fields selected. This is done in the view itself.

The structure of the query should be as shown in the following screenshot:

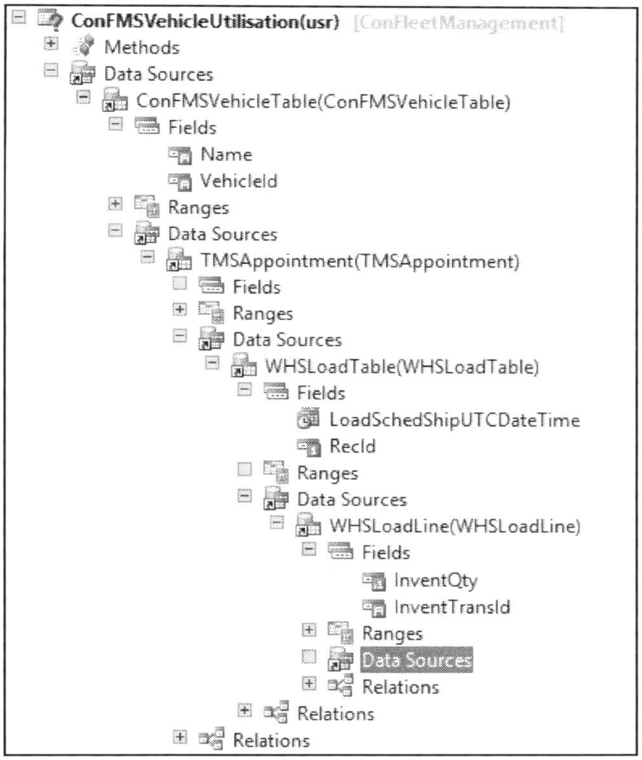

Creating the view using the query as a data source

We can now create the view, which is done as follows:

1. Create a new view under the **Views** node in your project called `ConFMSVehicleUtilisation`.
2. On the properties of the new view, enter the query name, `ConFMSVehicleUtilisation`, in the **Query** property.
3. Expand the node `ConFMSVehicleUtilisation`, and `ConFMSVehicleTable`.

4. Drag `LoadId` from the data source's **Fields** node to the view's **Fields** node, which is below the **Metadata** node.
5. Expand the data source's nodes further to locate the `WHSLoadTable` data source, and expand the data source's **Fields** node.
6. Drag the `LoadSchedShipUTCDateTime` field onto the view's **Fields** node. Collapse the `ConFMSVehicleUtilisation` node in order to use less vertical space.

> We will add the other fields manually as they are aggregated.

7. Right-click on the view's **Fields** node and go to **New** | **Field**.
8. On the new field's property sheet, enter `Number of loads` as **Label**, `WHSLoadTable` as **DataSource**, `RecId` as **Field** and `Count` as **Aggregation**.
9. Rename the field from the automatic name of `CountOfRecId` to a more useful name, `NumberOfLoads`.
10. Do the same for the remaining aggregate fields, as shown in the following table:

Name	Label	DataSource	Field	Aggregation
`NumberOfOrderLines`	`Number Of Order Lines`	`WHSLoadTable`	`InventTransId`	`Count`
`TotalItems`	`Total items (pieces)`	`WHSLoadLine`	`InventQty`	`Sum`

11. Save the view, then right-click on the view and choose **Synchronize**.
12. Test the view by right-clicking on the view and selecting **Open**.

There is probably limited data in this view. To make the testing more useful later, you should create some test data by creating new loads and appointments for your vehicles. The test data should span several months (including future dates) in order to validate that the filtering we will apply next actually works. This is best done using the unit test framework, which is explained in *Chapter 11, Unit and Performance Testing*.

Creating the query for the form part

On the form part, we want one aggregated view of the data, yet the view shows this grouped by `VehicleId` and `LoadSchedShipUTCDateTime`. AX automatically adds a group by clause for fields in the **Fields** node when any field in the view is aggregated.

Therefore, we can't simply add the view to our form part. We will have to summarize further by vehicle for a given data range.

We can write display methods, where we can calculate the totals on the `LinkActive` data source event. But in this case, we will use the aggregate features of a query, and add them to our form. The query will have three aggregate fields and a `group by` clause of `VehicleId`.

To create the query, follow these steps:

1. Create a new query called `ConFMSVehicleUtilisationPart`.
2. Add the `ConFMSVehicleTable` table as the root data source and set the **Dynamic** property on the **Fields** node to `No`.
3. Add the `VehicleId` field to the **Fields** list.
4. Then, add the `ConFMSVehicleUtilisation` view to the **Data Sources** node under `ConFMSVehicleTable`. Again, set the **Dynamic** property on the **Fields** node to `No`.

> In many places where a table can be specified, we can also select a view. AX treats views as read-only tables.

5. We now need to add fields aggregated as `Sum` to this data source, which is done by right-clicking on the **Fields** node and going to **New** | **SUM**.
6. On the new fields property sheet, set **Field** to `TotalItems`.

> The next two fields won't be selectable from the **Field** property dropdown, as this will only allow numeric fields. Even though they are actually numeric fields in the view, the extended data type is passed down to the view field, making AX think that the field is a different type; for example the InventTransId's base type is string, even though it is now a count field.

7. To add `NumberOfOrderLines` and `NumberOfLoads`, create the new field as a sum but paste in the field name. Do not try to edit this afterwards, as AX will change it to the first valid field it finds.
8. Add a relation to the `ConFMSVehicleUtilisation` data source using `VehicleId` as the key. Setting the **Relations** data source property will not work in this case because we don't have a relation on the view—we can't add relation definitions on views.
9. Finally, we need to tell the query to group by `VehicleId`. To do this, right-click on the **Group By** node and select **New Field**.
10. Enter `ConFMSVehicleUtilisation` as **DataSource** and `VehicleId` as **Field**.

Creating the form for our form part

The next part is to create a form for our new form part, which is done as follows:

1. Create a new form called `ConFMSVehicleUtilisationPart`.
2. On the **Data Sources** node, set the **Query** property to `ConFMSVehicleUtilisationPart`.
3. Do not set the designs' **Style** to `FormPart` as before, as this will make the form read-only and we want to be able to edit two date filters.
4. Add two group controls, `FilterGroup` and `ContentGroup`. Complete these by setting the appropriate labels.
5. Drag the three aggregate fields onto the `ContentGroup` field group.
6. We now need to write two edit methods and filter the `ConFMSVehicleUtilisation` data source when the user changes the dates.
7. In the `classDeclaration`, add the following lines of code. This will hold the variables we need for the from date and to date ranges:

```
public class FormRun extends ObjectRun
{
    FromDate    fromDate;
    ToDate      toDate;
}
```

8. Now create two edit methods. Press *Ctrl* + *N*, clear the method body (*Ctrl* + *A* and *Delete*), type `edit`, and press *Tab* to open the `edit` method dialog.
9. In the dialog, enter `FromDate` as **Extended data type name** and `fromDate` as the **Variable** name. These methods simply maintain the `fromDate` and `toDate` variables.

10. Drag these two methods onto the `FilterGroup` control, which will create two date controls bound to the methods. When the user edits the date controls, the bound edit method is called, with `_set` passed as `true`.
11. We now need to write a method that updates the query to filter on a date range.
12. The first part is to convert the dates into `UtcDateTime` variables. The `fromDate` variable should be the midnight of the date entered and `toDate` should be the end of the day.
13. Then we need to find or create a range on `LoadSchedShipUtcDateTime` and use the `fromDateTime` and `toDateTime` variables as a query range. Finally, we need to tell the root data source to execute. The completed method is as follows:

```
public void updateFilter()
{
    utcDateTime     fromDateTime, toDateTime;
    QueryBuildRange dateRange;

    if(toDate == dateNull())
        toDate = dateMax();
    // Convert the dates in to utcDateTime variables
    fromDateTime = DateTimeUtil::newDateTime(fromDate, 0);
    toDateTime   = DateTimeUtil::newDateTime(toDate,
                                  str2time(""23:59:59""));
    // Find of create the QueryRange on LoadSchedShipUTCDateTime
    dateRange = SysQuery::findOrCreateRange(
        ConFMSVehicleUtilisation_DS.queryBuildDataSource(),
        fieldNum(ConFMSVehicleUtilisation,
                 LoadSchedShipUTCDateTime));
    dateRange.value(queryRange(fromDateTime, toDateTime));
    // Execute the query
    ConFMSVehicleTable_DS.executeQuery();
```

14. We now need to alter our edit methods so that the preceding method is called if the user changes the date controls. The complete code for both methods is the following:

```
public edit ToDate editToDate(boolean _set, ToDate _toDate)
{
    if (_set)
    {
        toDate = _toDate;
        this.updateFilter();
    }
    return  toDate;
```

```
    }
    public edit FromDate editFromDate(boolean _set,
                                      FromDate _fromDate)
    {
        if (_set)
        {
            fromDate = _fromDate;
            this.updateFilter();
        }
        return  fromDate;
    }
```

15. Finally, we want the form to update when the vehicle selection changes on the list page where the form is placed. Since `LinkActive` will be called, we override this method on the `ConFMSVehicleTable` data source and call `this.updateFilter()` after the super call.

The rest of the process is as before, create the form part from the form you just created, create a method item for the form part, and add it to the form. The only deviation is that once we have added the form part to `ConFMSVehicleTableListPage`, we should set `DataSourceRelation` to `SelfLink`, as the target form has the same table as the root table. Once we have suitable data, we should see that the form part refreshes for each vehicle and the dates show different totals as we change the date ranges.

We could extend this further by adding a **Refresh** button and an **Auto refresh** checkbox, in case performance is affected. Feel free to add these features yourself. You don't need to use any events or features that we haven't used so far.

More on queries and forms

There is one more important point to explain here about queries and form data sources, which is partly why the preceding example was chosen.

When a table is added as a data source, the system will create a `Query` object and a `QueryRun` object, as well as the `FormDataSource` object. The system names these after the data source name with a suffix (`_Q`, `_QR`, `_DS`). This happens automatically when you add a data source to a form. Query is the design-time definition and when the form is run, the `QueryRun` and `FormDataSource` objects are initialized, essentially from `Query`. The `Query` object then takes no further part. When we add ranges to the data source, we are adding a range to the `QueryRun` object. When we call `ExecuteQuery` to refresh the form, we are actually calling on the `QueryRun` object through the `FormDataSource` object.

Using the query to build the data source definition, which in this case created two data sources, AX simply builds the form's data source definition from the query that we defined. We did this as we needed to aggregate the data, which the user interface doesn't allow on the form. We could have programmatically built the query, but there is no benefit in this case.

Creating links between forms programmatically

In some cases, we can't rely on the relations described in the data dictionary. Views, for example, can't have a relation to a table or another view. AX can make a reasonable job of sensing relations through the EDT, but this doesn't always work. For example, the primary key for `InventBatch` is `ItemId` and `InventBatchId`. If we want to link this to an order line (such as production order or sales line), we have a problem. The item ID is stored on the order line record, but the batch ID is stored on the related table, `InventDim`. AX doesn't stand a chance at sensing this relationship.

To handle this, we modify a form's `init` method, sense the calling table, and create a link to the caller.

Let's say we have a view called `ConInventBatchStatistics`, which is the data source of a form part. The view will have the fields `ItemId` and `InventBatchId` as they form the primary index for `InventBatch`.

The relation to `InventDim` (the table that stores all combinations or item and storage dimensions) is based on the table's primary key `InventDimId`.

```
public void iniFromCaller()
{
    SalesLine      salesLine;
    ItemId         itemId;
    InventBatchId inventBatchId;
    QueryBuildRange ItemRange;
    QueryBuildRange inventBatchRange;

    switch(element.args().dataset())
    {
        case tableNum(SalesLine):
            salesLine = element.args().record();
            itemId = salesLine.itemId;
            inventBatchId = salesLine.inventDim().inventBatchId;
            break;
```

```
        // add a case for each table required
        }

        itemRange = SysQuery::findOrCreateRange(
            ConInventBatchStatistics_DS.queryBuildDataSource(),
            fieldNum(ConInventBatchStatistics,
                     ItemId));
        inventBatchRange = SysQuery::findOrCreateRange(
            ConInventBatchStatistics_DS.queryBuildDataSource(),
            fieldNum(ConInventBatchStatistics,
                     InventBatchId));
        itemRange.value(itemId);
        inventBatchRange.value(inventBatchId);
        ConInventBatchStatistics_DS.executeQuery();
    }
```

We would call the preceding method after the `super()` call in `init` and the data source's `linkActive` method.

There is a more dynamic way to do this using metadata. We can use the function `fieldName2Id` to test whether the caller has the required fields and use the field ID to create a dynamic link. An example of how to do this is in the following code:

```
    private void initFromCaller()
    {
        //BP deviation here for brevity, we would actually
        // write code to sense the field's EDT instead
        str itemIdFieldName         = "ItemId";
        str inventBatchIdFieldName = "inventBatchId";
        RefFieldId          itemIdField;
        RefFieldId          inventBatchIdField;
        QueryBuildDataSource qbds;

        if(element.args().dataset() == 0)
            return;

        itemIdField        = fieldName2id(element.args().dataset(),
                                          itemIdFieldName);
        inventBatchIdField = fieldName2id(element.args().dataset(),
                                          inventBatchIdFieldName);
        if(itemIdField == 0 || inventBatchIdField == 0)
            return;
```

```
    qbds = ConInventBatchStatistics_DS.queryBuildDataSource();
    qbds.addDynalink(fieldNum(ConInventBatchStatistics, ItemId),
                    element.args().record(),
                    itemIdField);
    qbds.addDynalink(fieldNum(ConInventBatchStatistics,
                            InventBatchId),
                        element.args().record(),
                        inventBatchIdField);
}
```

In this example, we only need to call the preceding code in the form part's `init` method, and not the `linkActive` method. We can also just add this to any form with the required fields without modification to the form part's code. However, this is difficult to implement for the sales order scenario. We could still use `fieldName2Id` to make the form part easier to implement without making further code changes.

In both the examples, when we add the part to the form such as `InventBatch`, we must set the part's **IsLinked** property to **Yes**, otherwise, the system won't trigger the `linkActive` event, which is required by both the preceding methods.

Summary

In this chapter, we saw how to put several pieces of key business information at our users' fingertips without them having to navigate away from where they are. By making this data easily accessible, they save time and are able to make decisions quickly and accurately.

We also introduced some new general concepts, such as using queries to create views and form data source definitions, allowing us to display aggregate data both at view level and using a query that we can adjust at runtime. We also stepped into using metadata to make our code more flexible and the resulting parts easier to implement.

In the next chapter, we will extend the solution further by adding more advanced functionality.

6

Extending the Solution

In the chapters so far, we have covered most of the functionality required to write a business application that is focused on creation and maintenance of data. In this chapter, we will add some new features to the solution and then delve into some more advanced functionality.

In this chapter, we will cover the following topics:

- Adding secondary list pages
- Using menu items to change the vehicle status
- Adding a drop dialog to change the vehicle group
- Exposing the vehicle group logic as a custom web service

Adding secondary list pages

Secondary list pages allow us to display a subset of data without having to write a new list page, interaction class, or query. Typically, these are used to show data based on a status, for example, open purchase orders, sales orders for customers on hold, and so on.

We will create two types of secondary list pages: one for a status field on the vehicle, and the other to list vehicles that have an appointment.

Adding a list page for active vehicles

An active vehicle is determined by the `VehicleStatusId` field, so we will use this in order to filter the data in the list page. Prior to AX 2012, this was done by modifying the form to add a range to the form data source's query. This led to the code being written onto the form itself, which isn't possible on a list page. This is a good thing, as it forces us to use a better, more extendable practice.

Another method would be to simply duplicate the query, but this means duplication of effort and maintenance—always to be avoided!

Instead, we will create a query that extends the main vehicle list page query. These are termed as **composite queries**. Composite queries act like an extension of the main query, allowing ranges to be added, but we cannot change the structure of the query. This is desirable because the main use of composite queries is on secondary list pages, and this forces the query to be compatible.

A composite query for active vehicles is created by the following steps:

1. In your project, create a new blank query called `ConFMSVehicleTableListPageActive`.
2. Drag the `ConFMSVehicleTableListPage` query onto the **Composite Query** node of the `ConFMSVehicleTableListPageActive` query. This adds a reference to the query structure of `ConFMSVehicleTableListPage`.
3. In our new query, navigate to **Composite Query** | **ConFMSVehicleTableListPage** | **Data Sources** | **ConFMSVehicleTable**.
4. Right-click on the **Ranges** node and select **New Range**.
5. Select `VehicleStatusId` for **Field** and enter the enum value for `Active`, which is `2`, in the **Value** field.

This new query is tied to the original by the composite query reference. If a new field, range, or method is added to `ConFMSVehicleTableListPage`, then it will also apply to `ConFMSVehicleTableListPageActive`.

We now need to create a menu item that opens the `ConFMSVehicleTableListPage` list page with the query we have just created. This is done with the following steps:

1. Locate the menu item named `ConFMSVehicleTableListPage` by navigating to **Menu items** | **Display**.
2. Right-click on the menu item and select **Duplicate**.
3. Rename the duplicate menu item to `ConFMSVehicleTableListPageActive`.
4. Change **Label** to `Active vehicles`.
5. In the **Query** field, select the `ConFMSVehicleTableListPageActive` query.
6. Now save the menu item and then open it.

You will see that the `ConFMSVehicleTableListPage` form has been run, but using the results of the `ConFMSVehicleTableListPageActive` query. The form requires a query that looks and acts just like the `ConFMSVehicleTableListPage` query, and thanks to the composite query reference, our new query does just that.

Next, we will add the new menu item to our `ConFleetManagementSystem` menu structure.

Adding a list page for inactive vehicles

In order to show a list of an active vehicles (those without an active appointment) using a query, we would add a `join` to the `TMSAppointment` table as well as a query range. The problem is that the composite query method will not allow us to add a child data source, so we have to find another solution.

Adding a child data source won't actually make the query incompatible with the form. Notice what happens to the list page when we associate the query. It creates a data source for each table in the query and defines the relations between them. Adding a data source doesn't change the structure; it just adds a source that the form doesn't need. The composite query is being a little overprotective in this case.

We have two possible solutions: duplicate the query and add `TMSAppointment` as a data source under `ConFMSVehicleTable`, or modify the list page interaction class to modify the query when the form opens. Modifying the interaction class is preferable, as we avoid having to maintain two queries, so this is the method we will use.

First of all, we need a way to tell the interaction class when this should occur. The interaction class is aware of the menu item that called it, so we can use metadata on the menu item to control this.

There are three menu item properties that we can use:

- `Parameters`: A free text string
- `EnumTypeParameter`: A base enum
- `EnumParameter`: A numeric value of the base enum in `EnumTypeParameter`

It is more structured to use the Base enum method than a free text string, as this leads to typographical errors that are hard to debug.

Before we start updating the class, we need to perform the following steps:

1. Create a new Base enum called `ConFMSVehicleListPageType`. Add the All and `InactiveWithAppointment` elements in sequence, each with appropriate labels.

> We need **All** to have a value of `0`, as we want this to be the default option. It is easier to create them in the desired sequence to save changing the values afterwards.

2. Duplicate the `ConFMSVehicleTableListPage` menu item. Set `EnumTypeParameter` to `ConFMSVehicleListPageType` and `EnumParameter` to `1`—the value of `InactiveWithAppointment`.
3. Change the label for the new menu item to `Inactive vehicles with appointments`.
4. Finally, add this to the menu, just below the previous secondary list page.

We now need to update the interaction class to update the query based on the menu item parameters. We will break the code into methods to make it easier to read. The first method we will create is used to get the list page type from the menu item. The interaction class has access to a `listPage` object, which has an object called `listPageArgs`. This object has the properties we need. We will then write a method to update the query, and call this based on the list page type. We do this using the following steps:

1. Locate the `ConFMSVehicleTabeListPageInteraction` class.
2. Create a method called `listPageType` to determine the list page type from the menu item. The following method does this by using the list page's `listPageArgs` object. It returns the value from the `EnumParameter` property method if the type (`listPageArgs.enumTypeParameter`) is the `ConFMSVehicleListPageType`:

```
private ConFMSVehicleListPageType listPageType()
{
    ConFMSVehicleListPageType pageType =
                                ConFMSVehicleListPageType::All;

    if(this.listPage().listPageArgs().enumTypeParameter()
       == enumNum(ConFMSVehicleListPageType))
```

```
    {
        pageType =
            this.listPage().listPageArgs().enumParameter();
    }
    return pageType;
}
```

3. Although we don't need to assign a value to `pageType` in the first line of our method, in the case of enums, it is good for readability and to show that we do intend the default to be `All`.

> There is no `else` clause, as we set the default type earlier in the method. This is faster, as the else clause consumes a little CPU time. Using this simple pattern is a good habit to adopt for cases where we are working with lots of records and every clock cycle matters.

4. Next, we need a method that adds a status range, and a `join` operation to the TMSAppointment table. This is done by the following lines of code:

```
private void updateQueryInactiveWithAppointment(Query _q)
{
    QueryBuildDataSource apptQBDS;
    QueryBuildDataSource vehQBDS;
    QueryBuildRange      statusRange;

    vehQBDS = _q.dataSourceTable(
                        tableNum(ConFMSVehicleTable));

    statusRange = SysQuery::findOrCreateRange(vehQBDS,
                        fieldNum(ConFMSVehicleTable,
                                        VehicleStatusId));
    statusRange.value(
          SysQuery::valueNot(ConFMSVehicleStatus::Active));

    apptQBDS =
        vehQBDS.addDataSource(tableNum(TMSAppointment));
        apptQBDS.addLink(fieldNum(ConFMSvehicleTable,
RecId),
                     fieldNum(TMSAppointment,
                          ConFMSVehicleTableTruck));
}
```

> We will dissect the preceding method just after this section.

5. Finally, if the list page type is `InactiveWithAppointment`, we need to call this method, and this should happen after the query is initialized. This is done by overriding the `initializeQuery` method (right-click on the class's **Methods** node and select **Override | initializeQuery**).
6. We modify this so that we can update the query after the `super()` call, as follows:

```
public void initializeQuery(Query _query)
{
 super(_query);
 switch(this.listPageType())
 {
   case ConFMSVehicleListPageType::InactiveWithAppointment:
        this.updateQueryInactiveWithAppointment(_query);
        break;
 }
}
```

7. Save the class and open the new menu item created earlier to test.

The `updateQueryInactiveWithAppointment` method introduces some new concepts, in that we are modifying a query at runtime.

There are two main object types we work with, `QueryBuildDataSource` and `QueryBuildRange`. The data sources we add to a query are created as objects of the `QueryBuildDataSource` type. The ranges we add to the data source are of the `QueryBuildRange` type.

The query object allows access to the data sources through the `dataSourceName`, `dataSourceNo`, and `dataSourceTable` methods. Unless we have two data sources for the same table, `dataSourceTable` is the safest to use; otherwise, we can use its name. We won't use `dataSourceNo` in this context. This is used when iterating through the query's data sources.

We used this method to get the `QueryBuildDataSource` object for the vehicle table:

```
vehQBDS = _q.dataSourceTable(tableNum(ConFMSVehicleTable));
```

The first task with this data source is to add the `VehicleStatusId` range for inactive vehicles. We don't know whether the query already used has this range, so we use the `SysQuery` class to find or create this for us:

```
statusRange = SysQuery::findOrCreateRange(vehQBDS,
                    fieldNum(ConFMSVehicleTable, VehicleStatusId));
```

We pass this method to the `QueryBuildDataSource` object and the field we want the range to filter on. The next part is to add a new data source under the vehicle table data source. This is done by the following line of code:

```
apptQBDS = vehQBDS.addDataSource(tableNum(TMSAppointment));
```

We use `vehQBDS` because we are adding the appointment table as a data source to the vehicle table.

This command has created a join without relations, which will create a Cartesian join. This joins every record to every other record—possibly the worst thing you can do to your already busy SQL Server. The following adds the required relation:

```
apptQBDS.addLink(fieldNum(ConFMSvehicleTable, RecId),
                 fieldNum(TMSAppointment, ConFMSVehicleTableTruck));
```

We could also use the relations parameter method, and in most cases, this is preferable. This would be written as follows:

```
apptQBDS.relations(true);
```

We chose to add this manually in order to demonstrate how to programmatically create links between data sources. Since the query is dealt with by reference, we don't need to pass this back to the class.

To see what has happened behind the scenes, open the new menu item. Then right-click on the list page and choose **Personalize**. Select the **Query** tab, which should look like what is shown in the following screenshot:

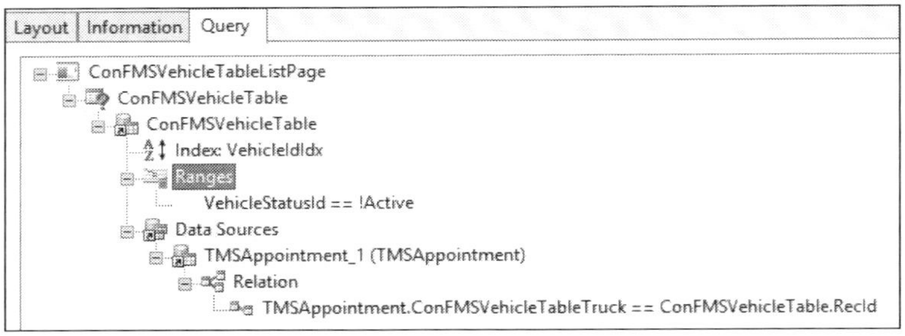

The table we added programmatically is there and is joined as requested, as is the range.

Using menu items to change the vehicle status

Status fields are set either manually by the user or by an external event; for example, the purchase order status is changed based on status change of the associated purchase order lines.

In the case where a status field is set manually by the user, which is our case, it is not normally appropriate to allow the user to edit this field directly. A change in status is an important event, and we should make this more of a deliberate action.

There are two patterns we can choose to edit a status: a menu item per status that is added to the form in a button group, or a drop dialog with a drop-down list control.

The menu item method gives us scope to disable or enable the buttons based on the current record. Since the status is an enumerated type, it has a fixed list of options; this is therefore the best method. You can see this used within the **Project management** module.

This also allows us to demonstrate further decoupling of the user interface and business logic. Decoupling the user interface from the business logic makes the code reusable. We will demonstrate this later in the chapter when we create a service to change the vehicle status.

We will start with writing the code to update the vehicle status. This class will need a vehicle ID and the desired status to change to. We can do this by adding public parameter methods or making the constructor accept these variables as parameters. This is how it used to be done before AX 2012, but in order to get the most out of the pattern, we will use a data contract class. This method has the additional benefit of being used more easily by a service, something we should always be conscious of when designing our solutions.

We define a class as a data contract class by adding the `[DataContractAttribute]` decoration to the class declaration and the `[DataMemberAttribute]` decoration to every method that should be exposed as a parameter.

These come into effect when we use the SysOperation framework, or if we ever want to use this contract as a service, as it is used to generate the **Web Service Definition Language** (**WSDL**).

Creating the data contract class

We will call the class that changes the `ConFMSVehicleStatusChange` status. Therefore, we will call the `ConFMSVehicleStatusChangeContract` contract class.

This class is quite straightforward. It should be written as follows:

```
[DataContractAttribute]
class ConFMSVehicleStatusChangeContract
{
    ConFMSVehicleId vehicleId;
    ConFMSVehicleStatus status;
}
```

The two parameter methods do not need the `parm` prefix; this is true for all data contracts. You can add the `parm` prefix, and you may see this in some standard AX data contracts, but you will need to add a further decoration to tell the WSDL the exposed method name.

The `parm` prefix adds an automatic documentation for the method, and is mandatory for methods used in the AIF document service classes. Custom services such as this will never be used in this way, and the prefix is just inconvenient when used outside AX.

The two methods should be written as follows:

```
[DataMemberAttribute]
public ConFMSVehicleId vehicleID(ConFMSVehicleId
                                  _vehicleId = vehicleID)
{
    vehicleID = _vehicleID;

    return vehicleID;
}
[DataMemberAttribute]
public ConFMSVehicleStatus status(ConFMSVehicleStatus
                                  _status = status)
{
    status = _status;

    return status;
}
```

> The preceding code was written using the `parm` code snippet and was manually edited to remove the `parm` prefix.

Finally, we create a `construct` method as we have done previously.

Creating the class to process the update

We can now write our class to change the status, which will follow a pattern we will use many times. This pattern requires the structure to have the following methods:

- `construct`
- `newFromContract`
- `parmContract`
- `validate`
- `run`

The `run` method will call `validate`, and simply return if `validate` returns `false`. The `validate` method is expected to display messages to the user if it fails.

If we intend to use this class with the SysOperation framework, the `run` method needs the `contract` as a parameter. We can, however, add a method called `runContract` that accepts the `contract` class and then calls `run`. The `run` method will usually call the various private methods to perform the required action, unless the code is very simple.

Our class will contain the following methods:

- `construct`
- `newFromContract`
- `parmContract`
- `validate`
- `run`, which calls validate and then `updateVehicleStatus`
- `runContract`, which updates `contract` and calls `run`
- `updateVehicleStatus`

Based on the preceding methods, we can call the class like this:

```
ConFMSVehicleStatusChange::newFromContract(<contract>).run();
```

Alternatively, we can use the following line of code:

```
ConFMSVehicleStatusChange::construct().runContract(<contract>);
```

The reason for the first method is that we could call the classes validate to first check whether the process will succeed, like this for example:

```
//...
ConFMSVehicleStatusChange change;

change = ConFMSVehicleStatusChange::newFromContract(<contract>);
if(change.validate())
{
  change.run();
}
else
{
  //perform an action
  //...
}
```

> The preceding code will mean that `validate` is called twice, so we should do this only if we need to know whether the update will fail validation before calling run. This is true if we are hooking the code with the UI and wish to give our user the opportunity to correct the error.

We will use this method later in this chapter when we use this pattern with a drop dialog. This is because it allows more control over the dialog. If the validate method returns false, we will not close the dialog, allowing the user to correct the issue.

The code for the class is again straightforward, and it should be written as follows:

```
class ConFMSVehicleStatusChange
{
    ConFMSVehicleStatusChangeContract contract;
}
```

Here is the code used to construct the class from the contract:

```
public ConFMSVehicleStatusChangeContract
            parmContract(ConFMSVehicleStatusChangeContract
                         _contract = contract)
{
    contract = _contract;

    return contract;
}
public static ConFMSVehicleStatusChange construct()
{
    return new ConFMSVehicleStatusChange();
}
public static ConFMSVehicleStatusChange
                 newFromContract(ConFMSVehicleStatusChangeContract
                                 _contract)
{
    ConFMSVehicleStatusChange instance =
            ConFMSVehicleStatusChange::construct();
    instance.parmContract(_contract);
    return instance;
}
```

The code used to validate and perform the required actions is as follows:

```
public boolean validate()
{
    if(contract.vehicleID() == "")
```

```
        {
            return checkFailed("Vehicle id is required");
        }
        if(!ConFMSVehicleTable::exist(contract.vehicleID()))
        {
            return checkFailed(strFmt("Vehicle %1 does not exist",
                               contract.vehicleID()));
        }
        return true;
    }
```

The run method calls validate, and if this returns true, it starts a transaction, calls the method to update the vehicle, and completes the transaction. The code for both the methods is as follows:

```
    public void run()
    {
        if(!this.validate())
            return;
        ttsBegin;
        this.updateVehicleStatus();
        ttsCommit;
    }
    private void updateVehicleStatus()
    {
        ConFMSVehicleTable vehicle = ConFMSVehicleTable::find(contract.
    vehicleID(), true);

        if(vehicle.RecId != 0)
        {
            vehicle.VehicleStatusId = contract.status();
            vehicle.update();
        }
    }
```

> Even though the validate method checks whether the vehicle exists, we should always check whether we've found a record using the RecId field.

Database transactions

The two preceding methods need to be looked at together. The `run` method first checks `validate` and then calls `ttsbegin`. This starts a database transaction, or adds a further level if a transaction has already been started by the code calling this class. Once inside a transaction, a call is made to `updateVehicleStatus()`. Finally, this transaction is committed by calling `ttsCommit`.

A transaction is mandatory for performing any update to a record in AX. If an update is attempted outside a transaction's scope, then AX will throw an error.

The next part is that we select the `forUpdate` vehicle by passing the `true` parameter to the `find` method. The record is not locked at this point, as AX uses optimistic concurrency for updates, but after `update` is called, the vehicle record is locked. This prevents any updates from elsewhere until after the final `ttsCommit`.

This means that if the `run` method had been called without a current transaction, then the call to `ttsCommit` will release the lock. However, if the calling method had started a transaction, then the `ttsCommit` in this method will not release the vehicle lock.

The following diagram shows the effect of a nested TTS:

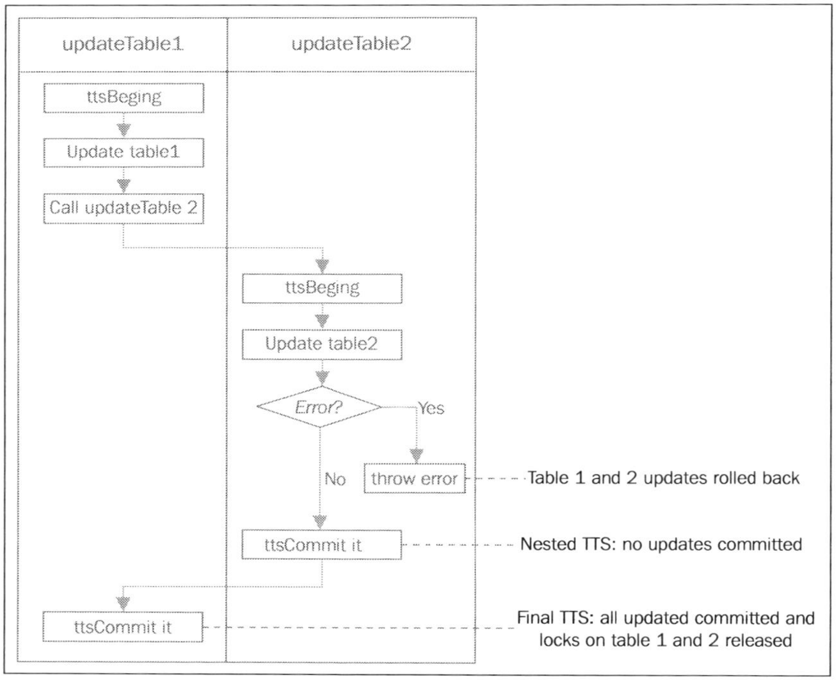

A transaction comprises of all updates from the first `ttsBegin` until the final `ttsCommit`. If you nest a transaction, it is the final `ttsCommit` that actually commits the transaction. If an error is thrown (or `ttsAbort` is executed) at any point before the final `ttsCommit`, all updates from the `ttsBegin` that started the transaction are rolled back.

This is closely linked with exception handling; see the *Exception handling* section in *Chapter 10, Advanced Development Techniques*.

This is important, as transactions should always be ACID, which means transactions should be:

- **Atomic**: If a transaction involves more than one entity, either all or none are committed to the database.
- **Consistent**: Should any part of the transaction fail, all of the data is rolled back to the state before failure.
- **Isolation**: Any update in the transaction must be isolated from any other transaction until the transaction is complete. So, reading a vehicle record in a separate transaction after `update` is called will not return the new data until the transaction is committed.
- **Durable**: Once the transaction is committed the records must remain committed, even after subsequent system failure, for example, if SQL server fails.

All of this is done by specifying `ttsbegin` before we start and `ttscommit` once we are done.

For more information, see *Transaction Integrity [AX 2012]*: `http://msdn.microsoft.com/en-us/library/aa622564.aspx`.

A problem arises if, during the action, we produce an output that can't be rolled back; such as an e-mail. In this case, we would have to manually write a method to deal with this. This is called **compensation**, and it follows the coffee shop transaction scenario. For "performance," you pay before you have your coffee, completing a transaction. Should there be no coffee, you have to be compensated with your money back. This is a paradigm when designing high-performance data systems, for example, when we use asynchronous database updates using the SysOperation framework—something AX utilizes to a great effect when posting ledger updates. We will cover this in *Chapter 9, Advanced Features and Frameworks*.

Adding further validation to the status change

We can take this further; let's say that the vehicle is on an appointment. Should we be allowed to make the vehicle status anything other than active? Well, if the vehicle is damaged, we have no choice, but we need to tell the user that they have to deal with this situation.

To do this, we will add a check method, as we want to show the user message. We will add it to the `validate` method as well, but ignore the result, as we will still want to update the status.

In this method, we are introducing an underused feature of the info log system, called `SysInfoAction`. This allows us to add a button to the **Infolog** that will perform the required action; in our case, open the `TMSAppointment` form with the appointment that the vehicle is on. We want to do this only if the vehicle is currently active, it is on an appointment in the future, and we are making the status not active. The code required is as follows:

```
public boolean checkAppointment()
{
    TMSAppointment              appt;
    ConFMSVehicleTable          vehicle;
    SysInfoAction_MenuFunction action;

    vehicle = ConFMSVehicleTable::find(contract.vehicleID());
    //if vehicle is found and we are changing it
    // from active to a non-active status.
    if(vehicle.RecId            != 0 &&
       vehicle.VehicleStatusId == ConFMSVehicleStatus::Active &&
       contract.status()        != ConFMSVehicleStatus::Active)
    {
        // look for an appointment in the future
        select appt
            where appt.ConFMSVehicleTableTruck == vehicle.RecId &&
                  appt.ApptFromUTCDateTime >
                                 DateTimeUtil::getSystemDateTime();
        if(appt.RecId != 0)
        {
            // the action adds a button to the info log
            // to take the user to the appointment
            action = SysInfoAction_MenuFunction::newMenuItem(
                              menuitemDisplayStr(TMSAppointment),
```

```
                                MenuItemType::Display);
            action.parmCallerBuffer(appt);

            return checkFailed("Vehicle has a future appointment",
                                  "", action);
        }
    }
    //vehicle does not exist, but return true
    //as this isn't the point of this check
    return true;
}
```

Add the following line to the `validate` method, just above the `return true;` line:

```
this.checkAppointment();
```

Hooking up the code with the interface

We have written the code, but we now need to add it to the UI. This will be done by creating a menu item for each status and a class to handle the menu item. We will start with the class.

Menu items will look for the entry point `main` on the class, and will pass in an object of type `Args`. The `args` object contains several pieces of useful information. We will use the following:

- `dataset`: This is the table ID of the calling record on the form. It must be a vehicle record.
- `parmEnumType`: This is the enum type on the menu item. It must be `ConFMSVehicleStatus`.
- `parmEnum`: This is the value of the enum, in this case our status.
- `record`: This is the record passed from the form.

We could, technically, add a main method to `ConFMSVehicleStatusChange`. But we won't, as this blurs the separation between the user interface and the code that performs the update, and more importantly, they have very different purposes. The main method is written purely to handle a menu item, whereas the class is designed to be used in any place that requires the vehicle status to be changed. This is a very important point, especially for those used to procedural programming.

Creating the menu item handler class

We will call our class `ConFMSVehicleStatusChangeHandler`, and add a `main` method, as follows:

```
public static void main(Args _args)
{
    ConFMSVehicleStatusChangeContract contract;
    ConFMSVehicleTable                vehicleTable;
    ConFMSVehicleStatus               newStatus;
    FormDataSource                    vehicleTable_DS;
    // use the dataset to check we have a
    // vehicle table in the record buffer
    switch(_args.dataset())
    {
        case tableNum(ConFMSVehicleTable):
            // get the record buffer
            vehicleTable = _args.record();
            break;
    }
    if(vehicleTable.RecId == 0)
    {
        //show standard message and abort the update
        // 'Active buffer required'
        throw error("@SYS79604");
    }
    if(_args.parmEnumType() != enumNum(ConFMSVehicleStatus))
    {
        //show the standard message on being
        //incorrectly called
        //'Function %1 has been incorrectly called.'
        // and format it with the class name with strFmt
        throw error (strFmt("@SYS22828",
                       classStr(ConFMSVehicleStatusChangeHandler)));
    }

    //construct the contract
    contract = ConFMSVehicleStatusChangeContract::construct();
    contract.vehicleID(vehicleTable.VehicleId);
    contract.status(_args.parmEnum());
```

```
        // construct and run the update
        ConFMSVehicleStatusChange::newFromContract(contract).run();
        //if this was called from a form the
        //vehicle will have isFormDataSource set
        //if so, get the formDataSource object
        //and call research, true keeps the
        //current set
        if(vehicleTable.isFormDataSource())
        {
            vehicleTable_DS = vehicleTable.dataSource();
            vehicleTable_DS.research(true);
        }
    }
```

The `command throw error` command is new. This will show an **Infolog** window type of error and abort the entire transaction, rolling everything back. We will cover this in more detail in the *Exception handling* section in *Chapter 10, Advanced Development Techniques*.

Creating the menu items

You can create the menu items by dragging the class onto the **Action** node under **Menu items** in our project. Try this and then right-click on the new menu item. You will get the `Active buffer required` error.

We need to configure the menu to have the following properties set:

- **Name**: `ConFMSVehicleStatusChangeCreated`.
- **Label**: The label of the first status is `Created`. Copy this from the base enum's `Created` element.
- **EnumTypeParameter**: `ConFMSVehicleStatus`.
- **EnumParameter**: `Created`.

We could, for completeness, also populate the **NormalImage** property. This is an image resource number, and you can see the full list by going to **Tools | Embedded resources**. Enter the number of the desired resource in the **NormalImage** property and set **ImageLocation** to `Embedded resource`.

Duplicate this menu item for each status, setting the **Name**, **Label**, and **EnumParameter** properties appropriately.

Adding the menu items to the list page

For this, we need to add a form control of type **MenuButton** and drag our new menu items onto this new control. This is done as follows:

1. On the `ConFMSVehicleTabeListPage` form, go to **Designs** | **Design** | **ActionPane** | **HomeTab** | **MaintainGroup**.
2. Right-click on **MaintainGroup** and go to **New Control** | **MenuButton**.
3. Rename this to **StatusMenuButton** and set the label to `Change status`.
4. Drag the new menu items onto this **MenuButton**.

> Should the form have more than one data source, we can ensure that the menu item uses the correct data source using the **Datasource** property. This property inherits its value from its container, **MaintainGroup** in this case, and so on until it reaches the **Design** node.

5. Open the form to test.

Of course, we could have written all of this in the last class we wrote, but there wasn't much more effort, and we have the added advantage of making the code reusable. We can even write a service that will use this with very little effort.

Adding a drop dialog to change vehicle group

We can use a similar pattern to use a drop dialog to update data on a record, the vehicle group in this case.

To do this, the contract and update classes are nearly identical to the earlier status change logic. We are simply updating the vehicle group. The steps required for this are similar as before, except that we will use a drop dialog form instead of menu items. It is not ideal to use menu items, as vehicle groups are defined in data. It is, therefore, far more natural to select the vehicle group with a drop-down list control.

We will be following the same pattern as before, so a summary of the first part of this task is listed as follows:

1. Create a data contract class called `ConFMSVehicleGroupChangeContract`, adding the `[DataContractAttribute]` decoration above `classDeclaration`.
2. Create variables in the `classDeclaration` for the `vehicleId` and `vehicleGroupId` using their EDTs.
3. Create the data member methods as we did in the vehicle status data contract class. Remember the `[DataMemberAttribute]` decoration.
4. Create the `construct` static method as usual.
5. Create the class that will perform the update. Following the earlier pattern, name this class `ConFMSVehicleGroupChange`, and use the following methods:
    - `public static ConFMSVehicleGroupChange construct()`
    - `public ConFMSVehicleGroupChangeContract parmContract(...)`
    - `public static ConFMSVehicleGroupChange newFromContract(..)`
    - `private void updateVehicle`
    - `public boolean validate()`
    - `public void run()`
    - `public void runContract(...)`
6. Next, you should write a job to test this, supplying both valid and invalid data; this is more important this time because the dialog won't allow the user to enter a vehicle group that does not exist.

There is a temptation to duplicate the vehicle status classes and then modify them for the new situation. This isn't necessarily a bad idea, but it is very vitally important to ensure that every part is modified appropriately. Failure to do this is one of the biggest causes of errors. AX's helpfulness in casting between EDTs of the same base type will allow us to use a vehicle group ID to check whether a record exists in the vehicle table. It will assume that we intended to cast the types. This is another benefit of using data contracts; we will not be allowed to cast between them.

Creating a drop dialog form

The next step is to create the user interface—a drop dialog. This is done by the following steps:

1. Right-click on the AOTs Forms node and select **New from form template | DropDialog**.
2. Rename this form to `ConFMSVehicleGroupChange` and drag this onto your project.
3. We do not need a data source for this; we are going to use the data contract.
4. In the `classDeclaration`, we declare our contract as follows:

```
public class FormRun extends ObjectRun
{
    ConFMSVehicleGroupChangeContract contract;
}
```

5. We now need to construct our contract and get the vehicle ID from the caller. The `element` object (the instance of the form) contains an `args` object, which we will use to construct the `contract` class:

```
public void init()
{
    ConFMSVehicleTable callerVehicle;
    super();
    switch(element.args().dataset())     {
        case tableNum(ConFMSVehicleTable):
            callerVehicle = element.args().record();
            break;
    }
    if(callerVehicle.RecId == 0)
    {
        throw error("@SYS79604");
    }
    contract = ConFMSVehicleGroupChangeContract::construct();
    contract.vehicleId(callerVehicle.VehicleId);
    contract.vehicleGroupId(callerVehicle.VehicleGroupId);
}
```

> The `this` variable has a different meaning in the context of forms. It means the element or control within the form that the current method is acting on. This could be the form, a data source, a field, or a control. The `element` object always refers to the instance of the form. If we are in the `Methods` node of the form, `this` and `element` are the same thing, but it is good practice to use element regardless when we are referring to the form instance.

6. We now need to create an `edit` method that acts on a data source for the vehicle group drop-down control, but unlike before, we are using the `contract` as our storage:

```
public edit ConFMSVehicleGroupId editVehicleGroupId(
                      boolean _set,
                      ConFMSVehicleGroupId _vehicleGroupId)
{
    if (_set)
    {
        contract.vehicleGroupId(_vehicleGroupId);
    }
    return  contract.vehicleGroupId();
}
```

7. Create a method that will update the vehicle and refresh the calling record. It will be called from the clicked method of the **OK** button, so we need to know whether the update succeeded. The code is as follows:

```
public boolean updateVehicle()
{
    ConFMSVehicleGroupChange change;
    FormDataSource           callerDS;

    change =
       ConFMSVehicleGroupChange::newFromContract(contract);
    if(change.validate())
    {
        change.run();
        if(element.args().record().isFormDataSource())
        {
            callerDS =
               element.args().record().dataSource();
```

```
                callerDS.research(true);
                return true;
            }
        }
        Return false;
    }
```

8. Enter a brief instruction in the `MainInstruction` control. We don't really need the `SupplementalInstruction`, so we can delete this control.
9. Drag the `edit` method onto the `DialogContent` group so that it is below the `MainInstruction`.
10. Finally, locate the `OKButton` and override its `clicked` method.
11. The `super()` method triggers several form events, one of which closes the form. We only need our `updateVehicle` to be called, and we need to close the form only on success, allowing the user to correct any data entry uses without having to reopen the form:

```
void clicked()
{
    if(element.updateVehicle())
    {
        super();
    }
}
```

12. We now need to create a menu item. We do this by dragging the saved form onto our project's **Display** node (which can be found under **Menu items**), remembering the label.

> The final step is to add this menu item to our vehicle list page. If we simply drag this onto the form, it will not create a drop dialog. It will display the form as a normal dialog, so we have to create this manually.

13. From the **ConFMSVehicleTableListPage** form, go to **Designs** | **Design** | **ActionPane** | **HomeTab** | **MaintainGroup**.
14. Right-click on **MaintainGroup** and go to **New** | **DropDialogButton**.
15. Rename the control to `ConFMSVehicleGroupChangeButton`.

16. Change the new button's **MenuItemName** property to `ConFMSVehicleGroupChange`.
17. Feel free to look for a nice icon in **Embedded resources** under **Tools**, and adjust the button's **Big**, **NeedsRecord**, and **Primary** properties as required.

Finally, it is important to understand what is happening and feel comfortable with this pattern. To challenge yourself, try the preceding steps for the vehicle schedule, and consider what might happen to the existing vehicle service records.

Exposing the vehicle group logic as a custom web service

To further highlight the benefits of writing coding decoupled from the user interface and the use of data contracts, we will create a service and use it in a C# project.

Writing services in AX is straightforward; for example, to create a service that returns "Hello world", we simply need to return the "Hello world" string. We do have to describe the service to the outside world, however, and this is done by a decoration at the method header.

Firstly, we need to tell the compiler that this is a web method, and the return type. In the case of the Hello world example, it is simply the following:

```
[AifCollectionTypeAttribute('return', Types::String),
SysEntryPointAttribute(true)]
```

The `AifCollectionAttribute` determines that the return is of type string, and `SysEntryPointAttribute` states that this is a web method.

A complete method that returns Hello world is as follows:

```
[AifCollectionTypeAttribute('return', Types::String),
SysEntryPointAttribute(true)]
public Name helloWorld()
{
    return "Hello world";
}
```

We can add parameters too, so to return "Hello world my name is <parameter>", we would write this code:

```
[AifCollectionTypeAttribute('return', Types::String),
SysEntryPointAttribute(true)]
public Name helloWorldMyName(Name _myName)
{
    return strFmt("Hello world my name is %1", _myName);
}
```

Apart from the decoration, this is just like any other X++ method.

Creating the service class and service

Let's try this and test this by creating a service and calling it from Visual Studio.

1. Create a class called `ConFMSVehicleServices` and create the two methods in the same way as you just saw.
2. Right-click on the **Services** node in your project and go to **New** | **Service**.
3. Rename the service to `ConFMSVehicleServices`. Enter this in the **Class** property as well.
4. Enter `ContosoFMS` in **Namespace**. This acts as a scope where the service only has to be unique within this namespace.
5. Right-click on the service's **Operations** node and select **Add Operation**.

> AX will display a dialog with the two methods in the class. If they don't appear, check whether `SysEntryPointAttribute` was specified in the method and that it was `public`.

6. Check both the method names and press **OK**.

> Next, we need a **Service** group. It is a group that is deployed through the AIF and is the lowest level by, which we can control its availability. It is appropriate to have one service group for each area of functionality.

7. Right-click on the **Service groups** node and go to **New** | **Service Group**.
8. Rename this group to `ConFMSServices`.
9. We drag your service onto the new service group. We should now have the structure similar to what is shown in the following screenshot:

10. We right-click on our service group and choose **Deploy Service Group**.

> This will cause AX to generate an incremental CIL and deploy our service as a WCF service. This may take up to 15 minutes, but if we have been building CILs frequently, it should happen within 2 minutes.

Once this is complete, you should see an info log with various information messages, including this line:

```
The port 'ConFMSServices' was deployed successfully.
```

Should there be a compilation error anywhere in the X++ code, AX will not be able to complete the CIL generation from the p-code. Also, if you receive an error that doesn't relate to a specific X++ compilation error, you will need to generate a full CIL, which is done from the **Build** menu.

This also created an inbound port within the **Application Integration Framework** (**AIF**). To see this, navigate to **System administration** | **Setup** | **Services and Application Integration Framework** | **Inbound ports**.

You should see a record for your port, as shown in the following screenshot:

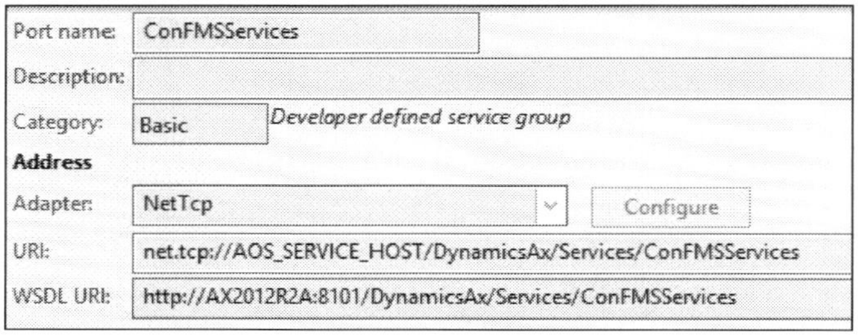

We will use the WSDL URI when including a reference in our Visual Studio project, which will differ from the preceding example, based on the AOS on which it was deployed.

Creating the Visual Studio test project

To create the test project, please follow these steps:

1. Start Visual Studio (2010 or later) and go to **File** | **New** | **Project...**.
2. Select **Console Application** from the **Visual C#** node, which can be found under **Installed Templates**.
3. Enter `ConFMSVehicleServicesTest` in **Name** and press **OK**.
4. You should now have the **Solution Explorer** window open, which is normally docked on the right.
5. On the **References** node, right-click and select **Add Service Reference**.
6. Paste in the WSDI URI from the AIF port configuration, `http://AX2012R2A:8101/DynamicsAx/Services/ConFMSServices` in our case.
7. Press **Go**.
8. You should see our service group name, `ConFMSServices`, and on expanding this node, you will see the **Operations** you added.
9. Enter `ConFMSServicesReference` in **Namespace** and press OK.
10. Open the `Program.cs` CS file from the **Solution Explorer**, which has one static method, named `Main`.

> In order to call a web service in AX, we have to define a call context. This would normally define the security context and various login properties. We don't have to provide these details in this case, as we are logged on as a valid AX user, and will run this interactively.

11. Write the following lines of code in the `Main` method:

```
ConFMSServicesReference.CallContext context = new
ConFMSServicesReference.CallContext();
//context.LogonAsUser = "Contoso\\administrator";
//context.Language = "en-gb";
//context.Company = "usmf";
ConFMSServicesReference.ConFMSVehicleServicesClient
  client = new
     ConFMSServicesReference.ConFMSVehicleServicesClient();
String responseMessage = client.helloWorld(context);
Console.WriteLine(responseMessage);
responseMessage = client.helloWorldMyName(context,
                                         "Tyler");
Console.WriteLine(responseMessage);
responseMessage = client.helloWorldMyName(context,
                                         "Isabella");
Console.WriteLine(responseMessage);
Console.ReadKey();
```

12. Press *F5* to run the project. You should see the following response in the console window:

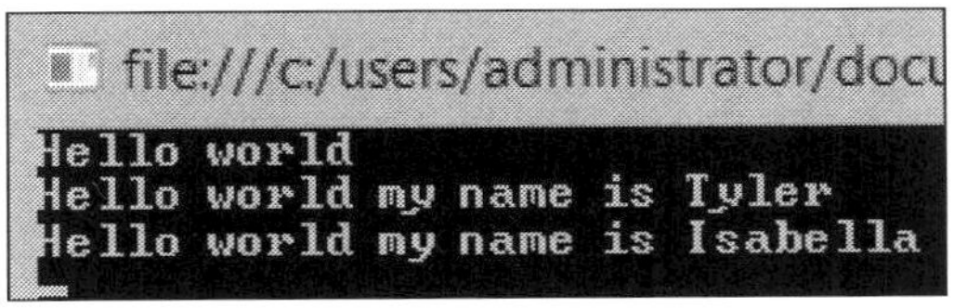

Creating a service method to change the vehicle group

Since we have done all of the hard work, we just need to create a method that accepts the `contract` and calls the `update` class.

Getting information from the infoLog object

We will need to return the error should the validation fail, which means we have to interrogate the `infoLog` object. Whenever we call `info`, `warning`, `error`, `checkFailed`, or `throw exception` (plus others), AX will add this to the session global `infoLog` object.

The data is stored in a container. A container is an unsorted, untyped set. There is no enumerator either, so we access its data through the `conPeek` command. We can test whether it is null using the `conNull` command.

We get the `infoLog` data using `infoLog.copy(from, to)`. This returns a container that will contain two or more elements from the range specified. The first is another container with one element of type integer. This describes the compatibility level of the data returned, and it should always be `1`. The subsequent elements are also a container each, containing the actual data from the requested `infoLog` records.

Each `infoLog` record container contains five elements:

1	An integer representing the exception level from the `Exception` enum.
2	The message text.
3	`HelpUrl` specified when the `infolog` was added. Usually, this is empty.
4	Class ID of the `SysInfoAction` class. 2071 is the default; it is the `SysInfoAction_Editor` class, which adds the `Edit` button to the `infoLog`.
5	A container that holds the call stack. `element 2` of this is the string AOT reference to the class that triggered the `infoLog` message.

If the `infoLog.copy(from, to)` command returns no data or the `infoLog` object is empty, it returns a null container.

To get the current `infoLog` line number (the last message), we use the `infologLine()` command.

The following job highlights how we would use this to get the last message from the `infoLog` object:

```
static void conGetInfoFromInfoLog(Args _args)
{
    container infologData, infologInnerData;
    str       message;
```

```
        info("Message 1");
        info("Message 2");

        infologData = infolog.copy(infologLine(), infologLine());
        if(infologData != conNull())
        {
            //get data (2nd element) from the outer container
            infologInnerData = conPeek(infologData, 2);
            //get message text (2nd element) from the inner container
            message = conPeek(infologInnerData, 2);

            info(message);
        }
    }
```

> When we need to write snippets of code similar to what was just covered, it is often easier to write it first as a job to test that it works, before we use it in its correct place.

We just used a hardcoded number, where it would be ideal if there were a standard macro or function call that gets this information for us. In these cases, there isn't, so this will need to be documented for future upgrades. As it stands, we will need to verify that this code still works after an upgrade. We will use this technique to return validation errors, if any, to the caller.

Creating the updateVehicleGroup service method

To process the service request we need a `ConFMSVehicleGroupChangeContract` object, and we will return a status.

The method is like what we did before, and is done by the following steps:

1. On the `ConFMSVehicleServices` class, create a new method called `updateVehicleGroup`.
2. The code is very similar to the method we wrote in the `updateVehicle` method on the drop dialog form, and it should be as follows:

```
[AifCollectionTypeAttribute('return', Types::String),
 SysEntryPointAttribute(true)]
public str updateVehicleGroup (ConFMSVehicleGroupChangeContract
_contract)
{
```

```
    str returnMsg;
    container infologData, infologInnerData;
    ConFMSVehicleGroupChange change =
  ConFMSVehicleGroupChange::newFromContract(_contract);
    if(change.validate())
    {
        change.run();
        returnMsg = "OK";
    }
    else
    {
        infologData = infolog.copy(infologLine(),
                                   infologLine());
        if(infologData != conNull())
        {
                  //the data we need is in the 2nd element
                  //of the outer container
                  infologInnerData = conPeek(infologData, 2);
                  //the message is in the 2nd element of the
                  //inner container
            returnMsg = conPeek(infologInnerData, 2);
        }
    }
    return returnMsg;
}
```

3. We now need to add this new service method as an operation to our service. Right-click on the `ConFMSVehicleServices` service and choose **Add Operation**.
4. Check the `updateVehicleGroup` method and press **OK**.
5. We now need to redeploy the service group, which is done as before—by right-clicking on the `ConFMSServices` service group and choosing **Deploy Service Group**.

Updating the Visual Studio service test project

We will simply update the project to run some tests on the service method and see yet another benefit of the pattern of decoupling the data contract from the object that processes it.

Before we write the test project, create a vehicle group, `Fleet`, and ensure that we have a vehicle with `V0001` as the vehicle ID, or change the following code so that it references a matching vehicle. We will test each combination to ensure that the validation works with the following steps:

1. In Visual Studio, using the same project you used earlier, right-click on **ConFMSServicesReference**, which is under **Service References**, and select **Update** Service Reference.

   > We now have a new class, `ConFMSVehicleGroupChangeContract`, which we can use. We will use this to test the service.

2. To reduce the typing, add a `using` command at the top:

   ```
   using ConFMSVehicleServicesTest.ConFMSServicesReference;
   ```

3. Let's move the code around a little; create a new `static` method as follows:

   ```
   public static void updateVehicleGroup()
   {
       CallContext context =
           new ConFMSServicesReference.CallContext();
       ConFMSVehicleServicesClient client =
           new ConFMSVehicleServicesClient();
       ConFMSVehicleGroupChangeContract contract =
           new ConFMSVehicleGroupChangeContract();

       Console.WriteLine("Should work");
       contract.vehicleGroupId = "Fleet";
       contract.vehicleId = "V0001";
       string msg =
           client.updateVehicleGroup(context, contract);
       Console.WriteLine(msg);

       Console.WriteLine("Vehicle Id should be invalid");
       contract.vehicleGroupId = "Fleet";
       contract.vehicleId = "ILB001";
       msg = client.updateVehicleGroup(context, contract);
   ```

```
        Console.WriteLine(msg);

        Console.WriteLine("Vehicle group should be invalid");
        contract.vehicleGroupId = "TLB001";
        contract.vehicleId = "V0001";
        msg = client.updateVehicleGroup(context, contract);
        Console.WriteLine(msg);

        Console.ReadKey();
    }
```

4. Update the code in the call to this in the `Main` method to read like this:

```
static void Main(string[] args)
{
    Program.updateVehicleGroup();
}
```

5. Press *F5* to run the code. The result should be similar to the following screenshot:

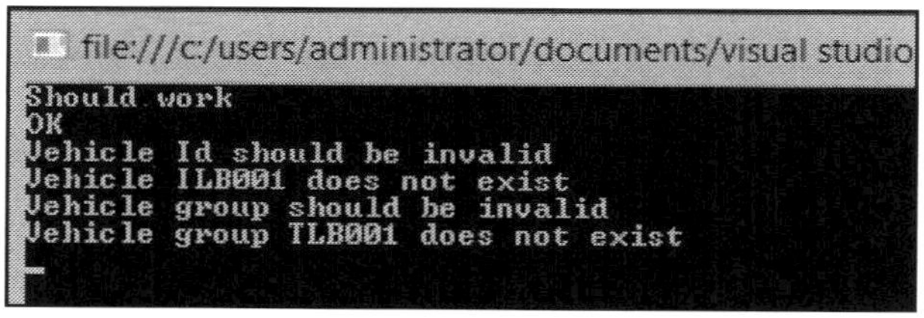

Creating a service method to return a list of vehicle groups

In this example, we will create a service method that returns a list of vehicle group records as data contracts. Rather than returning a full list, we will use a technique so that the caller can specify a query that we will process within the service method.

The way in which we can pass a generic query definition is by using the class `AifQueryCriteria`. This allows us to create a generic query definition, but in order to use it, we need to convert it to a `Query` object.

The fact that `AifQueryCriteria` is generic also means that there is no type-based validation when we come to use it; we could add elements for tables and fields that could cause our service method to fail. Although we can validate the object inside the service method, it doesn't help a developer who doesn't understand the data structures within AX.

Writing a data contract class to define the criteria can be complicated, especially if we need it to be flexible. So, a suitable solution to this would be to write a service method that provides a list of field names with their types.

Creating a utility method to convert an AifQueryCriteria object to a Query object

The utility method we will create ranges on a `Query` object from the criteria elements within an `AifQueryCriteria` object. It does this by looping through each criteria element, finding or creating a data source on the `Query` object, and adding the criteria element as a range to the data source. The `queryValue` method ensures that the value added to the range is safe, and prevents code injection.

On the class `ConFMSUtil`, create the following method:

```
public static Query buildQueryFromAifQueryCriteria(
                            AifQueryCriteria _criteria)
{
    counter                  idx;
    AifCriteriaElement       element;
    Query                    query = new Query();
    QueryBuildDataSource     dataSource;
    QueryBuildRange          range;
    for(idx = 1;
        idx <= _criteria.getCriteriaElementCount();
        idx++)
    {
        element = _criteria.getCriteriaElement(idx);
        dataSource = SysQuery::findOrCreateDataSource(query,
                   tableName2id(element.getDataSourceName()));
        switch(element.getOperator())
        {
            case AifCriteriaOperator::Equal:
                range = SysQuery::findOrCreateRange(dataSource,
                            fieldName2id(dataSource.table(),
                                        element.getFieldName()));
                range.value(queryValue(element.getValue1()));
                break;
            case AifCriteriaOperator::Greater:
                range = SysQuery::findOrCreateRange(dataSource,
                            fieldName2id(dataSource.table(),
                                       element.getFieldName()));
                range.value(">" +
                            queryValue(element.getValue1()));
```

```
                break;
            case AifCriteriaOperator::GreaterOrEqual:
                range = SysQuery::findOrCreateRange(dataSource,
                            fieldName2id(dataSource.table(),
                                        element.getFieldName()));
                range.value(queryValue(element.getValue1())+"..");
                break;
            case AifCriteriaOperator::Less:
                range = SysQuery::findOrCreateRange(dataSource,
                            fieldName2id(dataSource.table(),
                                         element.getFieldName()));
                range.value("<" +
                            queryValue(element.getValue1()));
                break;
            case AifCriteriaOperator::LessOrEqual:
                range = SysQuery::findOrCreateRange(dataSource,
                            fieldName2id(dataSource.table(),
                                         element.getFieldName()));
                range.value(".." +
                            queryValue(element.getValue1()));
                break;
            case AifCriteriaOperator::NotEqual:
                range = SysQuery::findOrCreateRange(dataSource,
                            fieldName2id(dataSource.table(),
                                         element.getFieldName()));
                range.value("!" +
                            queryValue(element.getValue1()));
                break;
            case AifCriteriaOperator::Range:
                range = SysQuery::findOrCreateRange(dataSource,
                            fieldName2id(dataSource.table(),
                                         element.getFieldName()));
                range.value(queryValue(element.getValue1())+".."+
                            queryValue(element.getValue2()));
                break;
        }
    }
    return query;
}
```

Creating a vehicle group data contract

Next, we need to create a data contract based on the table `ConFMSVehicleGroup`. This is no different from the contract created earlier, and should be written as follows:

```
[DataContractAttribute]
class ConFMSVehicleGroupContract
{
    ConFMSVehicleGroupId vehicleGroupId;
    Description          description;
}
[DataMemberAttribute]
public ConFMSVehicleGroupId vehicleGroupId(ConFMSVehicleGroupId
                               _vehicleGroupId = vehicleGroupId)
{
    vehicleGroupId = _vehicleGroupId;
    return vehicleGroupId;
}
[DataMemberAttribute]
public Description description(Description
                               _description = description)
{
    description = _description;
    return description;
}
public static ConFMSVehicleGroupContract construct()
{
    return new ConFMSVehicleGroupContract();
}
```

To simplify its usage, we will add a method to the `ConFMSVehicleGroup` table to construct the contract. Create the following method:

```
public ConFMSVehicleGroupContract contract()
{
    ConFMSVehicleGroupContract contract;
    contract = ConFMSVehicleGroupContract::construct();
    contract.vehicleGroupId(this.VehicleGroupId);
    contract.description(this.Description);
    return contract;
}
```

Creating the service method

The interesting part of this method is the decoration. We need to return a typed list of objects to the caller, and in AX, we do this using the following decoration:

```
[AifCollectionTypeAttribute('return', Types::Class,
                            classStr(ConFMSVehicleGroupContract)),
                            SysEntryPointAttribute(true)]
```

Even though we will return a `List` object, the preceding lines of code will tell the caller what type of the list is `ConFMSVehicleGroupContract[]`.

The equivalent code in C# is:

```
public ConFMSVehicleGroupContract[] vehicleGroups(...)
```

The method we will write next will perform the following:

- Have an `AifQueryCriteria` object as its parameter
- Convert the `AifQueryCriteria` object to a `Query` object
- Process the query and add matching records as data contracts to a `List` object
- Return the resulting `List` object

This is accomplished by the following code:

```
[AifCollectionTypeAttribute('return', Types::Class,
                            classStr(ConFMSVehicleGroupContract)),
                            SysEntryPointAttribute(true)]
public List retrieveVehicleGroupQuery(AifQueryCriteria _criteria)
{
    List                groupList = new List(Types::Class);
    Query               q;
    QueryRun            qr;
    ConFMSVehicleGroup vehicleGroup;

    q = ConFMSUtil:: buildQueryFromAifQueryCriteria(_criteria));
    qr = new QueryRun(q);
    while (qr.next())
    {
        vehicleGroup = qr.get(tableNum(ConFMSVehicleGroup);
        groupList.addEnd(vehicleGroup.contract());
    }
    return groupList;
}
```

Finally, we need to add the method as an operation to the `ConFMSVehicleServices` service and deploy the `ConFMSServices` service group.

> If you have renamed or deleted any types, you must generate a full CIL, otherwise, the deploy action will generate an incremental CIL for us.

Using the new service within the Visual Studio test project

In this example, we will return a list of all vehicle groups that matches a specified criterion. To test this, we will need the following setup data in the `ConFMSVehicleGroup` table:

Vehicle group	Description
Fleet	Fleet
Group	Description
I-Artic	Own fleet-Articulated truck
I-Car	Own fleet-Car
I-Van	Own fleet-Van
J-Car	J-Car

We have updated the service, so the first step is to refresh the `ConFMSServiceReference` service reference within the Visual Studio project we created earlier. To do this, right-click on it and select **Update Service Reference**.

Create a new method in `Program.cs` as follows:

```
public static void retrieveVehicleGroups()
{
    CallContext context =
        new ConFMSServicesReference.CallContext();
    ConFMSVehicleServicesClient client =
        new ConFMSVehicleServicesClient();
    ConFMSVehicleGroupContract[] vehicleGroups;

    QueryCriteria criteria = new QueryCriteria();
    CriteriaElement criteriaElement = new CriteriaElement();

    criteriaElement.DataSourceName = "ConFMSVehicleGroup";
```

```
        criteriaElement.FieldName = "VehicleGroupId";
        criteriaElement.Operator = Operator.Range;
        criteriaElement.Value1 = "I";
        criteriaElement.Value2 = "J";
        criteria.CriteriaElement = new CriteriaElement[1];
        criteria.CriteriaElement[0] = criteriaElement;
        vehicleGroups = client.retrieveVehicleGroupQuery(context,
                                                  criteria);
        foreach(ConFMSVehicleGroupContract contract in vehicleGroups)
        {
            Console.WriteLine("Vehicle Group: " +
                          contract.vehicleGroupId +
                          "(" + contract.description +  ")");
        }
        Console.ReadKey();
    }
```

> If the `ConFMSVehicleGroupContract` type does not exist, ensure that CIL is generated and the service group is redeployed.

We used `Operator.Range` as the operator because we couldn't use wildcards. To make the calls safe, we used the function `queryValue` in the code that converts the `AifQueryCriteria` object to a `Query` object. This has the effect of replacing the `*` with a literal, that is, `I*` would return vehicle groups that have the ID `I*`.

In the `Main` method, replace the call to `updateVehicleGroup` to call `retrieveVehicleGroups`, instead. When it is run this time, you should get the following output:

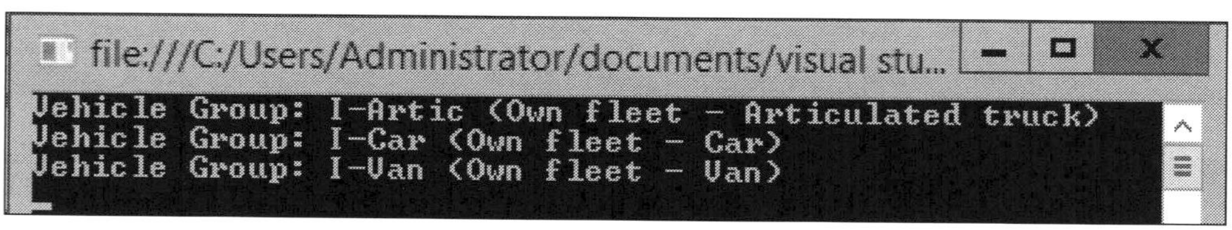

You will see, from this demonstration, that it is quite simple to expose the Dynamics AX functionality as a service that can be consumed by other external applications throughout the organization. This could be on production control systems, door entry systems, tablets, phones, or any other type of device.

The work required to extend the solution outside of AX was minimal. We could very easily write a service method that allows us to change the vehicle status via a mobile device; we would just reuse the code that we wrote in the *Using menu items to change the vehicle status* section.

> This is not a way to get free user CALs. When using code in this way, they are licensed as a device CAL. You can download the Dynamics AX 2012 licensing and pricing guide from `http://www.microsoft.com/en-us/dynamics/resource-library.aspx?SortField1=Microsoft%20Dynamics%20AX&SortField2=Licensing`.

Summary

In this chapter, we extended our solution to see how we can easily extend list pages to show pertinent data to users with minimal effort. We also saw that writing code in a service-oriented approach (with data decoupled from the processing classes) allowed us to easily reuse the business logic, even outside AX.

In the next chapter, we will cover creating the security model for our solution.

7
Designing Your Security Model

In this chapter, we will go through the design of the security for our application, which will be used by the security administrator to assign relevant roles to users.

We will cover the following topics:

- Setting up license and configuration keys
- Designing the security structure
- Creating privileges
- Creating duties
- Creating roles
- Providing access to server methods—code permissions
- Designing and creating process cycles
- Restricting access to data using policies

Setting up license and configuration keys

These are most relevant to organizations that create solutions that are used by more than one end user organization, such as an ISV.

License keys are only available for ISVs and allow them to control access to their software. These are not relevant to users, except that we may remove a license key if a block of functionality is not required.

Configuration keys allow us to enable or disable functionality system-wide. We typically associate these keys with extended data types, tables, and menu items, and if the associated key is disabled, it will appear to the user interface as if the associated entities do not exist.

> Configuration keys can be associated with other types of objects, even buttons on forms, but this would involve a lot of maintenance and is to be avoided. The rule of making a change at the lowest level applies here too.

Configuration keys are sometimes used by end user organizations if they are creating a solution that is also used by sister companies, or by a VAR that creates a vertical solution for their customers. In this way, we can write an application, allowing the customer to decide which elements of the solution are available.

Configuration keys are managed by navigating to **System administration** | **Setup** | **Licensing** | **License configuration**, as shown in the following screenshot:

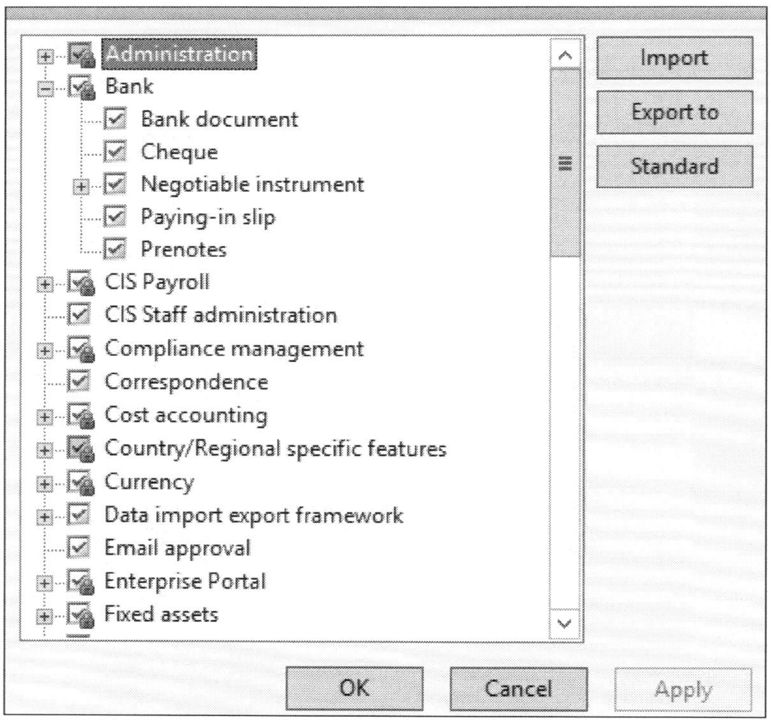

In the preceding example, you can see that configuration keys are nested and some of the root elements are locked. This is because the configuration key is linked directly to a license key. To disable these keys, the license code must be disabled using the neighboring **License information** form.

We can see this in the AOT by navigating to **Data Dictionary** | **Configuration Keys**, as shown in this screenshot:

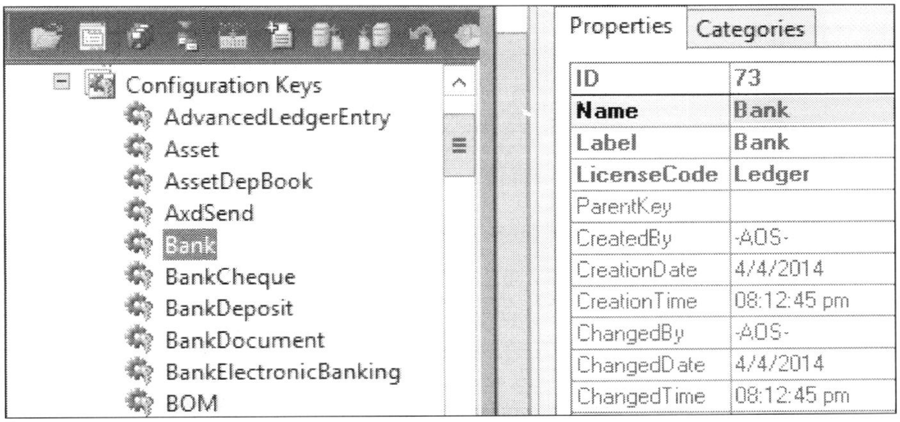

The `BankCheque`, `BankDeposit`, and other configuration keys have the **ParentKey** property set to `Bank`, causing it to be nested in the **License configuration** form.

The configuration keys are then associated with extended data types, menu items, tables, and views by the element's **ConfigurationKey** property. Be careful! Disabled configuration keys remove data from tables, although the physical table will still exist, which is useful if we have analysis services cubes that use the tables in their data view definition.

Should a view include data from a table that is disabled through a configuration key, you will get a warning when synchronizing the database that the view cannot be created.

Legacy security features

In prior editions of Dynamics AX, security was also based on keys, which are still in the AOT under **Security Keys** in **Data Dictionary**. These were complicated to set up, and were based on the idea of placing users in user groups. The new security design does not use security keys or user groups.

Designing the security structure

The new design is role-based and has been created with the organization's roles in mind, making it a much more natural fit. We can even automate the assignment of security roles based on the user's position in the organization, so by promoting a user to a production manager in human resources, we automatically assign them the appropriate role in the security model.

The security system in AX operates by controlling access to menu items. Much of the security architecture is based on this. When we added form parts, you may have wondered why we don't just drag the part onto the form. It is because we control access to the form part through the menu item, wherever it may appear. This is also why every button we add is linked to a menu item.

Dynamics AX is shipped with many roles controlling access to the standard features, and when we write a new module, we should do the same so that users can simply be assigned a security role. When extending an existing module, we will also need to adjust the security of the standard role to include the new feature(s) so that we can control who has what access, and at what level.

The security model in AX 2012 is broken down into the following structure:

- Process cycles
- Roles
- Duties
- Privileges
- Policies
- Code permissions

The primary structure of the security model includes process cycles, roles, duties, and privileges. We will explore these first, before taking a look at policies and code permissions.

Process cycles contain duties, and each duty belongs to a process cycle. They have no security function, but instead provide a logical grouping for the security administrator that reflects the business process that its duties are part of. If you are to create a new duty, it must be created within a process cycle.

The remaining parts are structured as follows:

- **Roles**: These contain duties, privileges, permissions, and subroles
- **Duties**: These contain privileges
- **Privileges**: These contain entry points and permissions

So, assigning a role effectively boils down to the assignment of privileges, and with them, their entry points and permissions.

Entry points define the access level of entry to AX functionality granted to methods, such as menu items, and services.

Permissions define access to tables, fields, server methods (code that runs on the server tier), and form controls (buttons, fields, or other controls placed on a form).

As part of the solution design, business processes are analyzed along with the roles that perform them. The business processes will then be mapped to AX's system processes. This is used for many purposes, including gap fit level, training plans, testing plans, and so on. This method of analyzing roles and processes also fits nicely into the AX security model, allowing the security model to be designed based on it.

The security model that we design and implement should always be simple to use, following the pattern of the standard roles provided by Microsoft. An important design principle is to think of the users' roles, and not of specific users, which should result in the following outcomes:

- Reduced number of roles
- Less complicated assignment of users to roles
- Roles are easier to maintain, with reduced risk of errors, such as unintended assignment of a privilege to a user

Impact on licensing

AX is licensed based on named users of a certain type (enterprise, functional, task, and self-service). Based on your organization's requirements, a mix of **client access license** (CAL) types can be bought.

> A device CAL can also be bought, but this is not determined by the application logic.

The user's CAL type is determined by the entry points (effectively, the menu items) to which they have read access or higher. For each menu item, we have two properties that control which license type will be required:

- `ViewUserLicense`: When a user is given read access to this menu item
- `MaintainUserLicense`: When the user is given `Update` or higher access to this menu item

The CAL type is determined by the highest user license type to which the user is assigned. We are not forced to enter values in these menu item properties, but it would be a breach of the license agreement to create a menu item to open a standard form if we don't match the user license type of the original menu item. Microsoft reserves the right, at their expense, to inspect the system.

> Security administrators should plan a cyclic approach to security. Check with the **Named User License Counts** report and adapt the security setup to ensure that you are complying with the license.
>
> Checking and maintaining license compliance is the license holder's responsibility.

For more information, from a system administrator's perspective, please see the book *Microsoft Dynamics AX 2012 R2 Administration Cookbook, Packt Publishing*.

Designing the security structure

The first part of the design is to determine the roles and duties of the users who will use our Fleet Management System.

As part of the analysis, the system will be used by the following roles:

- **Fleet management supervisor**: This is responsible for the vehicle and associated service data, and has full access to fleet management data.
- **Fleet management clerk**: This is responsible for checking vehicle and service data. It can fully maintain vehicle service records and edit the basic vehicle data. It must not be able to change the vehicle group or status.
- **Fleet management service clerk**: This is responsible for updating service data. It can create new service records but cannot delete existing records. It can also view vehicle data.

This description gives us the roles and duties, and from these, we can add the necessary privileges to the appropriate duty.

Adding roles is typical when we are extending the reach of Dynamics AX into new areas of our organization. If we are providing new functionality for existing roles within the organization, we may just create duties and privileges and leave it to the security administrator to add the new duties to the appropriate security role.

This goes for privileges too. If we are merely adding a new feature to a form that is part of an existing role's duty, we would just create a privilege for that menu item and add it to the existing duty. The roles that have that duty would automatically get the new privilege.

In our case, we are replacing a paper-based system, so the roles, duties, and privileges are all new. The statement of the roles earlier implied that the roles have certain duties—what they are responsible for. From each role, the duties will be mapped as follows:

Role	Responsible for / duties
Fleet management supervisor	Maintaining vehicle information Maintaining vehicle service records Maintaining fleet management setup Maintaining vehicle status Maintaining vehicle group
Fleet management clerk	Updating vehicle information Maintaining vehicle service records
Fleet management service clerk	Creating and updating vehicle service records Viewing vehicle records

The requirement of the `Maintain vehicle status` and `Maintain vehicle group` duties is implied in the role's description, as it is stated that the fleet management clerk should not have access to these features.

The design of the duties should be granular enough to be able to define the roles' permissions, while limiting the number of duties so that it is easy to maintain. We can add a privilege directly to a role, but this should only be done when absolutely necessary, as it increases the work required to maintain role permissions.

Privileges are related to one or more menu items, and each menu item must be in at least one privilege in order to be accessible to users. This is except for those in the system administrator role, who have full access to the entire system.

As the privilege determines the access level, we will often create at least two privileges for each set of menu items—one for view and one for maintain. The actual levels available are listed here in ascending order:

- `NoAccess`: The menu item will not display on the form.
- `Read`: The data opened from the menu item will be read-only.
- `Update`: The associated data can be edited, but the user will not be able to create new records.
- `Create`: This allows records to be created in the form opened via this menu item.
- `Correct`: This allows us to correct time-valid state records. This allows a user to correct time-sensitive data, such as employee information, where a change would normally create a new time-valid record. This is covered in the *Exception handling* section in *Chapter 10, Advanced Development Techniques*.
- `Delete`: This provides full access and allows us to perform all functions from read to delete to forms opened by this menu item.

When we add menu items to a form, there is a property on the button control called **NeededPermission**. If the access level on the privilege is less than the **NeededPermission** property, the button will not appear to the user.

We define a set as the menu items that make up the privilege. Since this is the most granular level, it is common to have privileges with just one menu item. Again, we want to keep this manageable, so if two menu items always have the same permission, they should be in the same privilege.

For further reading on role-based security in AX 2012, visit `http://msdn.microsoft.com/en-us/library/gg847971.aspx`.

Creating privileges

Before we start, we have to decide which model the security elements will go into. The consideration is that security is often configured by a consultant or someone in the organization responsible for maintaining security. The reason this is relevant is that the changes made in the client persist the changes back to the AOT, and therefore have to be deployed in the same way as our code is deployed.

Therefore, we often create a model specifically for security changes. In this way, they can be deployed separately in our code. Designing security is often an iterative process, and often there are many updates made during and after implementation.

We would create the security design in the same model as the main development if it is a vertical add-on. The end user organization will make changes in a specific model in their layer so as to not interfere with their other developments.

There is no specific rule for creating privileges, but we should ensure we provide enough granularity to enable the required duties to be created. We should also consider that privileges might be added to other duties by the security administrator.

The following is an example structure that would be appropriate, based on our menu items and required duties:

Privilege	Menu item	Access level
`ConFMSVehicleView`	`ConFMSVehicleTableListPageActive`	`Read`
	`ConFMSVehicleTableListPageInactiveAppt`	`Read`
	`ConFMSVehicleTable`	`Read`
	`ConFMSVehicleTableForNew`	`NoAccess`
	`ConFMSVehicleTableForEdit`	`Read`
	`ConFMSVehicleTableListPage`	`Read`
`ConFMSVehicleEdit`	`ConFMSVehicleTableListPageActive`	`Update`
	`ConFMSVehicleTableListPageInactiveAppt`	`Update`
	`ConFMSVehicleTable`	`Update`
	`ConFMSVehicleTableForNew`	`NoAccess`
	`ConFMSVehicleTableForEdit`	`Update`
	`ConFMSVehicleTableListPage`	`Update`

Privilege	Menu item	Access level
ConFMSVehicle Maintain	ConFMSVehicle TableListPageActive ConFMSVehicleTable ListPageInactiveAppt ConFMSVehicleTable ConFMSVehicleTableForNew ConFMSVehicleTableForEdit ConFMSVehicleTableListPage	Delete Delete Delete Delete Delete Delete
ConFMSVehicleSetup Maintain	ConFMSVehicleGroup ConFMSVehicleSchedule	Delete Delete
ConFMSVehicleAcquire	ConFMSVehicle StatusChangeCreated ConFMSVehicle StatusChangeAcquired	Update Update
ConFMSVehicleActive	ConFMSVehicle StatusChangeActive	Update
ConFMSVehicleUnavailable	ConFMSVehicle StatusChangeUnavailable	Update
ConFMSVehicleDispose	ConFMSVehicle StatusChangeDisposed	Update
ConFMSVehicleTable GroupMaintain	ConFMSVehicle GroupChange	Update
ConFMSVehicleInfoParts	ConFMSVehicle UtilisationPart ConFMSAppoint mentPart ConFMSAppointment VehicleCue ConFMSVehService TableCuePart ConFMSVehicle RelatedInfoCueGroup ConFMSVehicle TablePart ConFMSVehicle AppointmentPart ConFMSVehService TableListPageCue	Update Update Update Update Update Update Update Update

Privilege	Menu item	Access level
ConFMSVehicle ServiceMaintain	ConFMSVehService TableListPage ConFMSVehService Table ConFMSVehService TableEditGrid ConFMSVehService TableForEdit ConFMSVehService TableForNew	Delete Delete Delete Delete Delete
ConFMSVehicle ServiceView	ConFMSVehService TableListPage ConFMSVehService Table ConFMSVehService TableEditGrid ConFMSVehService TableForEdit ConFMSVehService TableForNew	Read Read Read Read NoAccess
ConFMSVehicle ServiceCreate	ConFMSVehService TableListPage ConFMSVehService Table ConFMSVehService TableEditGrid ConFMSVehService TableForEdit ConFMSVehService TableForNew	Create Create Create Create Create

The parts have `Update` access, as the data is read-only and the form parts may have controls that require the user to complete, such as the vehicle utilization part.

To create this structure, follow these steps:

1. In our project, create a new privilege named `ConFMSVehicleView` by navigating to **Security** | **Privileges**.
2. Set the **Label** property to `View vehicle information`. The label will appear to the user configuring security in the client.
3. Enter a longer description for the privilege as required. This also appears when configuring security in the client.
4. Drag the required menu items (as listed in the preceding table) onto the **Entry Points** node and set the **AccessLevel** appropriately.

Repeat this for each privilege.

How privileges affect security and user experience

A user with the `ConFMSVehicleView` privilege will have the following available in the **Fleet management system** menu:

- Vehicles
- Active vehicles
- Inactive with appointment

The **Setup** menu and forms related to service data are not visible. Furthermore, the action bar on the **Vehicles list** page will look like this:

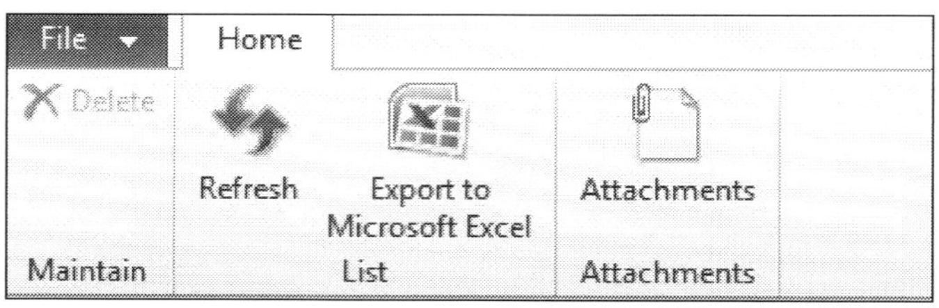

The buttons for the vehicle status, vehicle group change, and service details have been taken away, which is expected because the privilege did not have these as entry points.

However, the buttons for **New**, **Edit**, and **Edit in grid** are also not visible. The reason is that these menu items have the **OpenMode** property set to higher than **View**. The **Delete** button appears, but it is disabled. This is because it is a `CommandButton`, and so it is automatically disabled because the user only has `Read` access.

Without the **Edit** button the user has no obvious way to open the details form, unless they remember that they can double-click on the vehicle record on the grid. The template form we created this form from does have a **View** button, which is triggered by the double-click event, but this is hidden by default. To solve this issue, we can change the button's **Visible** property to `Yes`. On the details form, the following is shown:

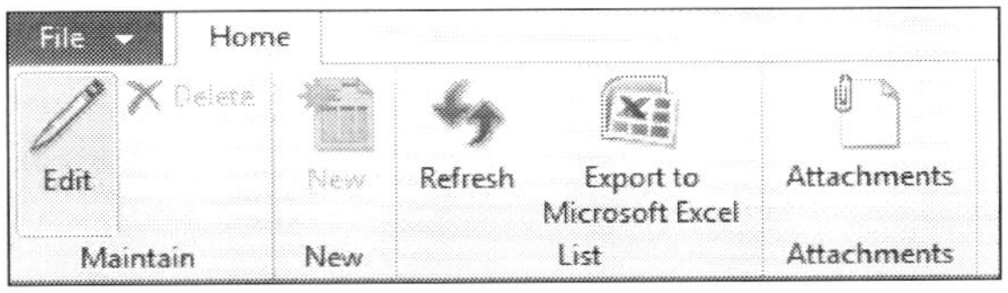

The buttons for **Edit**, **Delete**, and **New** are `CommandButtons` and will therefore not be hidden from the user. The interesting part here is that the **Edit** button is not disabled. It still triggers the form event, but even so, the user will not be able to edit records. This is not ideal, and the action bar would be much cleaner if the buttons didn't display at all.

Hiding buttons that the user has no access to

To hide these buttons, we have two options: adjusting the form control or adding the form control to the privilege.

There is a reason that there are two options. Adding the control to the privilege avoids modifying standard forms (or any that are in a layer lower than our own). But if we are the authors of the form, adjusting the form is by far the better option, as we will see.

To add a control to the privilege, follow these steps:

1. Drag the form onto the **Permissions** | **Forms** node of the privilege.
2. Right-click on the new node and choose **New Control**.
3. In the **Control** property, type the name of the control
4. Select the appropriate value for the `EffectiveAccess` property. To hide the control, make it `NoAccess`.

Since we are the authors of the forms, we will not do it in this way. Instead, we will achieve the same result by adjusting the form controls. Since we understand that, for example, the edit buttons require an access level of update, we can simply tell control it requires this permission. Each form control has a **NeededPermission** property. This functions as a minimum requirement for the control to be displayed to the user.

We should modify our forms, setting the **NeededPermission** property on the buttons not linked to a menu item, as follows:

Edit button	`Update`
Delete button	`Delete`
New button	`Create`

After this change is made to the `ConFMSVehicleTable` form, the action pane then looks like what is shown in the following screen shot:

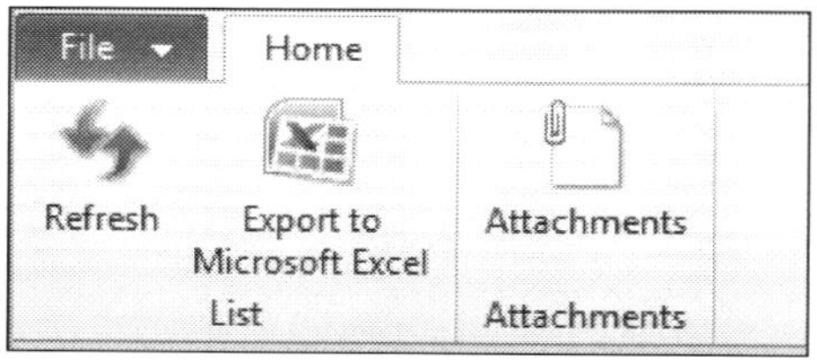

This is much cleaner, and only gives the options that the role requires.

Refining access to the data

By setting the **AccessLevel** on the entry point, we also determine the maximum access level for the data sources in the form that the menu item opens. By maximum access, we mean that the **AccessLevel** can't be used to override the **AllowEdit** property of the data source or table.

On occasion, we may need to override this, and we have a requirement for the `ConFMSVehicleEdit` privilege: we don't want the user to be able to edit the status or group fields.

To do this, we add the table and the applicable fields to the privilege, as follows:

1. Drag the `ConFMSVehicleTable` table to the **| Tables** node (found under **Permissions**) of the `ConFMSVehicleEdit` privilege.
2. **EffectiveAccess** will default to `Read`; we should change this to `Update`. The permission should be able to edit vehicle data, and this would override the **AccessLevel** on the `ConFMSVehicleTable` **Entry point**.
3. Right-click on the new node and select **New Field**.

> You can also drag the field from the table to this node.

4. Change **Field** to `VehicleStatusId`.
5. Change **EffectiveAccess** to `Read`. You will see that the maximum access is `Update`. This is because we set the table's `EffectiveAccess` to `Update`.
6. Repeat this for `VehicleGroupId`.

Providing access to services

We also need to create a privilege so that a service can be invoked by external applications. Currently only the system administrator role can execute services in our `ConFMSVehicleServices` class, such as the `updateVehicleGroup` method.

The privilege we need is created as follows:

1. Create a new privilege named `ConFMSVehicleServices` by navigating to **Security | Privileges**.
2. The label should be clear that this is providing access to service methods and not the service data, for example, `Access to vehicle service methods`.
3. Add description to describe what this will do.
4. Create a new entry point under the privilege's **Entry points** node named `VehicleServiceUpdateVehicleGroup`, and open the property sheet.
5. Set **ObjectType** to `ServiceOperation`.
6. Select `updateVehicleGroup` in **ObjectChildName**; this lists the appropriate server methods.
7. Change **AccessLevel** to `Invoke`.

Server methods

Server methods are used to provide code permission to a static method that runs on the server tier. These will be covered later when we discuss code permissions.

Creating duties

When designing the security model, duties were decided upon. Creating the duties and adding the relevant permissions is therefore straightforward.

There is one set of privileges that we didn't include in the role duties—the `ConFMSVehicleInfoParts` privilege. The reason these were created in a separate privilege is that we may add these parts to other parts of the system, as we did on the appointment form. The security administrator can then add this privilege to the appropriate duties and/or roles.

We will create a specific duty for this privilege in order to avoid having to add the privilege directly to a role. We may later develop new parts that should be included in this duty, adding the new privileges to the duty avoids the need to adjust the role.

The mapping from duties to privileges is as follows:

Duty	Privilege
`ConFMSVehicleMaintain` Maintaining vehicle information	`ConFMSVehicleMaintain`
`ConFMSVehicleServiceMaintain` Maintaining vehicle service records	`ConFMSVehicleServiceMaintain`
`ConFMSVehicleSetupMaintain` Maintaining fleet management setup	`ConFMSVehicleSetupMaintain`

`ConFMSVehicleStatusMaintain`
Maintaining vehicle status
	`ConFMSVehicleActive`
	`ConFMSVehicleUnavailable`
	`ConFMSVehicleDispose`
	`ConFMSVehicleAcquire`

`ConFMSVehicleTableGroupMaintain` Maintaining vehicle group for a vehicle	`ConFMSVehicleTableGroup` `Maintain`
`ConFMSVehicleEdit` Updating current vehicle information	`ConFMSVehicleEdit`
`ConFMSVehicleServiceView` Viewing vehicle service records.	`ConFMSVehicleServiceView`

Duty	Privilege
`ConFMSVehicleServiceCreate` Creation of vehicle service records	`ConFMSVehicleServiceCreate`
`ConFMSVehicleInfoParts` Viewing vehicle and service information parts	`ConFMSVehicleInfoParts`
`ConFMSVehicleServices` Invoking vehicle service server methods	`ConFMSVehicleServices`

To create the duties, follow these steps for each duty in the preceding table:

1. Create a new duty under the project's **Security** | **Duties** node named according to the table.
2. Provide a label that provides a short description of the duty, and **Description** as appropriate.
3. Drag the appropriate privileges onto the **Privileges** node of the duty.

We can now add the duties to roles.

Creating roles

As with duties, creating roles is a simple process and we have already covered most of the concepts. The role has four nodes:

- **Duties**
- **Privileges**
- **Permissions**
- **Sub Roles**

The **Sub Roles** node is interesting, as it allows us to create a nested role. The parent inherits the attributes from the **Sub Roles** node, and can tailor them further.

> You can have only three levels of roles. The warning AX gives you only counts roles that have the **Enabled** property set to `Yes`; but the compiler requires that three is the maximum level, regardless of whether or not it is enabled.
>
> The three-level limit may seem to be a limitation at the first glance, but **Sub Roles** are actually rarely used. They tend to bring more complexity than benefits.

In our case, we will only add duties to the roles, although you can add a specific privilege to a role if it simplifies the role definition. Adding privileges directly to a role should be the exception. Adding permissions directly should be avoided. The roles will map with duties as follows:

Role	**Duties**

`ConFMSFleetManagementSupervisor`
Fleet management supervisor
	`ConFMSVehicleMaintain`
	`ConFMSVehicleServiceMaintain`
	`ConFMSVehicleSetupMaintain`
	`ConFMSStatusMaintain`
	`ConFMSVehicleTableGroupMaintain`
	`ConFMSVehicleInfoParts`

`ConFMSFleetManagementClerk`
Fleet management clerk
	`ConFMSVehicleEdit`
	`ConFMSVehicleServiceMaintain`
	`ConFMSVehicleInfoParts`

`ConFMSFleetManagementServiceClerk`
Fleet management service clerk
	`ConFMSVehicleServiceCreate`
	`ConFMSVehicleView`
	`ConFMSVehicleInfoParts`

To create the aforementioned roles, follow these steps:

1. Create a new role under the project's **Security** | **Roles** node named according to the preceding table.
2. Drag the appropriate duty onto the role's **Duties** node.

Testing the security roles

Although we may have spent some time ensuring that the security setup is correct in theory, we need to test this. One method is to create a user for each role.

We're using the Contoso demonstration data. We need three users that do not have the `System Administrator` role, and have at least the `System User` role assigned.

The following users are appropriate for this:

User account	Role
`ELLEN`	Fleet management supervisor
`NANCY`	Fleet management clerk
`OSCAR`	Fleet management service clerk

We can assign the new roles to each user, or users to the roles. Either is fine; it depends on the situation. When testing roles, it is generally good practice to ensure that the user has only the `SystemUser` role assigned. In the following example, the users were selected such that their roles do not conflict.

In our case, we will do this from the **Users list** page, as follows:

1. Navigate to **System administration** | **Common** | **Users** | **Users**.
2. Filter the form to the relevant users: select the **Alias** column and press *Ctrl* + *F*. Enter `Ellen`, `Nancy`, `Oscar`.
3. Press **OK**.
4. Double-click on `ELLEN`.
5. In the User's roles fast tab, click on **Assign roles**.
6. Select **Fleet management supervisor** and press **OK**. The role should now be added to the list of roles in the User's roles fast tab.
7. In the same way, add the roles to the remaining users.

There are many ways to test this. One is to use a separate remote desktop session. A quicker method is to do the following:

1. Start Command Prompt.
2. Type `runas /user:Contoso\nancy cmd`.

3. Type the password when prompted; the standard password for Contoso is `pass@word1`.
4. Windows will open a new Command Prompt window; in it, type `ax32`. This runs the default configuration, which is fine in our example. In real life, we would use a `.AXC` shortcut that contains the connection details to the correct AX instance.

The Dynamics AX 2012 client will open under the security context of Nancy. See how to test the role-based security configurations under AOT security at `http://msdn.microsoft.com/en-us/library/gg845089.aspx`.

The relationship between client security tools and the AOT

When adjusting the roles, duties, and privileges, we have a choice between the AOT and the security tools within the client.

You can see the role definition by navigating to **System administration** | **Setup** | **Security roles**. Here, the **Label** and **Description** properties are displayed as fields and can also be edited. We can also add and remove duties and privileges and override the permissions.

One nice feature that is available in the client is that we can see the effective permissions for a role. The **Override permissions** button will open a form that evaluates all the duties and privileges, and then enumerates the resulting permissions. The form is intended to allow overriding these permissions, but it is useful to us as an inquiry tool. The following screenshot shows an example of this:

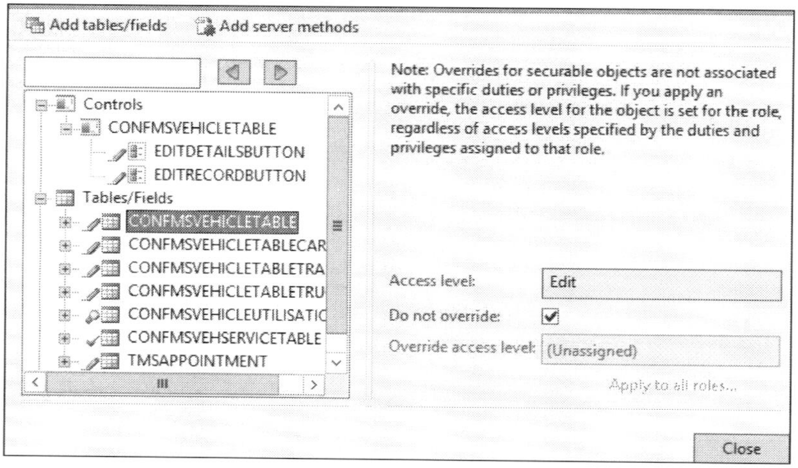

Pay attention to the warning on the form, and also note that there is no **Apply** button. If you make a change, it is written to the AOT, and there is no undo. It seems natural to assume that we are editing records in a table, but we are actually editing AOT elements effectively stored in the model store database, in the current layer and model. This is more important to security administrators, who may not understand the implications and the methodology around deploying code between environments.

The other effect of the AOT being the security form's effective data source is that if we have version control enabled, we will not be able to adjust security through the client. The client cannot check out AOT elements.

This is not normally an apparent concern to a security administrator, as they will not have version control enabled, but it does mean they can lose their changes if we redeploy the security model in the same layer. This means that we need clear roles and responsibilities in the development of the security design. One method would be that the developer (us) creates the initial design and has ongoing responsibility for privileges and code permissions. The roles and duties devolve to the security administrator.

This further reinforces the point that we must complete the label and descriptions for our elements to make them clear to those responsible for assigning appropriate roles.

Providing access to server methods – code permissions

Microsoft has published a very good article on how to create a code permission under AOT security at `http://msdn.microsoft.com/EN-US/library/gg880012.aspx`. To augment this article with a real-world example, we will build a feature that calls the service that updates the vehicle group. Code access permissions come into effect when the method has the `SysEntryPointAttribute` decoration.

This decoration has three outcomes:

- The method can be added to a service
- The code must run on the server tier
- The code will not run unless the user is given the specific permission to do so

We are concerned with the latter, and this does offer protection from inadvertent access to server methods. Security can become quite complicated, and it is possible that a server method is called by our code, to which the user should not have access for execution.

Due to the design of AX, this can't happen in the case of server methods (those that have `SysEntryPointAttribute`). It does not, however, prevent code from running that simply executes on the server tier; nor should it. Services are different and are considered as a securable object. This is why we need a privilege for services.

The best way to demonstrate this is with a code example. Follow these steps to set up the example:

1. Create a new class called `ConFMSSecurityTest`.
2. Create a method as follows:

```
public server static void testService()
{
    ConFMSVehicleServices
         service = new ConFMSVehicleServices();
    ConFMSVehicleGroupChangeContract
         contract =
           ConFMSVehicleGroupChangeContract::construct();
    contract.vehicleId("V0001"); // any valid vehicle id
    contract.vehicleGroupId("Fleet");
    service.updateVehicleGroup(contract);
}
```

> We need the `server` tag to ensure that the method runs on the server tier. Try calling this from a job without the `server` keyword. AX will throw an error and the execution will be terminated.

3. Create a form called `ConFMSSecurityTest`.
4. Add a button to the form, labeled `Press me`.
5. Override the clicked method and call our code, as follows:

```
ConFMSSecurityTest::testService();
```

6. Create a menu item for this form, with a label. Drag it onto our menu under **Periodic**.
7. Add this as an entry point to the `ConFMSVehicleView` privilege.
8. Log in as `Nancy`, open the new form, and press the button. You will get the following error:

```
Access denied to method updateVehicleGroup in class
ConFMSVehicleServices.
```

> Nancy and the ConFMSVehicleView privilege were deliberately chosen to highlight another feature. It will be discussed later in this section.

This situation wouldn't normally occur so simply. It usually occurs when the user starts a routine that, at some point during the execution of events, calls a server method. Although we endeavor to get this right first time, we will often realize that during testing, we find errors like this.

The other important point here is that code changes can cause regression in unexpected places. Let's say we decide to rewrite our code to make better use of AX frameworks. Testing that the code executes as a system administrator is not sufficient. As our knowledge increases, we circumvent these issues, in this case by adding a code permission. However, we will still need to test that the user can do their job. Conversely, we must also be sure to test that users do not acquire more permissions unintentionally.

Code access permissions for a privilege

We can add a permission to a privilege so that it can invoke server methods. This is not commonly done, and it is often better to have a separate privilege, as this aids granularity, ergo more flexibility when we create duties.

The following demonstration is intended to show that a permission to invoke a server method is not sufficient. AX will also check table permissions. These steps will add a code access permission to invoke the `ConFMSVehicleServices.updateVehicleGroup` server method on the `ConFMSVehicleView` privilege:

1. Expand the `ConFMSVehicleView` privilege. Right-click on **Permissions | Server Methods**, and select **New Server Method**.
2. Enter `ConFMSVehicleServices` in the **Class** property and type `updateVehicleGroup` in the **Method** name.
3. Set **EffectiveAccess** to `Invoke`.
4. Log in as `Nancy` and try to click on **Press me again**.

This time, we (correctly) get another error message:

```
User 'NANCY' is not authorized to select a record in table
'ConFMSVehicleGroup'. Request denied.

Cannot select a record in Vehicle groups (ConFMSVehicleGroup).
Access Denied: You do not have sufficient authorization to modify data
in database.
```

This is a great catch by AX, as adding a server method that updates data to a view privilege was clearly a mistake.

We should now remove this server method from the `ConFMSVehicleView` privilege, as this was only to demonstrate that AX will also validate table permissions for tables accessed through server methods.

Creating a code permission

Code permissions are required when a menu item will, in the course of execution, call a server method. In the `ConFMSSecurityTest` class, create a `main` method that calls the `testService` method created earlier:

```
public static void main(Args _args)
{
    ConFMSSecurityTest::testService();
}
```

Drag this onto the project's **Menu items | Action** node, label the new menu item as Test server method, and drag it onto our menu's **Periodic** submenu. You will need to add this to an appropriate privilege, `ConFMSVehicleMaintain` in this case. This should give `ELLEN` the appropriate permissions to execute the code—it simply updates the vehicle group. When we test this, we get the following error:

```
Access denied to the updateVehicleGroup method in class
ConFMSVehicleServices.
```

We could add the server method to the privilege, but since we have added the menu item to the privilege, it is preferable to give the menu item this permission. This is done by creating a code permission and associating it with the menu item.

To create the code permission, we need to perform the following steps:

1. Create a new code permission named `ConFMSVehicleUpdateGroup` under your project's **Security | Code permissions node**. In our example, this is a specific permission for a single method.
2. Right-click on **Server Methods** and select **New Server Method**.
3. Set **Class** to `ConFMSVehicleServices` and **Method** to `updateVehicleGroup`.

> You may notice that **Method** becomes blank if you select the property. This is because the dropdown is expecting a static method. As long as the server method appears as shown in the following screenshot, it is correct:

4. Set **EffectiveAccess** to `Invoke`.

To complete the code permission, we need to associate it with the `ConFMSSecurityTest` menu item created earlier:

1. Change the menu item's **LinkedPermissionType** property to `CodePermission`.
2. Set the **LinkedPermissionObject** property to `ConFMSVehicleUpdateGroup`.
3. Save all changes.

To test this, go to the session for the user `ELLEN`, restart the client, and try to navigate to **Periodic** | **Test server method** again. No error is produced, and on checking the vehicle record, you can see that it is updated correctly.

Designing and creating process cycles

It seems that we have a fully functional security design that works for our three test users. But we aren't done yet. It is best practice that all duties must be in a process cycle. You may notice if you navigate to **System administration** | **Setup** | **Security** | **Security privileges** that you only have access to privileges by their association with a process cycle.

The reason is not just technical. Process cycles are an important part of the security design in Dynamics AX 2012. When a security administrator wishes to create new roles, the process cycle helps them better understand the duty, due to its inclusion within a process cycle. The security administrator can also build their own process cycles, based on the organization's process areas.

Within the **Security privileges** form, you will see the summary like this:

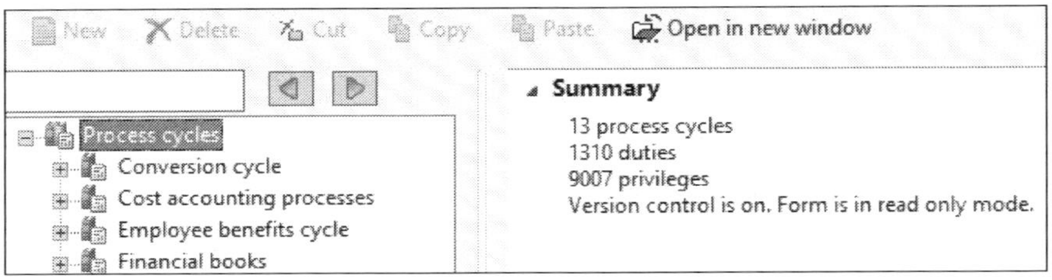

In our design, we have created a hierarchy where a privilege is largely exclusive to a duty and a duty is largely exclusive to a role. In our case, we will create one process cycle—Fleet management.

To do this, follow these steps:

1. Create a new process cycle under your project's **Security** | **Process cycles** node named `ConFMSFleetManagement`.
2. Set the **Label** property to `Fleet management system`.
3. Enter description again. This appears in the client.
4. Finally, drag all your duties onto the **Duties** node.

In the client's **Security privileges** form, you should now see the new process cycle.

Restricting access to data using policies

Policies in the context of security are also referenced as **Extensible Data Security** (**XDS**). The **Policies** node allows us to apply a data access policy to a rule based on a query. This feature is new in Dynamics AX 2012, and replaces the record-level security used in previous releases. Record-level security still exists, but this is considered a legacy functionality, and we will not use this. The policies are defined in the AOT and not in the application database, which means we can follow robust procedures for testing and deployment.

Here's a word of caution: the data policy is defined using a query, which could add significant server load, especially when the query is not written efficiently. In order to use policies, there should be a clear business case, and it may be more appropriate to have a secondary list page instead. The policies should be based on business process rules, where access must be restricted for security purposes.

So, creating a policy that is based on data the user enters, such as vehicles for a particular vehicle group, indicates that it isn't a policy but a filter on the vehicles list page. Policies are normally based on rules that are unaffected by user setup, such as an enum.

This could very easily have an impact on performance, so the ranges and joins we create in the query must be written correctly and covered by appropriate indexes.

The scenario we will follow is that Fleet management service clerks should only be able to see vehicles that are active.

First, we need a query that we will use to filter our data on. In this case, it will be based on `ConFMSVehicleTable`, and the range of `VehicleStatusId` will be `2`. This is done as follows:

1. Create a new query called `ConFMSVehicleTableServicePolicy`.
2. Add the `ConFMSVehicleTable` table.
3. Ensure that the **Dynamic** property on the **Fields** node is `No`.
4. Add the `VehicleStatusId` field to the **Fields** node.
5. Create a new range for `VehicleStatusId`, setting **Value** to `2`.

We now need to create our policy, using these steps:

1. Right-click on the project's **Policies** node (which is found under **Security**) and go to **New** | **Policy**.
2. Rename this to `ConFMSVehicleTableServicePolicy`.
3. Set **Label** to `Fleet service clerk vehicle table access policy`.
4. Set **PrimaryTable** to `ConFMSVehicleTable`. This tells AX the name of the primary table in the **Query** property.
5. Enter `ConFMSVehicleTableServicePolicy` in the **Query** property.
6. Leave **UseNotExistJoin** as `No`. Otherwise, this would have the effect of making the policy inactive vehicles only.
7. Set **ConstrainedTable** to `Yes`.
8. Leave **Operation** as `Select`; we are intending this policy to come into effect when selecting records.
9. Set **ContextType** to `RoleName` and enter `ConFMSFleetManagementServiceClerk` in the **RoleName** property.
10. Finally, set the **Enabled** property to `Yes`.

Test this using the user `Oscar`, noting the following:

- The vehicles list page contains only active vehicles
- When creating a new service, only vehicles that are active appear in the list

We can take this further, and in our case, we should. We can have service records for vehicles that are not active. Our service clerk should not be able to see these either:

1. Right-click on the policy's **ConstrainedTables** node and click on **New** | **Add table by relation**.
2. You will most likely get the following message:

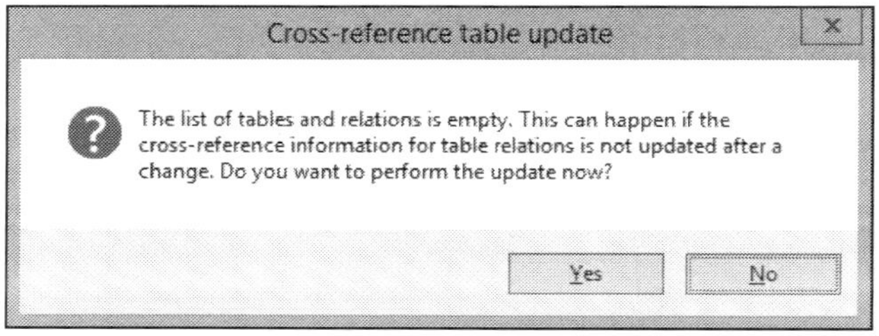

> This is because we haven't updated cross references, which we should do once our data model is complete. This is covered in *Chapter 8, Customizing Standard AX*.

3. Press **Yes** to update the cross references. This may take several hours sometimes.

> AX will then automatically add the first related table. Each time you add a table, it will find the first related table that isn't yet in the list.

4. On the new linked table, go to the properties and change **Table** to `ConFMSVehServiceTable`. This is the table that holds the vehicle's service records.

> **TableRelation** is correct in this case, but wherever we have more than one relation (different contexts), we should ensure that the correct relation is selected.

5. We can continue adding more related tables as required, and even restrict the records related to the linked table we just added by adding a linked table to this table.

We may get the situation where the table does not have a relation. This happens when the foreign key has multiple purposes. This occurs on views (which don't have relations) and some standard tables in AX, such as `InventTransOrigin`. The `ReferenceId` field could be a sales order, purchase order, production order, and so on.

In this case, we can use the **Add table or view using free form expression** option. If we were to add `ConFMSVehicleGroup` this way, we would complete the properties as follows:

`ConstrainedTable`	`Yes` (`No` if we are using the table to navigate relations to the intended constrained table)
`TableOfView`	`ConFMSVehicleGroup`
`Value`	`(ConFMSVehicleTable.VehicleGroupId == ConFMSVehicleGroup.VehicleGroupId)`

Since `Value` is a free type, AX will produce the following message if it is invalid:

Failed to generate query for constrained table `ConFMSVehicleGroup` for policy `ConFMSVehicleTableServicePolicy` for query `ConFMSVehicleTableServicePolicy`

What is happening behind the scenes is that AX generates a query that uses an `exists` join to the constrained tables. These joins are `inner` joins that don't select fields. You can actually use this technique in query ranges; these are covered in more detail in *Chapter 9, Advanced Features and Frameworks*.

When a user in the Fleet management service clerk role opens the vehicle services list page, only the service records for active vehicles are displayed. This is effective in all areas where the data is provided by the AOS, which includes services, the enterprise portal, and the Dynamics AX Microsoft Office add-in. Areas where data is accessed directly from SQL Server, such as OLAP, are not covered.

Summary

In this chapter, we covered the creation of security design in AX from the perspective of a developer. Although we focused mainly on securing new functionalities, the knowledge gained can be applied to adjust the standard security design to fit your organization's security requirements. Although developer-focused, the concepts and information covered in this chapter are equally relevant to security administrators, who work predominantly in the user interface but whose actions result in modifications to security objects, and thus to models and layers.

In the next chapter, we will cover how to customize standard AX while minimizing the impact on future upgrades.

8
Customizing Standard AX

For most developers, modifying standard code (or that supplied from a third party) is the most common task. It isn't sufficient to make a piece of code functionally correct. We have to ensure that the code is maintainable and has a minimal effect on future upgrades. This chapter covers this in the following topics:

- Key goals when customizing standard or third-party code
- How to determine where to make the change
- Adding fields to standard tables
- Integrating a custom module with standard AX
- Changing the behavior of a class
- Extending a framework: vendor electronic payments
- Using event handlers to reduce footprint on standard AX
- Using an extension table for additional fields

Key goals when customizing standard or third-party code

Any change we make that alters any element that is in a lower layer is effectively a modification. The terms **customization** and **modification** are used to imply the level of change, and somehow a customization has a lower impact. Customizations are often used to describe changes to the user interface, such as moving buttons into a more logical order for the organization.

This is a huge misconception; changes to forms are often the most time-consuming to upgrade, especially when changes are made to the form's code. One key aim we should adhere to when modifying code supplied by our VAR, ISV, or Microsoft is to ensure that further updates are easy to apply. We do this by the following:

- Minimizing the footprint. We use event handlers where possible, and avoid small changes in many places.
- Make modifications at the lowest level possible (see the hierarchy in the next section). In other words, we avoid code changes on forms, and try to make the changes at the table or class level.
- Make changes sympathetic to the code's intent, and avoid repurposing existing fields simply to avoid adding a new specific field.
- Do not hardcode current state business rules. Statements such as "We always / never..." are often followed by "Well, except when we order from that supplier, obviously." after implementation. In these cases, we would use a parameter to control the logic, which provides the benefit of allowing different legal entities to have different rules.

The last point is relevant to any development, but in the case of standard logic, the impact is often greater, as these are often more widely used across an organization. An example of a hard-coded business rule is as follows: place all export sales orders on hold for hold type `AUTH`.

Our role is to provide the ability for these rules to be implemented. Writing the rules in code often leads to them be changed frequently, as the business evolves, and therefore increases the cost of ownership and risk of regression elsewhere.

The request is a reasonable requirement, but the solution should use a table to store the conditions for placing the order on hold. Even making the hold type a parameter (for example, in the `SalesParameters` table) will most likely not be enough. Various exceptions will arise, resulting in a large, hard-to-read `if` statement.

How to determine where to make the change

The decision on where to make a change is based on many factors. These are to accomplish two goals: impact on future upgrades and reducing the number of changes to accomplish a task. These help keep the code maintainable, and when the code is handled by fewer changes, it is easier to read too. There may be other considerations, such as performance, that also need to be taken into account.

Both are accomplished by making the right modification in the correct place, and this should always be as "low" as possible. When making a change, we would rarely change standard code. Instead, we place a hook so that it calls our code.

> If we find ourselves rewriting a standard method, it indicates that we should really be creating new functionality. By changing the code's intent, we risk regression elsewhere in the application or in future upgrades.

The following list shows the preferred order and achieves both the goals:

- Event handler added to a class method
- Event handler added to a table method
- Modification to a class method
- Modification to a table method
- Modification to a method at the form level
- Modification to a form's data source event
- Modification to a form's data source field event
- Modification to a form control

We only make a change at a higher level if it is not possible to write the code lower or we wish only to affect the behavior at the current level. This can happen when we need information from another data source on a form. In this case, we have to place a change at the form's data source level, since a table instance (the current record) does not have access to the form's other data sources—they exist only in the scope of the form.

Many classes have levels of hierarchy, which can make it more difficult to determine where to make the change. The `SalesLineType` class, which handles table events for `SalesLine`, has several subclasses that handle specific types of sales order lines. The hierarchy is obvious in this case, as the classes are suffixed with each type of order line. When modifying the behavior here, we would modify the `SalesLineType_Sales` if we only want to affect the behavior for a standard sales order, or `SalesLineType` should the change need to affect all types of sales order lines. We will cover specific examples of this later in this chapter.

This hierarchy isn't always obvious, but AX provides some useful tools to help understand the hierarchy where objects are used. These are discussed next.

Cross-reference data

The Cross-reference data works with tables, classes, and types. A good example of how this affects day-to-day usage is when adding a table to a query in the advanced query editor. To see this in action, follow these steps:

1. Open the **Customer list** page by going to **Accounts receivable** | **Common** | **Customers** | **All Customers**.
2. Press *Ctrl* + *F3* to open the query editor form.
3. You will see a tree view at the top of the form, showing the data sources for the current form.
4. Right-click on the **Customers** data source and choose **1:N** (one-to-many or child relations). This displays the following menu:

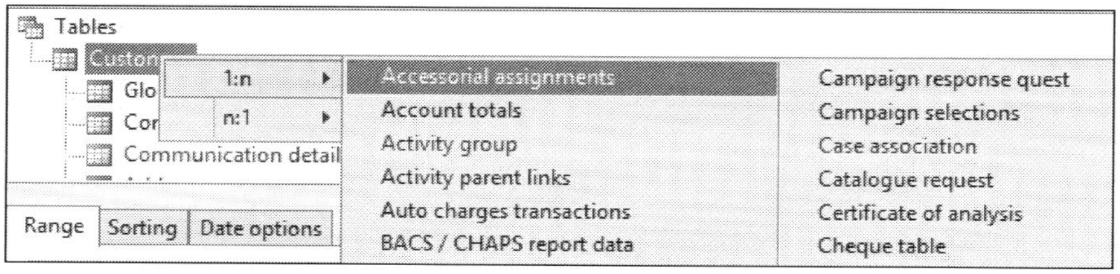

This list is built using the cross-reference data built from the relations specified on the tables, and provides the user with a very powerful query tool. Cross reference affects developers too, and is used to help work out which objects use or are used by the current AOT element.

Cross reference – Used by

There are two perspectives, `Used by` and `Using`. First, we will use the cross references to see what uses a field. We will do this in a few steps to highlight some important issues, the first being to update the element's cross reference:

1. In the `ConFMSVehicleTable` table, right-click on the `VehicleGroupId` field.
2. Go to **Add-Ins** | **Cross-reference** | **Update**. This will update the reference for all elements in the current table, not just the current field.

3. Once this completes, right-click on `VehicleGroupId` again and go to **Add-Ins | Cross-reference | Used by**. This will show a form similar to what is shown in the following screenshot:

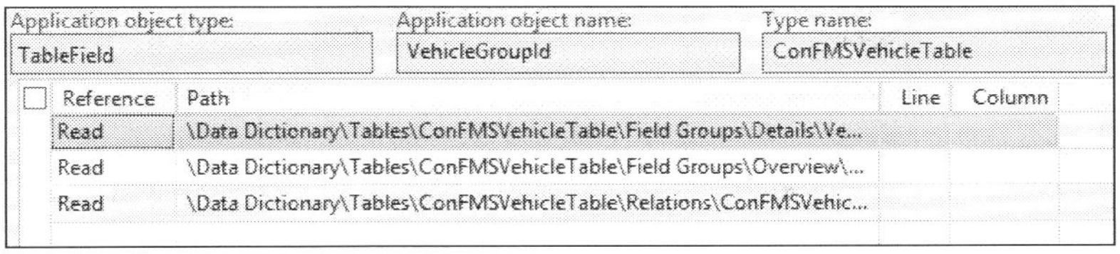

4. We can't be sure that the `Used by` list is complete, as this cross-reference update only processed the current table. We have to perform a full cross-reference update in order to ensure that this is complete. To include our classes in the cross reference, select the classes under our project's **Classes** node and go to **Add-Ins | Cross-reference | Update**.
5. Try the `Used by` list for the `VehicleGroupId` field again. The following is what you see:

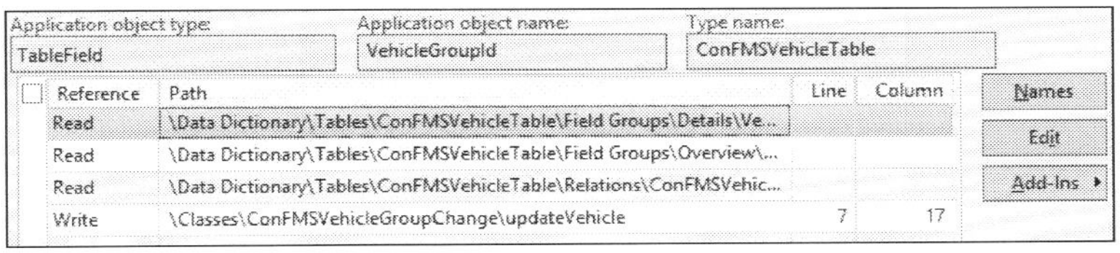

6. Select the last element and click on **Edit**. This will open the method for you. This is particularly useful if we have to rename a field.

Keeping the cross-reference data up to date

Because the AX code base is so large, the cross-reference data must be cached, otherwise looking up cross references would be too slow to be useful. In order for them to remain relevant, we will need to update the cross-reference data. This is done from the development environment's main menu by going to **Tools | Cross reference | Periodic | Update**.

In the **Update Cross Reference** form, check **Update data model** and press **OK**. The data model is important, as it updates the `1:n` and `n:1` relations used by the query editor. If any elements have been removed, renamed, or refactored, you should also check the **Delete** and **Update** options.

This will take a number of hours to complete, so it should only be done under the following circumstances:

- When we are about to start a new project
- When we are about to start an upgrade
- Nightly, if we are using shared development

In other scenarios, as required, if the cross-reference data is out of date and the benefit of getting it up to date outweighs the delay

We can also configure the compiler to automatically build the cross references as it compiles. This is done from the **Options** window under **Tools**. Click on the **Development** tab and then on the **Compiler** button. This will slow down the compilation, and should be turned off for full application compilations. It is quicker to rebuild the cross-reference data once the compilation has finished.

Cross reference – Using

We have two options on the **Add-Ins** | **Cross-reference fly-out** menu: **Using** and **Using (Instant view)**.

The **Using** option will use the stored cross reference information, and is only available after an update. This shows the data in the same form as the **Used by** options, but from the perspective of what the element is using.

For more information on the cross-reference tool, see *Cross-reference Tool [AX 2012]*, `http://msdn.microsoft.com/en-us/library/aa626961.aspx`.

Type hierarchy

The type hierarchy is a very useful feature when trying to understand how types (types, tables, and classes) relate.

Before we look at the browser, there is a useful tool when we want a quick look at the hierarchy as we move around the AOT. It is **Type hierarchy context**, from the **Tools** menu. This appears (by default) docked to the right of the IDE, showing the hierarchy to the base type of the selected AOT node.

An example for the `VehicleId` field on the `ConFMSVehicleTable` is as follows:

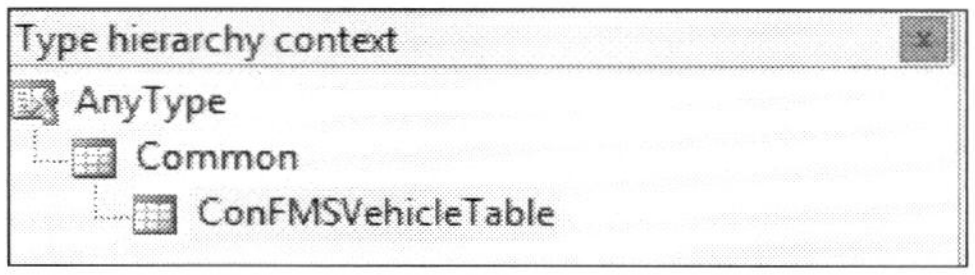

When an EDT is selected, such as `ConFMSVehicleId`:

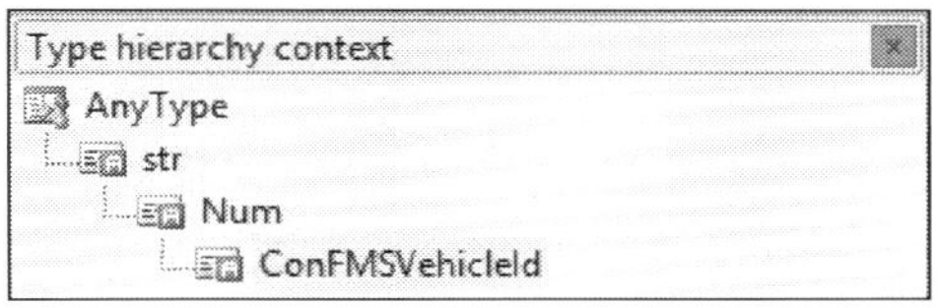

The more powerful type hierarchy browser is available from the **Tools** menu or the **Add-Ins** right-click menu—**Type hierarchy browser**. When opened from the **Tools** menu, it starts displaying just the base types, and you can navigate down the hierarchy. We will investigate the `SalesFormLetter_Invoice` class. So, either locate this class in the AOT and select **Add-Ins** | **Type hierarchy browser**, or open it from the **Tools** menu and use the search box.

Although it is very useful to see the hierarchy in this form, one of the more interesting features is seeing which of the parent class's methods are overridden. The hierarchy is shown in this screenshot:

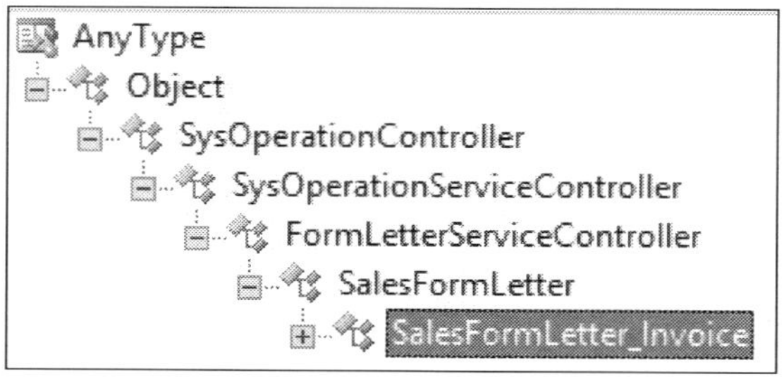

The graphic on the right-hand side displays this hierarchy, as shown in the following screenshot:

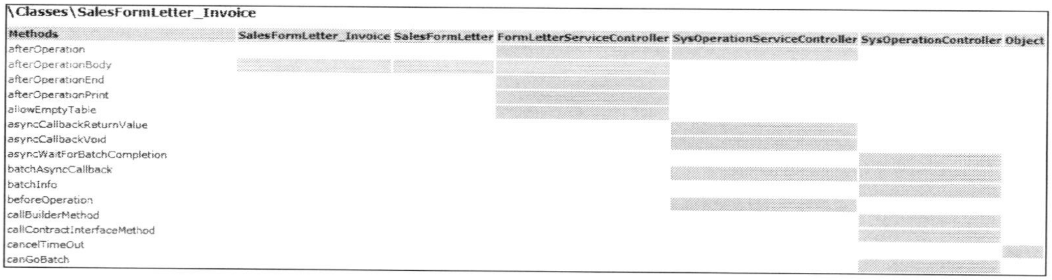

You can see from the preceding screenshot that the `afterOperationBody` method is introduced in the `FormLetterServiceController` class. It is overridden by `SalesFormLetter` and also by `SalesFormLetter_Invoice`.

Adding fields to tables

This is the most common modification, and we have done this many times. The only difference here is that when adding a field to an existing table, we must prefix the field; in our case, we would at least use the `Con` prefix, and if we want to highlight the fact that the field was specifically for the Fleet Management System, we would use `ConFMS`.

> There is a new pattern used from AX 2012 R2, wherein fields are added to an extension table instead. This would be joined to the primary table in a 1:1 join. This seems like a silver bullet—we can add fields to a standard table without modifying it!
>
> There are two main limitations with this from the foot print perspective.
>
> To maintain referential integrity, a `delete` action (or add an event handler to the `delete` method) must be placed on the parent table. Otherwise, we will have orphaned records if the parent is deleted.
>
> We have to modify the create and details forms to handle the extension table.
>
> Of course, we still have to modify the forms to show the fields. But this is likely to be the same for both methods. Therefore, adding a single field to a standard table involves more work, but with advantages such as these for example:
>
> - All of the table and field event handling for the new fields is completely separate from the standard table.
> - There is a performance benefit on updates when only the standard or extension table needs updating, although this is mitigated by having to first seek the parent table to get the extension table record.
> - Avoid potential buffer size issues when adding a large number of fields, such as note fields.

Field groups

Field groups are typically used to add a group of fields to a form. So, the form group controls referencing a field group are controlled by the field group. All we need to do to add a field to the form group control is add it to the table's field group. This helps reduce our footprint on standard code significantly by potentially removing the need to modify the form in order to add our new field to it.

To see this, in the AOT, navigate to **Forms** | **CustTable** and expand the following nodes under the form design: **Tab** | **TabPageDetails** | **TabHeader** | **TabDetails**.

Select the **Vendor** group and open the property sheet. In this, you will see that **DataSource** is `CustTable` and **DataGroup** is `Vendor`. Adding a field to the table's `VendGroup` field group will also add the field here, and anywhere else where the field group has been added to a form.

Not all form group controls reference a table field group, such as the `Administration` group (also on the `CustTable` form). This is normally done because we need more control over the fields in the group.

If we can't find a suitable field group to add our new field to, we should create a new field group (with our prefix) and add that field group from the data source to an appropriate place in the form's design. This is also best practice.

> Wherever possible, add fields to a table's field group. If not, it is preferable to have new fields in a separate field group. Try to avoid adding fields directly to a form.

Integrating a custom module with standard AX

Most modifications made to standard AX fall under the following categories:

- Adding a field to a master table that is used for reporting
- Adding a field to a table that is used by custom business logic
- Changing the behavior of the standard business logic in order to align it with our organization's processes or extend it with new functionality

We will demonstrate this in the form of a series of modifications, further integrating our fleet management application with standard AX. To demonstrate this, we will associate our haulier table with the vendor table so that we can identify a haulier as a supplier. Vehicles tracked by our Fleet Management System might be supplied by external hauliers. In order to track this, we require the following:

- Add a vendor ID reference to the vehicle table
- Add the ability to mark the vendor as a vehicle servicing vendor
- Add the ability to mark a purchase order as a vehicle service order

Adding the vendor ID reference to the vehicle table

This first part seems easy enough; we just need to drag the EDT for the supplier account into our vehicle table. To work out which EDT we should use, a good trick is to do the following:

1. Navigate to **Accounts payable** | **Common** | **Supplier** | **All suppliers** and open the details form for any supplier.
2. Right-click on the **Supplier account** field and choose **Personalize**.
3. On the form that opens, there is a **System name** field. It tells us the control name, form data source name, table name and field name, as shown in the following screenshot:

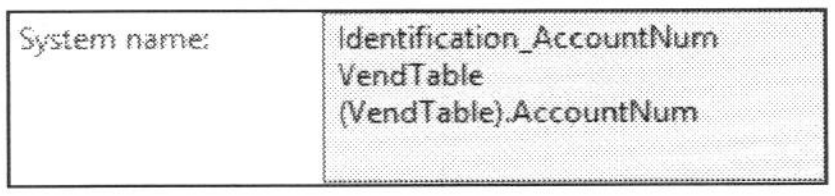

4. So, the field is `VendTable.AccountNum`. Open the AOT and then the properties for this field. The **ExtendedDataType** is `VendAccount`.
5. Locate `VendAccount` in the AOT and drag it into our `ConFMSVehicleTable` vehicle table.
6. You will receive this prompt: **Do you want to add the ForeignKey relation from the EDT to the current table?**. Click on **Yes**.
7. We want the field to appear on the list page and details form. Since we have constructed field groups, we simply add the new field to the **Overview** and **Details** field groups.
8. Go to **Fleet management system** | **Common** | **Vehicles**. Verify that the supplier account is there. If not, it means the grid doesn't reference the **Overview** field group, and it should be corrected.
9. Open the vehicle details for any vehicle, verifying that the field is there. Also verify that the lookup works and that the field only allows valid supplier accounts.

Marking a vendor as a vehicle service provider

To mark a vendor as a vehicle service provider, the most obvious change would be to add a flag to the `VendTable` table. The problem here is that over time, with the addition of other similar requirements, we could acquire many checkboxes. This increases the chances of errors due to incorrect data setup; the easier we make the setup of maintenance of the master, the better.

We will instead try to use an existing functionality, and there are several possibilities that we are going to consider. The first two are explained here:

- The first possible solution would be to declare that all members of a particular vendor group are considered vehicle service providers. We can do this by simply referencing the vendor group in a parameter, but this is limiting, especially since the vendor group is normally owned by the finance department and takes part in the integration with the general ledger.
- The second possibility is to set up a table of vehicle service providers. We can then use the `TableGroupAll` pattern or provide the ability to store a query that allows the user to define the criteria of a vehicle service provider.

An example of the `TableGroupAll` pattern can be found by going to **Accounts payable** | **Setup** | **Vendor posting profiles**. In order to determine whether a supplier matches, code must be written; we can't simply use the criteria in a query.

You can see the query method by navigating to **Warehouse management** | **Setup** | **Labor standard** | **Labor standards**. Here, we have two buttons, **Select items** and **Select locations**, that allow the user to associate items and locations with a labor standard using a user-defined query. Both of these methods will be covered in the *Exception handling* section in *Chapter 10, Advanced Development Techniques*.

However, it turns out that no modification is needed to do this; Dynamics AX provides this ability in the form of the procurement catalogue.

> The procurement catalogue feature allows vendors to be "tagged" as being approved to provide goods and services from one or more categories. The catalogue is a hierarchy of item categories, whereby if the vendor is tagged with a high-level category, then it is also expected to be able to supply items from a more specialist category.

Our requirement almost exactly matches the purpose of the procurement catalogue. This demonstrates the importance of broad system knowledge—so that we can identify when a requirement does and does not require significant modifications. It is common that, as we start work, we notice that the system can already perform the task. AX is a highly functional system, and a consultant or key user can miss this. We can also see that changes are requested that could cause a performance issue or conflict with the way AX is designed, ricking regression on when updates are applied. We should push back to the consultant or key user and discuss the correct action. Everyone involved will want the footprint of our modifications to be as small as possible and, where a modification is necessary, be sympathetic to AX's design.

To use the procurement catalogue, we simply choose a procurement category to represent a vehicle service provider and then tag the vendors as needed. We will still require a system parameter to know which category identifies vehicle service providers, and we will also need to write a lookup so that we allow only suitable suppliers to the vehicles.

First, we will configure a vendor to be a vehicle supplier. In the `USMF` company of the Contoso demo dataset, the procurement category contains a `VEHICLES` category. We will assign this to `US-102` and `Tailspin Parts`:

1. Navigate to **USMF** | **Accounts payable** | **Common** | **All vendors**.
2. Select **US-102** and the **General** tab and click on **Categories**.
3. In the form that opens, click on **Add category** and select **VEHICLES** from the **Category** drop-down list, as shown in the following screenshot:

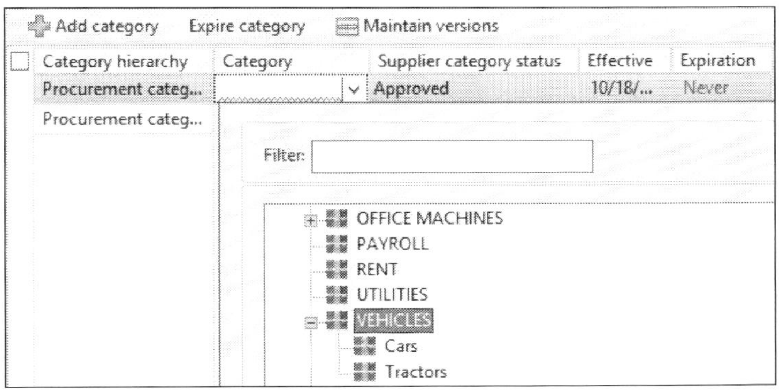

4. We can assign as many categories as we like to a supplier at various levels. Once this is done, close the form and jump back into the IDE.

Our requirement is to be able to mark the purchase orders as vehicle service orders, which we will do by checking whether the category to which the supplier is assigned is at or below the `VEHICLES` category. Therefore, we need to add a system parameter that will define which category identifies vehicle service providers. We will use this parameter to identify purchase orders as vehicle service orders, so we will add it to the **Vendor parameters** form. To do this, follow these steps:

We need to know which EDT to use in the same way as we did for the `VendAcount` EDT. Navigate to **USMF** | **Accounts payable** | **Common** | **All vendors**, select the **General** tab, and click on **Categories**.

Right-click on the **Category** field and select **Personalization**. This tells us that the form is `DirPartyEcoResCategory` and the field is `VendCategory.Category`.

The EDT we need is `EcoResCategoryId`. Drag this onto the field list of the `VendParameters` table. As usual, click on **Yes** when prompted to add a foreign key relation.

> We could use the personalization method to work out that the table name was `VendParameters`, but since it followed the naming conventions, it was easy to find. Using naming conventions makes development much easier for everyone.

1. Rename the field to `ConFMSServiceCategoryId`. Descriptive field names are critical for getting maintainable code. Set **Label** to **Vehicle service category**.
2. Save the changes, which results in the following error:

   ```
   'RelatedTableRole' conflicts with another 'RelatedTableRole' on
   relation EcoResCategory on table VendParameters.
   ```

3. There is already a relation, and we need to do two things to correct this.
4. First, the relation was created as `EcoResCategory1`. We should make this obvious with a proper name. Rename this to `ConFMSServiceCategory`. This won't fix the error but a correct name is very important.
5. To fix the error, we need to make the relation unique by populating the **RelatedTableRole** property. This is meant to describe the role of the `EcoResCategory` relation. Enter `ConFMSServiceCategory` in this property.

> The internal **RelatedTableRole** is a combination of the table name and this property. It doesn't use the relation name.

6. Complete the cardinality properties and save the table; the errors will be gone. You may need to compile the table again to convince the compiler that the relation is now unique.
7. By looking at the design for the `VendParameters` form, you will notice a suitable field group to use—`Vendor`. Drag your new field into this field group.
8. Drag the table into your project and save the project.
9. Before we continue, we open the `VendParameters` form. The drop-down list for the new field isn't very useful; it's just a flat list of categories. We need a nice tree view lookup.

Reference group controls

The `ConFMSServiceCategoryId` field is a record ID, so in order to make this usable for the user, we have to show data that the field's relation references. Dynamics AX provides a special control for this, called `ReferenceGroup`.

By adding the field to the `Vendor` field group, AX will automatically create the control on the forms that reference this field group. Since the record ID field has a primary-key-based foreign key relation, AX will create a `ReferenceGroup` control.

In the AOT, navigate to **Forms** | **VendParameters** and then look at the properties of the `Vendor_ConFMSServiceCategoryId` control. This is in **Designs** | **Design** | **Tab** | **GeneralBody** | **Vendor**.

The control has a property, called **ReferenceField**, that has a value for the `ConFMSServiceCategoryId` reference field, and also one for **ReplacementFieldGroup**. This references a field group on the referenced table in order to replace the record ID field with one or more fields from the reference table.

It defaults to `AutoIdentification`, in this case showing the `Name` field. You can see the fields added from the field group by expanding the control.

Creating a custom lookup for reference group controls

The `ReferenceGroup` form controls are different from other bound form controls in that they allow us to see fields from the referenced table. They do this by creating a reference data source as an outer join. This happens behind the scenes and is constructed using the table relation.

To use a custom lookup with reference group fields, we override the `lookupReference` method. The structure of this method is as follows:

```
public Common lookupReference(FormReferenceControl
                                  _formReferenceControl)
```

By investigating how Microsoft made the lookup work on the `DirPartyEcoResCategory` form, we see that they overrode the `lookupReference` and `resolveReference` methods. Since the category hierarchy is a complicated structure, Microsoft has provided a helper class for us.

For the lookup, the key method is `EcoResCategory::lookupCategoryHierarchy`. This requires a form control and a hierarchy to select from. Dynamics AX has the ability to have many types of hierarchies. We want the user to see those in the procurement category. This is done by locating the `EcoResCategoryHierarchy` for the `EcoResCategoryNamedHierarchyRole::Procurement` role.

To write the lookup method, follow these steps:

1. We are about to modify the `VendParameters` form, so we drag this from the AOT to the **Forms** node of our project.
2. On the `VendParameters` form, go to **Data Sources** | **VendParameters** | **Fields** | **ConFMSServiceCategoryId** | **Methods**.

> If you can't see this field, it means the form element was cached. Right-click on the form and choose **Restore**.

3. Right-click on the **Methods** node of this data source field and go to **Override method** | **lookupReference**.

4. Change the method as follows:

```
public Common lookupReference(FormReferenceControl
                                         _formReferenceControl)
{
  Common category;
  EcoResCategoryHierarchy     hierarchy;
  EcoResCategoryHierarchyRole role;

  select firstonly * from hierarchy
    join role
      where hierarchy.RecId == role.CategoryHierarchy &&
            role.NamedCategoryHierarchyRole ==
             EcoResCategoryNamedHierarchyRole::Procurement;

  category = EcoResCategory::lookupCategoryHierarchy(
                                       _formReferenceControl,
                                       hierarchy);

  return category;
}
```

5. Save the form and try the drop-down list again. We get a nice tree view as expected.

The `resolveReference` method is triggered if we enter a category manually. If we enter the `VEHICLES` category, we want to ensure that it finds a reference within the procurement hierarchy.

The code is actually similar; Microsoft provides a helper function to resolve the reference, and we have to supply the form control and the `EcoResHierarchy` record for the procurement role. The code we need is as follows:

```
public Common resolveReference(FormReferenceControl
                                         _formReferenceControl)
{
    Common category;
    EcoResCategoryHierarchy     hierarchy;
    EcoResCategoryHierarchyRole role;
```

```
        select firstonly * from hierarchy
            join role
                where hierarchy.RecId == role.CategoryHierarchy
                   && role.NamedCategoryHierarchyRole ==
                      EcoResCategoryNamedHierarchyRole::Procurement;

        category = EcoResCategory::resolveCategoryHierarchy(
                                   _formReferenceControl, hierarchy);

        return category.RecId ? category : null;
    }
```

The last line introduces a new command—the inline `if` statement. This is similar to C#, and is defined as follows:

```
<boolean condition> ? <statement if true> : <statement if false>
```

We can now enter values directly and be sure that the reference is resolved and the correct value is set in the table.

Creating a custom lookup for standard fields

Most of the time, the lookups we would create are based on string controls, such as the item lookup on the sales order line. A lookup on form control is performed by the control's `lookup` method. When a form control is bound to a data source, it calls the data source field's `lookup` method. This is where we would make the change to alter the lookup.

The following example is from the `InventTable`.lookupItem table:

```
public client static void lookupItem(FormStringControl _ctrl)
{
  SysTableLookup sysTableLookup = SysTableLookup::newParameters(
                                   tableNum(InventTable),_ctrl);
  Query           query = new Query();
  QueryBuildDataSource queryBuildDataSource =
                         query.addDataSource(tableNum(InventTable));

  sysTableLookup.addLookupField(fieldNum(InventTable,ItemId));
  sysTableLookup.addLookupMethod(tableMethodStr(
                               InventTable,defaultProductName));
  sysTableLookup.addLookupMethod(tableMethodStr(
```

```
                                    InventTable,itemGroupId));
    sysTableLookup.addLookupField(fieldNum(
                                    InventTable,NameAlias));
    sysTableLookup.addLookupField(fieldNum(InventTable,ItemType));
      sysTableLookup.addSelectionField(fieldNum(
                                    InventTable,Product));

    sysTableLookup.parmQuery(query);
    sysTableLookup.performFormLookup();
}
```

A `lookup` method is broken down as follows:

1. Construct the `SysTableLookup` class with a primary data source and a form control.
2. Construct a query and add a primary data source.
3. Add further child data sources and ranges as required.
4. Add the required fields and display methods to the `SysTableLookup` object.
5. Pass the constructed query object to the `SysTableLookup` object and tell it to perform the lookup.

To use this code, we would simply override the data source field's lookup method, as follows:

```
public void lookup(FormControl _formControl, str _filterStr)
{
    InventTable::lookupItem(_formControl);
}
```

You may notice that we aren't handling a return from the `lookup` method. The `lookup` class updates the form control for us if the user selects a record.

Adding a method to state whether this is a vehicle service provider or not

Using the procurement category not only provides the user with a method of identifying vendors as vehicle service providers, but also works with a standard process. We also have a minimal footprint on standard code.

This does present one problem, however; it is difficult to determine whether the vendor is a vehicle service provider. In order to solve this, `VendTable` should have a method that returns information on whether it is a vehicle service provider or not. This method sits naturally on the vehicle table, so it can be used wherever necessary.

We will write this method as a display method, so we can add it to a form or info part, if desired. Since we intend to use field groups wherever possible, we will create an EDT for the return type; in this way, a label will be added automatically.

Create the `ConFMSIsVehicleServiceProvider` EDT as a type enum, extending `NoYesId` and with the `Vehicle service provider` label.

Using personalization on the **Vendor Categories** form, we can determine that the list of categories a supplier is associated with is in the `VendCategory` table. We need a way to work out whether this category is a descendant of the **Vehicle service provider** category in vendor parameters.

Since this structure is complicated, we would expect a helper function to exist. The way to find such a function would be to first look at the `EcoResCategory` table, and then look for a class that provides this functionality. The `EcoResCategory` table has a method called `getAscendants`. This returns a set of records that are parents of the current category record.

We should test this first, to check whether it works for us. We will write a job that shows all ascendants of the `Cars` category. We are expecting to see `VEHICLES` and `CORP PROCUREMENT CATEGORIES`.

Since the `getAscendants` method returns a set of records, we will use a new method to iterate through them. The job is as follows:

```
static void ConFMSTestCategoryHierarchy(Args _args)
{
    EcoResCategory ascendants, child;

    select child where child.Name == "Cars";

    ascendants = child.getAscendants(false);
    while(ascendants.RecId != 0)
    {
        info(ascendants.Name);
        next ascendants;
    }
}
```

The `next` command will select the next record in the set of records returned by the `getAscendants` method, and the `while` command will execute as long as there is an active record in ascendants. The result should look like what is shown in the following screenshot:

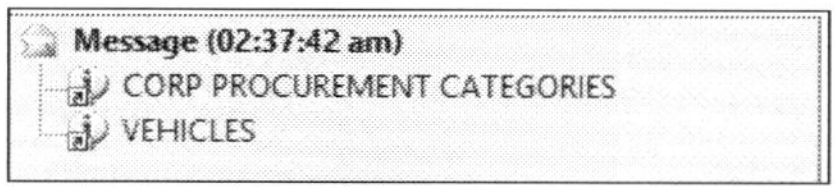

Now that we know that the method works, we can write our `display` method. Create a new method on the **VendTable** table and write the following lines of code:

```
public display ConFMSIsVehicleServiceProvider
conFMSDispIsVehicleServiceProvider()
{
    EcoResCategoryHierarchy     hierarchy;
    EcoResCategoryHierarchyRole role;
    VendCategory                vendCategories;
    EcoResCategory              ascendantCategories, category;
    VendParameters              parm;
    EcoResCategoryId            serviceCategoryId;

    parm = VendParameters::find();
    serviceCategoryId = parm.ConFMSServiceCategoryId;
    // if there is not category, return No now.
    if(serviceCategoryId == 0)
    {
        return NoYes::No;
    }

    select firstonly * from hierarchy
        join role
            where hierarchy.RecId == role.CategoryHierarchy
               && role.NamedCategoryHierarchyRole ==
                  EcoResCategoryNamedHierarchyRole::Procurement;
    // if a procurement hierarchy has not been
    //  configured, return No now
    if(hierarchy.RecId == 0)
    {
        return NoYes::No;
    }
```

```
        while select vendCategories
            where vendCategories.VendorAccount == this.AccountNum &&
                  vendCategories.VendorDataArea == this.dataAreaId
            join category
                where category.RecId == vendCategories.Category &&
                      category.CategoryHierarchy == hierarchy.RecId
        {
            // Check the current level
            if(category.RecId == serviceCategoryId)
            {
                return NoYes::Yes;
            }
            // get all parent category records for the
            // current category
            ascendantCategories = category.getAscendants();
            while(ascendantCategories.RecId != 0)
            {
                if(ascendantCategories.RecId == serviceCategoryId)
                {
                    return NoYes::Yes;
                }
            }
        }
        return NoYes::No;
    }
```

> It may be tempting to add this to the **Vendor** list page. This goes against best practice, as the method will execute for each row on the list page, affecting user experience.

Since the EDT extends `NoYesId`, we return its base enum value of `NoYes::No` or `NoYes::Yes`.

Using event handlers to reduce footprint on standard AX

Our organization needs us to provide a method to allow reporting on purchase orders for vehicle service providers. The solution we have decided upon is to record against a purchase order whether or not the order was a vehicle service order. The order should default as a vehicle service order if the supplier is a vehicle service provider, and allow the user to uncheck this flag. Orders that are not for vehicle service providers should not be allowed to have this flag set.

This provides the opportunity to demonstrate event handling, which allows us to hook into AX functionality with minimum footprint. We will also cover some of the tables used in the purchase order process.

First, the requirement to "record against a purchase order" is there to highlight common mistakes. Although fields on a purchase order can be used for reporting purposes, they shouldn't be. They should only be used to help manage the order-to-invoice process. Once invoiced, the purchase order can be deleted, and many organizations routinely delete invoiced purchase orders, either at the point of invoice or after a period of time.

To be used for reporting, we need this information to be stored somewhere more suitable, and this depends on why we need it. If it is for statistical reporting, it should be on the invoice journal record. Dynamics AX follows standard naming conventions for both sales and purchase orders, and the documents they generate fall under the same framework—`FormLetter`.

Each time a document, such as a purchase order invoice, is posted, it creates a set of records in a journal set. This allows the document to be reproduced as it was when first printed, and allows reprint on the invoice even if the order has been deleted.

These tables follow a naming convention: `<module><document>` followed by `Jour` for the header and `Trans` for the lines. The prefix for vendor documents is `Vend` and for customer documents is `Cust`. The following table shows the standard journal tables:

Module	**Document**	**Journal tables**
`Cust`	`Confirmation`	`CustConfirmJour` `CustConfirmTrans`
`Vend`	`Confirmation`	`VendPurchOrderJour`
`Cust`	`Packing slip`	`CustPackingSlipJour` `CustPackingSlipTrans`
`Vend`	`Packing slip`	`VendPackingSlipJour` `VendPackingSlipTrans`
`Cust`	`Invoice`	`CustInvoiceJour` `CustInvoiceTrans`
`Vend`	`Invoice`	`VendInvoiceJour` `VendInvoiceTrans`

In our case, it is statistical reporting, so this should go against `VendInvoiceJour`. This was determined using the **Personalization** form from the **Invoice journal** form.

The first step is to flag the order as a vehicle service order and allow the user to uncheck this. We will do this by adding a field to `PurchTable`, but we will handle the various events using event handlers.

To do this, follow these steps:

1. Create a new EDT called `ConFMSVehicleServiceOrder` of the enum type. It extends `NoYesId`. Set the label to `Vehicle service order`.

> Although we could just use the `NoYesId` EDT directly and set a label on the field, creating a new EDT adds benefits beyond property reuse. When used in a `display` method, EDT sets the label on the resulting form control.

2. Drag the `PurchTable` table into your project.
3. Drag the new EDT onto the **Fields** node on `PurchTable`.
4. Save the table, open the **Fields** node in a new window, and drag the new field onto the `Administration` field group.

> We would determine that this is the correct field group on the create form using the personalization technique.

5. Save the changes. You can test the field displays by creating a new purchase order.
6. To avoid modifying standard code, we will write a class that handles the events we are interested in. This class will have a specific purpose, so create a new class named `ConFMSPurchVehicleOrderHandler`.

> This method means that we will have one or more event subscriptions, which is perfect in our situation—it is a new module and allows it to be installed without any dependency on other customer elements. Sometimes, when making more generalized modifications, it is more convenient to have one class that handles the table or class, for example, `ConPurchTableHandler`.

7. In this class, we need to handle the `initFromVendTable` and `validateField` table methods, as we need to default our new fields and verify that it isn't set for vendors who aren't vehicle service providers. Right-click on the new class and go to **New | Pre-post event handler**.
8. Rename the method to `initFromVendTableEventHandler`.
9. We have written an event handler before, but this time, we need to get the `VendTable` record being passed to it. On inspection, we notice that the method has a `_vendTable` parameter, which we will use. The following lines of code will get the `VendTable` record, check whether the vendor is a vehicle service provider, and set our new field accordingly:

```
public static void initFromVendTableEventHandler(XppPrePostArgs
_args)
{
    VendTable vendTable;
    PurchTable purchTable = _args.getThis();

    if(!_args.existsArg("_vendTable"))
        throw error(strFmt("@SYS22828",
                    staticMethodStr(
                          ConFMSPurchVehicleOrderHandler,
                          initFromVendTableEventHandler)));
    vendTable = _args.getArg("_vendTable");

    purchTable.ConFMSVehicleServiceOrder = NoYes::No;
    if(vendTable.conFMSDispIsVehicleServiceProvider() ==
                                             NoYes::Yes)
    {
        purchTable.ConFMSVehicleServiceOrder = NoYes::Yes;
    }
}
```

> The `staticMethodStr` method validates at compile time that the static method exists, and returns the method name. This is for convenience if we later decide to rename the method. The `@SYS22828` label references the `Function %1 has been incorrectly called` label text.

10. Next, we need to write a method to handle the `validateField` method on `PurchTable` so that we allow the field to be set only if the supplier is a vehicle service supplier. This time, we need to read the `_fieldToCheck` parameter and alter the return value of the method. This is done by the following lines of code:

```
public static void validateFieldEventHandler(XppPrePostArgs _args)
{
    VendTable vendTable;
    PurchTable purchTable = _args.getThis();
    RefFieldId fieldToCheck;
    boolean ret = _args.getReturnValue();
    // no point checking further if the validation
    // has already failed.
    if(!ret)
        return;

    if(!_args.existsArg("_fieldIdToCheck"))
    {
        throw error(strFmt("@SYS22828",
                staticMethodStr(ConFMSPurchVehicleOrderHandler,
                                initFromVendTableEventHandler)));
    }
    fieldToCheck = _args.existsArg("_fieldIdToCheck");
    switch(fieldToCheck)
    {
        case fieldNum(PurchTable, ConFMSVehicleServiceOrder):
            vendTable = purchTable.vendTable_OrderAccount();
            if(vendTable.conFMSDispIsVehicleServiceProvider() &&
               purchTable.ConFMSVehicleServiceOrder == NoYes::Yes)
            {
                ret = checkFailed(strFmt(
                  "Supplier %1 is not a vehicle service supplier",
                  purchTable.OrderAccount));
            }
            break;
    }
    if(!ret)
    {
        _args.setReturnValue(ret);
    }
}
```

11. Finally, we need to add event handlers to the PurchTable's `initFromVendTable` and `validateField` methods.
12. In the `PurchTable` table, expand **Methods**, right-click on the `initFromVendTable` method, and select **New Event Handler Subscription**.
13. On the property sheet for the new event subscription, fill in the fields as per the following screenshot. **Post** is selected because we want our code to run after the method completes.

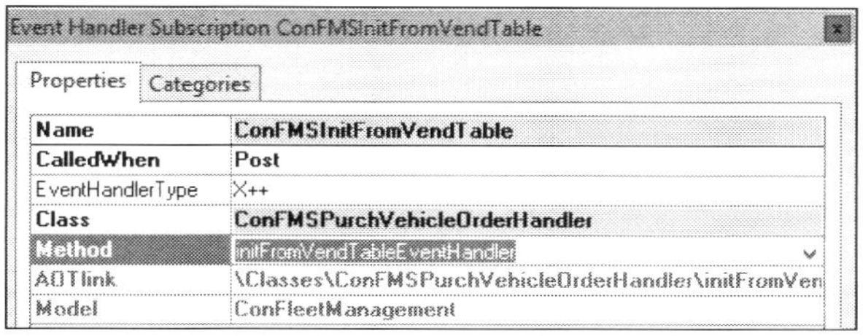

14. Next, add an event subscription to `validateField` and configure it as follows:

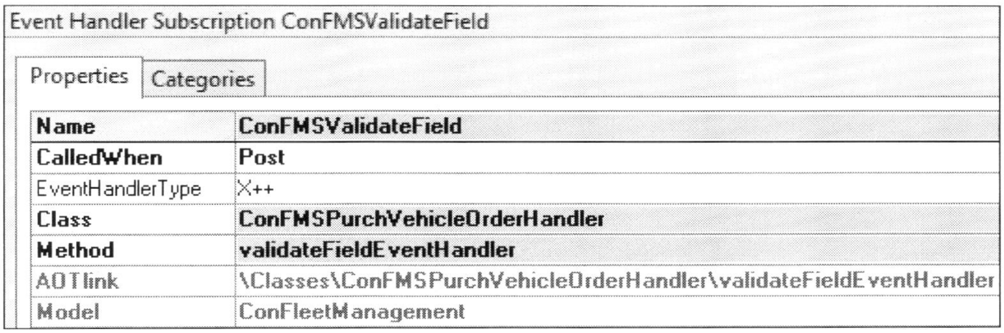

15. Again, the **CalledWhen** property is **Post**, otherwise the `validateField` method would have the final say on the return value.

We should test this now by creating a new order for a supplier that is a vehicle service provider, and one order for a supplier that isn't.

The next stage is to add our field to the `VendInvoiceJour` table and set the field based on the `PurchTable` record that it is created from. This is done by the following steps:

1. Drag the `VendInvoiceJour` table into the project. Then add a new field from the EDT just as you did for `PurchTable`.
2. For tables that take values as defaults from a source table, we expect that there will be a method that will initialize values from the source table. In this case, it is `initFromPurchTable`.
3. Rather than modify the `initFromPurchTable` method, we will add an event handler on the `ConFMSPurchVehicleOrderHandler` class, and create a new pre-post event handler method called `vendJourInitFromPurchTableEventHandler`.
4. We need to get the get the `VendInvoiceJour` record and set our new field based on the method's `_purchTable` parameter, which is done by the following lines of code:

```
public static void vendJourInitFromPTEventHandler(XppPrePostArgs
_args)
{
    PurchTable purchTable;
    VendInvoiceJour vendInvoiceJour = _args.getThis();

    if(!_args.existsArg("_purchTable"))
    {
        throw error(strFmt("@SYS22828",
                staticMethodStr(ConFMSPurchVehicleOrderHandler,

vendJourInitFromPurchTableEventHandler)));
    }
    purchTable = _args.getArg("_purchTable");
    vendInvoiceJour.ConFMSVehicleServiceOrder =
                        purchTable.ConFMSVehicleServiceOrder;
}
```

> The `VendInvoiceJour` table is passed by reference, so there is no need to send it back. We must not call update in this case because `initFrom` methods are often called before the record is inserted, and we would interfere with the normal execution of the code.

5. Add the event handler to the `VendInvoiceJour.initFromPurchTable` method as before.

You may notice on occasion that the drop-down list for the method is empty. AX uses a pattern to recognize event handler methods, and sometimes, this fails to execute correctly. This can be due to the method name length or compilation errors in the code. You can manually paste the method name, as the important parameter is `AOTLink`, which is set by the system based on the `Class` and `Method` parameters.

Using an extension table for additional fields

There is a new pattern for adding fields to standard tables that has been used from AX 2012 R2, wherein fields are actually added to an extension table. This would be joined to the primary table in a 1:1 join. This seems like a silver bullet—we can add fields to a standard table without modifying it!

There are two main limitations with this, from the footprint perspective.

- To maintain referential integrity, a `delete` action (or add an event handler to the `delete` method) must be placed on the parent table, otherwise, we will have orphaned records if the parent is deleted.
- We have to modify the forms to handle the extension table.

Of course, we still have to modify the forms to show the fields. However, this is the same for both the methods. Therefore, to add a single field to a standard table involves more work, but with advantages, for example, all of the table and field event handling for the new fields are completely separate from the standard table.

There is a performance benefit on updates when only the standard or extension table needs to be updated, although this is mitigated by having to first seek the parent table to get the extension table record. It also avoids potential buffer size issues when adding a large number of fields, such as note fields.

There is nothing new here that we haven't done before, so we will just list the steps required. We will take an example of `CustTable`; the steps involved in implementing this pattern are as follows:

1. Create the table named `ConCustTableExt` and add a primary key relation to `CustTable`, which will create a field named `CustTable` on our new table.

> This may seem odd to have the relation on the foreign table, but this helps reduce footprint and helps with referential integrity.

2. Add fields as required to the new table using fields groups to simplify adding them to the relevant forms.
3. Create a class to handle the delete event on `CustTable`; name it `ConCustTableExtHandler`.
4. Create a method `deleteEventHandler` that will locate and delete the extension record.
5. Add a subscription to the new event on CustTable's `delete` method.
6. Add the new data source to the form `CustTable` and set the **JoinSource** property to `CustTable`.
7. The relations are create in reverse for extension tables, so we have to modify the method, write for the data source `CustTable`, and add the following code after the call to `super()`:

```
if (!ConCustTableExt.RecId)
{
    ConCustTableExt.CustTable = custTable.RecId;
    ConCustTableExt.write();
}
```

You can then proceed to add fields as required to the form. In terms of deployment, you will have to handle the situation where there are customers without the extension table. This can be done by adding code to the form or writing a data initialization routine.

Changing the behavior of a class

If we intend to trigger a piece of logic when a method is executed, we would usually use an event. This is not always possible, for example, when we need to hook into a method during its execution. For this, we will use `PurchTableType` as an example, where the standard code synchronizes the delivery mode with the `tmpPurchTable` table, which is within the **Transport Management System** (**TRAX**).

This table is created within the `insert` method, and our example change is that we would reverse the vehicle service order flag if the delivery mode causes the standard code to select a carrier. The call stack for the standard code is as follows:

```
PurchLine.insert
Calls PurchLineType.insert
Calls PurchLineType.tmsModifiedDlvMode
Calls TMSDeliveryModeSyncAgentPurch.syncOnInsert
Calls TmsPurchTable.setCarrierFieldsFromDlvMode
Calls TmsPurchTable.setCarrierFields
```

Since we don't know whether the carrier fields were set until this code ran, and we must update our field before the record is inserted. We have to make a change to the insert method.

In order to maintain one of our design goals of reduced footprint, we need to take care when going about this. There are two methods in which we can solve the problem:

- Write a new method that contains our additional logic, and call this from the appropriate point in the standard method.
- Write a new class, extending the standard class, and override the method so that it performs the logic that we want it to.

> Remember that addition of an event subscription is not a modification to the table, and due to the way in which models are moved, there will be no conflict if an event subscription is already placed on the same method in the same layer. The only possible upgrade issues are if Microsoft moves the business logic elsewhere, or if a method parameter is changed from what we used within our handler.

The second method is a good technique, but does not remove the footprint on AX completely, and with the advent of event handling, the benefit is limited. For example, we could write a class that extends `PurchTableType` in order to override the `insert` method. This is limited because we only have two options available:

- Place the custom code before or after the call to `super()` in order to run that standard code
- Copy the insert method from `SalesLineType` and modify it in our class, without calling `super()`

The first option doesn't offer much more than creating a pre- or post-event subscription, except that we have access to all variables global to the class. Even so, it would be better to write a `parm` method to get this variable and use within an event subscription.

The second option offers the possibility to change the behavior as we desire, but at the cost of maintainability, as we have to manually compare these methods whenever we apply the upgrade; it is better to just place a call within the original method.

So, the solution to the problem in this case is to create a class that performs the required logic, which can be placed in a single line of code. If you are not sure, organize a peer review on the design, which (of course) should be a normal process as it is better to confront issues at the design stage than rewrite later.

The class's purpose is to perform actions on `PurchTable` and called from `PurchTableType`. We will therefore name the class `ConFMSPurchTableTypeHandler`, and construct it with a `PurchTable` record (which may not yet be inserted).

The pattern we are used to is to create a contract class, and pass it to a class that processes the request; this decoupling has been demonstrated as useful in earlier chapters. In this case, the `PurchTable` variable is already tightly coupled with the `PurchTableType` class—this is the class's sole purpose—so we will use `PurchTable` directly passed to our class:

1. Create the `ConFMSPurchTableTypeHandler` class, and add a `purchTable` class variable as `PurchTable` in the class declaration.
2. Create a `parm` method for `purchTable` like this: create a new method, delete the method content, type `parm`, and press *Tab*. Complete the dialog as prompted and press **OK**.

   Create a `construct` method as we have done before, and then a newFromPurchTable method. The code for this is shown here:

   ```
   public static ConFMSPurchTableTypeHandler
   newFromPurchTable(PurchTable _purchTable)
   {
       ConFMSPurchTableTypeHandler handler = ConFMSPurchTableTypeHand
   ler::construct();
       handler.parmPurchTable(_purchTable);
       return handler;
   }
   ```

3. Then, we need the method that performs our requirement to uncheck `ConFMSVehicleServiceOrder` if carrier information is present. To avoid multiple changes to `PurchTableType`, we will create a public method, `insert_preUpdate`, that calls the `checkSetConFMSVehicleServiceOrder` private method.
4. Crate a new private method, named `checkSetConFMSVehicleServiceOrder`, and enter the following lines of code:

   ```
   private void checkSetConFMSVehicleServiceOrder()
   {
       TMSPurchTable tmsPurchTable;
       if(purchTable.ConFMSVehicleServiceOrder == NoYes::No)
       {
   ```

```
        return;
    }
    tmsPurchTable = TMSPurchTable::find(purchTable.PurchId);
    // no need to check for rec id as CarrierServiceCode will
    // be empty if not found - not null.
    if(tmsPurchTable.CarrierServiceCode != "")
    {
        purchTable.ConFMSVehicleServiceOrder = NoYes::No;
    }
}
```

5. Create a new public method named `insert_preUpdate`. It simply calls our new method:

```
public void insert_preUpdate()
{
    this.checkSetConFMSVehicleServiceOrder();
}
```

> We do not call `update` or `insert` as `purchTable` is passed by reference. We can't update a record that does not exist yet, and calling insert will cause an error when the standard code inserts the record.

6. Finally, we can add our hook to `PurchTableType.insert`. To do this, we first drag the class into our project (as always) and open the `insert` method.
7. Locate the `purchTable.doInsert();` line and insert the following lines of code in the preceding line:

```
//Con FMS Modification by SB on 2014/11/06
//call custom update logic
ConFMSPurchTableTypeHandler::newFromPurchTable(PurchTable).insert_
preUpdate();
// Con end
```

> We are modifying standard code, so we should comment the change we have made.

8. We would also use this technique for the update method, by creating an `update_preUpdate` method and modifying `PurchTableType.update` in the same way.

This method should be used only when we cannot use an event subscription. Technically, we could have avoided it in this case. This would be done by adding a post-event handler to the `insert` and `update` methods.

We would then have to update the `purchTable` record using `doUpdate`, as the record will already be inserted or updated. We have to use `doUpdate` in order to avoid endless recursion, as it calls `purchTableType.update`.

There are two issues that arise out of this. Firstly, we are doubling the work for each insertion and update, and since updates to `PurchLine` also update the `PurchTable` record to maintain the status, it will cause many unnecessary writes.

The second issue is that it can cause errors on the user interface, as the record buffer on the form will be out of sync with the database record. This causes AX to produce an error for the user, asking them to refresh the form.

This can be solved, however, by refreshing the form data source for them. An example of this code is as follows:

```
FormDataSource purchTableDS;
//perform updates as required to the PurchTable record
// ...
if(purchTable.isFormDataSource())
{
    purchTableDS = purchTable.datasource();
    purchTableDS.research(true);
}
```

The `research` method will trigger the data source object to refresh its data from the database. Passing `true` as the parameter indicates whether or not it should maintain the current cursor position.

The following links explain the typical methods used to refresh data from the database:

- *FormDataSource.Refresh Method [AX 2012]*: `http://msdn.microsoft.com/en-us/library/formdatasource.refresh.aspx`
- *FormDataSource.reread Method [AX 2012]*: `http://msdn.microsoft.com/en-us/library/formdatasource.reread.aspx`
- *FormDataSource.research Method [AX 2012]*: `http://msdn.microsoft.com/en-us/library/formdatasource.research.aspx`

Extending a framework – vendor electronic payments

The electronic payments framework is designed to be extended, and when we dive into this framework, we can see that a lot of thought went into its design.

The first part of the problem that the designers faced was how to construct a specialized class that exports the required format. Since Dynamics AX is a global ERP solution, there can be many of these formats.

A common solution would be to use an enum, with an element for each format. We could use this enum within the user interface to configure which format to use, and also within code in order to construct the appropriate class. This is how the `PurchLineType` constructs its various specialized classes.

The problem is that this would require a modification to the base class's construct method, and there could be more than 256 payment methods worldwide—the limit for elements in an enum is 256.

> An enum is also a bad idea for this, as we should never modify a standard enum's elements. Microsoft may add their own, conflicting with the elements we added.

For a framework that was designed to be extended, this pattern has to be more flexible. Microsoft has created a clever design for this framework, as it avoids the need to modify the `construct` method to the base class.

This is our first look at using metadata in order to determine which class should be executed. During configuration, the user actually selects a class ID against the payment method. The interface shows them a nice description of the class, but behind the scenes, they are assigning a class ID to a payment method.

The framework's base class is `CustVendOutPaym`. In this class, the `construct` method is interesting:

```
public static Object construct(CustVendPaymModeClassId _classId)
{
    CustVendOutPaym custVendOutPaym;
    ;

    if (!SysDictClass::isSuperclass(_classId,
                                    classNum(CustVendOutPaym)))
```

```
        {
            throw error("@SYS55187");
        }
        custVendOutPaym = new DictClass(_classId).makeObject();
        return custVendOutPaym;
    }
```

The main part of this method is as follows:

```
custVendOutPaym = new DictClass(_classId).makeObject();
```

This constructs an instance of the `DictClass` object using a class ID (all objects in AX have an ID), and the `makeObject()` method to construct an instance of the class.

In long hand, the code is actually the following:

```
localDictClass = new DictClass(_classId);
custVendOutPaym = localDictClass.makeObject();
```

If we were to statically do this for the UK BACS payment method, it would read this:

```
custVendOutPaym = new VendOutPaym_UKBACS();
```

The preceding pattern is useful for allowing the user to select business logic through configuration. We will cover this in more detail in the *Exception handling* section in *Chapter 10, Advanced Development Techniques*.

For vendor payments, the classes begin with `VendOutPaym`, where many of the standard formats are already provided. Occasionally, a bank will require slightly different information for a standard format or have a format not currently available in Dynamics AX.

In either case, a new format should be created. There have been many cases where a format has been modified to suit a particular bank's requirements, only for a different bank to want to the standard format.

The best way to start here is to find a format that is similar and duplicate the set. In order to create a new format, the best way to start is by duplicating the `Format1` classes. These are designed to be templates to be copied for our own purposes.

The framework is instantiated with two classes, one that extends `VendOutPaym` and one that extends `VendOutPaymRecord`. The `VendOutPaym` is the class that is instantiated by the framework, and uses `VendOutPaymRecord` to output the data. Each format written adds a suffix to these classes.

For our format, we base it on `Format1`, which is made up of the `VendOutPaym_Format1` and `VendOutPaymRecordFormat1` classes. We will have to be very careful not to forget to refactor the various methods.

The format required by our bank ("My bank") is a fixed-width text file with no header or footer. The records must conform to the following:

Field	**Length**	**Example**
Receiving sort / routing code	6	001122
Receiving bank account	8	0011223344 (pad left with 0)
Receiving company, as known by the bank	20	Contoso Trading
Amount	20	The amount in the lowest currency unit prefixed with 0. For example: • £123.23 is 00000000000000012323 • $157.12 is 00000000000000015712
Your reference	12	YR000123
Senders sort / routing code	6	221100
Sender's account number	8	04332211 (pad left with 0)
Currency	3	The ISO currency code

To create the new custom payment format, follow these steps:

1. Right-click on **Classes** | **VendOutPaym_Format1** and choose **Duplicate**.
2. In `classDeclaration`, change the name of the class to `ConVendOutPaym_myBank`.
3. We copy the class to our project.
4. Right-click on **Classes** | **VendOutPaymRecordFormat1** and choose **Duplicate**.
5. In `classDeclaration`, change the name of the class to `ConVendOutPaymRecord_myBank`.
6. Again, we copy the class to our project.
7. Double-click on `ConVendOutPaym_myBank` in order to open all methods.

8. In description, refactor `VendOutPaym_Format1` to `ConVendOutPaym_myBank`.
9. In the open method and delete the following to lines, our format does not have a header or summary lines:

    ```
    openRecord = conins(openRecord,1,'Open Statement');
    file.writeExp(openRecord);
    ```

10. We also no longer require the `openRecord` container, so remove this line (the best practice compiler check will also point this out).
11. Change the string returned by `interfaceName` to `My bank format`, and create a label.
12. The `dialog` method allows us to add new options to the dialog presented to the user. In this case, we don't need to add further fields. Should we want to print a remittance, we would add the dialog field here, in the same way by which the standard code adds the control report option.
13. In `custVendOutPaymRecordRootClassId`, refactor `VendOutPaymRecordFormat1` to `ConVendOutPaymRecord_myBank`. This method tells the framework which output class to construct.
14. The `codepage` is usually fine, but you can use this to return create a file with a specific code page if required by the bank.
15. The sample close method inserts a footer line. Our format does not require this, so we remove the line:

    ```
    closeRecord = conins(closeRecord,1, 'Close Statement', total);
    ```

16. Close the code editor and double-click on the `ConVenOutPaymRecord_myBank` class to open all the methods.
17. The `checkValues` sample demonstrates how to add validation per `ledgerJournalTrans` record it processes. In our case, we will simply return super, as follows:

    ```
    boolean checkValues(LedgerJournalTrans
    _ledgerJournalTrans = null,
                       RunbaseProgress
    _progress          = null)
    {
        return super(_ledgerJournalTrans, _progress);
    }
    ```

18. We change the string returned by `interfaceName` to `My bank format` using the same label we created earlier.
19. To assist in formatting each field, we will create two new methods that will pad the values as required. This should contain the following code:

```
private str conFormatFieldRightAligned(str _field,
                                       int _length,
                                       str _prefix)
{
    _field = subStr(strLTrim(strRTrim(_field)),
                                       1, _length);
    return strRFix(_field, _length, _prefix);
}
private str conFormatFieldLeftAligned(str _field,
                                      int _length,
                                      str _suffix)
{
    _field = subStr(strLTrim(strRTrim(_field)),
                                       1, _length);
    return strLFix(_field, _length, _suffix);
}
```

20. We can now write our output method to conform to the specification provided by the bank. The code is as follows:

```
void output()
{
    str outRecord;
    str strAmt = num2str(custVendPaym.
paymAmountInForeignCurrency() * 100, 20, 0, 0, 0);

    paymStatus = CustVendPaymStatus::None;
    // Vendor Bank Sort Code
    // The method is spelt recievers...
    outRecord += this.conFormatFieldLeftAligned(
            custVendPaym.recieversBankRegistrationNumber(),
                                                6, " ");
    // Vendor Bank Account Number
    outRecord += this.conFormatFieldRightAligned(
             custVendPaym.recieversBankAccount(), 8, "0");
    // Vendor Name
```

```
        outRecord += this.conFormatFieldLeftAligned(
                custVendPaym.recieversCompanyName(), 20, " ");
        // Amount
        outRecord += this.conFormatFieldRightAligned(
                                              strAmt, 20, "0");
        // Our reference
        outRecord += this.conFormatFieldLeftAligned(
                custVendPaym.ledgerJournalTrans().Voucher,
                                                      12, " ");
        // Sender Bank Sort Code
        outRecord += this.conFormatFieldLeftAligned(
                custVendPaym.sendersBankRegistrationNumber(),
                                                       6, " ");
        // Sender Bank Account Number
        outRecord += this.conFormatFieldRightAligned(
                    custVendPaym.sendersBankAccount(), 8, "0");
        // Currency code
        outRecord += this.conFormatFieldLeftAligned(
                      custVendPaym.paymCurrencyCode(), 3, " ");

        custVendOutPaym.total(
                 custVendPaym.paymAmountInForeignCurrency());
        file.write(outRecord);
    }
```

> You may spot an apparent spelling mistake in recieve, but this is what the method is called.

21. This is the complete code. Before we try to use it, we should compile forward from `VendOutPaym` and `VendOutPaymRecord`. For each of these classes, right-click and go to **Add-Ins | Compile Forward**.

> We use the **Compile Forward** command to compile all classes that inherit from the select class.

To test this, we need to configure a payment method, which means venturing into the client user interface. A basic setup like this is something that you are expected to know over time, and understanding how the application works from a user perspective is very important for designing and developing high-quality code that works with the minimum number of test cycles:

1. Navigate to **Accounts payable** | **Setup** | **Payment** | **Methods of Payment** and click **New**.
2. Set **Method of Payment** to `MyBank`, **Description** to `My bank format`, and **Payment type** to `Electronic`.
3. Just below, in the **File formats** fast tab, click on the **Setup** button. The form that opens shows the allowable file formats, available to be selected against any method of payment, so don't remove any!
4. In the form, locate **My bank format** in the **Available** list and move it to the **Selected** list to the left, as shown in the following screenshot:

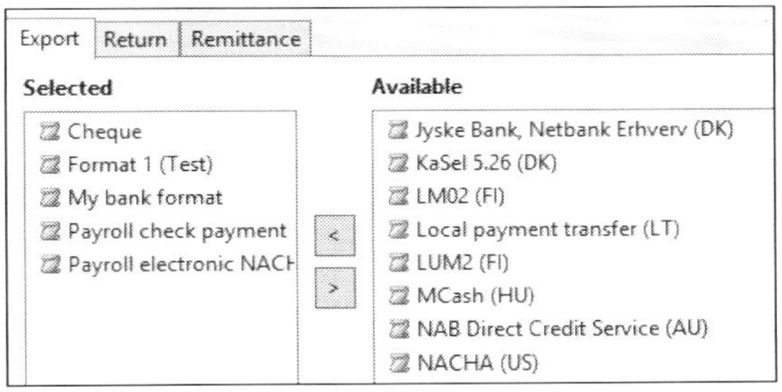

5. Close the form. You should now be able to select it in the **Export format** field.
6. For completeness, in the **General** fast tab, set **Account type** to `Bank` and **Payment account** to `USMF OPER` (if you are using Contoso data).
7. Close the form.
8. Navigate to **Accounts payable** | **Journals Payments** | **Payment journal**.
9. Click on **New** and select the first entry in the **Name** drop-down list in the grid.
10. Click on **Lines**.
11. In the **Account** field, select any supplier that is not stopped. Enter `1234.56` in the **Debit** column (we are paying them).
12. Select `MyBank` in the **Method of Payment** field, which will also set **Offset account** to the `USMF OPER` bank.

13. Go to **Functions** | **Generate payments**.
14. This form is intended to process one format at a time for a specific bank, so select `MyBank` in **Method of Payment** and `USMF OPER` in **Bank** account.
15. Before pressing **OK**, check **Show format** dialog. This displays the export format's dialog, allowing us to specify the filename.
16. Enter a filename, including the full path, and press **OK**.
17. Next, compare the output file to what is expected. We can reset **Payment status** to `None` by going to **Payment status** | **None** in the action pane strip.

Most of the errors we find are usually cases of missing or incorrect configuration, and to test fully, a new payment line should be created. This is because some of the values are set on the supplier and copied to the payment journal line.

Summary

The purpose of this chapter was to go through techniques of modifying standard or third-party code while keeping the footprint on AX at a minimum. We also covered where modifications should be made and the tools available for us to help determine this.

We took our first look at standard frameworks, and introduced the usage of metadata. In the next chapter, we will further explore the more advanced features of Dynamics AX, including the SysOperation framework, the global address book, and the financial dimension framework.

9

Advanced Features and Frameworks

In this chapter, we will introduce some advanced features and use them to extend our solution. The topics we will cover are as follows:

- Adding custom filters to list pages
- Advanced methods of adding query ranges
- Using the SysOperation framework
- Using the SysOperation framework's execution modes
- Customizing the user interface displayed by the SysOperation framework
- Tracking progress of scheduled tasks
- Understanding the global address book
- Accessing the financial dimension framework

Adding custom filters to list pages

Microsoft introduced a change in Dynamics AX 2012's List pages that meant that X++ can no longer be written directly on the form. This was, in part, to help provide a more seamless experience between the web interface (Enterprise Portal) and the Windows client.

One drawback of this is that the old method of using edit methods to add quick filters to a list page could no longer be used, as edit methods must run on the form if they are to access any data source other than the current record's form data source.

Microsoft obviously solved this and provided a new method to add custom filter controls. This, in many ways, is better than the previous method, as it does not require us to write code.

A list page created from the form template is made up of an action pane, a custom filter group control, and a grid.

When we add form controls to the `Filters` group control, they get three new properties:

- **FilterDataSource**
- **FilterField**
- **FilterExpression**

The first two properties define the field that the filter applies to, and the third property is the filter. The expression `%1` means the value the user entered. Setting the **FilterField** property and leaving **FilterExpression** at its default value of `%1` will simply filter the field by what the user enters.

AX does this in the same way as we construct a `QueryBuildRange` object against the data source, which means that the user can use wildcards and value ranges. This is fine for simple filters, but sometimes, we need to introduce more intelligence. Again, we can do this as we can treat it as a `QueryBuildRange` object.

Some examples of useful expressions are as follows:

FilterExpression	**Result**
`%1`	Pass the value directly to the resulting `QueryBuildRange` value
`..%1`	All values up to the value the user entered
`(dayRange(-%1, 0))`	Uses `SysQueryRangleUtil` to filter a `date` field from a number of days in the past until the current date
`(lessThanDate(%1))`	Uses `SysQueryRangleUtil` to filter the field for all records before the date the user entered

You can also be very creative with `FilterExpression`, but this can become hard to read; keeping it simple is important.

In order to add a simple filter to a list page, follow these steps:

1. On the `ConFMSVehicleTableListPage` form, expand **Designs** | **Design**.
2. The `Filters` form group control will be set as not visible by default. Change the **Visible** property to `Yes`.
3. Right-click on the `Filter` group control and choose **New** | **StringEdit**.
4. Rename the control to `FilterVehicleName` and complete the filter properties to filter the field `ConFMSVehicleTable.Name`. Leave `FilterExpression` as `%1`.
5. Save the form and open it.
6. Entering a partial match will return no result; you have to place a `*` sign. We wish to filter on the wildcard by default. Close the form and alter `FilterExpression` to `*%1*`.

Entering a partial match now returns all vehicles that contain the string entered.

Advanced methods of adding ranges to list pages

We can also do this for date controls, but we face a problem, should we wish to provide separate filter controls for from and to dates that act on the same date field. Filter controls alter the filter on the target field, so one filter control will override the filter set by the other. Also, if we specify a field of type `DateEdit` as a custom filter control, we can't enter a date range in that field—it will insist it is a valid date.

The only way around this is to use a form part, where we can add code to handle situations like this. The drawback is that the form part will not be visible, if we deploy it to the Enterprise Portal.

We will use the vehicle service list page as an example for this. The next part introduces programmatically controlling the form's data source query, by creating a range against the form's data source object.

The form part will initialize from the list page's data source, and use it to control the data sources query ranges.

To create the form part, follow these steps:

1. Create a new form under your project's **Forms** named `ConFMSVehServiceTableListPageFilterPart`.
2. In the `classDeclaration`, declare `callerDS` as a `FormDataSource`. We need to store a reference to the calling form's data source.
3. We need to initialize the `callerDS` from the caller, which must be `ConFMSVehicleTable`. Override the `init` method and enter the following lines of code:

```
public void init()
{
    ConFMSVehServiceTable caller;
    super();
    if(element.args().dataset() !=
       tableNum(ConFMSVehServiceTable))
    {
        // we would normally throw an error,
        // but this is silent method, which
        // may be useful.
        element.close();
        return;
    }
    caller = element.args().record();
    if(!caller.isFormDataSource())
    {
        //if it isn't a form data source,
        // it wasn't called from a form
        element.close();
        return;
    }
    callerDS = element.args().record().dataSource();
}
```

4. We can now work on adding `edit` methods, but since we aren't using a data contract, we need to declare the range values and query ranges as global to the form, which is done by adding the following to the `classDeclaration`:

```
FromDate        fromDate;
ToDate          toDate;
QueryBuildRange qbrServiceDate;
```

5. Before we create the `edit` methods, we should have a method that we call that handles the query ranges, create a new form method, and enter the following lines of code:

```
private void updateQuery()
{
    qbrServiceDate =
        SysQuery::findOrCreateRange(
                callerDS.queryBuildDataSource(),
                fieldNum(ConFMSVehServiceTable,
                     ServiceDate));
    qbrServiceDate.value(queryRange(fromDate, toDate));
    callerDS.executeQuery();
}
```

6. The `queryRange` function handles the conversion from the dates to a valid query range value, for example "03/03/2015..04/04/2015".

7. We now need two `edit` methods, as follows:

```
public edit FromDate editFromDate(boolean _set, FromDate _
fromDate)
{
    if (_set)
    {
        fromDate = _fromDate;
        element.updateQuery();
    }
    return fromDate;
}
public edit ToDate editToDate(boolean _set,ToDate _toDate)
{
    if (_set)
    {
        toDate = _toDate;
        element.updateQuery();
    }
    return toDate;
}
```

8. Finally, create a form group control with the following properties:

Name	`GroupDateFilter`
Caption	`Service date (using the existing label)`
Columns	`1 (default)`

   Since the **ArrangeMethod** property is set to its default value of `vertical`, if we set the **Columns** property to `2`, AX will place the controls in two columns. In this case, it uses too much horizontal space, so the default value of `1` is fine.

9. Drag the two `edit` methods onto the new group control.
10. Save the form, and create a form part called `ConFMSVehServiceTableFilterPart` and reference it to the new form using the **Form** property (set it to `ConFMSVehServiceTableFilterPart`).
11. Set **Caption** to `Filters`.
12. Create a menu item for the form part, as you have done before, under your project's **Menu items | Display** node. Set the **ObjectType** property to `FormPart` and the **Object** property to `ConFMSVehServiceTableFilterPart`.
13. Add the form part to the `ConFMSVehServiceTableListPage` list page by dragging the menu item onto the **Parts** node.
14. Ensure that you specify the data source as `ConFMSVehServiceTable`.
15. Save the changes and ensure that all objects are added to your project.

When you open the form, the new form part will be on the right, and you can use this to filter the form. This was a simple example, demonstrating how we can control a data source in a different object.

As discussed previously, AX will create a data source object for each table added to the form with the name of the table suffixed with _DS. The table will also have a reference to this, accessible through the `datasource()` method.

From there, we can access the `QueryBuildDataSource` object, which allows us (among others) to create and access the form's data source ranges. Although we can do this via methods on the `QueryBuildDataSource` object, the `SysQuery` class has a static method that makes this easier.

Using the SysOperation framework

Using the SysOperation framework may seem daunting at first, but it is not that different from the code we have written that utilizes data contract classes. The pattern is similar; we just get some features for free.

The framework replaces `RunBase` from prior versions of AX, and allows easy access to adding tasks to the batch processing framework. When using this framework, we have the option to perform the task synchronously or asynchronously or run it as a scheduled task.

The framework has some really cool features, such as an automatic UI builder from the data contract class, and a built-in ability to allow the user to submit the task as a batch task. The user interface that is displayed is also accessible from the batch task, should the task be submitted as a batch. The efforts we will make later to improve the user interface are not just for the initial dialog that the framework constructs for us.

To use the framework, we need three classes:

- **Controller**: This is a class that extends `SysOperationServiceController` that controls both the UI and instantiation of the processing class
- **Data contract**: This is a class that contains the properties required by the process class
- **Processing class**: This is the class that actually does the work

To step into this, we will extend our `ConFMSVehicleGroupChange` class to be called using the framework instead.

In its simplest form, the framework performs these tasks:

- Interrogates the data contract and builds a UI
- Constructs the processing class using a default constructor
- Calls a method on the processing class with the data contract

The target processing class in this case is `ConFMSVehicleGroupChange`, and the framework needs to call a `public` method that accepts the data contract the class needs.

For our class to be capable of being instantiated and called by the controller, it needs a default constructor and a public instance method that access the data contract. Luckily, our class already has a method that does this, `runContract`. We might pass this off as luck, but it was a natural design choice, and this is an example of where a little more investment in the design saves a lot of time later on.

To create the controller, follow these steps:

1. Create a new class called `ConFMSVehicleGroupChangeController`.
2. Modify the `classDeclaration` so that it extends `SysOperationServiceController`.
3. Right-click on the class and choose **Override | Caption**.
4. Simply change this to return `Vehicle group change`, selecting it as a label. This sets the caption if it is added to a batch queue.
5. Do the same for the `parmDialogCaption` method; this sets the title of the dialog that the framework creates from the data contract.

> When overriding methods that have default parameters, you may receive a compilation error. You will need to handle this, which in the case of these two methods is done by making the parameter default to `""`.

6. Finally, we need an entry point, which is a `main` method. The method should be created as per the following lines of code:

```
public static void main(Args args)
{
    ConFMSVehicleGroupChangeController  controller;

    controller = new ConFMSVehicleGroupChangeController(
                    classStr(ConFMSVehicleGroupChange),
                    methodStr(ConFMSVehicleGroupChange,
                              runContract),
                    SysOperationExecutionMode::Synchronous);
    controller.startOperation();
}
```

7. Save the changes, right-click on the class, and select **Open**.

We get a dialog with a field created automatically from the contract. We can even submit it to the batch queue. Pretty cool, and very little additional effort!

This witchcraft does deserve an explanation.

Since our class extends `SysOperationServiceController`, we get a lot of functionality, the first being that it can construct a dialog from the data contract. However, how did it know?

When the new method executed, the framework looked at the `runContract` method and determined the contract from the method's input parameter.

The call to `startOperation` caused the system to build the UI and handle the code execution based on what the user does. The dialog is constructed using the EDTs specified in the data member methods. Since we constructed the EDTs correctly with reference to the main table, it can also provide a simple lookup for us.

This explains why the new method requires the class and method names, but the third parameter is an execution mode. This comes into its own if we execute the controller programmatically. **Synchronous** means it will run in line with the current process; this is explained next.

> The `classStr` and `methodStr` intrinsic functions, as explained in the previous chapters, are used to check whether the functions refer to exists at compile time.

Using the SysOperation framework execution modes

We can also use the controller programmatically, without the dialog. For this, we need to interact with the contract and decide how it will be executed.

One of the benefits of this framework is that we can execute the code asynchronously or add it to a batch queue. To demonstrate this, we need a test class so that we can call the controller programmatically. To do this, create a new class called `ConFMSSysOpTest`, then create a main method, and enter the following lines of code:

```
public static void main(Args _args)
{
    ConFMSVehicleGroupChangeController  controller;
    ConFMSVehicleGroupChangeContract    dataContract;
```

```
        ConFMSVehicleId                       vehicleId;
        ConFMSVehicleGroupId                  groupId;
        ConFMSVehicleTable                    firstVehicle;
        ConFMSVehicleGroup                    firstGroup;

        // get any vehicle, clear the group and remember the id
        ttsBegin;
        select forUpdate firstVehicle;
        vehicleId = firstVehicle.VehicleId;
        firstVehicle.VehicleGroupId = "Invalid";
        firstVehicle.update();
        ttsCommit;
        info(strFmt("1: Vehicle group is %1",
                 firstVehicle.VehicleGroupId));

        // get any valid vehicle group
        select firstOnly firstGroup;
        controller = new ConFMSVehicleGroupChangeController(
                        classStr(ConFMSVehicleGroupChange),
                              methodStr(ConFMSVehicleGroupChange,
                                     runContract),
                          SysOperationExecutionMode::Synchronous);

        // Initialize data contract
        dataContract = controller.getDataContractObject("_contract");
        dataContract.vehicleGroupId(groupId);
        dataContract.vehicleId(vehicleId);
        controller.parmShowDialog(false);

        select firstVehicle where firstVehicle.VehicleId == vehicleId;
        info(strFmt("2: Vehicle group is %1",
                 firstVehicle.VehicleGroupId));
    }
```

Right-click on the class and select **Open** to test whether this works as expected.

Executing code asynchronously

The first mode we will try is asynchronous, which is done by altering the `SysOperationExecutionMode` parameter to `Asynchronous`, as shown in the following code snippet:

```
controller = new ConFMSVehicleGroupChangeController(
                    classStr(ConFMSVehicleGroupChange),
                        methodStr(ConFMSVehicleGroupChange,
                            runContract),
                     SysOperationExecutionMode::Asynchronous);
```

To verify that the code actually runs asynchronously, we will add a command to pause execution for 3 seconds.

Change the `ConFMSVehicleGroupChange.run` method to add the following line just before the `ttsbegin`:

```
sleep(3000);
```

Then add the following lines of code to the `main` method of the `test` class. The 5-second delay should be enough to allow the operation to complete, and we expect to see the vehicle group change when the second `info` statement executes:

```
sleep (5000);
select firstVehicle where firstVehicle.VehicleId == vehicleId;
info(strFmt("3: Vehicle group is %1",
            firstVehicle.VehicleGroupId));
```

The code executed by the SysOperation framework always runs in CIL, so we must generate an incremental CIL by going to **Build | Generate incremental CIL**. If we have deleted a method or renamed or deleted a type, we must generate a full CIL.

Once the incremental CIL generation is complete, right-click on the class and choose **Open**.

The output from the class indicates that the code didn't run asynchronously. Why? There are two main rules that govern this when the execution mode is asynchronous:

- The code has to be instantiated on the client, which may seem odd but there is a reason for it, which is as follows
- The class that the framework calls has to be registered in the AxClient service group

The client cannot execute the code in separate threads. It uses a `Wcf` call to execute code asynchronously. This means that we need to call a class that is registered as a service reference that is added to the `AxClient` service group. As another benefit of following good design patterns, we have already written the `ConFMSVehicleServices` class, with the `updateVehicleGroup` method, and referenced it in the `ConFMSVehicleServices` service.

First, we need to change our test `main` method in `ConFMSSysOpTest` so that we construct the controller as follows:

```
controller = new ConFMSVehicleGroupChangeController(
                    classStr(ConFMSVehicleServices),
                         methodStr(ConFMSVehicleServices,
                                updateVehicleGroup),
                   SysOperationExecutionMode::Asynchronous);
```

Then we need to add the service to the `AxClient` service group, do this with the following steps:

1. Right-click on the **AOT node Service Groups | AxClient**, and choose **New Service Node Reference**.
2. Change the **Name** and **Service** properties to `ConFMSVehicleServices`.
3. Finally, right-click on `AxClient` and choose **Deploy service group**, which also regenerates CIL.

Let's try again—right-click on `ConFMSSysOpTest` and choose **Open**.

The messages displayed show that the change happens between the two `info` statements. You may find, depending on the speed of your system, that you may need to alter the timing of the `sleep` statements, remembering to regenerate the CIL for each change.

This means that a task that we don't need to wait for can be executed asynchronously, releasing the user interface. We can use this method to make the user interface more responsive.

This technique isn't used very often, as it takes some effort to feed the result back to the user for saving them a slight delay. For heavy processing tasks, it is better to use the `ReliableAsynchronous` execution mode. But the technique has a place, as shown in the following concept:

1. Create the `controller` class that performs the update. Create an action menu item from it, and add the menu item as a button on a form. The form will need to create a correlation ID and pass it through the menu item parameters. The main method can use this to set a hidden data contract parameter.

2. The `controller` class, as part of the `afterOperation` event, creates or updates a tracking record from the correlation ID.
3. The form polls this record, tells the user when the task was completed, and displays the result.

We will cover a pattern similar to this concept later in this chapter.

Executing code using the batch framework

There are two other execution modes: `ReliableAsynchronous` and `ScheduledBatch`. In these cases, we don't need to call a service, and we could have left the original test code untouched.

Both of these methods submit jobs to the batch server for execution, where the `ReliableAsynchronous` method will auto-delete the jobs after execution.

The jobs do not execute immediately, but within a minute of submission. This is the rate at which the batch server polls for waiting jobs at this rate. We should use this method for performing asynchronous or scheduled jobs that require heavy processing.

Programmatically speaking, we wouldn't want to use the `ScheduledBatch` mode. It would only be used as a result of the user configuring the task to run as a batch using the **Batch** tab.

To submit the task as `ReliableAsynchronous`, simply change the code that constructs the controller to use this execution mode. On execution, you may notice that the info message indicates that nothing was done, but if you wait for about 1 minute and check the vehicle record, you will see that it has succeeded. You can also see the batch history for this.

Last value and usage data

You may have noticed that when we executed the controller, the system remembered the last values. It does this by serializing and deserializing the contract into the users' usage data.

If we try again now, the dialog doesn't display. It stored the value of the `ShowDialog` property, which we had set to false when trying asynchronous processing. This is not exactly desirable.

We may alter the code to be as follows:

```
public static void main(Args args)
{
    ConFMSVehicleGroupChangeController  controller;

    controller = new ConFMSVehicleGroupChangeController(
                        classStr(ConFMSVehicleGroupChange),
                        methodStr(ConFMSVehicleGroupChange,
                                  runContract),
                     SysOperationExecutionMode::Synchronous);
    controller.parmShowDialog(true);
    controller.startOperation();
}
```

But we are merely asserting the default, so the code will simply load the last values again and set it back, and the dialog will still refuse to display. We could call a method to save the last value, but then we would lose the saved values from the contract. This may be undesirable, especially if the user typically runs the routines with the same, or similar, values.

A technique we can use is to load the last values first, alter the `ShowDialog` property, and then save the values, using the following code before the call to `startOperation`:

```
    controller.loadFromSysLastValue();
    controller.parmShowDialog(true);
    controller.saveLast();
```

Handling the result of a task processed asynchronously

If we do decide to execute a task asynchronously within an update, we have to be aware of the implications if the task fails. Asynchronous tasks don't feed any result back to the caller. The main update task may already have completed and its database updates may have been committed to the database. These tasks run in a detached process, so if we offload a task to a server for asynchronous execution and continue as if the task will succeed, we will have to deal with this exception through a compensation pattern.

The compensation pattern is much like a coffee shop queue, as it is important to process the customers' requests quickly. In an ACID transaction, the customer makes the request at the till, the shop makes the coffee, customer pays, and the customer takes away the coffee. Should the shop not have coffee or the customer does not have the means to pay, the entire transaction is rolled back. The problem is that we have the baristas standing around waiting for an order and customers waiting for coffee.

The compensation pattern used by coffee shops allows the customer to place the order while queuing, and by the time they get to the till, the coffee is already being made. Should the shop run out of coffee after the payment is made, they either compensate the customer with an alternative or refund the payment.

If we consider the server as the barista, we would want to keep it as busy as possible all the time, and we can achieve this using the SysOperation framework.

We need to be careful when using this method, where appropriate users are sending e-mails, printing reports, performing some integration with third-party applications, or tasks where the asynchronous part of the update can be handled without affecting the stability of the system or reliability of the data.

The SysOperation framework has an `afterOperation` method that is called by the system calls on completion. We can override this on the controller by right-clicking on the `ConFMSVehicleGroupChangeController` class and choosing **Override | afterOperation**.

In this method, we would handle any failure using the `_asyncResult` object. We also have access to the data contract. In this method, we can write code to deal with the particular failure, which could be writing a log record, and potentially write code to retry the operation.

References

Introduction to the SysOperation framework, `http://www.microsoft.com/en-gb/download/confirmation.aspx?id=29215`, is useful for further reading on the SysOperation framework; the white paper does make some changes to the code, which in our opinion are unnecessary.

You can also refer to *Batch server overview [AX 2012]* at `http://technet.microsoft.com/en-us/library/dd309586.aspx`.

Customizing the user interface displayed by the SysOperation framework

Let's take a step back to the point where we were calling ConFMSVehicleGroupChangeController's main method directly.

The system very cleverly constructs the user interface; it does this simply by adding the data contracts data member directly to the dialog. There are some simple changes we can make to the data contract to control how they are displayed.

We make these changes by altering the decoration at the top of each data member. The following examples are useful for this:

SysOperationLabelAttribute("New vehicle group"),	Sets the label displayed on the dialog
SysOperationHelpTextAttribute ("Please select...");	Sets the help text for the resulting control
SysOperationDisplayOrderAttribute("2")	Causes the control to be placed second in the resulting dialog

An example decoration for the vehicleGroup method can be as follows:

```
[DataMemberAttribute,
 SysOperationLabelAttribute("New vehicle group"),
 SysOperationHelpTextAttribute("Please select...");
 SysOperationDisplayOrderAttribute("2")]
```

> As always, use labels in your code. To do this in the preceding code, use the literalStr(<Label Id>) command, for example, SysOperationLabelAttribute(literalStr("@CON123")).

Try to change the sort order and label; but before you test this, generate an incremental CIL and restart the client. This is easy to do, and any dialog that the SysOperation framework constructs from this contract will behave this way, whether it is a routine or a report.

We can go much further. We can attach a user interface builder to the data contract that can provide finer control over the interface, and programmatically hide or disable controls.

In the following steps, we will create a UI builder class that performs additional validation, and hides the vehicle ID if the controller was called from a vehicle record:

1. Create a class named `ConFMSVehicleGroupChangeUIBuilder`. Add extends `SysOperationAutomaticUIBuilder` to the class declaration.
2. We need two dialog fields that we will later bind to the data contract, the completed `classDeclaration` should look like this:

```
class ConFMSVehicleGroupChangeUIBuilder
      extends SysOperationAutomaticUIBuilder
{
    DialogField vehicleIdField;
    DialogField vehGroupIdField;
}
```

3. We now need to bind the contract's data member methods to the dialog fields. This is done in the `postBuild` method. Right-click on the class, select **Override | postBuild**, and enter the following lines of code:

```
public void postBuild()
{
    ConFMSVehicleGroupChangeContract contract;

    super();
    contract = this.dataContractObject();

    vehicleIdField = this.bindInfo().getDialogField(
            contract,
            methodStr(ConFMSVehicleGroupChangeContract,
                      vehicleId));
    vehGroupIdField = this.bindInfo().getDialogField(
            contract,
            methodStr(ConFMSVehicleGroupChangeContract,
                      vehicleGroupId));
}
```

4. In order to handle dialog field events, we need to create suitable methods, and register them as an override. Create a method called `validateVehicleGroup`, as shown here:

```
public boolean validateVehicleGroupId(FormStringControl
                                                  _control)
{
```

```
        ConFMSVehicleGroupChangeContract localContract;
        ConFMSVehicleGroupChange localValChange;

        localContract =
            ConFMSVehicleGroupChangeContract::construct();
        localContract.vehicleId(vehicleIdField.value());
        localContract.vehicleGroupId(_control.valueStr());

        localValChange =
                ConFMSVehicleGroupChange::newFromContract
                                            (localContract);
        return localValChange.validate();
    }
```

> The method declaration has to match the method we will register as an override. We can achieve this by overriding the required method on a form control of the right type. The first parameter will always be the form control object that triggered the event.

5. We have our validate method. We now need to hook it to the dialog field's event. In the `postBuild` method overriden earlier, add the following lines at the end of the method:

```
vehGroupIdField.registerOverrideMethod(
        methodStr(FormStringControl, validate),
        methodStr(ConFMSVehicleGroupChangeUIBuilder,
                validateVehicleGroupId),
        this);
```

Nearly done! But we haven't handled hiding the vehicle ID field if it was called from a vehicle record. How can we determine this from within the UI builder class? We can't; only the controller's `main` method knows this, which means we need a mechanism to tell the UI builder whether or not to hide the field. Since we attach the UI builder to the data contract, we will add a hidden field to the data contract, as follows:

1. First, change the decoration in the `classDeclaration` so that it is associated with the UI Builder:

```
[DataContractAttribute,
    SysOperationContractProcessingAttribute(
        classStr('ConFMSVehicleGroupChangeUIBuilder'))]
```

2. Then add a variable to the `classDeclaration`, as follows:

```
NoYesId hideVehicleId;
```

3. Add a data member method for the variable, with the `visibility` attribute:

```
[DataMemberAttribute,
 SysOperationControlVisibilityAttribute(false)]
public NoYesId hideVehicleId(
        NoYesId _hideVehicleId = hideVehicleId)
{
    hideVehicleId = _hideVehicleId;
    return hideVehicleId;
}
```

4. Finally, we need to modify our controller's `main` method to handle the case where it was called from a vehicle record, which is done like this:

```
public static void main(Args _args)
{
    ConFMSVehicleGroupChangeController controller;
    ConFMSVehicleTable vehicle;
    ConFMSVehicleGroupChangeContract contract;

    controller = new ConFMSVehicleGroupChangeController(
                    classStr(ConFMSVehicleGroupChange),
                              methodStr(
                              ConFMSVehicleGroupChange,
                              runContract),
                  SysOperationExecutionMode::Synchronous);

    controller.initParmDefault();
    controller.loadFromSysLastValue();
    controller.parmShowDialog(true);

    switch(_args.dataset())
    {
        case tableNum(ConFMSVehicleTable):
        case tableNum(ConFMSVehicleTableCar):
        case tableNum(ConFMSVehicleTableTrailer):
        case tableNum(ConFMSVehicleTableTruck):
            vehicle = _args.record();
            contract =
```

```
                    controller.getDataContractObject(
                                            '_contract');
                contract.hideVehicleId(true);
                contract.vehicleId(vehicle.VehicleId);
                break;
        }

        controller.saveLast();
        controller.startOperation();
    }
```

5. Since the `_args` object is initialized only when called from a menu item, we should do this now; drag `ConFMSVehicleGroupChangeController` onto the project node **Output**, which is under **Menu items**.
6. Change the label to `Change vehicle group`, selecting the appropriate label, and open it. The new property is hidden as expected, and the vehicle ID still appears.
7. Try to clear the value in the `Vehicle group` field; you should get a validation error.
8. Now drag the menu item onto the `ConFMSVehicleTable` form, onto the button group **MaintainGroup**, which is under **ActionPaneHeader | HeaderHomeTab**.
9. Save the form and open it to test the new button. The vehicle ID does not appear.

We should tidy this up by refreshing the calling data source if `_args.record()` was a form data source. This is done in the same way as we have done a few times before. Refer back if you need help with this.

There is clearly a lot more you can do with the framework, so feel free to explore the other methods that can be overridden on the UI builder class.

Tracking progress of scheduled tasks

In order to track the progress of a routine that isn't running synchronously, we need a method to write the state periodically. A table is clearly the best choice for this, and it may seem straightforward.

To do this, we will create a unique number and store it in the contract that acts as a correlation identifier. The calling routine would create this so that it can inquire about the status of that particular task. We could use a `guid`, which is a type in AX. Creating a new `guid` is done by this code:

```
guid myNewGuid = newGuid();
```

However, we are going to store this in a table, so we can simply use the record ID.

We will create the status record, which will contain fields to store the status (enum), the progress (such as the quantity processed and the total quantity to process), and details of any errors produced by the routine.

As the routine processes the data, it will update the record located via the record ID passed through the contract.

There is a problem, however. The routine will process its data in a transaction, and therefore, the updates to our status table will also be within that transaction. The record will appear unchanged until the routine finally issues a `ttscommit`. If the routine throws an error, the status record updates will also be rolled back.

The solution is to update the data in a separate transaction and make the code easier to use. This should be done as a static method on the status table.

Let's say our table is called `ConFMSSysOpStatus`. The method will then be as follows:

```
static void updateStatus(RefRecId _refId,
                         ConFMSSysOpStatus _status,
                         Qty _processed,
                         Qty _total,
                         ErrorMsg _errorMsg)
{
    UserConnection    conn;
    ConFMSSysOpStatus statusRecord;

    conn = new UserConnection();
    ttsBegin;
    statusRecord = null;
    statusRecord.setConnection(conn);

    select forupdate statusRecord
        where statusRecord.RecId == _recId;
    statusRecord.Status = _status;
    statusRecord.Processed = _processed;
    statusRecord.ErrorMsg = _errorMsg;
    statusRecord.Total = _total;
    if(statusRecord.RecId == 0)
```

```
        {
            statusRecord.insert();
        }
        else
        {
            statusRecord.update();
        }
        ttsCommit;
    }
```

With this method, we can also allow the task to be cancelled. We can add a field based on `NoYesId` that the routine checks each the batch routine executes, we can choose whether to commit and exit the routine or roll the transaction back with `throw error("Operation cancelled by user")`.

An example of this, with a progress bar on a submitting form, is included within the available downloads.

Understanding the global address book

The global address book normalizes the name and address data held against entities such as customers and suppliers. Changing the name, address, or contact information against a customer will also appear to change the address of the vendor if it is linked to the same address book entry and this information isn't actually stored in the vendor record.

It does so by associating the entity with a record in `DirPartyTable`. This table also has some special case tables that inherit from it, as shown in the following diagram (which was taken using the **Type hierarchy browser**):

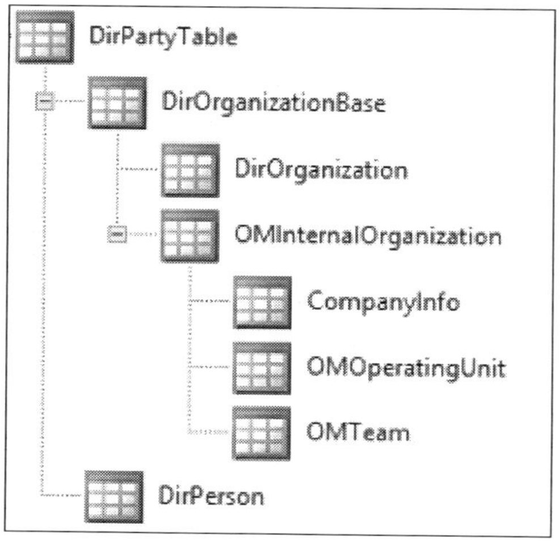

The tables generally used are `DirPartyTable` and `DirPerson`. Looking at these tables, there doesn't appear to be enough fields. We have the following fields against `DirPartyTable`:

- `KnownAs`
- `LanguageId`
- `Name`
- `NameAlias`
- `PartyNumber`
- `PrimaryAddressLocation`
- `PrimaryContactEmail`
- `PrimaryContactFax`
- `PrimaryContactPhone`
- `PrimaryContactTelex`
- `PrimaryContactURL`

The fields beginning with `PrimaryContact` are primary key relations to `LogisticsElectronicAddress`. The `PrimaryAddressLocation` relates to the entity's primary address location.

Electronic addresses

The structure of electronic addresses in AX is designed to be as flexible as possible so there isn't a field for each type of communication, such as phone, fax, and e-mail. There is a record that relates to a table that determines the type of communication.

The main tables used in this set are as follows:

Table	Relation	Purpose
`DirPartyTable`		A global address book record
`DirPartyLocation`	`Party ==` `DirPartyTable.RecId`	This relates the address book record to the location records
`LogisticsLocation`	`LogisticsLocation.RecId ==` `DirPartyLocation.Location`	The location we are associating with the address book record

Table	Relation	Purpose
LogisticsElectronic Address	Location == LogisticsLocation. RecId	This stores the communication address and type, such as e-mail or telephone number
LogisticsElectronic AddressRole	ElectronicAddress == LogisticsElectronic Address.RecId	This maps the address to the location role
LogisticsLocation Role	RecId == LogisticsElectronic AddressRole. LocationRole	This determines the location type, such as business, not the type of communication

Although this design is designed to be fully flexible, there has to be a basis by which we can determine the type. This is the LogisticsElectronicAddressTypes enum. This doesn't differentiate between types of telephones, a mobile or cellphone number is when Type is Phone and isMobilePhone is Yes.

This level of flexibility comes at a cost, and even when armed with relationships, it is still difficult to navigate at table level. Thankfully, we can use a view to simplify this. Locate the LogisticsEntityContactInfoView view and open the table browser. We usually won't use the tables to get the contact information data; we would normally use this view.

Postal addresses

The PrimaryAddressLocation field reveals how addresses are stored in Dynamics AX. This doesn't relate to an address but a location. A location could be something like 'main office', which in turn relates to an address record in LogisticsPostalAddress.

This design is made to handle situations such as this: a company has moved to a new address and this address might be known in advance. The LogisticsPostalAddress table is a ValidTimeState table, which means that changes to the records in this table create a new version. We can also say that the address will change at a specific date/time. When the interface shows the current record, it does so by selecting a record where the current date and time fall between the ValidFrom and ValidTo fields.

A good example of this in use is a sales order. Against a customer, we can set up a primary location, which is associated with an address. When the sales order is created, the current address from `LogisticsPostalAddress` is associated with it—not the location. Should the customer's address change, the address associated with the sales order record will not be changed, so the order will be delivered to the address that was set when the order was created.

The `ValidTimeState` tables will be discussed in *Chapter 10, Advanced Development Techniques*.

The logistics tables define locations (`LogisticsLocation`) and their addresses (`LogisticsPostalAddress`). But looking at the location associated with a customer, we can have multiple roles, such as delivery address, invoice address, and so on. These location roles are defined in data by the `LogisticsLocationRole` and `LogisticsLocationRoleTranslation` tables. The translation table allows the client to present the role in the any of the supported languages.

To take the example of a customer, the tables involved in this are listed in the following table:

Table	**Relation**	**Purpose**
`DirPartyTable`		The global address book record
`DirPartyLocation`	`DirPartyLocation.Party ==` `DirPartyTable.RecId`	Relates the address book record to location records
`DirPartyLocationRole`	`DirPartyLocationRole.PartyLocation ==` `DirPartyLocation.RecId`	Associates the location's role with the party location record
`LogisticsLocation`	`LogisticsLocation.RecId ==` `DirPartyLocation.Location`	The location we are associating with the address book record
`LogisticsPostalAddress`	`LogisticsPostalAddress.Location ==` `LogisticsLocation.RecId`	The address of the location

The other main address tables to be aware of are those starting with `LogisticsAddress`. These are the backing tables for the address element, such as country, city, and so on. This can seem a little complicated, especially if we wish to create an address programmatically. Fortunately, Microsoft has written views that flatten some of this information for easier access. Some useful views are:

- `DirPartyPostalAddressView`
- `LogisticsPostalAddressView`
- `LogisticsEntityPostalAddressView`

Creating addresses programmatically

The `DirPartyPostalAddressView` view is particularly interesting, as it also allows us to create records. Like all views in AX, it is read-only. However, we can write to the record buffer, and submit it to a class that will do all the hard work for us.

The code to create an address from a party record (for example,`CustTable.Party`) is as follows:

```
DirPartyPostalAddressView   addressView;

addressView.Party            = _partyRecId;
addressView.IsLocationOwner = NoYes::Yes;
addressView.IsPrimary        = _isPrimary;
addressView.State            = _state; // must exist or blank
addressView.County           = _county; // must exist or blank
addressView.City             = _city;
addressView.Street           = _street;
addressView.ZipCode          = _postalcode;
addressView.CountryRegionId = _country; // must exist
if(_isPrimary)
    addressView.LocationName = "Primary address";
addressView = DirPartyLocationEntity::createAddressForParty(
                                        addressView, _roles);
```

The `_roles` variable is a container of record IDs from `LogisticsLocationRole`. To get the business role, use the following lines of code:

```
RefRecId roleId = LogisticsLocationRole::findBytype(
                      LogisticsLocationRoleType::Business).RecId;
```

If we wish to pass a single role, we can use the syntax `[roledId]` as the parameter. We can use a similar technique to create an electronic address in this case:

```
private RefRecId createElectronicAddress(
                LogisticsElectronicAddressMethodType _type,
                Description _description,
                LogisticsElectronicAddressLocator _locator,
                PhoneLocal _extension,
                RefRecId _locationRecId,
                NoYes _isPrimary,
                NoYes _isMobile,
                NoYes _isSMS)
{
    LogisticsElectronicAddress  electronic;
    LogisticsLocation           location;
    RefRecId                    childLocRecId;
    // A location record id would be passed if we
    // were adding an electronic address
    // to a logistics address, for example, head office phone number
    select firstOnly RecId from location
        where location.ParentLocation == _locationRecId &&
                location.IsPostalAddress == false;
    childLocRecId = location.RecId;
    if(childLocRecId == 0)
    {
        childLocRecId = LogisticsLocation::create(_description,
                                                   false,
                                                   _locationRecId).RecId;
    }
    electronic.clear();
    electronic.initValue();
    electronic.Type = _type;
    electronic.Description = _description;
    electronic.IsMobilePhone = _isMobile;
    electronic.Locator = _locator;
    electronic.Location = childLocRecId;
    electronic.LocatorExtension = _extension;
    electric.IsInstantMessage = _isSMS;
```

```
        if(_isMobil == NoYes::No)
            electric.IsPrimary = _isPrimary;

        electric.insert();

        return electric.RecId;
    }
```

Accessing the financial dimension framework

Financial dimensions provide the ability to add structured analysis codes to source documents that are posted to the general ledger for later analysis. These appear as fields on forms such as the customer details form, but they are constructed from data. We can decide which analysis fields should display and whether they should be linked to custom lists or real tables in AX, such as the customer group table.

From the AOT, open (right-click and choose **Open**) the `CustTable` form and expand the **Financial dimensions** fast tab.

The fields that appear on the customer details form actually result in a single field on `CustTable`, named `DefaultDimension`. This is a foreign key to a set of records called a **dimension attribute value set**.

The fields displayed are built by looking up a record in `DimensionAttributeValueSet` and building the controls from the related records in `DimensionAttributeValueSetItem`. The field names are taken from the `DimensionAttribute` table.

From this perspective, the tables involved are as follows:

Table	Relation	Purpose
`DimensionAttribute ValueSet`		The foreign key found on the main table, such as `CustTable`. `DefaultDimension`
`DimensionAttribute ValueSetItem`	`DimensionAttribute ValueSet ==` `DimensionAttribute ValueSet.RecId`	A record for each value (a business unit), which is indirectly related to the type of value, (`BusinesUnit`)

Table	Relation	Purpose
DimensionAttribute Value	AttributeValueSet == DimensionAttribute ValueSetItem.RecId	Relates the set item, with some other information, to the attribute.
DimensionAttribute	DimensionAttribute == DimensionAttribute.RecId	The attribute, such as BusinessUnit.

There are many more tables, and this structure looks particularly complicated, where many tables in the data structure hold only foreign keys. The table browser is virtually unusable for investigating the data behind the scenes.

Although it may seem discomforting that looking at the physical tables doesn't really help us understand what is going on, we don't have to. The data structure wasn't designed to be modified or extended, and there shouldn't be a case where we would want to. There are tasks that are sometimes required, which require further explanation.

The most common tasks we may want to do are as follows:

- Add a dimension attribute entity to a record, such as Business unit
- Access a specific dimension from a dimension value set held against an entity, such as CustTable
- Merge two dimension sets

The first point is to be able to identify, in code, the attribute we want.

We do this by simply adding a primary key relation to the DimensionAttribute table, and we can then add the resulting field to a form as a ReferenceGroup control.

This is something we have done many times, and a good example is the InventParameters table, which has a SiteDimensionAttribute relation. The resulting foreign key field is presented in the InventSiteDimensionLink form.

This first part holds nothing new to us, so we can use it to demonstrate the second part. You can test your knowledge and add such a field to a suitable parameter table, but for demonstration purposes, we will use InventParameters.SiteDimensionAttribute.

To get and set the `BusinessUnit` dimension on the customer record, follow these steps:

1. In the `InventSiteDimensionLink` form, set the dimension attribute to `BusinessUnit`.
2. For the first customer, expand the **Financial dimensions** fast tab and set the `BusinessUnit` dimension to `001`. If you are not using Contoso data (`USMF`), set this to a specific value and note down another value.
3. Using the relations defined earlier, write a job to get the `BusinessUnit` from a customer. Use the following lines of code as an example:

```
static void ConFMSCustTabeGetBusinessUnit(Args _args)
{
    CustTable custTable;
    DimensionAttributeValueSetItem attrItem;
    DimensionAttributeValue attributeValue;

    RefRecId attributeRecId =
           InventParameters::find().SiteDimensionAttribute;

    custTable = CustTable::find("DE-001", true);

    select firstOnly attrItem
        where attrItem.DimensionAttributeValueSet ==
                                 custTable.DefaultDimension
        join attributeValue
        where attributeValue.RecId ==
                         attrItem.DimensionAttributeValue &&
              attributeValue.DimensionAttribute ==
                         attributeRecId;

    info(attrItem.DisplayValue);
}
```

4. The code required to set the same attribute value to a new one is as follows:

```
static void ConFMSCustTableSetBusinessUnit(Args _args)
{
    DimensionAttributeValueSetStorage storage;
    DimensionAttributeValue attrValue;
    DimensionAttribute      attribute;
    CustTable               custTable;
```

```
    RefRecId                  attributeRecId;
    DimensionDisplayValue     businessUnit;
    boolean                   updateRequired;

    custTable = CustTable::find("DE-001");

    // the new value to set
    businessUnit = "002";

    // get the attribute for the business unit
    attributeRecId = InventParameters::
                          find().SiteDimensionAttribute;

    // this is required in order to get the value record
    attribute = DimensionAttribute::find(attributeRecId);

    // this will find or create the
    // value record for the business unit
    attrValue = DimensionAttributeValue::
            findByDimensionAttributeAndValue(attribute,
                                            businessUnit,
                                            false, true);
    // construct the dimension value set
    // storage handler from the customer dimension
    storage = DimensionAttributeValueSetStorage::
                        find(custTable.DefaultDimension);
    storage.addItem(attrValue);

    ttsBegin;
    custTable.selectForUpdate(true);
    // this will trigger the class to persist the
    // new data structures to the database and return
    // the new DimensionAttributeValueSet RecId
    custTable.DefaultDimension = storage.save();
    custTable.update();
    ttsCommit;
}
```

The key commands here are described next:

```
attrValue = DimensionAttributeValue::
            findByDimensionAttributeAndValue(attribute,
                                             businessUnit,
                                             false, true);
```

The storage class needs a `DimensionAttributeValue` record, which needs to be found or created for the new business unit value:

```
storage.addItem(attrValue);
```

After the storage is constructed, we can update the data stored in the class. The preceding line will add the item or replace it if it exists.

The final key command is the following line, which writes the internal structures to the database and returns the new record ID:

```
custTable.DefaultDimension = storage.save();
```

References

Refer to *What's new: Financial dimensions framework [AX 2012]* at `http://technet.microsoft.com/en-us/library/dn527192.aspx`. This also contains a link to the white paper, and provides some great technical background information.

Summary

In this chapter, we covered some advanced functionality and hopefully simplified what can otherwise seem to be a daunting challenge. Beginning with some advanced techniques for handling list pages, we then progressed into three of the most important frameworks in Dynamics AX.

In the next chapter, we will cover more advanced development techniques, allowing your solutions to be more flexible and get more features.

10
Advanced Development Techniques

In this chapter, we will cover the more advanced techniques of Dynamics AX development. The topics we will cover are as follows:

- Making data date-effective
- Utilizing metadata within AX
- Making your code extendable with metadata
- Exception handling
- Controlling how and where code is executed
- Code access permissions
- More on views – computed columns

Making data date-effective

Date-effective tables, or `ValidTimeState` tables, allow us to see a record at a point in time, such as an employee's details in the past, or even planned future changes. This feature is part of the table definition in AX, which makes this technology much easier to use. There is, therefore, very little coding required in order to implement it.

This is pretty exciting, but we shouldn't get too carried away by it. Each edit will result in a new, time stamped record. Main tables, such as customer and vendor tables, should not be made date-effective, as it will create a lot of unnecessary records and complicate the foreign key relations to them. For example, if we did make the customer table date-effective, we would need to determine the version of the customer record that should be found when navigating back from a customer transaction.

In some cases, AX makes deliberate use of this technology. The `LogisticsPostalAddress` record is date-effective, yet the foreign key relation on `SalesTable` is based on `RecId`. This means that it relates to a specific version, which is suitable since the sales order should go to the address at the point when the order was taken.

For our example, we'll use the vehicle service records, which will consist of two parts. The first part is to configure the table as being date-effective and the second is to update the interface so that the user can see the record at a specific point in time.

To configure the table as a date-effective table, follow these steps:

1. Open the property sheet for the `ConFMSVehServiceTable` table.
2. Locate the **ValidTimeStateFieldType** property and select **UtcDateTime**. This makes the records valid at a point in time; `Date` will make the records valid on a day-by-day basis.
3. Expand the table's **Fields** node, and note that the table now has two new fields, `ValidFrom` and `ValidTo`. They are of the **UtcDateTime** type.
4. Now, open the table in the table browser, and try to save a record. You will receive the following error:

    ```
    Cannot edit a record in Vehicle service table
    (ConFMSVehServiceTable). Table does not contain a valid
    time state key. A unique index needs to be marked as a
    valid time state key.
    ```

5. It will also give the same message as a compilation error if we compile the table. This is meant to force us to create or update a primary index that contains the two new fields and drag the `ValidFrom` and `ValidTo` fields onto the `ServiceIdx` index.
6. Change the index's **ValidTimeStateKey** property to `Yes` and set **ValidTimeStateMode** to `NoGap`.
7. Open the table in the table browser and edit a record. On saving, nothing different happens. Also, if we write a job to update a record, it will update the record—it does not version the record.

8. Open the `ConFMSVehServiceTable` form and change the value of **Current odometer**. If you scan through the records or open the table's list page, it appears as if a version was not created. But, if you open the table browser to see what is actually stored, you will see that a new record was created, like this:

Curr...	HcmWorker...	NextServiceD...	Next...	ServiceDate	ServiceId	ValidFrom		ValidTo	
1301	0	8/17/2014	1900	8/17/2014	S001	1/3/2015	09:17:27 am	Never	
1300	0	8/17/2014	1900	8/17/2014	S001			1/3/2015	09:17:26 am

9. The final change to the table is as follows: we need to update the `find` and `exist` methods to handle the fact that `ServiceId` is no longer unique. By default, we want the current valid record, with the ability to select a record at a particular time. Modify the `find` method as follows:

```
public static ConFMSVehServiceTable find(
    ConFMSServiceId _id,
    utcdatetime _validFrom = DateTimeUtil::utcNow(),
    utcdatetime _validTo = _validFrom,
    boolean _forUpdate = false)
{
    ConFMSVehServiceTable service;

    service.selectForUpdate(_forUpdate);
    if(_id != "")
    {
        select validTimeState(_validFrom, _validTo) service
            where service.ServiceId == _id;
    }
    return service;
}
```

10. Make the same change for the `exist` method.

The next part is to update `ConFMSVehServiceTable` so that we can view the data at a point in time, which is done by the following steps:

1. Open the `classDeclaration` code window and add the following code inside the braces:

```
DateEffectivenessPaneController dePaneController
```

2. On the control to **Designs** | **Design**, right-click and select **New** | **Group**.

3. Rename the new group control to `VersionGroup` and set the following properties:

AutoDeclaration	`Yes`
VerticalSpacing	`0` (Pressing *Ctrl* + Space will change it so that numbers can be entered)
HideIfEmpty	`No` (this is populated by code, so we don't want AX to hide it)

4. Order the controls (*Alt* + up or down arrow keys) so that they appear as shown in the following screenshot:

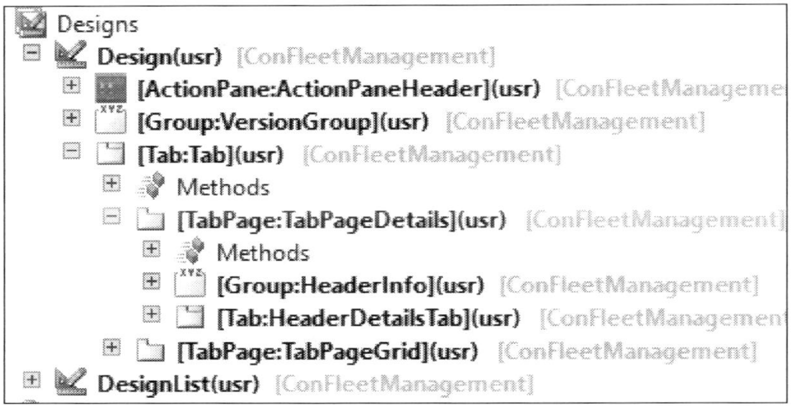

The reason that `VersionGroup` is above the tab is because we want the control to appear for both the detail and lines views of the form, which is made useful by allowing the control constructed in the next step to show all historic record versions.

5. Modify the `init` method so that it reads like this:

```
public void init()
{
    super();
    formHandler = ConFMSVehServiceTableForm::construct();
    switch(element.args().dataset())
    {
        case tableNum(ConFMSVehicleTable):
            formHandler.parmVehicleTable(
                                        element.args().record());
            break;
    }
```

```
        dePaneController =
          DateEffectivenessPaneController::constructWithGroup(
                        element,
                        versionGroup, // the form group
                        ConFMSVehServiceTable_ds,
                        false, // use plural labels
                        true, // allow show all records
                        true); // use datetime
    }
```

6. Save the changes and open the form.
7. Switch to the grid view using the controls at the bottom of the form, as shown in the following screenshot:

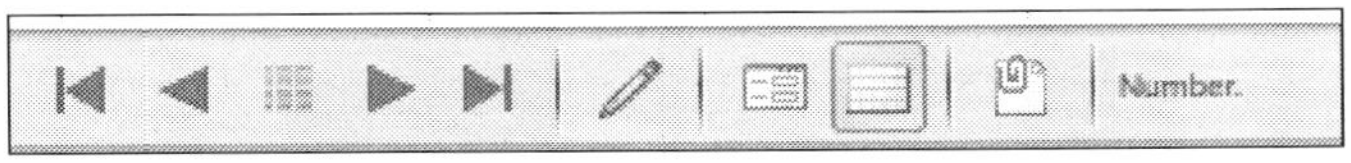

8. Click on the new **<| |>** control at the top of the form, which then expands, as shown in the following screenshot:

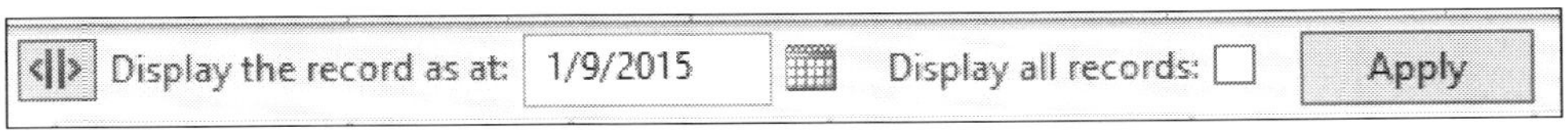

9. Check **Display all records** and note that the edits made earlier appear in the grid view. You may find adding the `ModifiedDateTime` and `modifiedBy` fields useful in this scenario.

Utilizing metadata within AX

We have already discussed that we can use metadata stored in the model store, such as a field's type or label. We can do much more, and in this section, we will cover techniques of using this to make our solutions even more flexible.

Accessing the data model using metadata

Every table and field in AX is identified internally by an identifier and by using the `DictTable` and `DictField` dictionary classes. With this information, we can select a record from a table and even access and update its data.

Create a new job and enter the following code:

```
static void ConDataModelUpdateJob(Args _args)
{
    Common buffer;
    DictTable dictTable;

    dictTable = new DictTable(tableNum(ConFMSVehicleTable));
    buffer = dictTable.makeRecord();
    select firstOnly buffer;
    info(buffer.(fieldNum(ConFMSVehicleTable, Name)));
}
```

The `tableNum` and `fieldNum` methods simply return the identifier of the element, so we aren't actually referencing the table or field at all.

We first construct a `DictTable` class using the table ID of our vehicle table, and then use `makeRecord` in order for an actual vehicle record to be constructed. We can assign this to buffer, as `Common` is the base class for all tables.

We can then work with buffer as if it is a vehicle record; it's just that it does not know at design time what type of table buffer is—only that it is of the type `Common`. Since, at runtime, it will be of type `ConFMSVehicleTable` we can work with the field number instead. This is what `buffer.(fieldNum(ConFMSVehicleTable, Name))` does.

Let's try something else—replace the line `select firstonly buffer;` with the following (replacing the vehicle ID with a value that exists in your data):

```
buffer = dictTable.callStatic("Find", "V0001");
```

Let's extend this a little by iterating through the fields in the table. This is done by the following code:

```
static void BclDataModelUpdateJob(Args _args)
{
    Common buffer;
    DictTable dictTable;
    DictField dictField;
    Counter idx;
    RefFieldId fieldId;
```

```
        dictTable = new DictTable(tableNum(ConFMSVehicleTable));
        buffer = dictTable.makeRecord();
        buffer = dictTable.callStatic("Find", "V0001");
        for(idx = 1; idx <= dictTable.fieldCnt(); idx++)
        {
            fieldId = dictTable.fieldCnt2Id(idx);
            dictField = new DictField(dictTable.id(), fieldId);
            info(strFmt("%1: %2",
                        dictField.label(), buffer.(fieldId)));
        }
    }
```

On running this code, we see a list of the field's label and value. Pretty clever stuff, but how can we use this in a practical manner?

One idea is to write a data import routine, where we can write a table that stores the field IDs and a column index that could import vehicle service data from a CSV or Excel file.

Accessing code using metadata

We can also access classes through metadata using the `DictClass` class.

The code is similar to the preceding section. We will use `DictClass` to access the `CustCreditCheck` class and store the instance of the class in an object of the `Object` type:

```
static void ConDictClassExample(Args _args)
{
    DictClass dictClass = new DictClass(
                              classNum(CustCreditLimit));
    Object    creditCheckObject;
    CustTable custTable;

    select firstOnly custTable
        where custTable.CreditMax > 0;
    //static server CustCreditLimit
    //      construct(Common _buffer,
    //               SalesTotals _salesTotals = null)
    creditCheckObject = dictClass.callStatic("construct",
                                         custTable);
    //AmountMST calcCreditAvailable()
    info(strFmt("Credit available: %1",
             dictClass.callObject("calcCreditAvailable",
                                 creditCheckObject)));
}
```

On running this code, we are given the credit available for the first customer that has a credit limit.

As before, we use a static method to construct the instance, this time by calling the construct method, which requires a customer record, and then calling an instance method on the class with the `callObject` method.

To take this thinking further, the class name and method could be fields on a table.

Again, this is clever stuff, but there is a lot more to metadata than this. This will be explored later in this chapter when we create a framework that is mainly based in metadata.

Making your code extendable with metadata

To bring together the earlier metadata techniques, we will create a simple framework that allows an end-user organization to extend our solution without making a modification to any object in our solution.

This could be to allow integration with data capture devices, or to simply allow them to add fields to the form without making a modification to it.

The way to do this is to create a configuration table in AX that allows our end user to add class names to it. This configuration table is then called at specific points in our code. In order to utilize `DictClass`, we either need to store the method name in the table, or simply insist that the classes conform to our pattern. The best method in many cases is to require that the end user implements a specific interface when creating the class.

Interfaces

An interface is a method by which we ensure that a class has a specific set of methods. The `interface` class itself has no code, just a definition of methods that a class that implements it must have.

To create an interface, we use the `interface` keyword instead of class in the **classDeclaration** and then add methods that our interface will enforce. The methods are abstract and must not contain code, even if they return a value.

Sample solution using metadata

Our example solution will be to provide a framework so that system administrators can add fields to the vehicle form without modifying it. We will do this by creating a framework that is implemented by a third-party (for example, an end-user organization developer), so our design must both be flexible and provide the necessary services to make the implementation as simple as possible.

In order to do this, we will design the solution in such a way that we will need a list of control definition contracts from one or more classes that are referenced in a table. This table will store the class ID of the table that implements our interface.

The design

The solution will consist of two main parts: a user interface that allows the user to select classes that implement our interface, and a class that will process the form control definition contracts that the implemented class must return.

The user interface must allow the user to select classes that implement our interface, and validate that the user does not enter a class that does not. There isn't an intrinsic function that does this, so we need to write one.

The other problem we will face is that we will deal with class IDs, and these can change between environments. This means that the class IDs may refer to a different class. We must therefore validate at runtime that the class is valid. We will write a reusable function that does this.

This design, as with most of the code referenced in this book, is available for download.

The solution from the framework's perspective isn't that complicated, and will consist of the following elements:

Type	Name	Description
Table	`ConFMSVehicleFormHandlerClasses`	This stores the classes that the framework will call to build the interface
Form	`ConFMSVehicleFormHandlerClasses`	
Interface	`ConFMSVehicleFieldsI`	Used to ensure the implementations have the `controlDefinitionList` method.
Class	`ConFMSVehicleFieldContract`	Defines the form control definitions

Type	Name	Description
Class	`ConFMSVehicle` `FieldsUIBuilder`	This will be constructed from the vehicle form, building the user interface from the control definition list defined by the classes in the `ConFMSVehicleFormHandlerClasses` table.

The UI builder class requires a little more thought in its design. First, it has to deal with one or more lists of control definitions, but it should also make itself extendable by offering events so that the end user can trap these for their own post processing.

The process will therefore be broken down into iterations; the method calls will be sequenced according the following diagram:

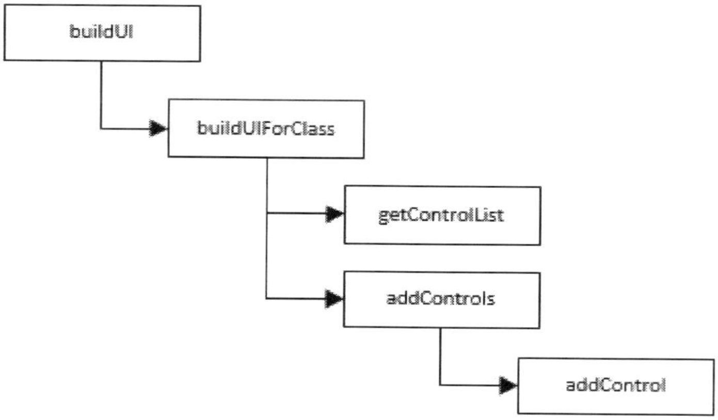

By breaking the design down as shown in the preceding diagram we simplify the code and make it easier to read, we can also add delegates such as `controlAdded(<ClassId>, <FormControl>)` so that a third-party developer can subscribe to for post processing. This design, as with most of the code referenced in this book, is available for download.

Creating a utility class

The first task will be to create a utility class. These are written to store functions that we either perceive as usable elsewhere or sometimes with hindsight. As we become more experienced, we will instinctively know to do this.

Our solution will make use of a function that can determine whether a class implements an interface.

Create a class named `ConFMSUtil` with the following method:

```
public static boolean implementsClass(DictClass _dictClass,
                                      ClassId _interfaceClassId)
{
    int impIdx;
    if(_dictClass)
    {
        if(_dictClass.implementsCnt() > 0)
        {
            for(impIdx = 1;
                impIdx <= _dictClass.implementsCnt();
                impIdx++)
            {
                if(_dictClass.implements(impIdx) ==
                   _interfaceClassId)
                {
                    return true;
                }
            }
        }
    }
    return false;
}
```

Creating the interface class

Create the interface class as per these steps:

1. Create a new class under your project's **Classes** node.
2. Replace the **classDeclaration** with the following:

   ```
   interface ConFMSVehicleFieldsI
   {
   }
   ```

3. Create this method:

   ```
   public List controlDefinitionList()
   {
   }
   ```

Creating the user interface

The next stage is to create a table and form that will allow classes that implement the preceding interface to be added.

To do this, follow these steps:

1. Create a table named `ConFMSVehicleFormHandlerClasses`, add the `ClassId` and `ClassName` fields, and specify the EDT of the same name.
2. Create a check method to check whether the class implements the interface, as follows:

```
private boolean checkClassId()
{
    DictClass dictClass;
    dictClass = new DictClass(this.ClassId);
    if(ConFMSUtil::implementsClass(dictClass,
       classNum(ConFMSVehicleFieldsI)))
    {
        return true;
    }
    return checkFailed(
            strFmt("Class %1 does not implement %2",
                    dictClass.name(),
                    classStr(ConFMSVehicleFieldsI)));
}
```

3. Override the `validateField` method to call `checkClassId` if the `ClassId` field changes.
4. Next, we need a lookup method that will offer the user classes that implement our interface. This is done using the following code:

```
static int pickInterface()
{
    Object      formRun;
    container   names;
    int         idx;
    DictClass   dictClass;
    ClassId     classId;
    #ResAppl
    Dictionary dict = new Dictionary();
    // classFactory is a globally initialized instance
    // of the class ClassFactory that provides function
    // to construct instances of types or elements
```

```
    // in this case we are using the function
    // createPickList to construct a FormRun
    // instance from the Form PickList
    formRun = classfactory.createPicklist();
    // we must always call init after a form is
    // constructed
    formRun.init();
    // iterate through all classes
    for (idx=1; idx <= dict.classCnt(); idx++)
    {
        // use Dictionary (dict) to get the ClassId
        // from the sequential counter
        classId = dict.classCnt2Id(idx);
        // construct a DictClass object
        // and use our utility to check if
        // it implements ConFMSVehicleFieldsI
        dictClass = new DictClass(classId);
        if(ConFMSUtil::implementsClass(
                        dictClass,
                        classNum(ConFMSVehicleFieldsI)))
        {
            names += dict.className(classId);
        }
    }
    // choices is a method on the form PickList
    // and since this doesn't exist on the base class
    // FormRun we declared formRun as type Object.
    formRun.choices(names, #ImageClass);
    formRun.caption("@SYS26387");
    formRun.run();
    // run will just execute the form - we want the code to
    // wait for the user's response
    formRun.wait();
    // choice is a method on the PickList form,
    // use to get the selected item from the list.
    if (formRun.choice())
    {
        return dict.className2Id(formRun.choice());
    }
    return 0;
}
```

> We can also write a method that initializes the table for all classes that implement our interface. Feel free to try this yourself; it is very similar to the preceding code.

5. Finally, override the `modifiedField` method to keep the class name and ID in sync, as follows:

```
public void modifiedField(FieldId _fieldId)
{
    super(_fieldId);
    switch(_fieldId)
    {
        case fieldNum(ConFMSVehicleFormHandlerClasses,
                      ClassId):
            this.ClassName = classId2Name(this.ClassId);
            break;
        case fieldNum(ConFMSVehicleFormHandlerClasses,
                      ClassName):
            this.ClassId = className2Id(this.ClassName);
            // if the class name was not valid the code
            // below will set the name to an empty string
            this.ClassName = classId2Name(this.ClassId);
            break;
    }
}
```

6. Next, create a form for the table using the simple list template.
7. Add the table to the form's data source and the `ClassName` field to the grid control; don't forget to set the grid control's data source.
8. Finally, override the lookup method for the `ClassName` data source field, as follows:

```
public void lookup(FormControl _formControl,
                   str _filterStr)
{
    ClassId classId =
           ConFMSVehicleFormHandlerClasses::pickInterface();
    ConFMSVehicleFormHandlerClasses.ClassName =
           classId2Name(classId);
}
```

To test the form and our framework, we need a test class that implements this interface. We create a class like this:

```
class ConFMSVehicleUserFields implements ConFMSVehicleFieldsI
{
}
```

Now create a constructor. On saving the `construct` method, you will be given the following compilation error:

```
Object could not be created because abstract method
ConFMSVehicleFieldsI.controlDefinitionList() has not been
implemented.
```

We can't choose override as we are not extending the class; we are simply forced to write this method. We can look at the interface class in order to see that it must return an object of type list.

Create the following method:

```
public List controlDefinitionList()
{
    return new List(Types::Class);
}
```

This will suffice in order to test our form, which should now allow us to add the class.

Creating the form control definition contract class

Create a data contract class, `ConFMSVehicleFieldContract`, as follows:

```
[DataContractAttribute]
class ConFMSVehicleFieldContract
{
    RefFieldId refFieldId;
    str fieldLabel;
}
[DataMemberAttribute]
public RefFieldId refFieldId(RefFieldId _refFieldId = refFieldId)
{
    refFieldId = _refFieldId;
    return refFieldId;
}
```

```
[DataMemberAttribute]
public str fieldLabel(str _fieldLabel = fieldLabel)
{
    fieldLabel = _fieldLabel;
    return fieldLabel;
}
public static ConFMSVehicleFieldContract construct()
{
    return new ConFMSVehicleFieldContract();
}
```

Creating the form builder class

The form builder class is the class that does its work by iterating through the records in our definition table, adding the controls to a form group control based on the list returned from each class.

To construct an instance of this class, we will need to know the form group control that the fields will be added to and the data source that the control will be bound to.

The first part of the class follows a pattern we have used many times before, and it should be created as follows:

```
class ConFMSVehicleFieldGroupUIBuilder
{
    FormGroupControl groupControl;
    FormDataSource dataSource
}
public FormGroupControl parmGroupControl(
                  FormGroupControl _groupControl = groupControl)
{
    groupControl = _groupControl;
    return groupControl;
}
public FormDataSource parmDataSource(
                  FormDataSource _dataSource = dataSource)
{
    dataSource = _dataSource;
    return dataSource;
}
public static ConFMSVehicleFieldGroupUIBuilder construct()
{
```

```
        return new ConFMSVehicleFieldGroupUIBuilder();
    }
    public static ConFMSVehicleFieldGroupUIBuilder
                    newFromFormGroupControl(
                            FormDataSource _ds,
                            FormGroupControl _control)
    {
        ConFMSVehicleFieldGroupUIBuilder
            builder = ConFMSVehicleFieldGroupUIBuilder::construct();
        builder.parmGroupControl(_control);
        builder.parmDatasource(_ds);
        return builder;
    }
```

We need to write the outer functions first (unless we use code placeholders for a method that don't exist yet), so we will create the class outside in, which again reinforces the need to design the class before we start writing the code.

The next part is to write the code that will get the list of control definitions from the classes in our setup table. Since we can have more than one set of fields, we should process each class separately.

So first, we need a method that returns a list for a class ID, as shown here:

```
    private List getControlList(ClassId _classId)
    {
        DictClass dictClass;
        List      list;
        Object    fieldListObj;
        dictClass = new dictClass(_classId);
        if(!dictClass)
        {
            throw error(strFmt("Class %1 could not be constructed",
                               classId2Name(_classId)));
        }
        if(!ConFMSUtil::implementsClass(dictClass,
                                        classNum(ConFMSVehicleFieldsI)))
        {
            throw error(strFmt("Class %1 does not implement %2",
                               classId2Name(_classId),
                               classStr(ConFMSVehicleFieldsI)));
        }
        fieldListObj = dictClass.makeObject();
        return fieldListObj.controlDefinitionList();
    }
```

In the preceding method, apart from the validation, the interesting elements are that the `controlDefinitionList` method does not exist on the `Object` class and the compiler allows the code to compile.

Let's write the method that adds the control to the group control, which is done as follows:

```
private void addControl(ClassId _classId,
                        ConFMSVehicleFieldContract _contract)
{
    FormControl control = groupControl.addDataField(
                                    datasource.id(),
                                    _contract.refFieldId());

    DictMethod testMethodExists;
    Object     formControlAsObject;
    // control will be a sub class of FormControl
    // but since FormControl doesn't have the
    // accessor 'label' we will declare it as type object
    if(_contract.fieldLabel() != "")
    {
        // use the intrinsic function methodStr to ensure
        // we spelt it right!
        testMethodExists = new
                DictMethod(UtilElementType::Class,
                           classIdGet(control),
                           methodStr(FormStringControl, label));

        // Check that if the control has the accessor method
        // label.
        if(testMethodExists && testMethodExists.compiledOk())
        {
            // Set the label using the instance
            // of control cast as an object.
            formControlAsObject = control;
            formControlAsObject.label(_contract.fieldLabel());
        }
    }
    this.controlAdded(_classId, control);
}
```

The preceding code suffices for a single property, but it should be split into separate methods for each property.

Since we don't know which class `FormGroupControl` created for us, we need to check whether the resultant control has the method `label`. Most data bound controls do, but we need to be sure. There is no function for this, so we attempt to instantiate `DictMethod` and check whether it created an instance.

The final call to `controlAdded` was to trigger the event, allowing a developer to perform special post-process event handling.

We now need to write the methods that will process the table and add the controls as per our earlier design. Create the methods in the order shown here:

```
private void addControls(ClassId _classId, List _controlContracts)
{
    ListEnumerator le = _controlContracts.getEnumerator();
    ConFMSVehicleFieldContract contract;
    while(le.moveNext())
    {
        contract = le.current();
        this.addControl(_classId, contract);
    }
}
private void buildUIForClass(ClassId _classId)
{
    List list = this.getControlList(_classId);
    if(list.elements() != 0)
    {
        this.addControls(_classId, list);
    }
}
public void buildUI()
{
    ConFMSVehicleFormHandlerClasses  formHandlerClass;
    while select formHandlerClass
        where formHandlerClass.ClassId != 0
    {
        this.buildUIForClass(formHandlerClass.ClassId);
    }
}
```

To test this, we need to update the form to call the class in the preceding code.

Updating the vehicle table form

We need to add a group control to the form and trigger our class to build it. This is done by performing the following steps:

1. On the `ConFMSVehicleTable` form, add a group control to **Designs** | **Design** | **Tab** | **HeaderDetailsTab** | **HeaderGeneral**.
2. Rename the control to `CustomFieldGroup` and set the **AutoDeclaration** property to `Yes`.

> **AutoDeclaration** is a `FormControl` property that will make the control globally accessible within the scope of the form.

3. On the `init` method, add the following code after the call to `super()`:

```
ConFMSVehicleFieldGroupUIBuilder::newFromFormGroupControl(
                    ConFMSVehicleTable_DS,
                    CustomFieldGroup).buildUI();
```

In order to test this, we need to modify our test class so that it returns at least one control definition in the list. Modify the `ConFMSVehicleUserFields` class so that the method `controlDefinitionList` reads like this:

```
public List controlDefinitionList()
{
    List fieldList;
    ConFMSVehicleFieldContract contract;

    fieldList = new List(Types::Class);

    contract = ConFMSVehicleFieldContract::construct();
    contract.refFieldId(fieldNum(ConFMSVehicleTable, Name));
    contract.fieldLabel("My vehicle name label");

    fieldList.addEnd(contract);

    return fieldList;
}
```

In order for the class to be processed, add the class to the list using the `ConFMSVehicleFormHandlerClasses` form.

Taking this further

Using the preceding technique, we can write an implementation of `ConFMSVehicleFieldI` to return a list of fields, which in turn are stored in a table by a user or security role, allowing each user to have their own specific design. Many ideas may spawn from this, which is the whole point of this section—to show how we can use metadata to make our solution more flexible. We could use the same technique to add event handlers defined in tables in AX, allowing third-party developers to create their own extensions without touching a single line of our code.

There is a limitation, however; the code will not be as quick as code written in line. There is an overhead when we use the dictionary classes to instantiate an object. Our test didn't make a noticeable difference, but we wouldn't use this technique on a per transaction basis where tiny overhead could make a noticeable difference.

Exception handling

Throughout the book, we have raised many exceptions through the `throw` command, but so far, we have simply allowed this exception to fall through the code, giving our user an error.

This is fine for many cases, but sometimes, we need specific handling. This is especially important when the error is a number of classes deep, and could produce an error message that makes no sense to the user. We may, in these cases, need to provide some context for the message or a different, more useful message for the user.

Handling general exceptions

In the previous section, an error could have been produced in many places, none of which are useful to the user. They are useful to the administrator or developer.

Looking at the code the errors we might expect are as follows:

- Invalid field ID in the control definition contract
- Class does not implement the interface
- Error thrown by the class that implements the interface

We do not, in any case, want an error to be thrown that stops the form from opening. Also, if there is an error, we need to decide whether the user actually needs to know that an error occurred. It may be enough for our purposes that the fields don't appear, and we can use the debugger to trace through the code to determine why.

In our `ConFMSVehicleFieldGroupUIBuilder` class, we throw an error in `getControlList` should the class not exist or not implement the interface. This will stop processing the code, issue a `ttsabort` command, and result in the vehicle form not being displayed. All we want to do is to skip the class.

The call stack `buildUI` calls `buildUIForClass` for each class in the setup table. The `buildUIForClass` class will call `getControlList` and pass the list to `addControls`. We therefore want to catch any errors thrown in `getControlList`, or anywhere down the stack triggered while adding the controls, and proceed to the next class. It is merely drawing the interface, and we are not performing a transactional update that requires the entire update to succeed or fail.

We would try and catch the error within the `getControlList` method, as the code in `buildUIForClass` would still continue. We need to try `getControlList` and `buildUIForClass` and catch any errors with a suitable message.

Update the method `buildUIForClass` to read like this:

```
private void buildUIForClass(ClassId _classId)
{
    List list;
    try
    {
        list = this.getControlList(_classId);
        if(list.elements() != 0)
        {
            this.addControls(_classId, list);
        }
    }
    catch
    {
        warning("Not all controls were added.");
    }
}
```

To test this, add the following line at the end of `getControlList`:

```
throw error("Confusing technical error.");
```

On running the form, we get the following message:

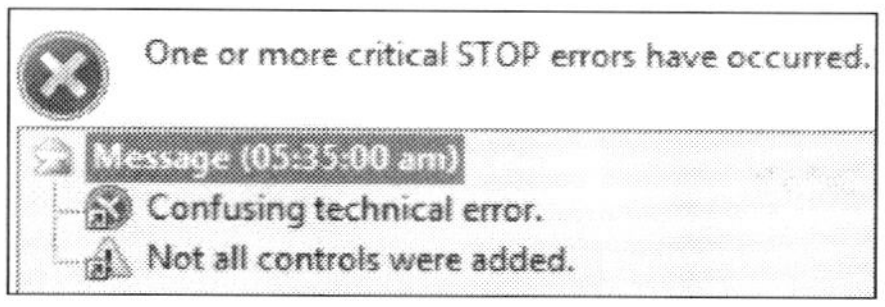

Our catch clearly caught the exception and the code continued (the form opened), but we still got a confusing technical error. This is sometimes desirable, but what do we do if we want to hide this message from the user?

We could clear the `infoLog` object of messages just before we add our warning to it, but this will clear all messages, including those created by other processes. The info log is global, so we need to be careful not to remove messages that we didn't create. The `infoLog` object has a method called `cut` that lets us remove log entries from it, so we simply store the current `infoLog` line at the start of our routine and clear the entries after that. We can amend the `buildUIForClass` method as follows:

```
private void buildUIForClass(ClassId _classId)
{
    List list;
    int infoLogLineBefore = infologLine();
    try
    {
        list = this.getControlList(_classId);
        if(list.elements() != 0)
        {
            this.addControls(_classId, list);
        }
    }
    catch
    {
        infolog.cut(infoLogLineBefore+1, infologLine());
        warning("Not all controls were added.");
    }
}
```

Within the `catch` block, we can write almost any cleanup code, but if this code fails, there is no fallback to handle errors within the `catch` block; the code in the `catch` block must be simple and not have any risk of failure. So, writing a log file or log database entry is not a good idea; currently, we don't have a `finally` clause in X++ to handle failures in the `catch`.

Handling CLR exceptions

The catch in the preceding example will catch all types of exceptions. Sometimes, we need to be more specific. Two common examples are handling CLR errors and database update errors.

If we call .NET code from AX, the error will not be passed to the `infoLog` object; we must get the CLR exception.

A catch statement for getting the CLR exception details is as follows:

```
System.Exception outerEx, innerEx;
try
{
    //CLR Code
}
catch (Exception::CLRError)
{
    outerEx = CLRInterop::getLastException();
    if(outerEx != null)
    {
        innerEx = outerEx.get_InnerException();
        error(strfmt("%1 \n %2",
              outerEx.get_Message(),
              innerEx.ToString()));
    }
}
catch
{
    warning("<suitable message on general failure>.");
}
```

The exception has a lot of details available. You should explore this with your own CLR code to see how to handle CLR errors.

The article *How to: Catch Exceptions Thrown from CLR Objects [AX 2012]* provides more information on how to catch the exception. You can find this document at `http://msdn.microsoft.com/en-us/library/ee677495.aspx`.

Handling table update exceptions

There are two main table update exceptions, `UpdateConflict` and `DeadLock`. An update conflict occurs due to the optimistic concurrency failing, whereas a deadlock is the classic database scenario where both transactions have each locked a table that the other needs.

Deadlocks should be rare in properly normalized database designs, where the transactions are kept as short as possible, but still they can occur. Deadlocks happen when we are frequently performing a transaction that affects many tables or where one or more tables are being updated by another routine that affects many tables. Examples of these are inventory journals, where one update will affect inventory transactions, inventory on hand, financial ledgers, and so on.

AX will handle the deadlock all by itself. The losing transaction will be rolled back, and the user will be given a message that is normally given straight to IT support for them to usually say "Try again."

We can, however, try again for the user with the `retry` option. The following code demonstrates this pattern:

```
static void ConFMSDeadLockExample(Args _args)
{
    boolean firstTime = true;

    try
    {
        ttsBegin;
        //post transaction
        ttscommit;
    }
    catch (Exception::Deadlock)
    {
        retry;
    }
}
```

Update conflicts are normally handled within the insert, delete, and update methods of a table. The BOM table is a good example of this. You may also find it hard to find many examples where this has been used. We use this pattern only if we deem it to be required. The code within the table's update method also updates other records, so it has been written to handle update conflicts.

The following code is an example pattern:

```
public void update()
{
    #OCCRetryCount
    try
    {
        ttsbegin;
        // code that updates records in other tables
        super(); // do the update
        // other code that updates records in other tables
        ttscommit;
    }
    catch (Exception::Deadlock)
    {
        retry;
    }
    catch (Exception::UpdateConflict)
    {
        if (appl.ttsLevel() == 0)
        {
            if (xSession::currentRetryCount() >= #RetryNum)
            {
                throw Exception::UpdateConflictNotRecovered;
            }
            else
            {
                retry;
            }
        }
        else
        {
            throw Exception::UpdateConflict;
        }
    }
}
```

It is important that we don't retry indefinitely, as this may cause the client to hang. To control this, we use `xSession::currentRetryCount()` to get the number of retries and check this against the `#RetryNum` macro. The macro defines the standard number of retries deemed appropriate by Microsoft, which is five.

The other new element here is `ttsLevel`. Since transactions can be nested, we do want the exception to fall through to the parent transaction if one exists. If `ttsabort` is issued (directly or due to a `throw` error) at any level, the whole transaction will be rolled back; we can't roll back just the level where the error is thrown.

See *Exception handling with try and catch Keywords [AX 2012]* from Microsoft for further reading, at `http://msdn.microsoft.com/en-us/library/aa893385.aspx`.

Controlling how and where code is executed

We haven't had to think much about where code is executed and how data is passed between the server and client, as this is normally handled for us. For instance, when a form is opened, the tables are created on the server-side, and the form and the form data source objects are created client. This makes sense if we consider the efficient transfer of data from machine to machine over the network. For the same reason, we would want a class that performs heavy data updates to be executed on the server. If it were executed on the client, data would have to travel all the way through the AOS from the SQL Server and back again. For single record updates triggered from a button on the client, it isn't so important where the code is executed, as the definition of the update (a result from a dialog, for instance) has to be transferred to the server anyway.

As passing data between client and server is actually something we want to avoid, we need to be mindful of where the code executes and where the data that the code needs resides. This should be part of the software design, but can be simplified using standard patterns or frameworks such as SysOperation.

Even so, there are some things we must keep in mind:

- Should the code ask the user for a file, the code must read the file on the client, as we can't be certain that the server will have access to the file.
- Temporary tables should be created and processed on the same tier.
- Event handlers must be constructed on the same tier as the subscription.
- Not all objects will pass between server and client tiers, such as objects of the `List`, `Set`, and `Map` types.

Typically, objects are constructed and executed on the tier they are called from. So, objects that are constructed within code that runs on the server side will be constructed on the server, as are objects constructed by code running on the client. Only by deliberately targeting a tier will code be constructed on a different tier to the calling object.

Constructing code on a specific tier

We control where code is executed by adding the `server` or `client` keyword to the `construct` method declaration. Only static methods can be declared to run on a specific tier, so we can modify the construct methods should we need to force the object to be created on the server tier. The following `construct` method will be created on the server:

```
public static server MyServerClass construct()
```

Should the caller construct the object with the `new` keyword, the code will still be constructed on the calling tier. To force a class to be constructed on the server, open the class's properties and set the **RunOn** property to `Server` or `Client`. Note that the default is `CalledFrom`.

We can test this by creating three classes:

- `ConFMSTierTestClient`
- `ConFMSTierTestServer`
- `ConFMSTierTestCaller`, which will call the two preceding classes

Complete the client class like this:

```
public static client ConFMSTierTestClient construct()
{
    return new ConFMSTierTestClient();
}
public void run()
{
    str runMode = "Client";
    if(isRunningOnServer())
        runMode = "Server";
    info(strFmt("%1 is running on the %2",
         classStr(ConFMSTierTestClient), runMode));
}
```

The `server` class is as follows. It additionally calls the client class to demonstrate what happens when server code tries to create a class on the client:

```
public static server ConFMSTierTestServer construct()
{
    return new ConFMSTierTestServer();
}
public void run()
{
    str runMode = "Client";
    if(isRunningOnServer())
        runMode = "Server";
    info(strFmt("%1 is running on the %2",
         classStr(ConFMSTierTestServer), runMode));
    ConFMSTierTestClient::construct().run();
}
```

Finally, create the following method on `ConFMSTierTestCaller`:

```
public static void main(Args _args)
{
    ConFMSTierTestClient::construct().run();
    ConFMSTierTestServer::construct().run();
}
```

Upon executing the caller class, the following info log is shown:

```
ConFMSTierTestClient is running on the Client
ConFMSTierTestServer is running on the Server
ConFMSTierTestClient is running on the Client
```

Somehow, the server managed to construct code to execute on the client. This may seem clever but it is dangerous; if our class was running as a batch task, it would fail—often dramatically.

It is rare that a class will be forced to run on the client. It is more usual to design software where the entry point is on the client and construct a contract that is passed to a class running on the server.

Passing data between client and server

Let's extend our test classes to pass data between them. First add a method to `ConFMSTierTestServer`, as follows:

```
public CustTable getAnyCustomer()
{
    CustTable customer;
    select firstOnly customer;
    return customer;
}
```

Then add the following method to the `ConFMSTierTestClient` class:

```
public void showAnyCustomerName()
{
    CustTable customer = ConFMSTierTestServer::
                              construct().getAnyCustomer();
    info(customer.name());
}
```

Finally, modify the main method in `ConFMSTierTestCaller` to read like this:

```
public static void main(Args _args)
{
    ConFMSTierTestClient::construct().run();
    ConFMSTierTestServer::construct().run();
    ConFMSTierTestClient::construct().showAnyCustomerName();
}
```

The resulting info log does get the customer name, which means that AX transferred the customer record to the client by value.

Let's try the same thing using a `List` object. Add the following method to `ConFMSTierTestServer`:

```
public List customerNameList()
{
    List customerList = new List(Types::String);
    CustTable custTable;
    select firstonly custTable;
    customerList.addEnd(custTable.name());
    return customerList;
}
```

We will call this from the `ConFMSTierTestClient` class, as follows:

```
public void showCustomerNameFromList()
{
    List custNameList;
    ListEnumerator le;

    custNameList = ConFMSTierTestServer::
                        construct().customerNameList();
    le = custNameList.getEnumerator();
    while(le.moveNext())
    {
        info(le.current());
    }
}
```

We call the preceding method from our `ConFMSTierTestCaller` class as before and execute it. Again, the code appears to work, but we said earlier that types such as `List` can't be passed to the client!

This works due to intelligence in the compiler. What actually happened was that the `List` object was created as a server-side object and `ListEnumerator` was also created as a server object, as they can't exist in different tiers. The value from the `List` object was transferred to the client using `ListEnumerator` with the `current` method—strings can pass freely between server and client tiers.

We should write this code differently if we want the list transferred to the client and therefore be safe. Many classes in AX are packable, which means that they can be packed or serialized into a container on one tier and then unpacked on another.

To ensure that the `List` object is transferred to the client, add the following method:

```
public Container customerNameListPacked()
{
    List customerList = new List(Types::String);
    CustTable custTable;
    select firstonly custTable;
    customerList.addEnd(custTable.name());
    return customerList.pack();
}
```

Finally, modify the `ConFMSTierTestClient.showCustomerNameFromList` method, as follows:

```
public void showCustomerNameFromList()
{
    List custNameList;
    ListEnumerator le;
    container packedList;
    ConFMSTierTestServer tierTestServer;

    tierTestServer = ConFMSTierTestServer::construct();
    packedList = tierTestServer.customerNameListPacked();
    custNameList = List::create(packedList);

    le = custNameList.getEnumerator();
    while(le.moveNext())
    {
        info(le.current());
    }
}
```

There is no visual difference, but the `List` and `ListEnumerator` objects are constructed on the client.

Serializing classes using the SysPackable interface

In order for classes to be passed between server and client tiers, they need to implement the `Pack` and `Unpack` methods using the pattern defined in `SysPackable`. This interface also contains a sample usage.

To create an example of this, we will use the `ConFMSVehicleFieldContract` class.

The **classDeclaration** is currently as follows:

```
[DataContractAttribute]
class ConFMSVehicleFieldContract
{
    RefFieldId refFieldId;
    str fieldLabel;
}
```

In order to make this packable, we need to follow the pattern defined in the **classDeclaration** of `SysPackable`:

```
[DataContractAttribute]
class ConFMSVehicleFieldContract implements SysPackable
{
    RefFieldId refFieldId;
    str fieldLabel;
    #define.CurrentVersion(1)
    #localmacro.CurrentList
        refFieldId,
        fieldLabel
    #endmacro
}
```

The preceding code is used by the `pack` and `unpack` methods to determine the version of the class to unpack and the class variables that should be packed or unpacked.

The `pack` and `unpack` methods are normally the same each time we write them and are written as follows:

```
public container pack()
{
    return [#CurrentVersion,#CurrentList];
}
public boolean unpack(container packedClass)
{
    int version     = runbase::getVersion(packedClass);

    switch (version)
    {
        case #CurrentVersion:
            [version,#CurrentList] = packedClass;
            return true;
        // should we add a class variable
        // we will copy #currentList and
        // save as the version's List, for example
        //case 1:
        //    [1, #Version1List] == packedClass
        //    break;
        // #version1List would be #currentlist
        // before it changed
```

```
            default :
                return false;
        }

        return false;
    }
```

Let's test this with our `ConFMSTierTestCaller` class by adding the following method to it:

```
    public void packAndUnpackTest()
    {
        ConFMSVehicleFieldContract fromContract;
        ConFMSVehicleFieldContract toContract;
        container packedClass;

        fromContract = ConFMSVehicleFieldContract::construct();
        fromContract.refFieldId(10);
        fromContract.fieldLabel("Test packed label");

        packedClass = fromContract.pack();

        toContract = ConFMSVehicleFieldContract::construct();
        toContract.unpack(packedClass);
        info(strfmt("Field %1, label %2",
                    toContract.refFieldId(),
                    toContract.fieldLabel()));
    }
```

Add a `construct` method (if one hasn't already been created) and add the following lines to the `main` method:

```
    ConFMSTierTestCaller::construct().packAndUnpackTest();
```

The code displays the expected result: `Field 10, label Test packed label`.

This technique is useful when we need the class to be reconstructed on a specific tier.

Executing code in CIL

To deliberately execute code in CIL (normally termed **IL**) we use the `runClassMethod` method for class methods and `runTableMethod` for table methods.

The method that runs in IL must accept and return a container type. To demonstrate this, create the following method in `ConFMSTierTestServer`:

```
public server static container getVehicleFieldsContractIL(
                                        container _packedContract)
{
    ConFMSVehicleFieldContract contract =
            ConFMSVehicleFieldContract::construct();
    contract.unpack(_packedContract);
    contract.fieldLabel("Changed by IL Code");
    return contract.pack();
}
```

To call this code so that it runs in IL, add the following method:

```
public void runCodeInILTest()
{
    container packedOutputContract;
    ConFMSVehicleFieldContract inputContract;
    ConFMSVehicleFieldContract outputContract;

    inputContract = ConFMSVehicleFieldContract::construct();
    inputContract.fieldLabel("Label set in prior to call");

    new XppILExecutePermission().assert();
    packedOutputContract = runClassMethodIL(
                        classStr(ConFMSTierTestServer),
                        staticMethodStr(ConFMSTierTestServer,
                                        changeFieldLabelIL),
                        inputContract.pack());
    CodeAccessPermission::revertAssert();
    outputContract = ConFMSVehicleFieldContract::construct();
    outputContract.unpack(packedOutputContract);
    info(outputContract.fieldLabel());
}
```

> We will cover code access permissions in the next section.

Modify the `main` method to call `runCodeInILTest` and execute the class. We will most likely receive the following error:

```
Error executing code: ConFMSTierTestServer object does not have
method 'changeFieldLabelIL'.
```

The reason is that when we compile a class, it will not automatically compile it to IL. To do this, navigate to **Build** | **Generate incremental CIL**.

> Whenever we change code that runs in CIL, we must generate an incremental CIL. If the types are renamed or deleted we must generate a full CIL.

Once the CIL is generated, running the `ConFMSTierTestCaller` class produces the following output:

```
ConFMSTierTestClient is running on the Client
ConFMSTierTestServer is running on the Server
ConFMSTierTestClient is running on the Client
Contoso Europe
Contoso Europe
Field 10, label Test packed label
Changed by IL Code
```

We should force code to run in CIL only if performance was particularly critical, such as an event triggered from the UI that would otherwise appear as a glitch to the user. An example of this is `SalesLine.modifiedSalseQty`, which fires whenever the `SalesLine.SalesQty` field is changed.

Code access permissions

Code running on the server requires that the developer deliberately assert access permissions when trying to access certain tasks. The common tasks are as follows:

- Executing X++ code in CIL
- Accessing a file
- Calling CLR code

The pattern of usage is this:

- Assert the permission
- Write the code that requires the permission
- Revert the access

File I/O permission

An example of accessing a file is as follows, and it should be added to the `ConFMSTierTestServer` and `ConFMSTierTestClient` classes:

```
public void checkFileExists()
{
    new FileIOPermission("C:\\NoFileHere.txt", "r").assert();
    if(!WinAPIServer::fileExists("C:\\noFileHere.txt"))
        info("The file does not exist");
    CodeAccessPermission::revertAssert();
}
```

Write a job as shown here:

```
public static void ConFMSCheckFileExists(Args _args)
{
    ConFMSTierTestServer::construct().checkFileExists();
    ConFMSTierTestClient::construct().checkFileExists();
}
```

When this job executes, the **InfoLog** window shows the following messages:

```
Message (09:52:47 am)
The file does not exist
Request for the permission of type 'FileIOPermission' failed.
(S)\Classes\FileIOPermission\demand
(S)\Classes\WinAPIServer\fileExists - line 14
(C)\Classes\ConFMSTierTestClient\checkFileExists - line 4
(C)\Jobs\ConFMSCheckFileExists - line 4
```

> The `(C)` and `(S)` prefixes indicate the tier the code is executing on.

As we can see from the preceding output, on line 4, the code that runs on the client has failed. This is because we must ask for permission on the same tier that requires it. The `WinAPIServer::fileExists` method is a static method that constructs on the server, so this is where the permission must be asserted.

> Microsoft wrote two classes for common Windows API calls, `WinAPI` for client code, and `WinAPIServer` for server code.

The CLR interop permission

In this case, we will use the CLR interop to determine whether the file exists. The permission for using the CLR interop is asserted using this code:

```
new InteropPermission(InteropKind::ClrInterop).assert();
```

We will use `System.IO.File::Exists` to do this, but it will also require that we assert the file I/O permission. In order to assert two permissions at the same time, we need to use a different command—`CodeAccessPermission::assertMultiple`.

This requires a set of permissions and is done using the following code:

```
public void fileExistsUsingCLR()
{
    Set permSet = new Set(Types::Class);

    permSet.add(new FileIOPermission("C:\\NoFileHere.txt", "r"));
    permSet.add(new InteropPermission(InteropKind::ClrInterop));

    CodeAccessPermission::assertMultiple(permSet);

    if(!System.IO.File::Exists("C:\\noFileHere.txt"))
        info("The file does not exist");

    CodeAccessPermission::revertAssert();

}
```

More on views – computed columns

The view we created earlier in this book was a simple view with an aggregation, serving as an introduction to views in AX. In this section, we will expand on this to cover some important features. For this section, we will need administrator access to AX SQL Server and have **SQL Server Management Studio** (**SSMS**) installed.

We won't use many of the features from SSMS, but it is worth reading the following:

- *Tutorial: SQL Server Management Studio* at `https://msdn.microsoft.com/en-us/library/bb934498.aspx`
- *Displaying Graphical Execution Plans (SQL Server Management Studio)* at: `https://technet.microsoft.com/en-us/library/ms178071%28v=sql.105%29.aspx`

How SQL Server executes views

When we create views, we are effectively storing a query definition that is executed by SQL Server, even though we treat them as read-only tables in AX. If we write a view that uses another view as its data source, SQL Server will determine the best execution plan based on the desired output columns and the queries defined by the views.

This is important to understand, and it will help us create more efficient views. For example, there is an almost natural belief that writing a view that filters data to be used by another view is more efficient, as the data source has fewer rows. This is incorrect because the base view's data doesn't physically exist; it is merely a query definition.

Another example is how aggregated columns in a base view are treated by views based on it. Let's say our base view has an aggregated column, and we write another view that uses this base view but does not use the base view's aggregated column. The aggregation will not be executed by SQL Server.

For example, suppose we created the following views using SSMS:

```
CREATE VIEW [baseView] AS
SELECT SalesId, Sum(QtyOrdered) totalOrdered
    FROM SalesLine
    GROUP BY SalesId
GO
CREATE view [otherView] AS
SELECT SalesId from baseView
GO
```

Enable Include actual execution plan in the **Query** menu, and write the following code:

```
SELECT SalesId FROM otherView
```

All of this produces the following execution plan:

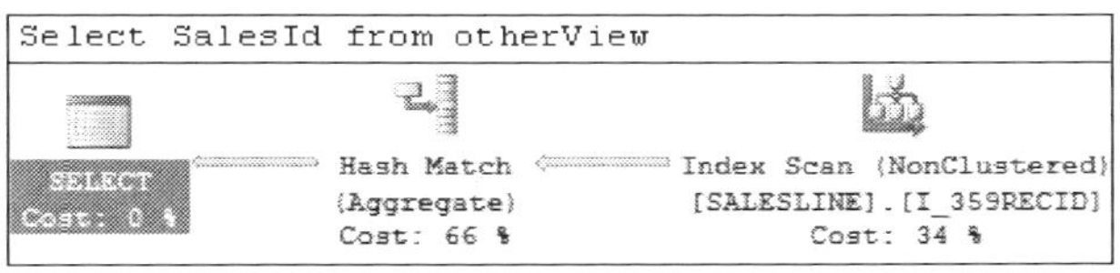

It is clear that the query executed by SQL Server is directly querying `SalesLine`.

> The preceding code was merely meant to explain quickly what happens when a view uses another view. We must never create tables or views directly in SQL Server.

Adding a computed column

One of the limitations of SQL views defined in AX is that you cannot use CASE statements or subqueries as columns. To solve this problem, Microsoft now allows methods to be created that return a SQL statement that can be used as a column in the view. These are called computed columns.

> For this section, you will need Microsoft SSMS.

View methods are static server methods that should return a string of valid **Transact-SQL** (actual SQL code).

This could be something like the following:

```
public server static str thisIsOne()
{

    return "SELECT 1";
}
```

When added to the view as an integer view method called `One`, it adds a column with the following code:

```
CAST((SELECT 1) as INTEGER) as One
```

> The returned string can largely be any valid Transact-SQL code that can execute under the security context of the AX server service account. Another reason we lock down service accounts is to minimize the exposed surface area.

A note on performance of computed columns

We can therefore write a computed column that returns a complicated subquery that is used as a column in a view. When we do this, we must ensure that SQL Server is executing the code efficiently, and it is hard to know this without testing it.

Although computed column methods may seem far easier to use than building a query with aggregations, if the aggregation can be done in the query that the view uses, that is where it should be done. The following example explains why:

1. Open the SQL Server Management Studio and select your business database.
2. Create a new query window and type the following:

```
SELECT InventTable.ItemId,
    ISNULL(SUM(SalesLine.QtyOrdered), 0.00) AS QtySold,
    ISNULL(SUM(PurchLine.LineAmount), 0.00) AS Purchased,
    ISNULL(SUM(PurchLine.QtyOrdered), 0.00) AS QtyBought,
    ISNULL(SUM(PurchLine.LineAmount), 0.00) AS Purchased
    FROM InventTable
  LEFT OUTER JOIN SalesLine
      ON SalesLine.ItemId     = InventTable.ItemId
     AND SalesLine.DataAreaID = InventTable.DataAreaID
     AND SalesLine.Partition  = InventTable.Partition
  LEFT OUTER JOIN PurchLine
      ON PurchLine.ItemId     = InventTable.ItemId
     AND PurchLine.DataAreaID = InventTable.DataAreaID
     AND PurchLine.Partition  = InventTable.Partition
  WHERE InventTable.DataAreaId = 'USMF'
    AND InventTable.Partition = 5637144576
    GROUP BY InventTable.DataAreaID,
             InventTable.Partition,
             InventTable.ItemId
```

3. Ensure that **Include Actual Execution Plan** and **Include Client Statistics** are selected in the **Query** menu.
4. Navigate to **Query** | **Reset Client Statistics**.

5. Execute the query and note the following graphic in the **Execution plan** tab:

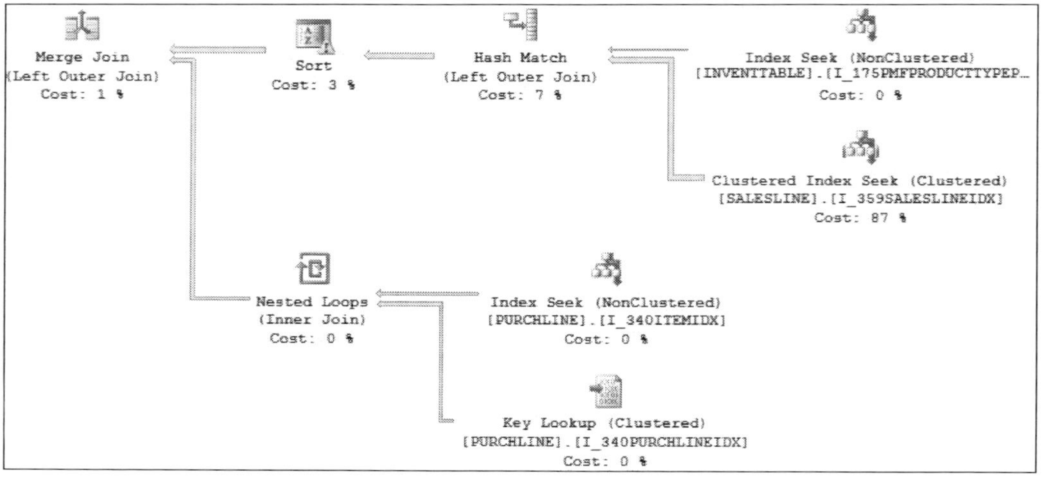

6. Let's try the same code, but using subqueries for the two aggregations:

```
SELECT IT.ItemId,
       ISNULL((SELECT SUM(SL.QtyOrdered)
              FROM SalesLine SL
              WHERE SL.ItemId = IT.ItemId
                AND SL.DataAreaID = IT.DataAreaID
                AND SL.Partition  = IT.Partition), 0)
       AS QtySold,
       ISNULL((SELECT SUM(SL.LineAmount)
              FROM SalesLine SL
              WHERE SL.ItemId = IT.ItemId
                AND SL.DataAreaID = IT.DataAreaID
                AND SL.Partition  = IT.Partition), 0)
       AS Sales,
       ISNULL((SELECT SUM(PL.QtyOrdered)
              FROM PurchLine PL
              WHERE PL.ItemId     = IT.ItemId
                AND PL.DataAreaID = IT.DataAreaID
                  AND PL.Partition  = IT.Partition), 0)
       AS QtyBought,
       ISNULL((SELECT SUM(PL.LineAmount)
              FROM PurchLine PL
              WHERE PL.ItemId     = IT.ItemId
```

```
                    AND PL.DataAreaID = IT.DataAreaID
                      AND PL.Partition  = IT.Partition), 0)
            AS Purchased
         FROM InventTable IT
       WHERE IT.DataAreaId = 'USMF'
         AND IT.Partition = 5637144576
       ORDER BY IT.DataAreaId, IT.Partition, IT.ItemId
```

7. The execution plan reveals the cost of doing it this way, as shown here:

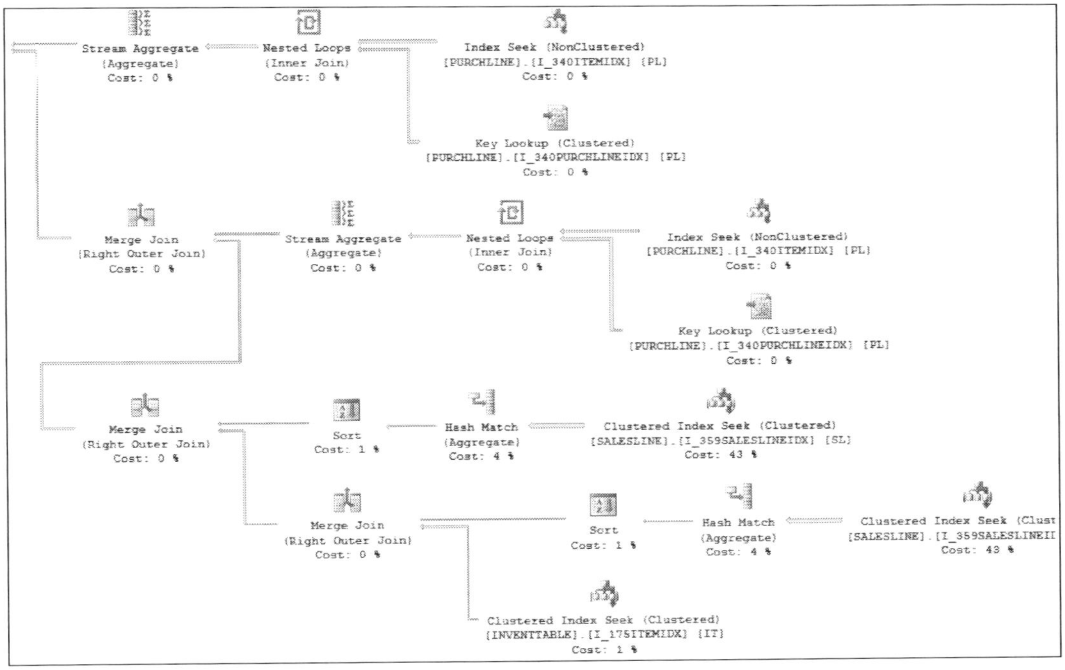

The execution plans look completely different, and the second example shows that some more work is being done in putting the results together before it is returned to the client. The cost of this additional work, however, is shown as **0 %**, so the execution plan makes the difference appear worse than it actually is. The subquery method can be faster, especially for simple aggregations where the table is used once. Should we have many complicated subqueries, the join method is usually much faster.

> Checking and understanding the execution plan is generally important, and it should be tested against a real-life data scenario—not just on our development machines.

Creating a computed column – concatenating two fields

To get started with our first computed column method, we will create a simple concatenation of two fields. The first part to understand is that we have access to the tables and fields in the view's data sources, and we can use them to perform calculations or join other tables not in the view's data source list.

We will use the `ConFMSVehicleUtilisation` view, which we created earlier in this book. The view's data sources include the `ConFMSVehicleTable` table and the `VehicleId` and `Name` fields.

To do this, create a new method under the view's **Methods** node and write the following code:

```
public server static str vehicleIdAndName()
{
    str viewName = tableStr(ConFMSVehicleUtilisation);
    str sql;
    // this is the data source's name,
    // which may not be the same as the table name
    str datasourceName = identifierStr(ConFMSVehicleTable);
    str vehicleIdField = fieldStr(ConFMSVehicleTable, VehicleId);
    str nameField      = fieldStr(ConFMSVehicleTable, Name);
    // to contain the actual SQL column name
    str vehicleId;
    str name;
    // the following will return a string similar to T1.VehicleId
    vehicleId = SysComputedColumn::returnField(viewName,
                                               datasourceName,
                                               vehicleIdField);
    name      = SysComputedColumn::returnField(viewName,
                                               datasourceName,
                                               nameField);
    sql = vehicleId + "+ '-' + " + name;
    return sql;
}
```

We use `SysComputedColumn::returnField`, as AX will sometimes use a different physical field name in the actual SQL table. It will also alias each table from T1 upwards, like this:

```
SELECT T1.SalesId from SalesTable T1
```

Next, add this to the view's field list by following these steps:

1. Right-click on **ConFMSVehicleUtilisation** | **Fields** and choose **String Computed Column**.
2. Open the property sheet for the new field.
3. Change the **Name** to `VehicleIdAndName`.
4. Enter a suitable label in the **Label** property.
5. Select `vehicleIdAndName` from the **ViewMethod** list.
6. Set **ExtendedDateType** to `Name`.
7. Save and synchronize the view (right on the view and choose **Synchronize**).

This fails because we used the `Name` field, which is not included in the group by the clause of the query. The `VehicleId` field is fine because AX automatically adds fields in the output list as a group by for aggregated views.

In this case, it is okay to use the `MIN` command to select the `Name` field first. This is because the `VehicleId` and `Name` fields are on the same data source, and grouping `VehicleId` means that `ConFMSVehicleTable` is not aggregated. This may seem obvious in this case, but if we were grouping by `VehiceGroupId`, using `MIN` would return the lowest `Name` field for each grouped set of `ConFMSVehicleTable` records.

Change the code as follows:

```
sql = vehicleId + "+ '-' + MIN(" + name + ")";
```

When you open the view, you should see the new field. The cool part is that the calculation is done by SQL Server and is treated like a real view field in AX, which means we can filter and sort by it.

The actual Transact-SQL returned by this function will be similar to the following:

```
T1.VehicleId +'-'+MIN(T1.Name)
```

By adding this to the view as a string computed column, it adds a `CAST` command to ensure that it returns the correct type. The relevant portion of the actual Transact-SQL generated is as follows:

```
SELECT T1.VEHICLEID AS VEHICLEID,
--/
(CAST((T1.VEHICLEID+ '-' + min(T1.NAME)) AS NVARCHAR(60)))
AS VEHICLEIDANDNAME
--/
```

Creating a computed column – return data from related tables

The code is similar to the preceding code, but we have a big consideration here when joining a table as a subquery. AX will naturally join the two system fields, `Partition` and `DataAreaId`, and they are also added to the indexes. Simply, we must add these fields to our joins (depending on the table's `SaveDataPerPartition` and `SaveDataPerCompany` properties) when writing a subquery as a view method.

The following method will sum records from `ConFMSVehServiceTable` for each vehicle:

```
public server static str vehicleServiceCount()
{
    str viewName = tableStr(ConFMSVehicleUtilisation);
    str sql;
    // this is the data source's name,
    // which may not be the same as the table name
    str datasourceName = identifierStr(ConFMSVehicleTable);
    str vehicleIdField = fieldStr(ConFMSVehicleTable, VehicleId);
    str dataAreaFIeld  = fieldStr(ConFMSVehicleTable, DataAreaId);
    str partitionField = fieldStr(ConFMSVehicleTable, Partition);
    // to contain the actual SQL column name
    str vehicleId;
    str dataAreaId;
    str partition;
    // the following will return a string similar to T1.VehicleId
dataAreaId = SysComputedColumn::returnField(viewName,
                                            datasourceName,
                                            dataAreaFIeld);
    partition = SysComputedColumn::returnField(viewName,
                                            datasourceName,
                                            partitionField);
    vehicleId = SysComputedColumn::returnField(viewName,
                                            datasourceName,
                                            vehicleIdField);

    sql  = "SELECT COUNT(*) FROM ConFMSVehServiceTable LVS \n";
    sql += "    WHERE LVS.VehicleId  = " + vehicleId  + "\n";
    sql += "      AND LVS.DataAreaId = " + dataAreaId + "\n";
    sql += "      AND LVS.Partition  = " + partition + "\n";

    return sql;
}
```

> In the preceding code, we added a newline character. We do this when writing more complicated code so that we can read the resulting Transact-SQL in SSMS.

Next, add this to the view's field list by following these steps:

1. Right-click on **ConFMSVehicleUtilisation** | **Fields** and choose **Real Computed Column**.
2. Open the property sheet for the new field.
3. Change **Name** to `ServiceRecords`.
4. Enter `Service records` as the **Label** property.
5. Select `vehicleServiceCount` from the **ViewMethod** list.
6. Set **ExtendedDateType** to `Total`.
7. Save the view and synchronize it as before.

Other useful functions

Although we can write Transact-SQL directly, there are some useful functions that are provided to us. All of these are stored in the `SysComputedColumn` class.

The common functions we tend to use are as follows:

To return a fully-qualified SQL field name use the command `SysComputedColumn ::returnField`.

To create a Transact-SQL `CASE` statement use `SysComputedColumn::switch`. This has two parameters:

- `_controlExpression`: The value to be compared, such as a field. This is useful for mapping enum values to strings, for example, `SalesStatus`.
- `_comparisionExpressionMap`: The map of comparison and result values. The map's key attribute will be the value to be compared, and the value attribute will be the value returned. For the `SalesStatus` example it would replace the numeric value of 1 with 'Open order'.

You can use the `SysComputedColumn::if` command to create a simple `CASE` statement with on `CASE` and one `ELSE`.

> With regard to the switch method example using `SalesStatus`, since you have learned about metadata you can create the map using the `DictEnum` class.

The reason these methods exist is twofold: firstly, they are a helper to those not skilled in Transact-SQL, and secondly, the code returned will be valid for supported versions of SQL Server. This doesn't mean you can't use Transact-SQL, and in some cases, it will be easier to read and possibly perform faster. If you do write Transact-SQL, you are responsible for ensuring that the code will work on the current and future versions of SQL Server.

Common misconceptions

The most common mistake we have seen is using X++ functions when building the SQL statement, like this for example:

```
sql += "      AND LVS.DataAreaId = " + curExt() + "\n";
```

This will hardcode the company that was active when the view was synchronized into the statement; it will return a value only if the user is in that company.

Others are attempts to use X++ table methods when creating the statement. Again, the result of the method was determined when the view was synchronized, hardcoding the static result of the statement.

Finally, the data returned will bypass any security you have in place within AX. We therefore need to be mindful of this when writing the computed column. For example, if a user doesn't have access to `CustTabe.CreditMax` and we write a computed column that gets this value of AX on a view the user does have access to, they will see this data.

Summary

In this chapter, we covered many topics, including metadata, exception handling, code execution, passing data between tiers, and computed columns on views. We won't need to use all of this in every project we work on. What is important is that you understand the concepts, as you can always use this as reference when you have something where a technique covered here is appropriate.

In the next chapter, we will cover unit and performance testing to help us ensure that the code performs as expected in terms of functionality and performance.

11

Unit and Performance Testing

In this chapter, we will cover testing of both functionality and performance, as well as the tools used to debug code, in the following topics:

- Unit testing
- Using the debugger
- Automated unit testing
- Creating automated unit test cases
- Creating unit tests with data isolation
- How to run a test case
- Reviewing the results of the unit test
- Code and database performance testing through code profiling

Unit testing

In the last few chapters, we wrote some impressive code, and now it is necessary to make sure it functions as defined by the requirement. The term **unit testing** means we are testing whether the code fulfils the requirement only, and not how it fits into the whole process.

As part of the unit test process, the focus of the testing is as follows:

- Does the code fit the requirement?
- Is the user interface usable and does it follow AX conventions?
- Is the code efficient in terms of processing and database calls?

> Although we can't perform a true performance test on a development system, we can check whether the code is written in an efficient manner as part of the developer's own testing and the code review.

If any bugs are found, and subsequently fixed, during the course of testing, it will mean that all tests must be done again, as one fix could break something else, and dry-reading the code for this kind of regression testing is not sufficient.

Even though it is tempting to simply declare the work as done and ready for user acceptance testing, the apparent time saved can be very costly, not just financially, but also in terms of goodwill of the users helping out with the testing process. The end-user acceptance team is busy enough with additional workload on top of their normal tasks, so releasing unfinished code erodes the excitement they may have for the new software.

Code review

It may seem the easiest thing in the world to criticize someone else's work, which may seem negative until we consider that we want to deliver good-quality code that performs well and is easy to maintain.

Just because the code works, and even matches the requirement, does not mean that it is ready for release. Ensuring that the code is maintainable and performs well is partly accomplished using standard patterns, but this cannot replace the benefits of a code review by a trained peer.

Test-driven development

When planning the process for this book, we had a decision of whether to follow the more traditional bottom-up method, where we write code for a requirement or specification and then perform unit testing, or to use **test-driven development** (**TDD**).

We felt that following TDD would detract from this book's core aim of getting started with AX development, but this doesn't mean we won't recommend it. With TDD, we actually write the test case first and then write the code, which of course won't compile until the code is complete. This changes our way of thinking about the code we write, often resulting in better code and a different focus when writing the actual code.

Testing best practices for Microsoft Dynamics AX development can be found at `http://www.microsoft.com/download/en/details.aspx?id=27565`.

Using the debugger

One of the best ways to test code is through the debugger. This starts automatically when the code reaches a breakpoint, you are in the System Administrator security role, and your Windows account is in the local Windows user group called Microsoft AX Debugging Users Group.

To set up and run the test, follow these steps:

1. Create suitable test data (vehicles, trailers, and trucks), including data to test false positives. For the first test, use a test case that should succeed.
2. Open the `ConFMSAppointmentVehicleHandler::tmsAppointmentModifiedFieldEventHandler` method.
3. Set a breakpoint by selecting the `TMSAppointment appointment = _args.getThis();` line, and press *F9*.

> A red dot will appear in the left-hand-side margin. A list of breakpoints can be seen by pressing *Shift* + *F9*.

4. In the client, navigate to **Transportation management** | **Common** | **Driver check-in and check-out**.
5. Click on **Schedule an appointment**.
6. Enter a value (as per your test cases) in **Tractor number**, and tab out of the field.

> The debugger will open, highlighting the current line that is about to be executed. We are interested in watching the code execution and how the appointment record buffer is updated.

7. The default layout will show a window in the bottom-left corner, with the **Locals** active tab. Note that the `fieldId` variable is `0` and the `appointment` record has `<recid = 0>`, as shown in this screenshot:

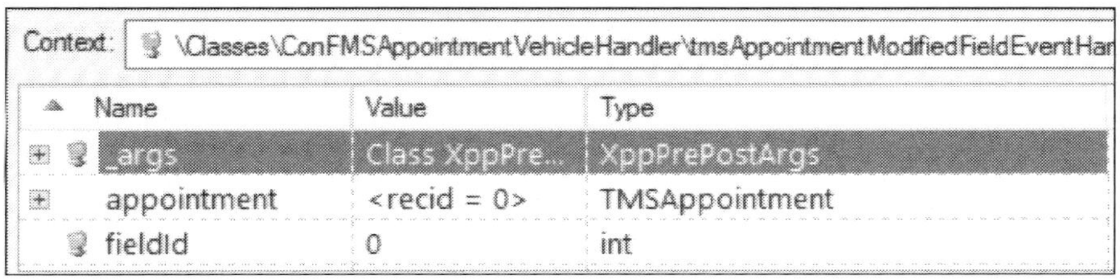

> <Recid = 0> means that the record has not been saved, which is also how we test whether a record was selected.

8. Step over the next calls using *F10* until the `handler.run();` line, watching how the values are changing.
9. The appointment will not appear to change because it is a new record, so expand this node to see that the `TractorNumber` field has changed to the value entered.
10. On the `handler.run();` line press *F11* to step into the method.
11. Step over (*F10*) the lines, and step into (*F11*) the `this.handlerTractorNumber();` line.
12. Verify that the `getVehiceReferenceForType` method succeeds, and then see that `appointment.ConFMSVehicleTableTruck` is set correctly.
13. As you step out of the method, note that the field remains set.
14. Step through `tmsAppointmentModifiedFieldEventHandler` using *F11* until you are returned to the closing brace of `TMSAppointment.modifiedField`, and check the value of `this.ConFMSVehicleTableTruck`. The record was therefore passed by reference.

> When stepping through a post-event handler and once it is complete, we are returned to the event to which the handler is subscribed, at its closing brace.

15. Continue your tests for each scenario using the debugger to trace the method flows. Should you wish to simply let the code run, press *F5*.

Automated unit testing

We can create unit test cases in AX to perform tests for us. We can also use them to test performance by robotically testing the code. We write the test, such as updating a field on a record, and the expected result. This is not always done in a project, and many opt to test manually. There are advantages that a coded unit test has over manual testing, which include the following:

- The test is repeatable, with little effort
- It can be used to simulate loads
- It can be used for regression testing

One of the main sources of end-user frustration, along with consulting and development costs, is regression. This is where a new feature breaks something that previously worked. Using unit test cases is a way to minimize this risk.

When writing automated tests, we focus on testing business logic and database updates where we can set the state or input parameters for the test and determine the result, matching it against the expected result. We will not, however, test the UI in this manner.

The steps involved in an automated test are as follows:

- Set up the test data required for the test
- Perform the tests
- Tear down (clean up) the data or other artifacts created by the test

Creating automated unit test cases

We will perform two tests, one to test the `ConFMSVehicleUtilisation` view and another that can be used to test performance.

The test case must reflect the requirement, such as this:

```
The vehicle utilization view is to show the number of items in
stocking unit added to a load.
```

To prove this, we will write a method that calculates this and matches it with the `TotalItems` column on the view. We will test for failure first, so we will deliberately code it to fail, and then change the code to perform the test we expect to succeed.

> In TDD, we would have already written the test case, which would only pass once the code is complete and working.

Creating the unit test project

For our test case, we need a test suite. This is done by creating a test project, as shown in the following steps:

1. Open the **Projects** window using the toolbar or the *Ctrl* + *P* shortcut.
2. Right-click on the **Shared** node and go to **New** | **Test project**. This will open the test project and a toolbar as shown here:

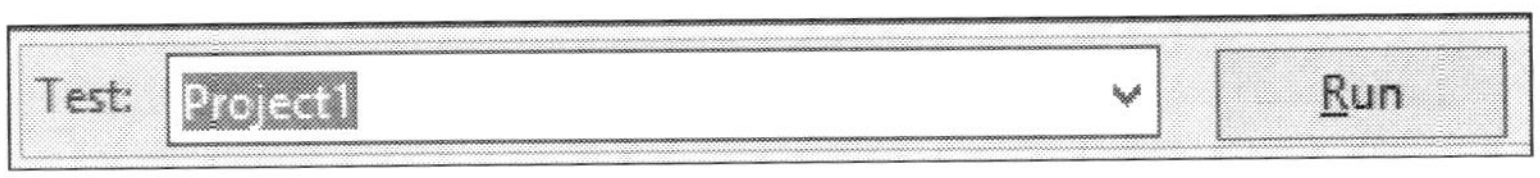

3. Rename the project to `ConFMSVehicleTestProject`. We should suffix the project with `TestProject` and name it according to the area of functionality we are developing.
4. In the toolbar, overtype the test project name from `Project1` to `ConFMSVehicleTestProject`.

Creating a unit test case

The test case is a class that extends the `SysTestCase` class, and is used to test an element. This is usually a table or class. In this case, we will test the `ConFMSVehicleUtilisation` view.

To create the test case, follow these steps:

1. Right-click on the **TestSuite** node and go to **New | Class**.
2. Rename the class to `ConFMSVehicleUtilisationTest`. The class must be named after the element we are testing and suffixed with `Test`.
3. We now bind this to the element within the `classDeclaration`, and declare the element we are testing, as follows:

```
[SysTestTargetAttribute(tableStr(ConFMSVehicleUtilisation),
UtilElementType::Table)]
class ConFMSVehicleUtilisationTest extends SysTestCase
{
    ConFMSVehicleUtilisation vehicleUtilisation;
}
```

4. To set up the data for the test, we override the method setup. Right-click on the class and select **Override method | setUp**.
5. Our setup data will simply be to select the first record in the view, as shown here:

```
public void setUp()
{
    select firstOnly vehicleUtilisation;
    super();
}
```

6. We now need to create our first test method. Again, the naming is important, and the code is written as follows:

```
[SysTestMethodAttribute]
public void testTotalItems()
{
    WHSLoadLine loadLine;
    TMSAppointment appt;
    ConFMSVehicleTable vehicleTable;
    str msg;
    // Action
    select sum(InventQty) from loadLine
        join appt
        where appt.ApptRefNum == loadLine.LoadId &&
              appt.ApptRefType == TMSApptRefType::Load
        join vehicleTable
        where vehicleTable.RecId ==
                    appt.ConFMSVehicleTableTruck &&
              vehicleTable.VehicleId ==
                    vehicleUtilisation.VehicleId;
    msg = strFmt("Testing vehicle %1",
                 vehicleUtilisation.VehicleId);
    // Assert result
    this.assertEquals(loadLine.InventQty + 1,
                    vehicleUtilisation.TotalItems,
                    msg);
}
```

> Use the test script to create this method in the same way you do for `parm` and `construct` methods—clear the method body, type `test` and press *Tab*.

7. Save and compile the class.

> The `+ 1` in step 6 is to deliberately make this test fail—we test for failure first.

The preceding pattern is actually best suited for testing a static class that is instantiated in the setup method and each method tested. We don't need to tear down the data in this case as we aren't creating or updating data.

Running the unit test case

Once we have completed our test cases, we can execute them. We have coded the test to fail, in order to prove the test.

To run the test cases in your suite, click on **Run** from the unit test toolbar. Once complete, we expect to see a message similar to this:

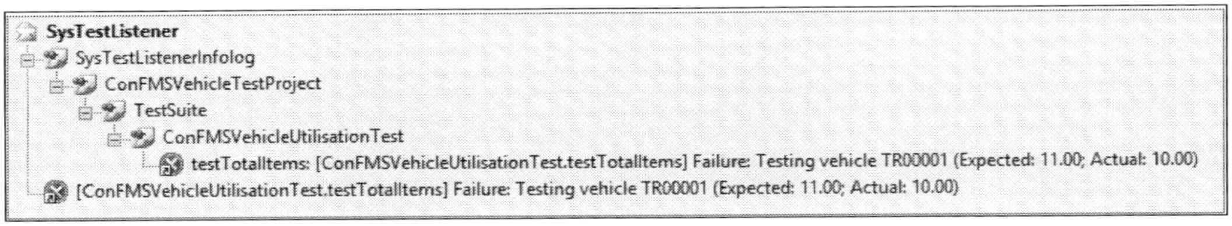

> We can also run the tests for a specific unit test class by going to **Add-Ins** | **Run tests** from the class's right-click menu.

The project window is also updated. The tests that failed are highlighted, as shown here:

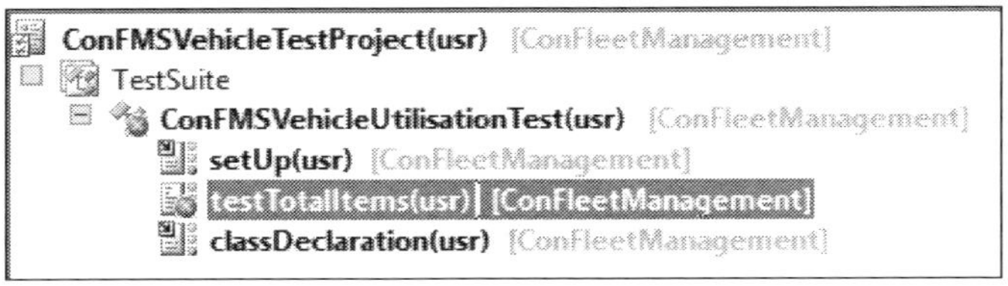

We should now test for success, so modify the `testTotalItems` method so that it should be a success; that is, remove the `+ 1`. Then compile the class, and this time, right-click on `ConFMSVehicleUtilisationTest` and go to **Add-ins** | **Run tests**.

This time, we get success, and the icon on the class and method is a green tick.

You can see the results for each test by clicking on the **Details** button in the unit test toolbar.

Creating unit tests with data isolation

In this instance, our test case will create data that will used to test that the records are inserted correctly and the methods perform the correct behavior.

The test will be to create a number of vehicle service records and test the `validateField`, `modifiedField`, and `insert` methods. We also want to test creating a number of these records to test performance of this table.

The steps involved in this scenario are the same as before, except that we need to tear down the data we created. We will also see that a test case can actually contain far more code than the code that we are testing. This is normal, and we expect to see a 3:1 ratio of test code to business logic.

The framework supports automatic teardown of test data using company isolation. This is done by creating a temporary company and deleting it after the test method or class completes.

> Do not try and tear down the data using `ttsAbort`, or else you will roll back the test result data.

We control the isolation of our test case by overriding the `createSuite` method and returning a new instance of one of the following methods:

- `SysTestSuite`: This does not provide automatic teardown, and must be manually cleaned up in the class's tear-down method
- `SysTestSuiteCompanyIsolateClass`: A company will be created, the test methods executed, and then the company is deleted
- `SysTestSuiteCompanyIsolateMethod`: A company will be created per test method, isolating each test method's data from each other

We will use the `SysTestSuiteCompanyIsolateClass` suite for our test, as we want to create a reasonable amount of setup data and test each method on this data.

There is a second part to this, and that is whether the test case should run in a single instance. The default is `false`, which means that the class is instantiated for each test method. This means that the setup method will be executed for each test method with no teardown or cognizance of the other instances of the class. So, if we are using company isolation by class, we normally do want the class to execute as one instance and prevent the data setup execution for subsequent test methods.

The steps used to create the unit test case are as follows:

1. Right-click on the **TestSuite** node and choose **New** | **Class**.
2. Rename the class to `ConFMSVehServiceTableTest`.
3. As before, we need to decorate the declaration, but we will have variables that we can use to build the test data, as follows:

```
[SysTestTargetAttribute(tableStr(ConFMSVehServiceTable),
UtilElementType::Table)]
class ConFMSVehServiceTableTest extends SysTestCase
{
    int numberOfServiceRecordsToCreate;
    int numberOfVehicles;
    // set up is run for each test method
    // we don't want the data created for each
    // test method as we will isolate at class level
    boolean dataIsReady;
}
```

4. The setup data method is a little more complicated, so we will create a method for this and we will call it from the overridden `setUp` method. It is written as follows:

```
private void createTestSetupData()
{
    ConFMSVehicleTable    vehicle;
    ConFMSVehicleGroup    vehGroup;
    ConFMSVehicleSchedule schedule;
    Counter               idx;
    ConFMSVehicleId       vehicleId;

    vehGroup.clear();
    vehGroup.VehicleGroupId = "TestGroup";
    vehGroup.insert();

    schedule.clear();
    schedule.VehicleScheduleId = "1";
    schedule.Days = 30;
    schedule.Distance = 2000;
    schedule.insert();
```

```
        schedule.clear();
        schedule.VehicleScheduleId = "2";
        schedule.Days = 60;
        schedule.Distance = 4000;
        schedule.insert();
        schedule.clear();

        schedule.VehicleScheduleId = "3";
        schedule.Days = 365;
        schedule.Distance = 30000;
        schedule.insert();

        for(idx = 1; idx <= numberOfVehicles; idx++)
        {
            vehicleId = strFmt("V%1",
                            strReplace(
                                strRFix(int2str(idx),5),
                                " ", "0"));
            vehicle.clear();
            vehicle.VehicleId = vehicleId;
            vehicle.Name = strFmt("Vehicle %1", vehicleId);
            vehicle.VehicleGroupId = vehGroup.VehicleGroupId;
            vehicle.VehicleSchedId = int2str((idx mod 3) + 1);
            vehicle.insert();
        }
        dataIsReady = true;
    }
```

5. To set up the data for the test, we override the `setUp` method—right-click on the class and go to **Override method | setUp**.
6. Our setup data is used simply to select the first record in the view, as shown here:

```
public void setUp()
{
    // These parameter variables will be also
    // be used by the test methods
    numberOfServiceRecordsToCreate = 20;
    numberOfVehicles = 200;
    if(!isDataReady)
        this.createTestSetupData();
    super();
}
```

7. We now need to specify the isolation level, which is done by overriding `createSuite` so that it returns a new instance of `SysTestSuiteCompanyIsolateClass`:

```
public SysTestSuite createSuite()
{
    return new SysTestSuiteCompanyIsolateClass(this);
}
```

8. The final step, prior to creating our test methods, is to ensure the test case will run as a single instance, otherwise the `isDataReady` variable will always be `false`. Override the `useSingleInstance` method and return `true`, as shown here:

```
public boolean useSingleInstance()
{
    return true;
}
```

9. The code for the test methods is as follows:

```
[SysTestMethodAttribute]
public void testInitFromConFMSVehicleTable()
{
    ConFMSVehicleTable    vehicle;
    ConFMSVehServiceTable vehServices;
    while select vehicle
    {
        vehServices.clear();
        vehServices.initFromConFMSVehicleTable(vehicle);
        this.assertEquals(vehicle.VehicleId,
                          vehServices.VehicleId,
                          strFmt("Vehicle %1 initialised",
                                 vehicle.VehicleId));
    }
}
[SysTestMethodAttribute]
public void testValidateField()
{
    ConFMSVehicleTable    vehicle;
    ConFMSVehServiceTable vehServices;
    Counter               idx;
    ConFMSVehicleSchedId  serviceSchedId;
    Days                  serviceDaysExpected;
    Distance              serviceDistanceExpected;
```

```
    while select vehicle
    {
        for(idx = 1;
            idx<= numberOfServiceRecordsToCreate;
            idx ++)
        {
            vehServices.clear();
            vehServices.VehicleId = vehicle.VehicleId;
            // test invalid data
            vehServices.ServiceDate = systemDateGet() + 5;
            vehServices.NextServiceDate =
                            vehServices.ServiceDate - 2;
            this.assertFalse(vehServices.validateField(
                            fieldNum(ConFMSVehServiceTable,
                                      NextServiceDate)));

            vehServices.CurrentOdometer = 1000;
            vehServices.NextServiceOdo =
                            vehServices.CurrentOdometer-2;
            this.assertFalse(vehServices.validateField(
                            fieldNum(ConFMSVehServiceTable,
                                      NextServiceOdo)));
            // test valid data
            vehServices.ServiceDate = systemDateGet() + 5;
            vehServices.modifiedField(
                            fieldNum(ConFMSVehServiceTable,
                                      ServiceDate));
            this.assertTrue(vehServices.validateField(
                            fieldNum(ConFMSVehServiceTable,
                                      NextServiceDate)));
            vehServices.CurrentOdometer = 1000;
            vehServices.modifiedField(
                            fieldNum(ConFMSVehServiceTable,
                                      CurrentOdometer));
            this.assertTrue(vehServices.validateField(
                            fieldNum(ConFMSVehServiceTable,
                                      NextServiceOdo)));
        }
    }
}
[SysTestMethodAttribute]
public void testModifiedField()
{
```

```
ConFMSVehicleTable    vehicle;
ConFMSVehServiceTable vehServices;
Counter               idx;
ConFMSVehicleSchedId  schedId;
Days                  serviceDaysExpected;
Distance              serviceDistanceExpected;
TransDate             serviceDateExpected;
while select vehicle
{
    for(idx = 1;
        idx<= numberOfServiceRecordsToCreate;
        idx++)
    {
        vehServices.clear();
        vehServices.VehicleId = vehicle.VehicleId;
        vehServices.ServiceDate = systemDateGet();
        vehServices.modifiedField(
                        fieldNum(ConFMSVehServiceTable,
                                 ServiceDate));

        schedId = vehicle.VehicleSchedId;
        serviceDateExpected = dateNull();
        if(ConFMSVehicleSchedule::exist(schedId))
        {
            serviceDaysExpected =
                    ConFMSVehicleSchedule::
                              find(schedId).Days;
            serviceDateExpected =
                    vehServices.ServiceDate +
                    serviceDaysExpected;
        }
        this.assertEquals(serviceDateExpected,
                          vehServices.NextServiceDate);

        vehServices.CurrentOdometer = 1000;
        vehServices.modifiedField(
                        fieldNum(ConFMSVehServiceTable,
                                 CurrentOdometer));

        serviceDistanceExpected = 0;
```

```
                serviceSchedId = vehicle.VehicleSchedId;
                if(ConFMSVehicleSchedule::exist(schedId))
                {
                    serviceDistanceExpected =
                                vehServices.CurrentOdometer +
                                ConFMSVehicleSchedule::
                                 find(schedId).Distance;
                }
                this.assertEquals(serviceDistanceExpected,
                                  vehServices.NextServiceOdo);
            }
        }
    }
    [SysTestMethodAttribute]
    public void testInsert()
    {
        ConFMSVehicleTable    vehicle;
        ConFMSVehServiceTable vehServices;
        Counter               idx;
        while select vehicle
        {
            for(idx = 1;
                idx<= numberOfServiceRecordsToCreate;
                idx++)
            {
                vehServices.clear();
                vehServices.initFromConFMSVehicleTable(
                                                  vehicle);
                vehServices.ServiceId =
                             vehicle.VehicleId+int2str(idx);
                vehServices.insert();
                this.assertEquals(vehicle.VehicleId,
                                  vehServices.VehicleId,
                                  strFmt("Vehicle %1 inserted",
                                         vehicle.VehicleId));
                this.assertNotEqual(vehServices.RecId,
                                  0,
                                  strFmt("Vehicle %1 inserted",
                                         vehicle.VehicleId));
            }
        }
    }
```

10. In this instance, we expect the cases to pass, so we first go back to each test method and change them to what we expect to fail.
11. Close the code window and compile the class.
12. To execute this test case, right-click on the class and go to **Add-ins** | **Run test case**.

As before, the system will provide the results of the test in the **Infolog** window, marking the test methods as succeeded or failed. In the following example, a test method had a compilation error:

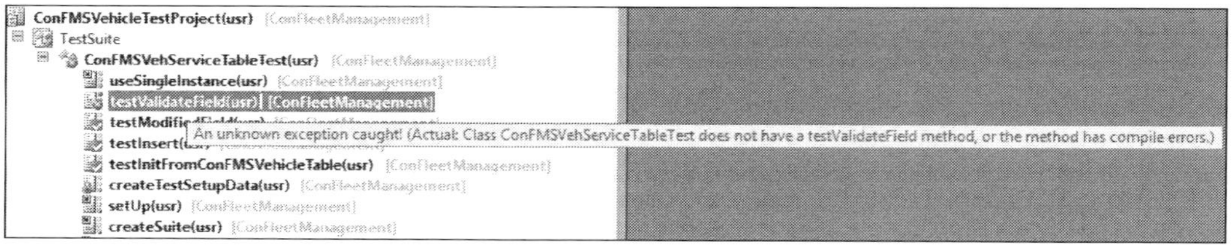

Setup and teardown of test data

In our example, we used company isolation of data. This creates a company for each class, runs the setup method to create the setup data, and deletes the company after the test class completes. This is sufficient in our custom code, as the test data is very simple. However, this is insufficient for many testing requirements, as the configuration data is just as important as the code. This is usually the case when we are running the tests to validate code on the test environment. In this case, we can run our test cases without isolation, use SQL database backup and restore as the setup and teardown steps. This is easily possible only when using the TFS development method, where each developer has their own instance, which is another advantage of using this method of development.

Reviewing the results of the unit test

Even the simplest code has some part that executes conditionally, and we need to be sure we have tested all of the code. The test framework allows us to assess how much of the code was actually tested. This is called **code coverage**.

This time, we will turn on code coverage, which is done by the following steps:

1. In the unit test toolbar, click on **Parameters**.
2. In the form, check both **Record code coverage** and **Record number of records**.

3. Run the test again, and click on **Details** once the test completes. This form shows a record for each test run and some statistics and details about the test.
4. Select the last test run and click on **Tests**.
5. Since the last test was just for one class, we will see one record in the list of test cases, and a record for each test method, as shown here:

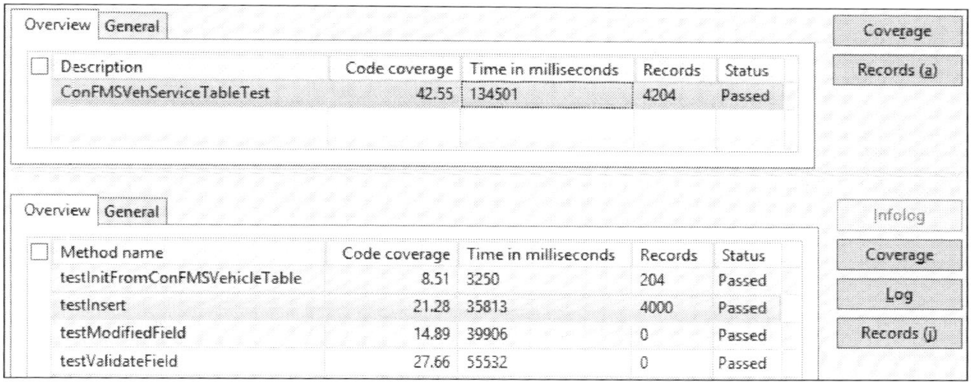

6. To check the code that was covered for the test case, click on **Coverage** in the top-right corner and press **Compare** on the **Code coverage** form.
7. Expand the **Methods** node, select `initFromConFMSVehicleTable`, and review the results, as shown in the following screenshot:

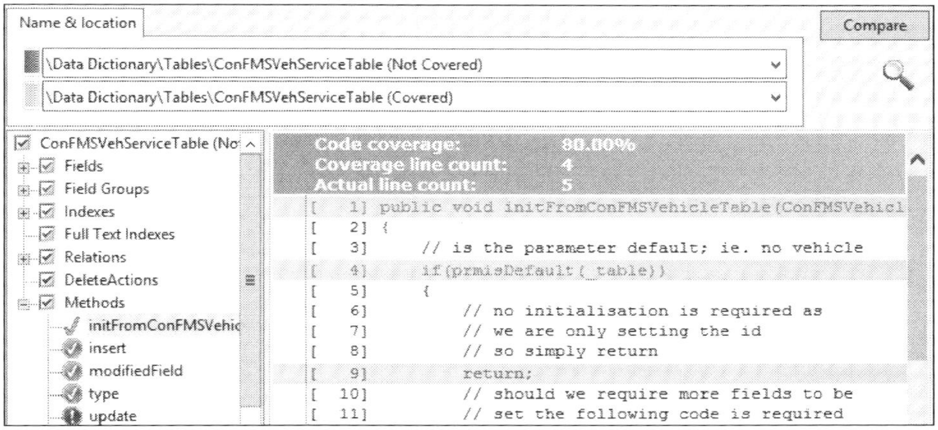

Here, we can see that line 9 was not executed or covered by our test, hence the tick symbol that is not in a green circle. We can also see that the update method was not covered at all.

Code and database performance testing through code profiling

Performance testing should be done to validate the effects of newly developed code, to test the production environment as part of environment validation, or as a way to investigate a reported performance issue.

The premise here is that we start the data capture, perform the task or tasks we wish to test, and then review the results. This is done using the Trace Parser, with the following steps:

1. Launch Microsoft Dynamics AX 2012 Trace Parser (if you're using Windows 8, search for Trace Parser).
2. In the **Register Database** dialog, select the SQL Server that will store the trace result's database.
3. Enter a database name for the trace file, for example, `MyTraceDatabase`:

4. Click on **Yes** when you are asked **The specified database does not exist. Would you like to create it?**.
5. Close the AX client if it is running and relaunch the client using **Run as administrator** (right-click on the client icon).
6. Launch the development environment (the quick way is to press *Ctrl* + *D*).
7. Click on **Tools** and **Tracing Cockpit**.
8. The defaults are fine, but to make the results more useful, you should also check **Xpp parameters** and **Bind parameters**, as shown in the following screenshot:

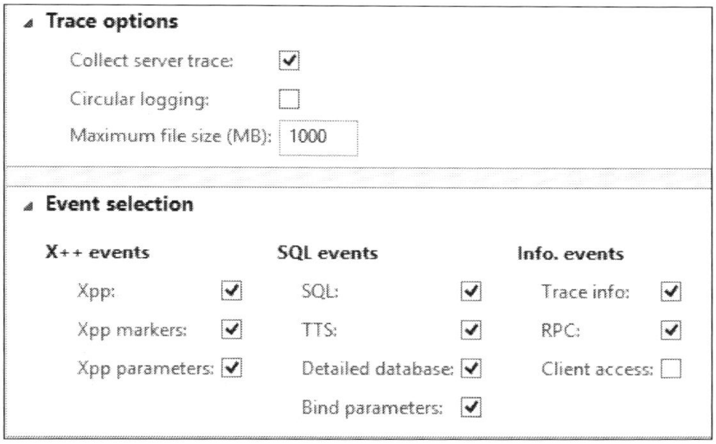

The reason **Xpp parameters** and **Bind parameters** are disabled by default is that they may reveal information (that is, actual data) as it is passed between the AX and SQL Servers. This could include sensitive information, for instance, salary details. You should therefore obtain approval for this before proceeding.

9. Click on **Start trace** to start the trace.
10. Enter a file for the trace to be stored within; this must be accessible by the server, so please use a UNC such as `\\server\share\ path\ trace20150703.etl`.

At this point, all database activity between the AX server and SQL Server is logged, and you may notice that the server load increases at this point.

11. Once the data has been captured, click on **Stop trace**.

> It is important to make sure that the trace is running only for the time needed, as this will add significant load to the system.

12. To view the trace, click on **Open trace**, which imports the trace file into the registered database.
13. The initial view of the trace is a brief summary. To view more details, select the user in question from the **Session** drop-down list.
14. Use **Call Tree** to examine the call stack. The darker the red highlight, the larger the impact of the event on performance. You can use the code window to see the code that was executed. This is useful for developers, where custom code may be the cause of poor performance. It is shown in the following screenshot:

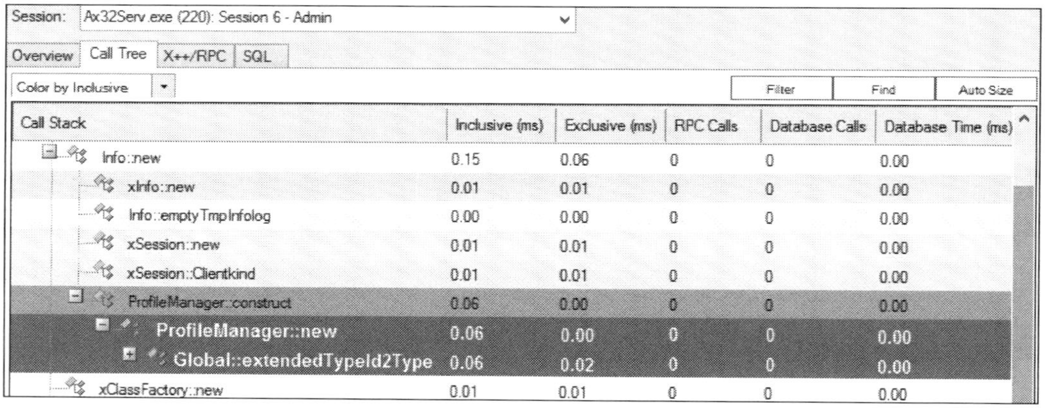

15. Use the **X++/RPC** tab to view aggregate X++ and server RPC call information. You can also see the call stack and the code that was executed.
16. Finally, the **SQL** section shows the aggregate or detailed SQL transactions. This will give you the Transact-SQL statement that was executed.

If the trace fails to start, check whether:

- The AX Server service account has write access to the file
- You have rights to create the file
- There is sufficient disk space
- The AX client was started with **Run as Administrator**

> You should perform the trace after the system has been in use for a period of time so as to simulate normal use and avoid having your results skewed by investigating the issues related to the system starting up. The system will behave slower than normal, as it takes time to initialize and cache. Always follow this advice, unless the issue is specifically that a task is slow the first time it is performed after system startup.

Interpreting the results

The trace is performed by the server monitoring the AX code and SQL activity and producing a file that you can import into Trace Parser.

The **Event Trace Log** (**ETL**) file can then be imported into Trace Parser (which is done by clicking on **Open trace**). The reason we created the database before starting the trace is that we can simply click on **Open trace**.

In undertaking a full performance test, we have analyzed the server counters for AX and SQL Server and also performed an AX trace with the tracing cockpit.

Each one in isolation will not always provide us with the reason for a performance problem, and even with all of these tools being run together, it will not always make the reason obvious. Users can experience performance problems even when all servers seem to be idling.

The information we now have in hand is as follows:

- AX Windows Server counters for the CPU, disk, memory, and network
- SQL Windows Server counters for the CPU, memory, and network
- Details of the tasks being performed by the user in the window
- Details of the SQL statements being executed and the ability to generate an execution plan

With this, we can correlate the information in order to determine the cause. The cause can be due to a hardware resource, indexing, statistics, code, or a combination of these.

Low resource utilization while you are experiencing a performance problem is also a clue; the resource in question might be waiting for something else.

The most likely causes of performance issues within SQL Server are as follows:

- **Disk subsystem**: This is indicated by high disk queue length, low CPU usage, and high page life expectancy.
- **Memory**: This is indicated by high disk queue length on the system disk, reducing the buffer cache hit ratio, and reducing the page life expectancy.
- **CPU**: This is indicated by high CPU usage, low disk queue length (less than one per spindle), and high page life expectancy.
- **Network**: This is often misreported. If SQL Server is slow to respond and the SQL counters are low, network latency could be the cause. It could also mean that there is a deadlock chain and the process causing the deadlock is "sleeping"; for example, AX has locked the record while communicating with an unresponsive service.

For AX Server, if a counter indicates high usage, either it is a case of badly written code, or the server is underpowered. Adding a second AOS may not solve the issue, as the code is not load balanced. If there is not a dedicated batch server, a batch task could be the cause. We should follow best practices by installing a dedicated AOS for batch tasks that are not part of the cluster to which users connect.

Enabling SQL execution plans

We have discussed execution previously, and one of the main reasons for which we enabled Bind parameters was to take the SQL statement into SQL Management Studio in order to determine its execution plan.

Do not try and use the `DELETE` or `UPDATE` statements. Even though we don't need to execute the statement in order to gain the execution plan, we will have to use the live database to gain an accurate plan. Not only that, there is little we can do to improve most `UPDATE` statements, and there is the risk that we could execute the statement by mistake.

The `SELECT` statements are safer, and when we are checking the resultant execution plan, we are looking primarily for:

- Table scans (unless the table has few records)
- Clustered index scans

As a lower priority, we are looking for index use and the corresponding bookmark lookups. It is always ideal to use clustered index seeks, and less ideal to use index seeks. Table or clustered index scans are expensive and indicated as incorrect indexing on the table or out-of-date data statistics.

Investigating the performance of views

Views are very powerful, and with the advent of computed columns, they offer large performance improvements, as calculations are performed by SQL Server. However, they can be a victim of their own success as we make them more and more complicated, which may result in them performing poorly. When a view performs slowly, the following points should be checked first:

- Are ranges used by the view covered by an index?
- Are relations correctly specified, and are these covered by an index?
- Could the data calculated in a computed column be placed in the query instead?
- For computed columns, are we joining correctly? For example, are `DataAreaId` and `Partition` in the `join` clause?

One of the best methods to test views is by using SQL Server Management Studio. Locate the view in the business data database, and from the view's context menu (right-click) navigate to **Script view as | ALTER To | New Query Editor Window**.

We don't actually want to alter the view, so we remove the lines prior to the `ALTER VIEW` statement, and the first part of the `ALTER VIEW` statement so that the `SELECT` statement is the first statement.

We can now use this as a normal `SELECT` statement, using SQL Server tools such as execution plans to determine whether the view could be improved. We can even target a different database that has more recent or appropriate data in order to test it before deploying it to the live environment.

> The `SELECT` statement will be a long, barely readable line of text. Use a SQL beautifier to reformat the text into formatted Transact-SQL.

References

The following references are useful when performance tuning:

- *Dynamics Ax Performance Team Blog*, `http://blogs.msdn.com/b/axperf/`
- *Tools for monitoring performance [AX 2012]*, `https://technet.microsoft.com/en-us/library/jj149695.aspx`
- *Display an Actual Execution Plan*, `https://msdn.microsoft.com/en-us/library/ms189562.aspx`

Summary

The concepts in this chapter are critical, as we plan and design the code that we will develop. Writing test cases before the code does change the mindset when developing code. Many developers write them in conjunction, which does help prevent errors in the code and even the design.

A

Efficient Design and Development with Microsoft Dynamics AX

In this appendix, we will cover the following topics:

- The technical overview of Dynamics AX
- Layers and models
- The MorphX IDE
- Source control – the options
- Patterns and frameworks

The technical overview of Dynamics AX

At the simplest level, Dynamics AX is designed as a three-tier architecture and requires three main components to function: a database server, an application server, and a client.

The database server performs two roles; it hosts both the business database and the model store database. The database server must be a supported edition of Microsoft SQL Server.

The application server is referred to as the **Application Object Server** (**AOS**) or AX Server. This provides many services, including web services, to the client Windows AX.

The Windows AX client is the application that the users use to perform their tasks. It also allows us to access the **integrated development environment** (**IDE**).

All requests for application elements (such as forms) and data are made to the AOS through **remote procedure calls** (**RPC**) or the **Windows Communication Foundation** (**WCF**). There is no direct communication between the client and the SQL Server. All data goes through the AOS; this is fundamental to the design. It ensures that all of the business logic is common across all clients and enforces data integrity and security.

The following diagram, which has been recreated from Microsoft TechNet, highlights this:

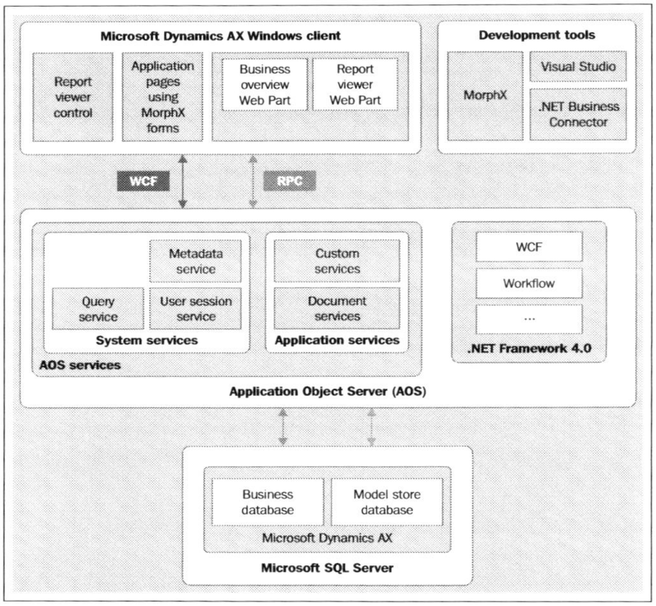

The full details can be accessed at `http://technet.microsoft.com/en-us/library/dd362112.aspx`.

The element named **Application pages using MorphX forms** in the preceding diagram represents the vast majority of all content viewed within the Windows AX client, for example, the Sales order details form.

> All forms written within the AX client development environment under the `Forms` node are MorphX forms; they may include .NET controls such as **Print preview** and custom .NET controls.

The client primarily uses RPC for communication between the client and the AOS, but certain elements within the client use WCF; for example, the **Report viewer control**. Applications such as Microsoft Office, **SQL Server Reporting Services** (**SSRS**), and custom applications also use WCF. These applications access services that are hosted by the AOS.

Much of the complexity is hidden from us, and we do not have to remember every nuance of the integration between the tiers. Gaining an understanding of the structure, however, is important.

For example, we will later be writing code that will run on a specific tier (AOS or client). In this case, it is important to pay attention to where the objects are instantiated and how they are marshalled between the client and server.

The model store database

The model store is a database hosted by the same SQL server as the business database. It is always named after the business database and suffixed with `_model`. For example, if the database is called `MsDynAXLive`, then the model store database is called `MSDynAXLive_Model`.

This model store contains the application code and metadata. The application code is stored in both the source code and compiled forms. This means that all objects in the AOT, such as database table definitions, forms, classes, reports, and Visual Studio projects, are stored in this database.

> There are many benefits of this design, one of which is that it is now more easily handled as part of our high availability and disaster recovery plans.

Each element (such as a class, method, database table, field, and so on) has an element ID. These have many uses, which are mainly internal. One such use is for handling the link between the elements' stored table definitions and the physical table definition within SQL Server.

> The important point here is that we cannot simply assume that we can use a model store database with a business database that was not generated from that model store database.

The compiler and CIL

The primary language for development in AX is X++, and it is syntactically similar to C#. AX compiles code as required to its intermediary language, p-code. This p-code is AX's native object code and AX will execute most code in this way. The compiled code stored in the Model store database is p-code.

Microsoft introduced a .NET **Common Intermediate Language** (**CIL**) compiler to AX 2012. This allows AX code to run under the .NET runtime and achieves better performance. This does not replace the p-code, and is generated from the compiled p-code—not directly from the source code.

> This means we have two sets of executable code, p-code and CIL. The form-level logic still uses p-code, but some table events and server-side code and all of the code accessed through WCF will run the CIL-compiled code.

CIL generation also creates physical DLLs and updates the WCF services (both those hosted by the AX Service and those hosted by IIS).

Layers and models

The Layers and Models section is taken from the Packt Publishing book, *Microsoft Dynamics AX 2012 R2 Administration Cookbook*. It has been amended to suit a software development audience.

One of the key founding features of Dynamics AX was the ability to modify the software easily without locking the solution into a version. This was so advanced, even when the software was first released, that it would often be cheaper and faster to write the functionality in Dynamics AX than to upgrade the incumbent system.

AX not only had an outstanding IDE (the MorphX IDE) but also a solution to the problem of upgradability, change tracking, and management of solutions written by various parties; for example, Microsoft **independent software vendors** (**ISVs**)/Partners and the end-user/customer.

The solution to this was the technology called the **layer system**.

Layers

Layers segregate modifications (or the creation) of an application object's elements (for example, a field on a table or a control on a form). This allows Microsoft partners/ISVs and the customer to write a new functionality or change an existing functionality in a specific layer without directly modifying the standard software or the software supplied by the partner or ISV.

The following layers are available from the highest layer down:

Layer	Description
USR	The user layer is for end-user modifications, such as reports. It often has changes written by the development team of the end-user organization.
CUS	The customer layer is for modifications that are specific to a company.
VAR	**Value-added Resellers** (**VAR**) can make modifications or new developments to the VAR layer as specified by the customer or as a strategy of creating an industry-specific solution.
ISV	When an ISV creates their own solution, their modifications are saved in the ISV layer.
SLN	The solution layer is used by distributors to implement vertical partner solutions.
FPK	The FPK layer is an application object patch layer reserved by Microsoft for future patching or other updates. For more information, see *Patch Layers [AX 2012]* at `https://msdn.microsoft.com/en-us/library/aa891248.aspx`.
GLS	When the application is modified to match country- or region-specific legal demands, these modifications are saved in the GLS layer.
SYS	The standard application is implemented at the lowest level, the SYS layer. The application objects in it can never be deleted.

This information is taken from `http://msdn.microsoft.com/en-us/library/aa851164.aspx`.

Each layer has a patch layer, where SYP is the patch layer for SYS, and so on. The patch layer is used to ship hotfixes and service packs. A range of tools can be used to compare and merge code into a higher layer (that is, USR), where it has been changed by the patch.

> Although it may seem logical to use the patch layer for updates to your system, this actually just adds more work and detracts from its goal of maintainability. It was sometimes useful before we had models, but with the model technology, it is used for a different purpose.

The current layer is set in the AX configuration utility, and to use any layer other than the USR layer, you need an access code, which Microsoft provides as part of your license.

When a change is made to individual elements (methods, fields, form controls, and so on), it is copied to the current layer. This copy then hides the element in lower layers. The compiler does this by looking down at the elements from the highest layer down—as if it were looking through the panes of a glass—as shown in the following image (which is taken from Microsoft TechNet):

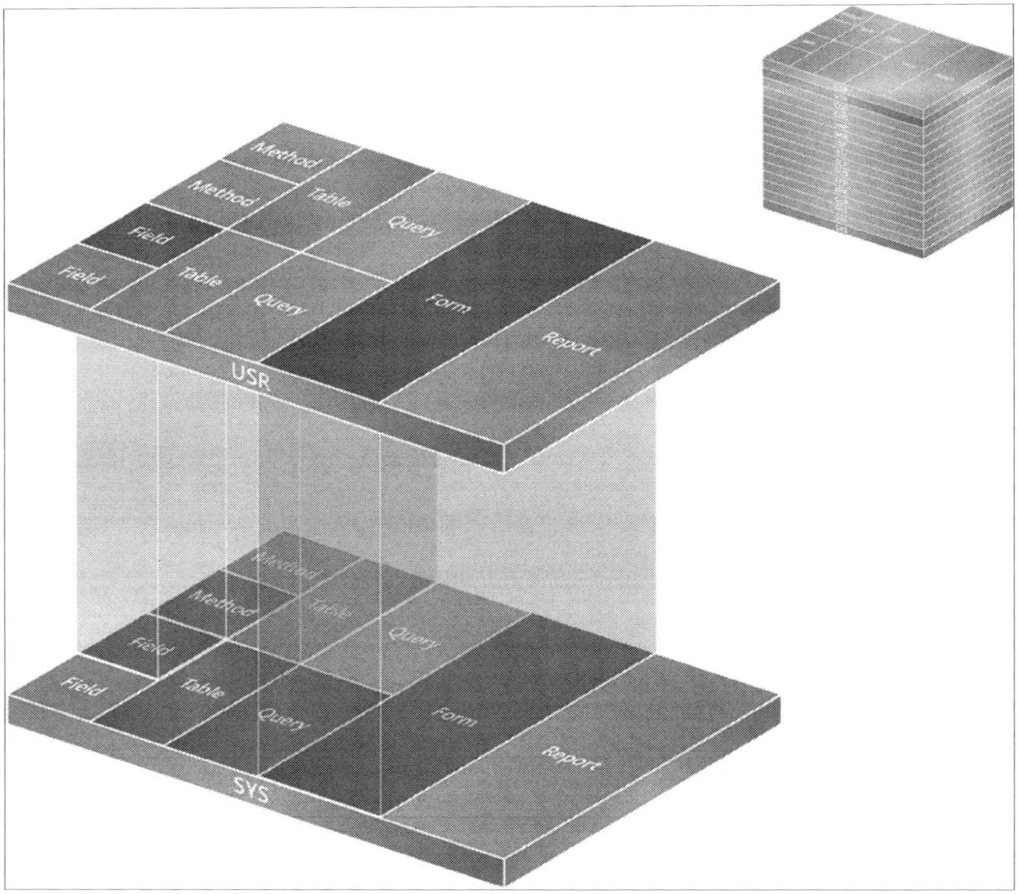

The exception to this is if we modify an object that is already in a higher layer. In this case, the change is done in the higher layer—if there is any change in the current layer, it is not used. This is by design; if the change was made in the lower layer, it would not be used, as it would be masked by the higher layer change.

This means that your changes are protected, allowing you to merge the changes as required.

Commonly, your partner will develop features or customize AX in the VAR layer, and the end user (the customer) in either the CUS or the USR layer.

On rare occasions, the customer may use both CUS and USR. One example would be a global organization that has systems in several countries and employs an internal development team. In this case, the internal development team will develop the core system in the CUS layer, leaving the country to develop its own specific requirements in the USR layer.

Prior to AX 2012, the elements were not shredded to a sufficient level. In other words, forms were treated as one element and therefore copied in their entirety to your layer, should you simply add a field to a grid. This posed a problem for Microsoft because it limited the amount of add-on solutions that could coexist in a system without a developer merging the code.

This shredding of elements, into individual controls on a form for instance, exposed another problem for ISVs developing add-ons on AX.

An ISV would write their add-on in a specific layer: for example, SLN or ISV (in the previous versions, it would be the BUS layer). They would deliver their solution as an entire layer (which used to be a file ending in AOD) along with labels.

This, therefore, limited the number of ISV solutions you could use within your implementation without greatly increasing the complexity of implementing them.

The answer to this issue came in the form of models.

Models

Every element in a layer belongs to one model; if a layer does not have a model, the system will create a default model for it when a modification is made; for instance, the USR model. These are not normally used and, in my opinion, should never be used, as we cannot be sure whether this was intended.

A model exists in a specific layer, and elements in a layer can only belong to one model; this is by design and should not be thought of as a limitation. Thus, a model is a collection of elements in a specific layer.

If you import an add-on as a model, it will be imported into its original layer. The only thing you have to do is to synchronize, compile the application, and regenerate the CIL. This model can also be removed; again, all you need to do is synchronize, compile the application, and regenerate CIL.

You can then, in your layer and model, make changes to the add-on for your specific requirements; and when the ISV releases an upgrade, you simply have to import the model and use AX's tools to highlight the changes that may conflict with yours.

Models have many benefits, and I suspect more than what were initially intended when designed:

For ISVs, models create the following abilities:

- Digitally sign the models
- Ship the model in a way that is easy to deploy on their customers' systems
- Send patches and upgrades to customers that are relatively easy to apply

For partners, the benefits of models are the following:

- Easy alignment with development, deployment, and quality assurance processes
- Simplified deployment of builds during the system's implementation
- The partner can more easily use ISV solutions in their offering to their customers, which allows the partner to focus on their specific value offering
- Environments such as live, **User Acceptance Testing** (**UAT**), and development are more easily kept aligned

There are advantages for customers too, which are as follows:

- The ability to have more control of their system, where they can choose to install or remove add-ons with PowerShell commands. Earlier, the customer could only remove the whole layer and not add-ons within a layer.
- Simplified deployment of internally developed solutions
- As a side effect of the benefits to ISVs and partners, better value and quality of implementation are achieved, thereby reducing the risk

> Don't fall for the trap of creating a model for each requirement because even with the object model's shredded control or field level, you will find overlaps (that is, changes required to a method across two requirements).

In our experience, partner and customer layers typically have the following models.

Typical partner (VAR) models are as follows:

- The main functionality model (often named as a prefix and the customer name, for example, axp<CustomerName>)
- Labels
- Security roles
- Add-on models

Here are the typical customer (CUS or USR) models:

- The main functionality model
- Labels
- Customer-specific security roles

> A label file is a dictionary of label codes that that the Dynamics AX client uses to display labels and text in the user's language.

The reason a label file is in its own model is that the label file is not shredded into elements, and therefore, all labels in a label file exist in one model. Each party would normally maintain one label file, which has a three-letter name, and is therefore limited.

The MorphX IDE

The development environment is accessed from within the Windows AX client, which is also referred to as the MorphX IDE. It opens a new application window, tailored specifically for development. This environment is still the AX client, and forms can be opened and code executed as if it were opened from the main client window.

The quickest way is through keyboard shortcuts:

- *Ctrl* + *D*: This opens the IDE, with the **Application Object Tree** (**AOT**) open.
- *Ctrl* + *Shift* + *P*: This opens the development environment, with the **Projects** window open.
- *Ctrl* + *Shift* + *W*: This performs an action equivalent to *Ctrl* + *D*.

The development environment is structured into the following main components:

- **Title bar**: This tells us which server the client is connected to.
- **Main menu**: This is a classic MDI menu that runs across the top of the window. There are customization options for some parts of its structure.
- **Content area**: This contains the AOT, **Projects** window, and code editing windows.
- **Properties**: This shows the properties of the selected element. It floats when opened for the first time, but is usually docked to the right.
- **Compiler output**: This appears when an object is compiled. It is docked at the bottom by default, but can be made to float. It can occupy some of the valuable content area.
- **Status bar**: This is configurable through your user options. The most important information shown here is about the company, layer, and current model.

AOT

The typical centerpiece of the IDE is the AOT. This contains the entire application code of AX. The following screenshot shows a tree view, which is organized by object type:

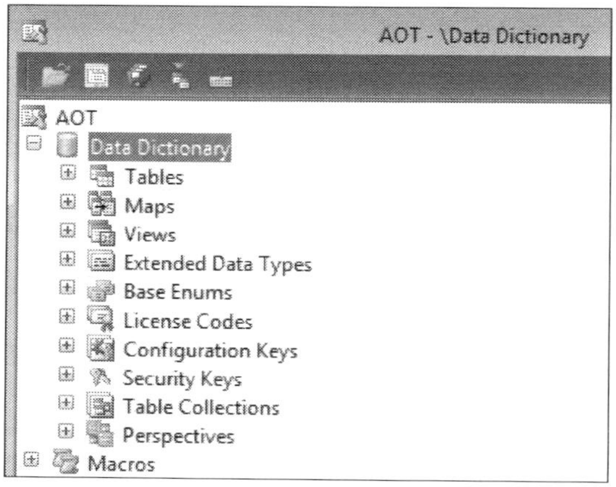

The button ribbon at the top of the window is context sensitive to the selected node, and in sequence, they are as follows:

- **Open**: This will open the selected object, such as a form. It is actually an execute action. So, for a table, it will open the table browser, and for a class, it will try to execute if it contains a static `Main` method.
- **Properties**: This will open the property sheet. This action can also be done by pressing *Alt* + *Enter*.
- **Save all**: This will save all unsaved elements. This action can also be done by pressing *Ctrl* + *Shift* + *S*.
- **Import**: This will open the XPO import dialog, allowing code to be imported into the system.
- **Compile**: This will compile the selected object or node. If a node is selected, this button compiles all objects within that node. This action can also be done by hitting the *F7* key.

> If we click on the compile icon while the AOT node is selected, the entire system is recompiled. This can take over an hour to complete.

To navigate around the AOT, you can use the mouse, but the most efficient method is to use the keyboard. The AOT behaves intuitively, that is, the right arrow key will expand a node and the left arrow key will collapse. Partially typing an object name will move to that object. For example, to navigate to the table named `CustTable` from the AOT node, perform the following steps:

1. Press the right or down arrow key. This will move to the first node, called `Data Dictionary`, under the AOT.
2. Press the right arrow key again to expand this node.
3. Press the right arrow key again to move down to the first node, `Tables`.

4. Expand the `Tables` node with the right arrow key, and then press the down arrow key to move to the first table, as shown in the following screenshot:

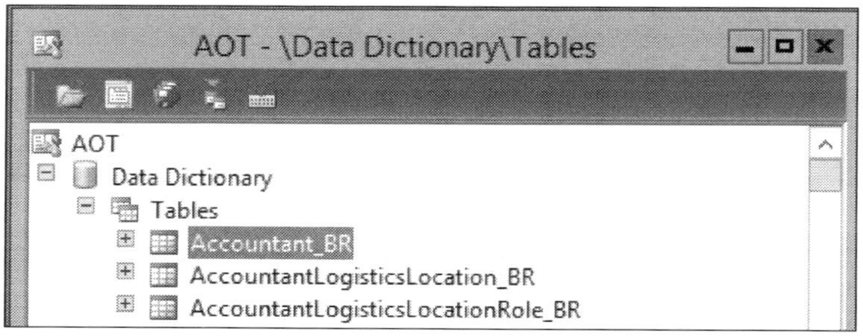

5. Start typing `CustTable`; AX will move the cursor down as you type, displaying the text typed in the status bar at the bottom of the application's window.

This may seem quite simple, but it is very important that we are fast at navigating around the environment so that it is second nature.

We can now look at the property sheet for `CustTable`. We could use the button on the AOT window, but this takes time. Instead, use the *Alt* + *Enter* keyboard shortcut.

> Using keyboard shortcuts is much faster than using the mouse, so this should always be the preference. You might be slower at first, but it pays off later.

The following links contain useful shortcuts. You don't need to learn them all, but it is useful to use the keyboard shortcuts for the commands we frequently perform:

- **Shortcut Keys: Code Editor [AX 2012]**: `http://msdn.microsoft.com/en-us/library/aa865357.aspx`
- **Shortcut Keys: AOT [AX 2012]**: `http://msdn.microsoft.com/en-us/library/aa623612.aspx`

The property sheet will show the properties relevant to the current object type, in the case where the properties are pertinent to a table.

> Although these may seem safe to adjust, any change made to any property sheet is still a modification and will move the object into your layer and model, even if you change the property back.

We access most of the tasks we perform on an object through the right-click context menu (or the Windows context menu key). This menu is context aware, and we will go through this when we perform the task.

The following screenshot is of the context menu for `CustTable`, accessed by right-clicking on the `CustTable` node:

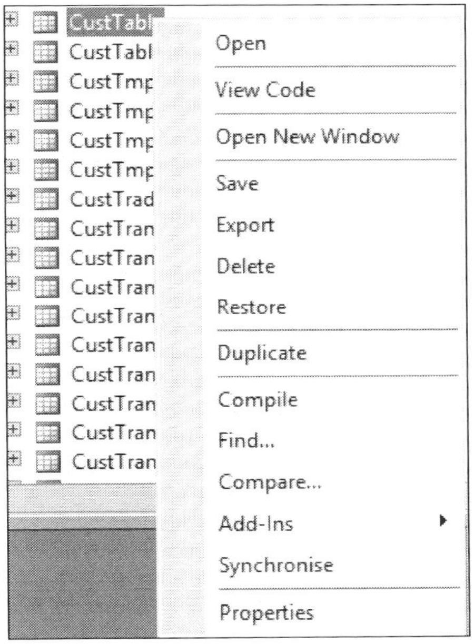

Here are some generic options on this menu:

- **Open**: This is not always available, and should be thought of as an execute command. Its behavior depends on the selected object type:
    - **Tables and Views**: This opens a table browser, a grid view form showing all visible fields and the possibility to edit (beware!).
    - **Table maps**: This opens a table browser for fields in the map, but will show no data. This is of limited value.
    - **Forms**: This opens the form as if it were opened from the AX client. It is useful for testing forms as we modify them.
    - **Classes**: This will execute the class if it has the `Main` static method. Many have assumed that it would open the code editor.
    - **Queries**: This will open the **Query** tool with the query loaded. It is of limited use.

    - **Menu items**: This will open the object referenced as if it were opened from the Windows client.
    - **Jobs**: This will execute the job; beware here, as many assume that this opens the code editor!

- **View code**: This opens the code editor with all methods visible.
- **Open New Window**: This is a very useful feature. It will open a new AOT window starting from the currently selected node. This is great for the drag-and-drop functionality.
- **Save**: This will save the changes made to the currently selected object.
- **Export**: This exports the objects from the currently selected node to an XPO file—a file that contains the object definition—so that it can be imported to a different system.
- **Delete**: This deletes the element at the select level from the current layer. So, if you change `CustTable`, you can delete your changes and revert to the next layer below. This is discussed in more detail in the next section.
- **Restore**: This will revert the selected objects to what is stored in the model store database, losing unsaved changes. Also, this is useful for loading the changes made by another developer working in the same system, or to refresh a form's data source if we add fields to the table it references.
- **Duplicate**: This will create a duplicate of the object. If the object is a table, it does not copy the data. If the copied object contains static methods, they are not refactored to the new object name.
- **Compile**: This will compile the current object, or in the case of a node, the objects within that node.
- **Find...**: This will open the **Find** tool, allowing you to search for an element or the source code text.
- **Compare...**: This opens the **Compare** tool (discussed in detail later), which allows you to compare the object across layers.
- **Add-Ins**: This a submenu of options that will be discussed when required.
- **Properties**: This opens the property sheet.

Saving your work

When you make a change to an object in the AOT, AX highlights this with a vertical red bar, as shown in the following screenshot:

Objects can be saved automatically, based on a timeout in your user options. This automatic save does not occur while editing the code in the code editor, which is good.

You can save all unsaved changes with the *Ctrl* + *Shift* + *S* option. This works everywhere in the IDE except the code editor. This is because the code editor is actually the code editor from Visual Studio, where this particular hotkey makes whitespace characters visible.

When the work is saved, AX writes the changes to the model store database. If the element (for example, a class method) is new, AX will create a unique element ID for it. If two developers open the same method, the first person to save the method "wins"; the other developer will be told that the method is newer on the server. Using the **Restore** option from the right-click menu will retrieve the version from the server.

The Projects window

A project is a subset of objects taken from the AOT. This could be thought of as a painter's palette. Any changes made to an object in a project are not sandboxed into that project. The change is also made to the same object in the AOT; the project merely contains references to the AOT object.

There are two types of project: private and shared. Private projects are collections only visible to the user who created them, and are generally of little use. Some projects automatically created by AX are an exception to this, as the elements (tables, methods, and so on) can contain a status indicating whether the object is complete or not.

Therefore, all projects we create will be shared. To create a shared project, we follow these steps:

1. Open the **Projects** window (*Ctrl* + *Shift* + *P*).
2. Right-click on the **Shared** node and choose **Project**, which is under **New**.
3. This will create a new project named **Project1** (if not, it means we have not given a previously created project a proper name).
4. We should rename this with a suitable name. This is done by double-clicking on the object (as you do to rename a file in Windows explorer) or choosing **Rename** from the right-click context menu. The double-click method is faster.

> Naming conventions are critical to getting maintainable code. These are discussed later in this chapter.

To open the project, simply double-click on it. AX will display a window with a single node. Elements can now be dragged from the AOT as required.

The next step is to create the project structure. The best structure to use is the same structure as that of the AOT, as this makes items easier to find. This is done by the following steps:

1. Right-click on the root node and choose **Group**, which is under **New**.
2. Rename this node to be the same as the AOT node we are creating, for example, `Data Dictionary`.
3. Open the properties of this node and change `ProjectGroupType` to `DataDictionary` (from the drop-down list), as shown in the following screenshot. You would then continue this process for the nodes in the AOT.

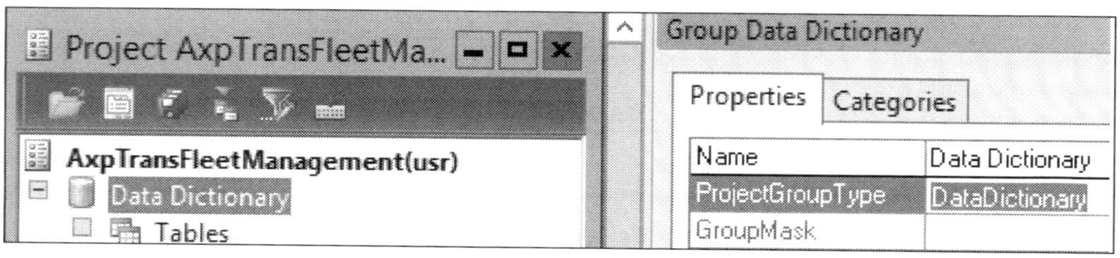

> This is clearly time-consuming. The good practice is to do this once and name the project `ProjectTemplate`. Then, simply duplicate the project every time you need it.

As you change `ProjectGroupType`, you will see that the icon in the project node changes to the icon in the equivalent AOT node.

> Creating a project and changing the project group type has an additional benefit; AX now understands that the element contains objects of that type, and the **right-click** | **New** menu will then offer to create an object of that type.

The options for source control

Source control has become more prevalent with AX development in the last 5 years. Initially, there was no specific source control with the development environment, but we survived. This was done through heavy use of comments and adding a dummy method for the development history to each modified object.

We have had version control for a few versions now, and in AX 2012, it has been improved further. The source control options we have are as follows:

- Source depot
- Visual SourceSafe
- MorphX VCS
- TFS

What Microsoft recommends here is either MorphX VCS or TFS. We prefer to avoid shared development and use TFS internally, which is integrated with our project management methodology.

Microsoft provides a good reference for this in MSDN at `http://msdn.microsoft.com/en-us/library/aa639568.aspx`. The following table, taken from the preceding article, shows the key differences:

	MorphX VCS	**TFS**
Concurrent development	No	Yes
Isolated development	No	Yes
Change description	Yes	Yes
Change history	Yes	Yes
Quality bar enforcement	Yes	Yes
Branching	No	Yes
Work item integration	No	Yes
Labelling support	No	No

The isolated development feature means that each developer has an isolated AX environment. The developer's machine (usually a virtual server) would need to be reasonably powerful in order to run the environment at a suitable speed.

It also has a more involved process; that is, the developer has to check in their work (which is file-based), and then a build has to be created.

The main advantage of TFS over MorphX VCS is the integration with work items, which can be used alongside your sure-step agile methodology. We also have an advantage in that the source is also held in a separate repository.

The MorphX VCS provides features similar to TFS (except branching), but it allows the development server to be shared by multiple developers. Objects are still checked out (and therefore locked) and checked in with comments. It also allows the use of the built-in code compare tool to review the changes between different versions.

This is a simple, yet clever, version control solution, but it also has one drawback. The version control information is stored in a set of tables in the business database. This means you lose the version control data if you rebuild the business database from the live business database.

General development practices

Efficient software development means following good and consistent development practices. This is not just about creating fantastic, well-designed code, but also about the seemingly little things such as naming conventions and comments.

We will not cover all the best practice guidelines here, as it is more pertinent to explain them as we use them. We'll cover some general guidelines before we start.

Naming

First, all the objects you create or elements added to an object authored by another party must be prefixed. The prefix is usually specific to your organization; in the case of Binary, we use two prefixes—BCL for all work we carry out as a VAR, and AXP for our ISV work. The prefix cannot be of any three characters; for example, `Sys` would be a bad prefix because it is also used by Microsoft for their system objects.

When adding element to your own objects, do not prefix them. All type names (extended data types, tables, classes, and so on) must begin with a capital letter, and all instance variables and methods must have a lowercase first letter.

Although the AX compiler is not case-sensitive, the CIL is; thankfully, this compiles from the p-code, so it isn't normally a problem. It is nonetheless good practice to write code as if it is case-sensitive. This also helps make the code much easier to read.

The second part of naming is that you should capitalize the first letter of each word in the type, method, or variable name; for example, `CustTable` and the `initFromCustTable` method. This, again, makes the code much easier to read.

Commenting

A version control system cannot replace good code commenting. Any change made to an object that was not authored by you should be tagged with the following:

- Your organization's prefix
- Your initials
- Reference to the business requirement (for example, a **Technical Definition Document** (**TDD**) reference or a **Functional Requirements Document** (**FRD**) reference)
- The date
- A few words as to the reason for the change and what the change is intended to do
- A second line (as required) to explain what the change is intended to do

Let's take a look at the following example:

```
// BCL 5.2.4 (var) by SB on 2014/06/07: Set the focus to the item id
control
SalesLine_ItemId.setFocus();
// BCL 5.2.4 end
```

> Use yyyy/mm/dd as a date format because dd/mm/yyyy or mm/dd/yyyy can cause confusion across continents. However, if you do see a date that is not YMD, it is most likely to be DMY, not MDY.

If you add a method to an existing object, you should add a header comment. This can easily be done by entering /// in the first line of the method. It should contain the comment line, as shown in the preceding code snippet.

If you have made a change to a form layout, you should add a method called `DevelopmentHistory` highlighting the changes. Otherwise, you may realize that it gets lost when another developer applies an update or hotfix. This content format is up to your organization; this would normally be a list of changes formatted in a table in the same format as the earlier change tag.

Adding comments is often a pain and, when focused on writing an exciting piece of code, they are easily forgotten. One way to solve this is by making the addition easy by modifying the `EditorScripts` class.

The `EditorScripts` class has methods that create code blocks and even entire methods for you, either through the right-click menu or by typing a keyword. The class can be modified by adding a public method that accepts an `Editor` instance. *Appendix C, Code Editor Scripts*, covers this topic.

Editor scripts

Editor scripts are code snippets that insert code into the current method, and can even ask for information as part of the process. They insert either statement blocks, such as a `switch` statement block, or an entire method. They are simple to enter; simply type the script name and press the *Tab* key.

For example, if we have a class called `BclFleetVehicleTableType` and enter the text construct in a method, the following code is inserted:

```
public static BclFleetVehicleTableType construct()
{
    return new BclFleetVehicleTableType();
}
```

The available scripts can be seen by right-clicking on the method and navigating to **Scripts** | **template**, as shown in the following screenshot:

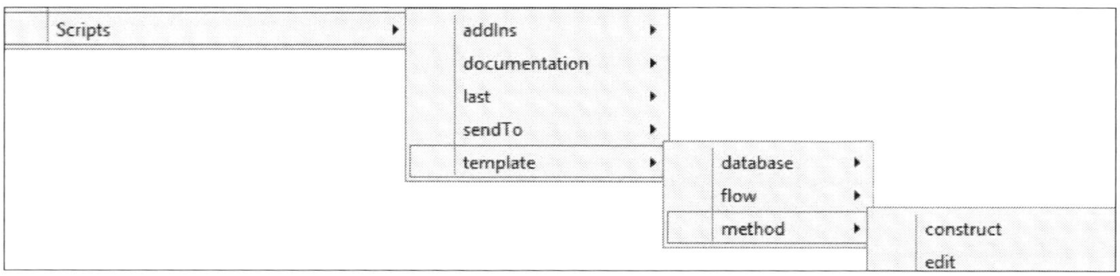

Patterns and frameworks

The easiest way to describe patterns and frameworks is to state that patterns describe how we perform a task, and a framework is the existing code that we use or extend. Both are very important.

Although patterns do not contain actual code, they are critical for ensuring that what we write is consistent, extendable, and easy to understand by members of our team. This removes a lot of thinking about how a task is performed, so we can focus on the actual problem.

Patterns

A good example of how patterns can be used is demonstrated by the following requirement: we require a method to edit the customer credit limit from the customer list page. This should be a button on the action page that will open a dialog, showing the current credit limit and allowing the user to update it. When the user clicks on **OK**, it will update the customer's credit limit.

There are many ways to do this, and it may seem appropriate to create a form that initializes from the current customer on the list page, and updates the record when the user presses **OK**.

This is until we get the next series of requests:

- Can we add the button to the collections list page?
- Can we add the button to the sales order form?
- Can we run a routine that validates the open sales order?
- Can we place the resulting sales orders that fail the credit limit in a workflow?

The preceding requests are clearly additional work, but the code should require only extending and not rewriting. What often happens is that the design is changed to such an extent to try to fit the requirement that it is barely readable by the original developer.

The actual design we should have adopted would be similar to the following:

- The form, instead, interacts with a data contract, which is initialized from the caller
- A handler class is written to take the data contract (which contains the new credit limit and the customer to be updated) and makes the necessary updates

A data contract is a class that has a set of public properties that form a structured dataset, allowing the data to be passed to and among objects. They can also cross tiers across the architecture and be marshalled to external services.

The additional work is to create two classes and about 10 lines of code. This will make the solution much easier to extend, and if adopted by a team, easier to read and maintain.

Many development teams spend some effort in adopting patterns, and sometimes evolving them over time. We have many patters in AX, and most of the tasks we need to perform can be done by following an existing pattern.

Microsoft has published the reference patterns that we should follow at *Microsoft Dynamics AX Design Patterns*, `http://msdn.microsoft.com/en-us/library/aa851876.aspx`.

Frameworks

The frameworks in Dynamics AX are designed to be either used or extended. They are often a complicated set of tables and classes, and sometimes contain a user interface. We take advantage of them by extending and/or implementing a specific class.

Most of the key functionality in AX is accessed through the existing business logic; this is true for some master data tables, and certainly true of all transactional data.

For example, in order to post a sales order confirmation, we would use the `FormLetter` framework. In this case, the framework provides the `FormLetterService` class, which has the `postSalesOrderConfirmation` method.

Other frameworks are designed to assist us in common development patterns or provide access to features that are not directly accessible from X++. In the preceding example, we could've used the `SysOperation` framework, which allows us to interact with the batch framework, thereby allowing asynchronous code execution.

We will use and extend these frameworks as we progress through the chapters.

B

Using Version Control

While working on the tutorial project, we used TFS with Visual Studio Online. There are some practices, which we use internally, that help us to be more efficient while using version control. This information was omitted from the main flow of the book in order to focus on the specific topics in each chapter. The information in the following sections is based on using TFS.

When to add to version control

All objects we create, must be added manually to source control, and this is by design. The reason for this is that we may not be at a stage where the code, which we're working on, is ready for other developers. It could also be that we have various code snippets that are just for our personal use, and we don't want them published to the team.

You can add a new object to version control as soon as it is created, but we delay checking in the code until we are at least approaching code complete for a section of the work. This is because checked-in code is available to other developers (and the build process) when they choose to synchronize.

In some cases, we will be writing foundation code and data structures that are required by other team members; internal communication is therefore important.

We tend to use a discrete project for each packet of work, which is owned by one developer. The code is added to source control once the basic framework of objects is complete, but is not checked in until it is code complete. If an element needs to be renamed, it has to be checked in first, so don't add it until you are sure your objects (such as classes and tables) don't need to be refactored. It may be argued that a good technical design should avoid this scenario, but it can still happen.

Working with version control

We can add any object, such as a table or class, to source control as long as it is modified in the current layer and not in a higher layer.

Adding a model to version control

When we created the models in *Chapter 1, Preparing Our Solution*, we added them to source control. This can be done afterwards by following these steps:

1. Navigate to **Version Control** | **Add model to version control**.
2. The **Check-in description** field is **Check in** by default and is usually suitable, but this can be changed if required.
3. Select the model ID to add to source control.

> The **Model repository folder** field must be changed so that the last part is a folder for this model (you may have to create the folder).

4. Ensure that a folder exists for the model under the folder set by navigating to **Version Control** | **Version Control Parameters**. If the `Repository` folder is `C:\Projects\VCS\AX` and the application root folder is `3579GettingStarted`, create the folder under `C:\Projects\VCS\AX\3579GettingStarted`. Use the model's name as the folder name.
5. Enter or select the folder in the **Model repository** folder, as shown in the following screenshot:

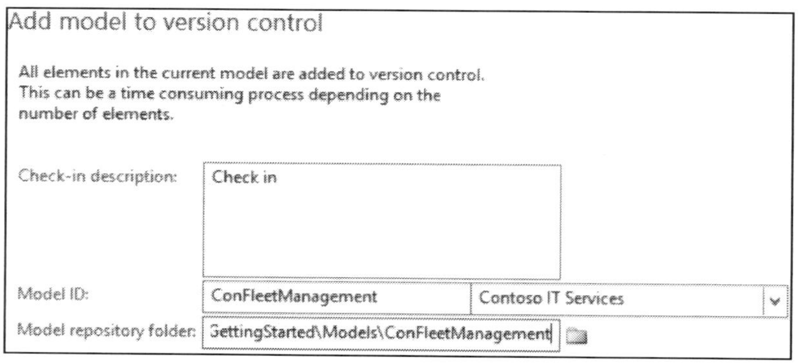

Managing AOT elements with version control

The integration with TFS from AX is done by importing and exporting XPOs of the changed parts of an element. If we add a method to the table `TMSParameters` and add it to source control, it will create a file called `TMSParameters.xpo`, which only contains that method. Let's take a look at the following code example:

```
Exportfile for AOT version 1.0 or later
Formatversion: 1

***Element: DBT
; Microsoft Dynamics AX Table : TMSParameters unloaded
; ----------------------------------------------------------------------
-------------
  TABLEVERSION 1

  TABLE #TMSParameters
    EnforceFKRelation 0
    FIELDS
    ENDFIELDS
    GROUPS
    ENDGROUPS

    INDICES
    ENDINDICES
    FULLTEXTINDICES
    ENDFULLTEXTINDICES
    REFERENCES
    ENDREFERENCES

    METHODS
      SOURCE #conFMSNumRefConFMSVehicleId
        #server static NumberSequenceReference
conFMSNumRefConFMSVehicleId()
        #{
        #    return NumberSeqReference::findReference(extendedTypeNum(
ConFMSVehicleId));
        #}
      ENDSOURCE
    ENDMETHODS
  ENDTABLE
***Element: END
```

Handling whether an object is checked in or out is done by telling TFS to check in and check out the XPO. AX understands whether the element is checked in or not by requesting the status for the file stored in the TFS repository. There is no table that holds this reference; it is done purely using the folder structure we configured in the version control settings.

Once source control is active, we get six new options available to us in the context/ right-click menu:

Option	Action
Add to Version Control	This adds the element to source control and exports an XPO of the changes in the element to the TFS folder structure. The element is marked as checked out and won't be available to the team until checked in. This is only available if the element is modified in the current layer, and not in a higher layer.
Check In	This will export the element as an XPO to the appropriate folder within TFS and send a request to TFS to check it in to the main repository.
Check Out	This instructs the source control system to check out the element. This simply tells TFS to mark the XPO in its folder structure as checked out. This is only visible when the element is not already checked out.
Undo Check Out	This will reverse the check-out process by importing the XPO from the TFS folder structure, thus reverting the changes made since check out.
History	This opens the check in history and also allows you to compare the versions using the compare tool.
Get Latest	This will get the latest version of the XPO from the TFS repository and import it.

These options are also available on the toolbar ribbon on the AOT and project windows.

Version control options

We also have some useful tools on the **Version Control** option from the main menu.

Changes

The **Changes** option lists all change sets that have been checked in to TFS, and by whom. You can view the contents of each change set and compare the change to the current version or prior versions.

Pending Objects

The **Pending Objects** option lists all objects that are pending to be checked in. This can be to add, edit, or delete from TFS. You can start the check in from this form. You can also create a project, which is useful when we wish to export the changes in case they need to be shelved.

Synchronise

The **Synchronise** option will synchronize the TFS repository with your local environment, applying all changes made by other developers; this includes any deleted elements, and this option does so without any warning. This may sound scary, but it is no different from a developer deleting an element in a shared development environment, except for the fact that we can get it back!

This can be run with a **Force** option that will fetch everything, and not just the changes made since the last synchronization.

When we start this, we are asked which model we need to synchronize, and will default to the layer. We must always change this to the model we are working with, and repeat the process for each model we wish to synchronize with.

Synchronisation log

The **Synchronisation log** option shows a list of the elements affected by the last synchronization and is worth checking in case an element did not synchronize. You can see this by the **Completed** field on the list. You can reprocess the incomplete items using the **Process** button. Each synchronization will be added to this list, so we should use the **Clean up log** (all records for the current synchronization) or **Clean all** button to clear this. The following screenshot shows this:

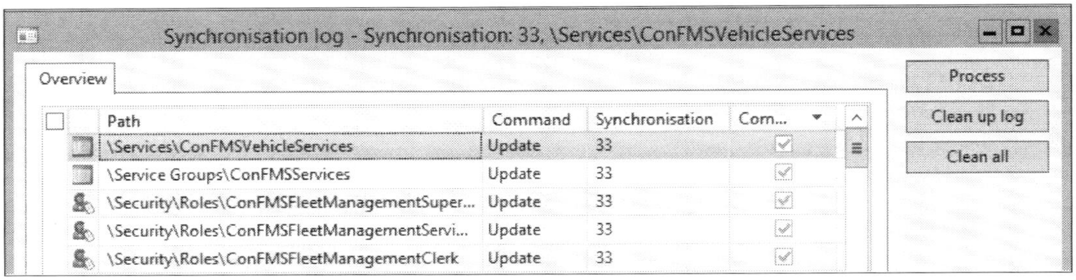

The main reason for a failure is that the element has been modified in a higher layer.

TFS interaction with models and layers

An element, such as a table, is stored down at the field level. Changes to a field will only place that field in the current layer. This also means that the same table can have two different fields in different models in the same layer. When we export a model, it will only export the changes within that model; any fields that are in the model will not be exported. This is by design, and has many benefits when deploying a release or applying a hotfix.

TFS integration is file-based and works by AX, exporting an XPO of each element to the local repository when the element is saved. The link between the file and AX is held at the element level, as shown in the following example from our local development environment:

`\Data Dictionary\Tables\ConFMSVehicleGroup` maps to `C:\Projects\VCS\AX\6015GettingStarted\ConFleetManagement\Data Dictionary\Tables\ConFMSVehicleGroup.xpo`.

Even though the resulting XPO will only contain the changes, it means the changes in the layer, not the specific model.

To demonstrate what happens with version control when we add a field to an element in a different model, follow these steps:

1. Check out the `ConFMSVehicleGroup` table.
2. Add a new field to this table by dragging the `CustAccount` EDT onto its **Fields** node.
3. Save the table and ensure that the new field's model is `USR Model`.
4. Check in the table.

Open the XPO for the table under the `ConFleetManagement` model's folder structure, and you'll see that the new field will be there. The folder structure for `USR Model` will not contain the element at all.

This means that an element must only be in one model—we must not have fields, methods, or controls in different models in the same layer. This is good practice and should not be considered as a limitation.

In terms of layers, there is a technical limitation where elements under source control must not also be modified in a higher layer. For example, if we are working in the VAR layer, the same object must not also be in the USR layer. This shouldn't pose a practical problem in normal deployment procedures.

For example, where the VAR has vertical solutions or add-ons, they should be brought in at the lowest layer possible (ISV or VAR), and the modifications made under source control should be made in the layer above that, such as the VAR or CUS layer.

If the customer also has an internal development team working on a separate functionality set in a separate layer, such as the USR, their environment will be built from the partner or ISV supplier models, and when ready for deployment, they will move their model to the build server.

Designing a deployment procedure

When building a deployment procedure, there is a point that can cause quite intense discussion. How do we prevent code that is not ready for release from being released?

There is no easy way to shelve code in AX, and many would panic at the thought of synchronizing to the tip. We can create a branch and update the VCS settings with this branch, but we can't easily merge this back into the main branch after release.

The solution we use is to create shelvesets. In order for this to work, there are some dos and don'ts; this is the list that we use:

- Do not check in every small change. Check in a block of changes that we have unit tested.
- Plan development work to minimize the overlaps in changes being made to similar areas of the system.
- Check out the label file when work begins.
- Once the piece of work is complete and has passed the unit testing, check in the work including the label file. We also tag it with the appropriate TFS task so that the checked-in code is linked to the requirement.

Let's say we have two pieces of work in progress, and one is not ready for release. We can check in the code that is ready and create a shelveset within Visual Studio for the code that should be shelved. We can then synchronize the code with TFS in AX to remove the shelved changes. To check for regression, we would run a full compile and rerun our test cases. The full compile is required as the p-code for a shelved method may still be there, and a call to this shelved method may actually still work! This has caught many out when they say, "It worked in my environment!" only to find that recompiling the affected objects highlights the problem as being a compilation error.

We can bring the shelved changes back into our repository after the release has been done and synchronize AX with TFS.

Once all releasable code is checked in, we create a build that we can then release to the appropriate environment, such as a user acceptance test server.

We may also need to remove the checked-in code; a useful trick is to check out the elements and create a project from the **Pending Objects** form in order to export it. You can then revert the changes as required, create the release build, and eventually, reimport the XPO after the release is done.

> Be careful when importing XPOs. When they are exported, they contain the entire object, even though only one field or method was changed or added. You may need to use the compare tool to merge the changes back in again.

Building the solution

There are many scripts to help us build the solution, which can be very complicated. To get us started, the following scenario can work well for many implementations.

In this scenario, we have several developers working on a solution for the VAR, and a team of two working on security and reports in the USR layer.

The customer's environment consists of the following:

- A shared development server or a VM for each developer
- A build sever
- A test server
- The production or live server farm

The VAR's environment will consist of these:

- A virtual machine for each developer (and also per customer they are working)
- A build server, which also acts as a unit test machine

The process starts at the VAR when all developers have checked in the code-complete unit tested code. The following steps cover the general process:

1. The build server at the VAR will be rebuilt from an AX 2012 VM template of the correct service pack level.
2. It will then be configured to link to the TFS repository.
3. The developer will then navigate to **Version Control** | **Synchronise**, check **Force** in the dialog, and press **OK**.
4. This will be repeated for each model.

The models will then be exported and delivered to the customer's site. At the customer's site, the following steps are performed:

1. The customer's build server will be refreshed from live (using database backup and restore for at least the model store database, and the business database too if policies allow).
2. The models will be installed from the VAR.
3. If using version control, one developer will synchronize his/her virtual machine with source control.
4. The models will be exported from the developer's VM or the shared development environment.

5. The models are then imported into the build server and then fully compiled.
6. The test server will be refreshed from live using database backup and restore of both the databases (the baseline is not relevant for this).

The model store can now be moved to test in its entirety. This is because the build server was refreshed from live, and therefore, the element IDs will match the live server. Importing models will only create element IDs if they don't already exist. Once we have performed our user acceptance test in test, it can then be deployed in live.

This is a simplistic method, which avoids the use of build scripts. Build scripts may seem complicated, but once they are set up, the whole process can be automated. The following material is useful for more detail on the best practices with source control as well as for creating your own automated build process:

- *Build and deploy scripts for Microsoft Dynamics AX 2012*: `https://gallery.technet.microsoft.com/scriptcenter/Build-and-deploy-for-b166c6e4`
- *Change management and TFS integration for multi-developer projects (white paper) [AX 2012]*: `http://technet.microsoft.com/en-us/library/jj713631.aspx`

Label files

Label files will have their own model, and are checked in and out using the label editor. You may notice that it assigns an odd-looking label ID, such as `@$AA101`. This is a temporary label ID that will be used until the label is checked in, at which time it works out the next label ID.

This is usually seamless but you may notice odd labels might start to appear, like this:

```
Label @$AA101 is replaced by @BCL101
```

The problem makes sense when we understand what happens when labels are checked in. The label check-in process is as follows:

1. Replace the temporary label ID with next global label ID from TFS.
2. Replace all instances of the temporary label with the new global label ID.
3. If the target element is not checked out, change the text of the temporary label to assist the developer in manually assigning the correct global label ID.

So, don't check in the objects before the labels are checked in, otherwise you will need to check each label and correct it.

C
Code Editor Scripts

At the start of this book, we promised to provide examples of how to create our own editor scripts. To get you started, we have created examples of two common types of scripts that are similar to what is used internally:

- Code editor snippet: code commenting
- Code editor snippet: the `find` method

Editor scripts

Microsoft provides a simple how-to on adding a script to the code editor at `http://msdn.microsoft.com/en-us/library/aa676080.aspx`. In the following sections, we will create some scripts that save us time while writing code.

To add an editor script, we modify the `EditorScripts` class. Looking at the `classDeclaration`, we see this comment:

```
// This is a framework class. Customizing this class may cause
problems with future upgrades to the software.
```

In this case, the warning means that Microsoft may change this class or the technology in future versions, and this is likely given the direction they are going in with rationalizing development tools. We will therefore proceed under the knowledge that we may need to remove this code when upgrading to the next release.

The scripts context menu is opened while in the code editor, using the scripts icon or by selecting **Scripts** from the right-click menu. This is shown here:

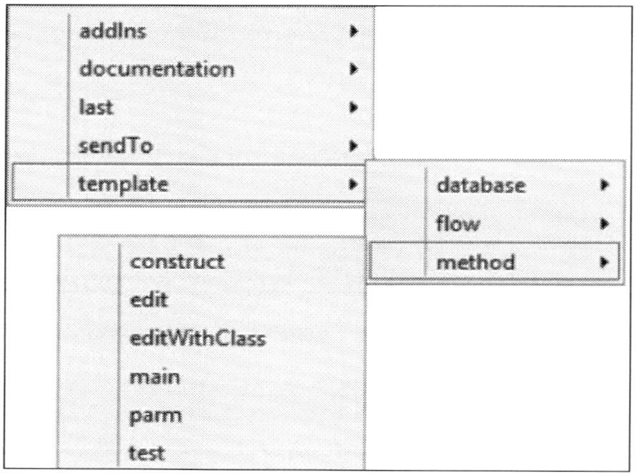

Now look at the methods in the `EditorScripts` class. You can see from the following screenshot that the method name actually creates this menu structure:

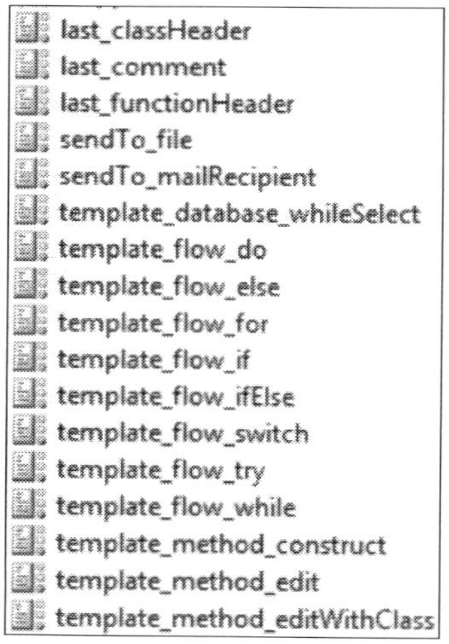

Code snippet – code commenting

To simplify and bring consistency to code commenting, we use an editor script to add comments. This is a simplified version of what we use internally.

We need to edit a standard class to do this, and since some scripts are better when split into methods, we'll create a new class in order to minimize the number of changes.

Create a new class, `ConXppCodeSnippets`, and add the following method:

```
public static NotesLine commentText()
{
    return strFmt("%1 modification by %4 on %5: ", "Con",
                  currentAOLayer(), curUserId(),
                  date2str(systemDateGet(), 321,2,4,2,4,4));
}
```

We can also use this in other methods and extend it, so that we can get data from a parameter table. In the `EditorScripts` class, create the following method:

```
public void contoso_comment(Editor editor)
{
    int currentLine = editor.currentLineNo();
    int currentCol = editor.columnNo();
    str prefix = "";
    editor.unmark();
    if(currentCol == 0)
    {
        currentCol = 4;
        prefix = strRep(' ', 4);
    }
    editor.insertLines(prefix+'// ' +
                       ConXppCodeSnippets::commentText() + '\n');

    editor.gotoLine(currentLine+2);
    editor.insertString(strRep(' ', currentCol));

}
```

Restart AX, and look at the **Scripts** menu. It has created the **Contoso** submenu, with **Comment** as an option.

Code snippet – the find method

In this example, we'll create a simple `find` method using information about the currently selected AOT node.

When the script methods are called, they are created with an instance of an `Editor` class. This class contains, among other information, the tree node of the method we are editing. Like this, for example:

```
\Data Dictionary\Tables\ConFMSVehServiceTable\Methods\method1
```

The following code uses this to get the table name. Again, add this to the `EditorScripts` class:

```
public void contoso_method_find(Editor editor)
{
    str             path = editor.path();
    TreeNode        treeNode;
    TableName       tableName;
    str             prefix = strRep(" ", 4);
    #TreeNodeSysNodeType

    treeNode = path ? TreeNode::findNode(path) : null;

    if (treeNode)
    {
        treeNode = treeNode.AOTparent();
        if(treeNode)
            treeNode = treeNode.AOTparent();
        if (!treeNode)
            return;
        if (treeNode.treeNodeType().id() == #NT_DBTABLE)
        {
            tableName = treeNode.treeNodeName();
        }
    }
    if(tableName == "")
        return;

    editor.insertLines(
        strFmt("public static %1 find(%2 _id, boolean _forUpdate =
false)\n",
```

```
                tableName, "RefRecId"));
    editor.insertLines("{\n");
    editor.insertLines(prefix + strFmt("%1 table;\n\n",
                                       tableName));
    editor.insertLines(prefix +
                    "table.selectForUpdate(_forUpdate);\n");
    editor.insertLines(prefix +
                  strFmt("select table where table.%2 == _id;\n",
                         tableName, "RecId"));
    editor.insertLines(prefix + "return table;\n");
    editor.insertLines("}");
}
```

We can extend this further by interrogating the table's metadata, using `DictTable` to find the keys in the primary key.

Finally, you might wonder how the scripts work where you just type the script name. We can do this using the following steps:

1. Rename the method to `template_method_find`.
2. On the `ConFMSVehicleTable` table, create a new method.
3. Delete the content of the method, type `find`, and press *Tab*. We'll see that it creates a `find` method for us.

We have broken our naming convention by dropping the prefix, and doing this can cause some issue when you perform an upgrade. And, in this particular case, it could also be affected by cumulative updates or service packs.

Index

A

B

C

D

G

H

I

L

M

N

O

T

U

V

W

[PACKT] PUBLISHING enterprise
professional expertise distilled

Thank you for buying

Mastering Microsoft Dynamics AX 2012 R3 Programming

About Packt Publishing

Packt, pronounced 'packed', published its first book, *Mastering phpMyAdmin for Effective MySQL Management*, in April 2004, and subsequently continued to specialize in publishing highly focused books on specific technologies and solutions.

Our books and publications share the experiences of your fellow IT professionals in adapting and customizing today's systems, applications, and frameworks. Our solution-based books give you the knowledge and power to customize the software and technologies you're using to get the job done. Packt books are more specific and less general than the IT books you have seen in the past. Our unique business model allows us to bring you more focused information, giving you more of what you need to know, and less of what you don't.

Packt is a modern yet unique publishing company that focuses on producing quality, cutting-edge books for communities of developers, administrators, and newbies alike. For more information, please visit our website at `www.packtpub.com`.

About Packt Enterprise

In 2010, Packt launched two new brands, Packt Enterprise and Packt Open Source, in order to continue its focus on specialization. This book is part of the Packt Enterprise brand, home to books published on enterprise software – software created by major vendors, including (but not limited to) IBM, Microsoft, and Oracle, often for use in other corporations. Its titles will offer information relevant to a range of users of this software, including administrators, developers, architects, and end users.

Writing for Packt

We welcome all inquiries from people who are interested in authoring. Book proposals should be sent to `author@packtpub.com`. If your book idea is still at an early stage and you would like to discuss it first before writing a formal book proposal, then please contact us; one of our commissioning editors will get in touch with you.

We're not just looking for published authors; if you have strong technical skills but no writing experience, our experienced editors can help you develop a writing career, or simply get some additional reward for your expertise.

[PACKT] enterprise
PUBLISHING
professional expertise distilled

Microsoft Dynamics AX 2012 R2 Services

ISBN: 978-1-78217-672-5 Paperback: 264 pages

Harness the power of Microsoft Dynamics AX 2012 R2 to create and use your own services effectively

1. Learn about the Dynamics AX 2012 service architecture.
2. Create your own services using wizards or X++ code.
3. Deploy your services in a variety of ways using high availability.

Microsoft Dynamics GP 2013 Implementation

ISBN: 978-1-78217-784-5 Paperback: 430 pages

Successfully implement Microsoft Dynamics GP 2013 with easy-to-follow instructions and examples

1. Plan, install, and implement Microsoft Dynamics GP 2013 with real-world advice from a Microsoft Dynamics GP MVP.
2. Learn how to set up the core modules in Microsoft Dynamics GP effectively following detailed, step-by-step instructions.
3. Discover additional tools and resources available for your Dynamics GP.

Please check **www.PacktPub.com** for information on our titles

20171341R00264

Printed in Great Britain
by Amazon